PENGUIN BOOKS

THE SCOTTISH CLEARANCES

A *Daily Telegraph*, *Herald* and *Scotsman* Book of the Year 2018

'Scotland's best modern historian . . . he make history accessible backed up with formidable original research . . . a balanced, detailed and extremely readable account of one of the saddest events in Scotland's history' Ewen MacAskill, *Guardian*

'It is his magnum opus . . . also provides a final and exquisite stitching underpinning the tapestry woven through his other great Scottish histories: *To the Ends of the Earth*, *Scotland's Empire* and *Independence or Union*' Kevin McKenna, *The Herald*

'Devine treats the subject with sensitive intelligence . . . in providing us with the material which makes it more possible to see history as it actually was, Sir Tom has written a necessary book' Allan Massie, *Scotsman*

'In this powerful book Devine lays out the history with admirable lucidity and comprehensive depth . . . The processes of dispossession related in this important book continue to mark contemporary Scotland. The emptiness of the countryside, north and south, is marketed as a natural and positive state of affairs. Solitude and wilderness are valuable commodities today. Tom Devine lays out, in comprehensive depth, the traumatic process that created these conditions' Ewen Cameron, *Irish Times*

'In a meticulously detailed history Devine sets the record straight . . . there are some notable myth-busting moments and a lot to admire in this book' Stuart Kelly, *Spectator*

'A giant of Scottish intellectual life, Professor Sir Tom Devine is always a clear eyed guide to the country's history . . . this book is a history which still matters' *The Herald*

'Devine's book should be in every Scottish library, private as well as public. He is a master . . . expert in moulding the morass of new historiographic material into a digestible whole. He writes with admirable clarity, sticking closely to verifiable information, with two audiences in mind, one his peers in universities, the other the reading public' Alan Taylor. *Scottish R*

'This book is very much in the Devine mould: eloquent,
erudite and comprehensive . . . his usual trenchant style is also
on display. These features will ensure its relevance to Scottish
historical studies for some considerable time to come'
D. S. Forsyth, *Literary Review*

'So much British History is London-centric but T.M. Devine,
probably the foremost historian of Scotland, challenges that'
Simon Heffer, *Daily Telegraph*, '50 Books that Blew Us Away 2018'

'Likely to represent the definitive word for at least
an academic generation on this most controversial of
topics in Scottish history' *The National*

'Sir Tom Devine has swept away much of the misunderstanding
but has not deadened the story. What he tells is in many
respects even more dramatic' Brian Morton, *The Herald*

'A massively researched work' Magnus Linklater, *The Times Scotland*

'Scotland's most important current historian . . . When it
comes to the Clearances, Devine is again an exhilarating
puncturer of myths and resolver of mysteries. Devine is rigorous,
factual, endlessly curious and unafraid to draw big conclusions.
He has made a superb book. It is crammed with data but is
colourful and passionate as well. Anyone interested in Scottish
history needs to read it . . . it is also a great contribution
to British history' Andrew Marr, *Sunday Times*

'A great historian punctuates a national myth. This superb book is
written by a member of the Scottish intellectual aristocracy (Tom Devine
is a knight as well as a professor) which renders its conclusions almost
unassailable. This is a life work . . . what is obvious is that the book is
massively researched' David Aaronovitch, *The Times*

ABOUT THE AUTHOR

T. M. Devine has written four books for Penguin: *The Scottish Nation*,
Scotland's Empire, *To the Ends of the Earth* and *Independence or Union*.
He is Sir William Fraser Professor Emeritus of Scottish History and
Palaeography at the University of Edinburgh. In 2001 he was awarded the
Royal Gold Medal, Scotland's supreme academic accolade, and has won all
three major prizes for Scottish historical research. He was knighted in 2014
for services to the study of Scottish history. In 2018 he received the UK
Parliament's All Party History and Archives Group Lifetime Achievement
Award for Historical Studies.

T. M. DEVINE

The Scottish Clearances

A History of the Dispossessed
1600–1900

PENGUIN BOOKS

PENGUIN BOOKS

UK | USA | Canada | Ireland | Australia
India | New Zealand | South Africa

Penguin Books is part of the Penguin Random House group of companies
whose addresses can be found at global.penguinrandomhouse.com.

First published by Allen Lane 2018
Published in Penguin Books 2019

010

Set in 9.35/12.50 pt Sabon LT Std
Typeset by Jouve (UK), Milton Keynes
Printed and bound in Great Britain by Clays Ltd, Elcograf S.p.A.

A CIP catalogue record for this book is available from the British Library

ISBN: 978–0–141–98593–0

www.greenpenguin.co.uk

Penguin Random House is committed to a
sustainable future for our business, our readers
and our planet. This book is made from Forest
Stewardship Council® certified paper.

In memory of
Malcolm Gray

1918–2008

Historian of Scottish rural society

Few things cry so urgently for rewriting as does Scots history, as in few aspects of her bastardised culture has Scotland been so ill-served as by her historians.

The chatter and gossip of half the salons and drawing-rooms of European intellectualism hang over the antique Scottish scene like a malarial fog through which peer the fictitious faces of heroic Highlanders, hardy Norsemen, lovely Stewart queens, and dashing Jacobite rebels.

Those stage-ghosts shamble amid the dimness, and mope and mow in their ancient parts with an idiotic vacuity but a maddening persistence.

Lewis Grassic Gibbon and Hugh MacDiarmid,
*Scottish Scene or The Intelligent Man's
Guide to Albyn* (1934)

Contents

CONTENTS

Annexes

Tables

Maps

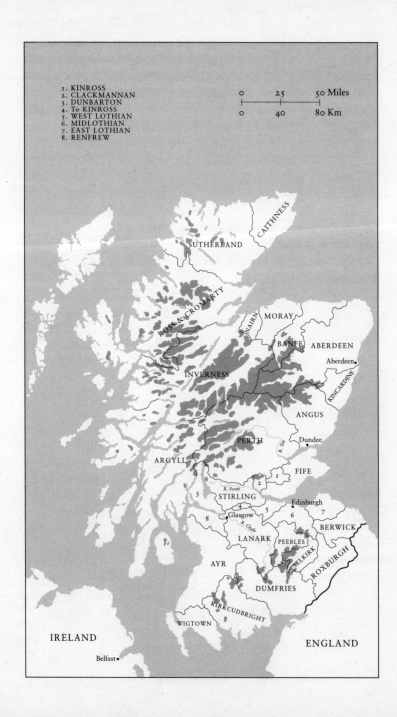

1. KINROSS
2. CLACKMANNAN
3. DUNBARTON
4. To KINROSS
5. WEST LOTHIAN
6. MIDLOTHIAN
7. EAST LOTHIAN
8. RENFREW

0   25   50 Miles

0   40   80 Km

CAITHNESS

SUTHERLAND

ROSS & CROMARTY

NAIRN

MORAY

BANFF

ABERDEEN

Aberdeen•

INVERNESS

KINCARDINE

ANGUS

PERTH

R. Tay

Dundee•

ARGYLL

FIFE

2   1

R. Forth

3   STIRLING

Edinburgh•

4   5

7

8   Glasgow•

6

R. Clyde

BERWICK

LANARK

PEEBLES

SELKIRK

AYR

ROXBURGH

DUMFRIES

KIRKCUDBRIGHT

WIGTOWN

IRELAND

ENGLAND

Belfast•

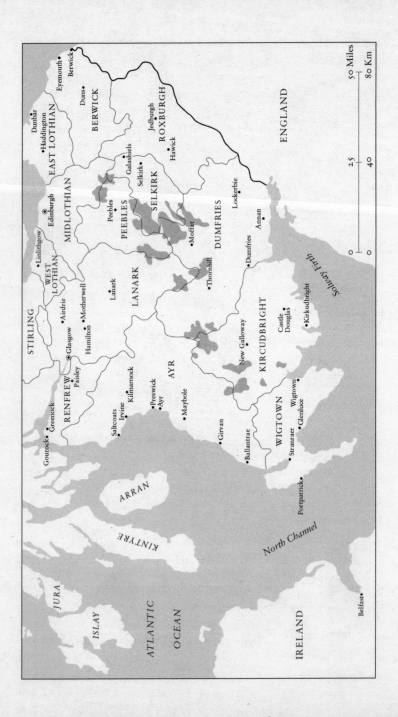

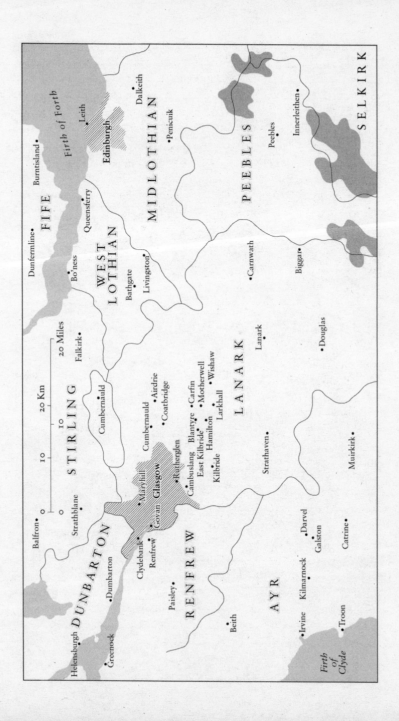

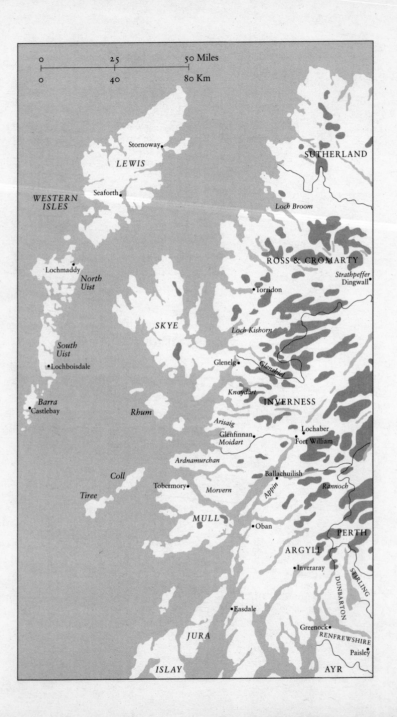

Stornoway•

LEWIS

SUTHERLAND

WESTERN
ISLES

Seaforth•

Loch Broom

ROSS & CROMARTY

•Lochmaddy
North
Uist

Torridon•

Strathpeffer
Dingwall•

SKYE

Loch Kishorn

South
Uist
•Lochboisdale

Glenelg•

Glenshiel

Knoydart

INVERNESS

Barra
•Castlebay

Rhum

Arisaig
Glenfinnan•
Moidart

Lochaber•
Fort William•

Ardnamurchan

Ballachuilish•

Rannoch

Coll

Tobermory•

Morvern

Appin

Tiree

MULL

•Oban

PERTH

ARGYLL

•Inveraray

JURA

•Easdale

DUNBARTON

STIRLING

Greenock•
RENFREWSHIRE
Paisley•

ISLAY

AYR

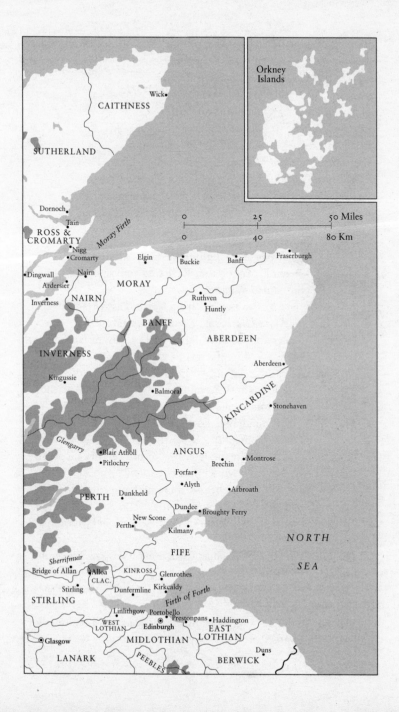

Orkney
Islands

CAITHNESS
Wick

SUTHERLAND

Dornoch
Tain
ROSS &
CROMARTY
Nigg
Cromarty
Dingwall
Ardersier
Nairn
Inverness
Moray Firth
Elgin
Buckie
Banff
Fraserburgh

NAIRN

MORAY

Ruthven
Huntly

BANEF

INVERNESS

ABERDEEN

Kingussie

Aberdeen

Balmoral

KINCARDINE
Stonehaven

Glengarry
Blair Atholl
Pitlochry

ANGUS

Brechin
Montrose

Forfar
Alyth

Arbroath

PERTH
Dunkheld

Dundee
Broughty Ferry

New Scone
Perth
Kilmany

Sherrifmuir
Bridge of Allan
Stirling
STIRLING
Alloa
CLAC.
KINROSS
Glenrothes
Dunfermline
Kirkcaldy

FIFE

NORTH

SEA

Linlithgow
Portobello
Prestonpans
Haddington
WEST
LOTHIAN
Edinburgh
Glasgow
MIDLOTHIAN
EAST
LOTHIAN
Duns
LANARK
PEEBLES
BERWICK

Firth of Forth

25   50 Miles

40   80 Km

List of Illustrations

1. The ruins of Castle Tioram on Loch Moidart in the western Highlands (Getty)
2. The cairn at Culloden Moor (Alamy)
3. The Runrigs of Corsehill, Eglinton estate, Ayrshire, 1789 (National Records of Scotland, RHP3/20 copyright © Rt Hon Earl of Eglinton and Winton)
4. A view of the Scottish Borders from Carter Pass (Alamy)
5. *Horsefair on Bruntfield Links, Edinburgh*, Paul Sandby, 1750 (National Gallery of Scotland. Purchased by Private Treaty 1990)
6. Culzean Castle, Ayrshire (Getty)
7. An improved farm steading, Wester Kittochside, South Lanarkshire (copyright © Royal Commission on the Ancient and Historical Monuments of Scotland; C/44446)
8. The village of Tyninghame, East Lothian (copyright © The Scotsman Publications Ltd)
9. Ploughman and horse team, later nineteenth century (Scottish Life Archive, National Museums of Scotland)
10. The township of Ormsaigbeg, Ardnamurchan peninsula (copyright © Heritage Ardnamurchan)
11. Private soldier of 42 Regiment of Foot (© National Museums Scotland)
12. *The Last of the Clan*, Thomas Faed, 1865 (Glasgow Museums/Bridgeman Images)
13. The ruins of the township of Arichonan, Argyll (Alamy)
14. The *Hercules* (Getty)
15. Marines landing at Uig, Skye, in 1884 (Illustrated London News Ltd/Mary Evans Picture Library)

Abbreviations in References

HPL	Hamilton Public Library
IC	Inveraray Castle Archives
NA	National Archives
NLS	National Library of Scotland
NRA(S)	National Register of Archives (Scotland)
NRS	National Records of Scotland
NSA	New Statistical Account
OSA	First or Old Statistical Account
PP	Parliamentary Papers

Glossary

A' Chlann	The clan, literally the children
An Gaidhealtachd	Scottish Gaeldom, literally 'the Place of the Gael'
Ariage	Labour services from tenants
Baile	Traditional Highland township or settlement
Bard	Poet
Bere	Hardy, four-row form of barley
Boll	A dry measure; a boll of meal amounts to 140lb avoirdupois
Bonnage	Services rendered by a tenant
Buannachan	'Household men'; specialist warrior cadre within clanship
Carriage	Labour services involving transport of commodities
Cas-chrom	Foot-plough used for turning rough ground, where a horse-drawn plough could not easily work
Ceann-cinnidh	Head of the kindred
Cess	Land tax
Commonty	Rough pasture land possessed jointly by different proprietors
Cottar	Occupier of a small patch of land in return for providing labour services to a tenant farmer
Cottoun	Row of cottar cottages
Croft	A small individual agricultural landholding
Crofter	Occupant of a croft

Division of Commonty	Dividing a commonty into individual and separate properties by landowners who have rights to it
Duthchas	Collective heritage; obligation on clan gentry to provide protection to members of the clan in return for service
Factor	Estate officer or manager
Feannagan	See *Lazy beds*
Fencibles	Regiments raised at home and in the colonies in the second half of the eighteenth century for home defence
Fermetouns	Traditional pre-improvement farming townships
Fine	Clan élite; the chief and leading gentry
Fir-tacsa	See *Tacksman*
Heritable Jurisdiction	Grants of jurisdiction to a lord and his heirs. Usually accompanied by feudal tenures and conferring considerable power on landed families
Heritor	Proprietor of heritable property with land subject to payment of taxation and other public burdens
Hirsel	Number of sheep looked after by one shepherd
Houghing	Cutting the hamstrings of livestock
Laird	A landowner below noble rank
Lazy beds	Parallel banks of ridge and furrow cultivation with the beds formed into sandwiches of soil topped with peat and seaweed for fertilizer
Loamings	Tracks between cultivated fields
Machair	A strip of sandy, grassy, often lime-rich soil just above the high-water mark on shores; used as grazing or arable land
Moss	Deep basin peatland
Muir	Shallow hill peat
Na Daoine	Literally 'The Men', a lay religious élite

Non-Jurors	Those who refused, normally on religious grounds, to swear allegiance to the monarchy of William and Mary after the Revolution of 1688
Park	An enclosure for animals, grass or crops
Reiving	Cattle thieving
Runrig	A 'rig' was a narrow strip of cultivated land. A 'runrig' involved each tenant being allocated several detached rigs or pieces of land, often on a yearly basis
Sept	Division of a clan
Sliochden	Branches of a clan
Sorning	Extraction of food and shelter by fighting men of the clan from the other members of the clan
Souming	The limit of number of animals which tenants could graze on pasture land
Strath	Broad river valley
Tack	A lease of property
Tacksman	Leaseholder of land within the clan structure which he sublet to clansmen below him in the social hierarchy; invariably related to the chief and ruling family
Testificat	Certificate, usually of a person's good character
Thirlage	The process by which tenants were bound to grind their grain at the landowner's mill
Wadset	A mortgage of land to a creditor who was enabled to draw rents from it as interest on the money lent. The borrower retained rights of reversion

Introduction

I have thought, written and taught on several of the issues in this book for nearly forty years. But this is the first time I have tried to bring all the parts of a fascinating historical jigsaw into a single framework. The main purpose of doing so is to consider through a comparative investigation the dispossession of people from land in the Highlands and rural Lowlands during that extraordinary period almost three centuries ago when it can truly be said the modern nation of Scotland was born.

In 1814 Sir Walter Scott published *Waverley, Or, 'tis Sixty Years Since*, a novel which opened at the time of the last Jacobite rising in 1745–6. The book quickly became an international bestseller and launched Scott into literary stardom. In the preamble to the text he has the anonymous narrator look back and comment on the previous six decades of Scottish history from the standpoint of an observer living in the second decade of the nineteenth century:

> There is no European nation, which, within the course of half a century, or little more, has undergone so complete a change as this kingdom of Scotland . . .
>
> The increase of wealth, and extension of commerce, have since united to render the present people of Scotland a class of beings as different from their grandfathers as the existing English are from those of Queen Elizabeth's time.

For Scott, then, the transformation of his native land was rapid, profound and comprehensive. A trio of radical developments, all interacting and taking place simultaneously from the 1760s, had changed the face and character of the country. These powerful forces were industrialization, urbanization and agricultural revolution. This book focuses on the social effects of the last of these at the time when an old Scotland began to fade into history and the new age of market capitalism was in the early stages of formation. In the history of the Scottish Highlands this period has become known as the Age of the Clearances.

The Highland clearances have not only been a central topic of historical interest but have also long entered into the popular and cultural consciousness of Scots both in the homeland and throughout the global diaspora. It is widely assumed that the removal of peasant communities took place exclusively north of the Highland line with the empty glens and remains of crumbling townships in the hill country bearing mute physical testimony to that fact. The Canadian writer of Highland ancestry Alistair MacLeod, in his short story 'Clearances', has his main character pay a visit to Ardnamurchan on the west Highland mainland during the Second World War. There, in the land which his forefathers had left many years before to sail across the Atlantic for a new life in Cape Breton, he begins to grasp for the first time the original meaning of 'clearance':

> Where once people had lived in their hundreds and their thousands, there stretched out only the unpopulated emptiness of the vast estates with their sheep-covered hills or the islands which have become bird sanctuaries or shooting ranges for the well-to-do. He is himself as the descendant of victims of history and changing economic times, betrayed perhaps by politics and poverty as well.

In similar vein, the Scottish novelist Neil Gunn wrote of the deserted lands of Sutherland from where his own kinfolk, the MacKeamish Gunns, had long disappeared:

> In Kildonan there is today a shadow, a chill, of which any sensitive mind would, I am convinced, be vaguely aware, though possessing no knowledge of the clearances. We are affected strangely by any place from which the tide of life has ebbed. (*Caithness and Sutherland*, published 1935)

Few would deny that these evocations are both haunting and compelling. The Scottish Highlands, contrary to the image projected in countless tourist brochures, are not one of the last great wildernesses in Europe but in many parts can be more accurately described as a derelict landscape from where most of the families who once lived and worked the soil have long gone. Numerous townships which had existed from medieval times were cleared or abandoned in the late eighteenth century and the nineteenth, never again to be inhabited. A number of commentators then and since have taken the view that the dispersal of the people across the seas was caused by greedy landlordism and the brazen subordination of human need to human profit.

Yet the actual historical record shows that the realities of diaspora were far from simple. Many more Gaels left the Highlands after the removals came to an end in the later 1850s than during the age of the clearances itself. Nor did evictions necessarily cause widespread depopulation in all parts of the region as they undeniably did in specific estates, glens, coasts and straths. The decennial censuses confirm that the population of the Highland counties, with the exception of Argyll, which reached its peak in 1841, continued to rise during the clearance period and only started to fall into decline after the removals came to an end. A thorough scholarly study of one parish, Morvern in west Argyll, which suffered from clearance on a particularly extensive scale, estimates that of all the people who left there in the nineteenth century probably only around a quarter did so as a direct result of eviction, and it is by no means certain that all those who were forced from their homes left the parish for elsewhere.

Nevertheless, the profile of the Highland clearances, nationally and internationally, is remarkable. By no means confined to historical writing alone, the subject has also become embedded in works of fiction, poetry and across the genres of music, drama, film, art and museology. A selection of the creative output on the subject could include: Neil Gunn, *Butcher's Broom* (1934) and *The Silver Darlings* (1945); Fionn MacColla, *And the Cock Crew* (1945); Iain Crichton Smith, *Consider the Lilies* (1968) and *Collected Poems* (1992); Kathleen Fidler, *The Desperate Journey* (1964) – a widely read story for primary schoolchildren; John McGrath, *The Cheviot, the Stag and the Black, Black Oil* (1974), a hugely popular stage play which has been reprised several times over the years; and the television film *Yet Still the Blood is Strong* (1984). The clearances not only have profound historical resonance but have

metamorphosed into an even broader Scottish cultural and political phenomenon. Even those who would not claim to know much about the
history of the nation have usually heard about the Highland clearances.

None of the works cited above, however, has ever had the popular
appeal of the biggest selling Scottish history book of all time, John
Prebble's *The Highland Clearances*, published for the first time in
1963. Since then it has achieved world-wide sales of more than a
quarter of a million copies and remains to this day the most widely
read text on any aspect of Scottish history in North America. Recent
research among the diaspora across the Atlantic has confirmed that
the clearances are known there primarily by a reading of Prebble's
book, some historical fiction, consulting a few websites and visiting
heritage centres on trips to Scotland which draw on the same written
sources. *The Highland Clearances* is part of a Highland trilogy, *Fire
and Sword*, which also includes *Culloden* (1961) and *Glencoe* (1966).
In the foreword to *Glencoe*, Prebble wrote: 'I have written this book
because its story is, in a sense, a beginning to what I have already
written about Culloden and the clearances – the destruction of the
Highland people and their way of life.'

John Prebble (1915–2001) was born in England but emigrated,
aged six, to Canada with his parents, later returning to the UK as a
young boy of twelve. It is suggested that early friendships among
members of the Scottish emigrant communities in Canada first stimulated his interest in Highland history. He joined the Communist
Party of Great Britain as an adult but left it after the end of the Second
World War. However, Prebble never lost his critical approach to the
human impact of market capitalism, or sympathy for its victims.

Some scholars have rubbished *The Highland Clearances* as a work
of faction, or a fusion of fact and fiction, rather than a serious history. Predictably the book rarely features in the prescribed reading
lists of Scottish universities, except perhaps as an exemplar of parti-
san historical interpretation. I recall a colleague once setting students
the essay question: 'Prebble's *The Highland Clearances* is not a good
history but it is a good novel. Discuss.'

But most readers seem not to care about the ferocious criticisms
which the volume has sometimes attracted from members of the
academy. For the general public, Prebble tells a compelling story in

very readable prose presented as a dramatic saga of betrayal, loss, tragedy and forced exile of the Highland clans from their native glens which in his interpretation remain empty to this day as silent memorials of man's inhumanity to man.

The author makes his own position perfectly clear from the outset: 'This is the story of how the Highlanders were deserted and then betrayed. It concerns itself with people, how sheep were preferred to them, and how bayonet, truncheon and fire were used to drive them from their homes.' The book is an accessible and fluent read, in part because the author does not even try to come to grips with any of the many challenging complexities of Highland history. Those in the dock are always the former chieftains of the clans, by the later eighteenth century transformed into commercial landlords, whose greed, Prebble insists, led them to sacrifice their erstwhile clansmen for filthy lucre. At root, indeed, the volume is concerned with a classic struggle between the forces of good (the defenceless people of the Highlands) and evil (the brutal landlords and their callous lackeys, the notorious factors (estate managers) of ill fame). Prebble's perspective on clearances had been fashioned by almost a century of polemic, political and fictional writing which stretched back into the Victorian era. Most of the documentation in the book relies on these earlier works with little evidence of original research by the author. Almost all of this passionate *oeuvre* was produced at the height of Victorian controversies about clearances between the 1840s and the 1880s. It was deeply sympathetic to the people who had been displaced, strongly supportive of the vital need for land reform and bitterly hostile to what was seen as oppressive and brutal landlordism.

However, there was one significant and salient gap in the genre. No academic history of clearance based on original sources was published until the second half of the twentieth century. Popular accounts were therefore in the vanguard over many decades while the professionals lagged very far behind in their research and writing. Scottish historians in the universities before the great expansion from the 1960s were few and far between, and most of those who were active in research and writing tended to focus on the history of the independent nation before 1707. The new Burnett-Fletcher Professor of History at Aberdeen stated in his inaugural lecture in 1964 that modern Scottish history was less studied than the history of York-shire. Malcolm Gray's pathbreaking *The Highland Economy 1750–1850*, published in 1957, was an exception, but even in that book clearances appeared only incidentally in the text. Not until 1982 did a professional historian attempt to tackle the subject in a comprehensive fashion, with the appearance of Eric Richards's *A History of the Highland Clearances*. Since then a number of books have been published on aspects of clearance. The new interest in the subject from the 1960s has helped to influence current political debates in the devolved Scottish Parliament on land reform.

At the time of the clearances, there were vitriolic contemporary condemnations of landed iniquity from the pens of Robert Allister, Eric Findlater, Thomas Muloch, Donald Ross and others, though their writings have now been largely forgotten and are mainly of interest to scholars of Highland history. More influential and potent by far in the fashioning of modern thinking were the books by Donald MacLeod and Alexander Mackenzie published in the later nineteenth century. Prebble himself admitted that it was reading MacLeod's *Gloomy Memories of the Highlands of Scotland*, subtitled *The Extirpation of the Celtic Race from the North of Scotland*, which first drew him to write on the history of the Highlands. Mackenzie's *History of the Highland Clearances* (1883) was published at the time of the great crofting agitation of the 1880s and the Royal Commission chaired by Lord Napier into crofting conditions in that same decade. The book brought reports of several evictions together in one volume and catalogued the misdeeds of landlordism at considerable length. It was a formidable compendium, overtly propagandist and designed to support the crofters' cause by publicizing the injustices of clearance. The volume was published at a time when the Liberal Party and some radical politicians were engaged in a much wider assault on the privileges of landlordism throughout Britain. Indeed, at the time clearances came to epitomize the abuse of landed power and the vital need for land reform, which from that point on was rarely off the political agenda in the years before the Great War.

The events in the Highlands also stirred much interest and condemnation outside Scotland. Most famously, Karl Marx, in Chapter 27 of *Das Kapital* (1867), railed against the clearances as a primary exemplar of peasant expropriation and the 'reckless terrorism' which had usurped communal rights in the name of private property.

Until John Prebble and Ian Grimble's *The Trial of Patrick Sellar*, published in the early 1960s, few other focused accounts of the removals appeared. But literary works by Neil Gunn and Fionn MacColla had kept interest alive in the 1930s and 1940s. Earlier, scathing attacks on landed élites in general had been integral elements of the polemics by the Labour politician Tom Johnston, later Secretary of State for Scotland in Churchill's government during the Second World War. His bestselling *Our Scots Noble Families* (1909) and *History of the Working Classes in Scotland* (1920) skilfully linked the political quest for political reform directly with the story of the removals in the Highlands.

Since Prebble wrote, others have followed his lead and sometimes gone even further in the intensity of their rhetoric. Clearances in some texts have taken on a modern meaning as harbingers of twentieth-century ethnic cleansing while others even claim in works published over the last few decades that a genocide had been committed in the Highlands and the fate of the cleared Gaels bears comparison to that of the Jews, gypsies, mental patients and homosexuals who suffered in the Nazi death camps. (See Annex A for a sample of these views.) The campaign mounted in recent years to tear down the massive statue to the first Duke of Sutherland, which towers on Ben Braggie, above the town of Golspie on the east coast of Sutherland, has been justified because it is 'the Murderer's Monument'. The 100-foot memorial to the Duke, or the 'Mannie' as it is known locally, has had graffiti sprayed on it with the word 'Monster' in green paint. As recently as 2011 two large sandstone sections of the plinth were removed and more stones have been extracted from it since then. The police believe there is an ongoing campaign to topple the edifice once and for all.

It was of some significance that *The Highland Clearances* first achieved bestseller status in Scotland during the late 1960s and 1970s, when the country first began to experience the early stages of deindustrialization and rising levels of unemployment as the postwar boom petered out and politically Scotland started to move mainly to the left. For some the history of the evictions became a symbol for the emerging tragedy of an economy in decline, the social impact of deindustrialization sometimes being described as a modern clearance.

This was also the time when Scottish nationalism finally achieved some electoral purchase with Winnie Ewing's famous victory in the Hamilton by-election of 1967. Nationalism, clearances and victimhood soon became intimately linked by some polemicists, a tendency which has continued to the present day through the proliferation of social media. The contentions were that the historic tragedy of the Gaels had taken place during the Union and sometimes also, against all the evidence, that English landowners and sheep farmers were mainly responsible for the draconian acts of eviction.

The roots of Scottish heritage were starting to attract new interest at the same time as part of a broader ethnic revival in folk culture, tales and song which was proving popular throughout the Western world. Genealogy and family history became fashionable as more and more people became interested in finding out where they had come from and the origins of their personal identities. It was in those decades too that the first glimmers of sartorial neo-Highlandism started to come to the fore. Kilts, sporrans and tartans, formerly favoured almost exclusively by the county set and Scottish military, began to be worn more often at weddings, formal events and graduation ceremonies, though the remarkable universality of Highland dress at those occasions still lay in the future. As Highlandism became more influential, Highland symbolism came to be even more significant as an important marker of Scottish identity, so ensuring that the saga of the clearances could now be incorporated into the heritage of all Scots whatever their ancestral local and regional background. This neo-Highlandism built on the huge earlier influence of Sir Walter Scott's Waverley novels in Victorian times which invested the Highlands with an extraordinary romantic aura and magical appeal.

John Prebble himself never claimed to be a historian and always referred to himself as a historical writer. He seems to have been surprised and somewhat taken aback by the storm of criticism generated by his book. Some thought the furore simply reflected jealousy on the part of an academic establishment whose works might be scholarly and rigorous but could never hope to achieve a fraction of Prebble's sales. It is also fair to say that he had tackled an important and controversial subject which most historians up until that point had studiously ignored or consciously avoided. But scholars were also right to be concerned that a book which some of them believed to be riven by bias and distortion, as well as being under-researched and devoid of much critical perspective, had been widely accepted by the public as the authentic chronicle of clearance.

Yet Prebble's publishing success is only the most remarkable example of the lure of the Scottish Highlands for all kinds of writers and artists. Academic historians have also succumbed to the same seduction in recent times. At the last count, more than fifty research-based books have been published since about 1980 on aspects of the history of the Highlands since the eighteenth century. The appeal and romance of the Jacobite Risings partly explain this phenomenon, though books on that subject make up a relatively small proportion of the overall publication list. One distinguished but sceptical professor a few years ago was so annoyed by this explosion of writing on one region that he wrote an article in a learned journal protesting that there was simply 'too much Highland history'. But his complaint had no effect as studies of the Highlands continued to pour from the university presses. The professor was undeniably correct, however, to claim a gross imbalance in scholarly productivity. Over the last four decades, fewer than half a dozen monographs have been published on the history of the rural Lowlands, the part of the country where the great majority of non-urban Scottish people lived, not only today but at the time of the evictions.

In terms of popular writing, and a range of genres from fiction to drama, which has sustained interest in the Highland story of loss of land, the imbalance is, if anything, even more striking. No oral tradition, folk memory of dispossession, poetry of tragedy or words of lament surround the Lowland experience of land loss. Only one book to date has the title *The Lowland Clearances* (2003). Published fourteen years ago, it was compiled by two former BBC Scotland journalists, Andrew Cassell and Peter Aitchison, and is based on an excellent Radio Scotland series they presented and which featured a number of historians as expert commentators. The book is written in an accessible style but its history since publication stands in stark contrast to Prebble's stellar success. The publishers only decided recently to go ahead with a first reprint after a campaign on the internet convinced them to do so. By way of comparison, the new edition of a popular guide to clearance sites in the Highlands, *The Highland Clearances Trail* (2006), has been reprinted eight times in the last six years.

Does this very low profile imply that a concept such as 'the Lowland clearances' is either myth or a most remarkable sidelining of a central part of modern Scottish history? Certainly the idea remains controversial, even for some historians, and as a modern coinage has yet to achieve much appeal or interest among the general public. Lowland rural society has in fact long been one of the Cinderella subjects of Scottish history. Scotland had become one of the most urbanized countries on earth by the middle decades of the nineteenth century, and it is perhaps not surprising that a nation which has overwhelmingly lived in towns and cities for generations has lost interest in much of its rural past.

Of course, in addition, and crucially, the Lowlands cannot match in any way the human appeal of the story north of the Highland line, set as it is against a background of romantic mythology and world-renowned natural beauty. The Highlands are more than a geographical region for most Scots but have become an iconic land which helps to define their identity and has repeatedly been used to imagine the Scottish nation in story, art, music and film. That unofficial national anthem (or dirge, depending on one's opinion), 'Flower of Scotland', has the famous line: 'That fought and died for / your wee bit hill and glen'.

For much of the rest of the world, indeed, a once renowned Victorian centre of industry has metamorphosed into a Highland country. The 'land of the mountain and the flood' adorns numerous tourist posters, and the familiar symbols of Scottish identity, tartan, kilts, clans and bagpipes, are all of Highland origin. When Europeans 'play Scots', as groups of people in several countries of northern Europe, stretching from Russia to Holland, have bizarrely begun to do in recent years, they wear Highland dress, take part in Highland games, become members of pipe bands and masquerade as kilted soldiers in military enactments.* It is said that, during his numerous

---

* In *Warrior Dreams: Playing Scotsmen in Mainland Europe* (2014), David Hesse identified at least 600 such activities in 2010, stretching from Moscow to Stockholm, involving 'affinity' Scots who had no blood or family ties to Scotland, with forty-six kilted pipe bands in the Netherlands alone.

popular concerts throughout the world, the renowned violinist/ conductor André Rieu and his orchestra achieve most emotional impact on audiences with the haunting tune 'Highland Cathedral', composed by two Germans, Ulrich Roever and Michael Korb, for a Highland Games held in Germany in 1982. The music is usually set against the backdrop of a Highland castle and massed pipe bands ranked across the stage. Highland culture, whether in authentic or invented form, has an extraordinary glamour which has marginalized the history of the rural Lowlands.

Nowhere is this more visible than in the USA. At the last count, there were 160 American 'clan societies', nearly 2,000 pipe bands, over 150 Highland-dancing schools and seventy Highland Games. The sense of identity of those who take part depends on a cult of Highlandism invented and embroidered in Scotland during Victorian times. Many third- and fourth-generation American Scots share the view that Scottish emigration across the Atlantic came from the Highlands and was initiated by force and coercion. The boring reality is that the vast majority left from the farms, towns and cities of the Lowlands and were mainly attracted to North America because they saw it as a fabled land of opportunity to achieve a better life. The mythology, however, has it that the ancestors were driven from their homeland by the collapse of the Jacobite Risings, post-Culloden ethnic cleansing and, above all, by 'the clearances'. The key sources for these beliefs are John Prebble's books, a few novels and films, and more recently the hugely popular *Outlander* fantasy series, now widely televised, by the American author Diana Gabaldon, which is based on time travel between the 1940s and the eighteenth century. 'Roots Tourism' to Scotland has a similar bias. Whatever the geographical origins of their families, visitors often admit to feeling a strong and special empathy with the Highlands and its history of exile, victimhood and dispossession. The story is told of one Texan lady of Scottish ancestry who was much disappointed when genealogical researchers reported that her forebears came from the industrial Lowland town of Motherwell rather than a cleared township in Skye.

It would be impossible to alter the marginalization of the rural Lowlands in popular culture as Highlandism and its associated mythologies are just too deeply embedded and potent in the popular imagination for such an attempt to have any chance of success. However, it might be more realistic to address the much more limited question of historiographical imbalance in relation to the single issue of dispossession from land. The definition of 'clearance' is now subject to broader scholarly interpretation than it was in the nineteenth century, when the term came into popular usage for the first time. Then it referred exclusively to the removal, usually by force, of traditional peasant communities in the Highlands in order to make way for sheep farms. But modern scholarship has shown that that time-honoured concept of 'the clearances' cannot capture the full range and complexity of the actual historical experience of dispossession.

The historical geographer Robert Dodgshon has argued convincingly on the basis of research published in recent years that:

> whilst the wholesale clearance of touns (the standard farm unit in Scotland before improvement) to make way for sheep is still rightly seen as the prime means by which many highland touns were restructured, it is clear that a significant number did not experience a clearance of this kind.
>
> We have long known that many along the western seaboard were tidied up into newly configured crofting townships rather than cleared. Others experienced a clearance but via a gradual reduction in tenant numbers. Still others were reorganised or divided up into small consolidated farms.
>
> Finally, a sizeable number of highland touns did not undergo any form of fundamental structural change at all, other than enclosure, in their transition to modern forms since, even by the time they first appear in late seventeenth century rentals, they were held and worked as single tenancies.[1]

This perspective now makes more achievable the task of carrying out a comparative analysis which covers both Highland history and the much less familiar narrative of what happened in the rural Lowlands. It might even be that the evolution of the two regions had more in common than implied in the older historiography. Equally, however, demographic, economic, cultural and geographical differences between the two might explain why dispossession in the Highlands is remembered while loss of land by communities in the Lowlands has for the most part been ignored and forgotten except by a few scholars.

The Scottish experience of rural transformation was a national variant of broader developments in Europe. A primary determinant across the Continent and in Britain as a whole was a sustained revolution of increasing population which soon generated immense pressures on traditional modes of food production. In the past, a significant rise in humans had usually hit barriers of disease, harvest failure and other natural disasters. As a result any surge in numbers eventually tended to fall away. Thomas Malthus in his seminal text, *An Essay on the Principle of Population* (1798), argued that population had a tendency to grow as increases in food supply improved human health and well-being. Equally, however, the rise in numbers would be transitory because more people would soon press upon the capacity of agriculture to feed extra mouths, thus causing susceptibility to disease and famine. Mortality crises would then cut back the size of populations to the earlier levels which had existed before the increase. This so-called 'Malthusian trap' was one explanation for the cataclysmic rise in death rates and mass emigration associated with the Great Famine in Ireland of the 1840s. Elsewhere, however, a revolution in food production based on higher grain yields, innovative crop rotations, developments in long-distance transportation and improved organization of farming ensured the trap was not sprung in most parts of Western Europe.

To achieve this positive result, different nations and regions took a wide spectrum of routes to agrarian modernization. In France it took the form of assertion of peasant individualism and the eradication of feudal controls during and after the Revolution. In Denmark it was the state which was influential and tried to achieve some social equity in the distribution of improved holdings. In Scotland, and much of mainland Britain, the pattern was different again with landed magnates deploying their power to introduce far-reaching changes from above. Some of their decisions resulted in dispossession of traditional rural communities on a large scale. As a result only a small minority of the many families who once had access to some land still remained in possession by the time this social and economic revolution had come to an end.

This is the first book to examine this historic transformation of Highland and Lowland Scotland in a single study which also tries to draw comparisons and contrasts between the two regions as well as showing awareness of the mosaic of differences within them. As such it does not claim to be a definitive study. The objective has rather been to mark out the parameters for what happened, engage with some of the more salient questions and attempt to provide interim answers to them. The themes of the book range across traditional society, clanship, the origins and impact of rural change, protest and stability, emigration, landlordism, peasant mentalities and migration. At its core, however, is the central issue of dispossession from land, how it came about and how such loss affected the peoples of rural Scotland wherever they lived. Predictably, most of the sources for the period record the perspective of landowners, managers, clerics, accountants, trustees and middle-class travellers rather than those directly affected by the momentous changes experienced by innumerable tenants, crofters, cottars and labourers. But, as the book will try to demonstrate, much invaluable information can be gleaned from these records about society at all levels, as long as the limitations of such sources are acknowledged and taken into account. Nevertheless, the people are not always mute and silent. Every effort has been made to allow them to speak, either through the evidence they gave to several government enquiries, the memories of observers sympathetic to their interest and, most crucially of all, their own repository of ballad, poetry, song and story.

What follows is organized in three parts. Part One considers the nature of traditional societies before widespread dispossession began. Part Two analyses the roots of fundamental social change and focuses on the loss of land in the Border and Lowland regions. Finally, Part Three concentrates on clearances, their origins and effects, in the Highlands. Throughout, comparative comment alerts the reader to similarities and differences between these areas of the country as well as within them.

The annexes that follow the main text are primarily for the interest of scholars and those who may wish to explore the more detailed evidence supporting some of the arguments in the book.

PART ONE

I

Land and Clanship

Nowadays the Scottish Highlands have immense global appeal as a region of magical natural beauty. Towering peaks, remote glens and silent lochs feature in innumerable films, works of art and countless tourist brochures. In that different place the jaded traveller can hope to escape to a world which promises spiritual renewal and restful refreshment far away from the strains and stresses of modern life. Yet, in the perspective of history, that popular image of the Highlands is a modern invention which became fashionable only from the very late eighteenth century. First created during the Romantic era as a direct consequence of a revolution in aesthetics and visual taste at that time, the iconography then became shaped by new concepts of scenic beauty, the picturesque and the sublime, which transformed how humans saw and experienced their natural environment.

Before that time the conventional perception of the Highland landscape was radically different. Mist-covered mountains situated alongside vast stretches of desolate moorland stirred feelings of foreboding and melancholy rather than emotions of awe. In his famous journey of 1773 to the Western Isles across the hill country of the mainland, Dr Samuel Johnson found himself repelled and ultimately depressed by the 'wide extent of hopeless sterility' which he encountered on his travels.[1] Nearly forty years before, the English military engineer Captain Edmund Burt saw the neighbourhood around Inverness as 'a dismal gloomy Brown ... and most of all disagreeable, when the Heath is in Bloom'. For Burt, bens and glens clothed in purple heather during the months of autumn were therefore ugly and sinister and not in any way bonnie or appealing.[2] Even in 1800, by which time the aesthetic revolution was already in its early stages, the author of *The General Gazetteer or Compendious Geographical Directory* could report on the 'North division of the country' as 'chiefly an assembly of vast dreary mountains'.[3]

This was the land of the Highland clans from their origins in early medieval times until their disintegration in the eighteenth century.

I

Scottish Gaeldom, *An Gaidhealtachd*, literally 'the Place of the Gael', lay north and west of the Highland Boundary Fault which crosses Scotland in a line from the town of Helensburgh in the south-west to Stonehaven in the north-east. The core geographical region includes the counties of Argyll, Ross and Cromarty, Sutherland and Inverness, but in earlier times 'the Highlands' also encompassed in linguistic and cultural terms the western and northern districts of Aberdeenshire, Angus, Perthshire and Stirlingshire. Not all the lands of the clans lay in impenetrable mountain country. Several of the inner and outer Hebridean islands, and especially the foothills of the main Highland massif to the east and south, contained districts of relatively flat and productive land. Even in the harsher landscape to the north and west, the people tended to settle mainly on the scattered pieces of arable land which could be found discontinuously across an otherwise barren terrain.

No matter where they lived, however, living conditions for the Gaels were hard and often challenging in the extreme. Only a small fraction of the land, later reckoned to be around 9 per cent of the whole, was suitable for cultivation. But even this scarce arable was often split into mere patches rather than formed in the continuous stretches characteristic of most parts of the Scottish Lowlands. Some places, such as the Kintyre peninsula, the islands of Tiree and Islay, and the western coastlands of the Outer Isles, did indeed have a reputation for fertility. But most other areas were much less favoured. It was said in Victorian times, for instance, that of four parishes in north-west Sutherland only a one-hundredth part of the soil there had ever been cultivated. Even in some more southerly districts, closer to the Lowlands, arable was often in short supply. Thus in the parish of Lochgilphead in south Argyll, nineteenth-century estimates suggest that only a tiny one-fifteenth of the land surface had ever been under the plough.

Settlement in the western Highlands and Islands was mainly confined to very limited areas because of the challenging constraints of geology, climate and geography. Therefore, when modern visitors contemplate hills and glens which are empty of people, they should not assume that they were inhabited in the past or that their present silence and loneliness were necessarily the consequence of later clearance or emigration.

A historical demographer has recently analysed General William Roy's great map of Scotland, drawn between 1747 and 1755 and hence before the period of convulsive change. He concludes:

> This [the Roy map] shows settlements as clusters of red dots reflecting small groups of houses that dominated settlement patterns before the reorganisations of the following hundred or more years.
>
> The overwhelming impression for the whole of the land north and west of the Great Glen is vast areas of higher land with no houses at all. Lower down, even the most densely populated inland straths seldom show sets of red dots located less than about half a kilometre apart in the lower reaches; in their middle sections there are rarely less than one per kilometre; and higher up they peter out almost entirely.
>
> Many straths and glens were much less settled than this, with just a few scattered settlements where the land allowed. Some strips of coastline had rather denser patches of settlement spread out for a few kilometres, but in the mid eighteenth century most of the coast was completely without houses or had just odd groups clustered on a headland or around the head of a small bay.*

Other constraints made the Highlands a risk-laden environment for the people who scratched a living from the land. Climatic conditions were among the most hazardous. A historical geographer has commented:

* Michael Anderson, *Scotland's Populations from the 1850s to Today* (Oxford, 2018), pp. 25–6.

extreme events, including gales, storms, floods and blizzards, were all capable of devastating crops and stock in a matter of hours. On a larger or longer time-scale, poor seasons, especially when two or more ran in succession, could have equally devastating effect on a regional scale. Cold, wet summers could leave farmers with a harvest barely sufficient to match the seed used whilst long, hard winters could thin herds and flocks dramatically if little shelter was available, or could make it difficult to sow crops until well into the normal growing season.[4]

The western Highlands and Islands in the fifteenth and sixteenth centuries were likely to experience partial crop failure once in every three years. Severe shortages were recorded in 1671, 1680, 1680, 1688, 1695 and 1702. Between 1647 and 1707, one of the most intensely cold and stormy phases of the Little Ice Age afflicted many parts of Europe. The migration of Arctic sea ice southwards caused mean temperatures to fall steeply in the Highlands while districts along the western seaboard and across the Hebrides were fully exposed to increased risk of storm. Some tounships in the most vulnerable parishes were temporally abandoned altogether by their inhabitants during this period. The worst crisis came with the onset of the so-called 'Lean Years' in the 1690s, when successive harvest failures resulted in famine, disease and increased mortality across the whole of Scotland. The most recent estimates suggest that the population of the country as a whole fell by as much as 15 per cent as a result of sharp rises in mortality and the related mass emigration of famine refugees from south-west Scotland and the southern Highlands across the North Channel to Ulster. The available evidence also indicates that death rates were probably higher in the Highlands and Islands than elsewhere in Scotland.

The disasters of the Lean Years were triggered by an especially acute but ephemeral climatic deterioration in the later seventeenth century, which for a time also gripped Scandinavia, France, Holland and the German states. More common were the routine natural hazards of life in Gaeldom. Many communities in the Uists, Harris, Bernera, Coll and Tiree grew their grain crop on the rich *machair* lands of the western coastal fringes. The *machair* was made up of calciferous sand which the people continuously fertilized by animal manure and seaweed. But cultivating these soils increased the risks of erosion especially when severe storms struck. In the 1750s, for instance, sandstorms frequently overwhelmed both settlements and arable in the Hebrides while the low-lying nature of the coastal areas also made them vulnerable to inundation by sea storms. A similar problem of flooding in cultivated stretches was common beside rivers in the glens of the central and northern Highlands. Estate surveys of the time were replete with evidence of lands lost and peasant holdings swept away. The experience of farmers in Glen Shira (near Inveraray in Argyll) would not have been unusual. It was said that the people there were able to catch salmon where they had previously ploughed because serious flooding had altered the river channels.

These natural challenges meant that the returns on grain to the people in most parts of the north and west in medieval and early modern times were often meagre at best and seriously deficient at worst. Life for the mass of the people must have been a constant struggle to survive. It was far from the idyllic existence portrayed by later writers politically sympathetic to the Gaels during the Age of the Clearances. The endemic poverty of the western Highlands was one reason why the Scottish state took so long to impose its authority throughout the territory. If the resource base of the region had been richer and more productive, governments would probably have been tempted at a much earlier time to establish a more effective dominion over the north-west and insular districts.

Yet, while much of the terrain only provided poor crops, having some land, however tiny, was vital to the survival of each family. For this was a subsistence-based society where virtually all the necessities of life had to come directly from the land. The common food and drink crops were oats and bere (a hardy form of barley), both grown for their resilience in a harsh climate rather than because they were likely to be a source of increased yields, especially as the growing season was shorter than elsewhere in Scotland. Oats were the dietary staple throughout the Highlands, while from bere came ale and, later, whisky. The universal fuel was peat or turf, dug out from the boglands in spring, stacked and dried during the summer months as fuel for the long Highland winter.

Construction of the dwellings of the people also drew on perishable organic materials such as turf, straw, heather and ferns, not only for roofs but also for walling. The stone-built houses whose remains litter many parts of the western Highlands and Islands today came much later. Indeed, passing travellers often found it difficult to make out at a distance the settlement clusters of township huts as they merged so completely into the surrounding heath and moorland. Contemporary accounts also suggest that these habitations were rarely permanent fixtures. Thatch was recycled annually and turf walls and wattle interiors were usually taken down every three years or so, with the organic matter then used as compost and field manure. The extent and frequency with which the most basic materials used in the traditional house were renewed meant that most dwellings seem to have passed through regular cycles of construction and deconstruction.

Wool from the small sheep of the region was a primary raw material for spinning, weaving and dyeing, routine labours throughout the year. That the amount of cloth worked up was considerable is confirmed by the volume of plaid which is often documented in rental accounts. The household crafts also turned out brogues made from raw hides with leather tanned from bark. Until the sixteenth century, when some cash payments started to become more common, the rentals paid by the peasantry to their chiefs and leading gentry consisted overwhelmingly of produce extracted from the land. These payments in kind included livestock, grain, fish, poultry, cloth and whisky. As will be shown later, the distribution of land was also fundamental to the cohesion of clanship and to the prestige and power of those at the top of the social pyramid.

A few items, of course, had to be imported from elsewhere. These included salt, for preserving fish, and iron in small quantities for some farming implements and the fashioning of weapons. Most crucial, however, was wood. The evidence from Major-General William Roy's military map of 1755 suggests that on the Highland mainland woodland cover was only a little over 3 per cent of the whole, though later figures place it slightly higher. Wood for the making of ploughs, hoes, spade handles and room partitions was therefore very highly prized. Above all in importance were the roof-couples for dwellings. They would be carried from place to place as families moved and were often passed down from one generation to another. The value of timber can be confirmed by the fact that on leaving a holding tenants were usually allowed to take both roof-couples and doors with them on their departure.

2

The universal unit of settlement in the pre-clearance Highlands was the township or *baile*. Usually consisting of around four to twenty families, and sometimes more, they were scattered across the landscape in pockets of scarce arable along the glens and coastlands of the west. Some took the form of nucleated holdings, but most were dispersed settlements reflecting the patchy nature of good land outside the richer terrain of the southern and eastern fringes of the Highlands and the more fertile lands of some of the islands. Two key aspects of these communities stand out. First was the universal social need for a stake in the land, however small. Second were the close links of kindred which meant that tenants with married children by custom divided land among them. If population only rose and fell within traditional limits, these traditions were tolerable. But when in the future numbers increased in any sustained way, this form of partible inheritance threatened demographic disaster by pulverizing holdings which were originally only ever enough to support single families.

In addition to the tenants, the *bailes* were also populated by people whose names did not feature in the rental books. These 'cottars' held even tinier plots of land because of familial ties to tenants or in return for labour services on bigger holdings. Communities were therefore held together seamlessly with all having some access to land, however minuscule, so vital was it for daily existence and subsistence. Almost all families were able to graze a few cattle, goats and sheep on the grasslands of the less fertile areas around the township and the hill country beyond. But the distribution of land also had a key social and economic purpose as the resource foundation of clan society:

> Land in the Highlands . . . was laid out not so much to ensure an effective agricultural economy as to stabilize a class structure and to verify mutual obligations. It passed from proprietor to tacksman to small tenant, from tenant to subtenant, from subtenant to cottar or servant. At each stage

some ground would be kept in immediate occupation, but the rest would be handed down, as an earnest of kinship, or to ensure rent, loyalty, service, each linked with the next in mutual obligation.[5]

To eighteenth-century 'improving' writers the weaknesses of a social system of this kind were self-evident. They took the view that it was impossible for a class of richer peasants to emerge from a society where limited land was so fragmented and the potential for capital accumulation further constricted by communal working and traditional custom. But these thinkers judged the past in terms of their own age rather than by those of the world of clanship. The effects of kinship obligation and the use of land in return for labour services meant that the precious asset had to be distributed widely rather than settled in a small number of dominant peasant families. Differences in wealth between tenants do not seem to have been thought significant and little evidence of any striving for greater social status or more material gain within the structure of clanship has come to light. Crucially, also, in the heyday of clanship chiefs had a powerful rationale to pack large numbers of warriors into their lands at a time when the building up of military power was much more important than the augmentation of rent rolls.

Nevertheless, this tribal society was not lacking in enterprise or the creative ability to adapt to the challenges of living in a harsh environment. Township land was laid out in the runrig tradition by which the shares of each tenant were scattered across the arable in intermixed strips which were often regularly subject to reallocation in order to ensure reasonably fair access to good and bad soils. Rarely, outside the southern and eastern Highlands and some other favoured areas, was the arable configured in compact blocks, as in most of the Highlands the good ground was separated out by ridges, moor, bog and waterlogged areas. The traditional township and runrig cultivation are sometimes depicted as unchanging archaic structures inherited from an antique past and frozen in time. In fact adaptation and change were integral features of the townships in the old Highlands. The most striking change was an increase in the region's capacity to rear cattle and with that the great expansion of the droving trade to the Lowlands and England.

This was a salient example of how the comparative advantage of Gaeldom could be exploited. Deficient in arable resources, the Highlands had rough pasture in plentiful supply, enabling the region to become a specialist centre for the breeding, though not fattening, of small black cattle. Costly investment in transport infrastructure was unnecessary. Stock went on the hoof to the Lowland cattle markets of Crieff and Falkirk for onward sale. So much did their tracks become accustomed to the repeated imprint of man and beast that they came to be known in time as the 'drove roads'. By the middle decades of the seventeenth century, the export trade in cattle embraced all the Highlands and Islands. In the 1680s, for instance, herds of 1,000 head of cattle making their way south were not an unusual sight. Indeed, clan society provided an effective business structure for the droving trade. The contract covering the whole of the land settled by a clan and its satellites was negotiated by leading families with drovers from the Lowlands. Gathering in of stock would then be organized from individual townships by the clan gentry, and the market value of the tenants' cattle was settled and recorded as payments against their book rentals.

This major increase in cattle exports provided a novel flexibility to this subsistence-based economy and, not surprisingly, the balance of activity within the peasant holdings soon began to change as a result. The mixed economy of the townships was able to switch more land from arable to pasture and use the purchasing power released by droving to buy meal from more favoured Lowland areas on the fringes of the Highlands. Meat was rarely consumed in Gaeldom as animals were too precious a potential cash commodity for them to be sacrificed as a source of food. So sales of stock provided the purchasing power to buy in the vital supplies of meal. Indeed, by the middle decades of the eighteenth century, contemporaries observed that large parts of the central and western Highlands were only able to subsist by large importations of meal. It was said, for instance, that: 'This country [Gairloch] and all the West coast, are supplied in the summer with meal by vessels that come from the different parts at a distance; such as Caithness, Murray [sic], Peterhead, Banff, Aberdeen, Greenock etc.'[6]

Nor was the arable economy inflexible. The people had learned how to respond to some of the problems of shallow soils, marginal land and regular waterlogging. The techniques which were adopted called for a great deal of labour, but that was the one resource in abundant supply in most parts of the north and west. The common method was the labour-intensive construction of lazy beds (*feannagan*) and then working them by the spade or foot-plough (*cas-chrom*). The *feannagan* were raised sandwiches of soil with furrows between which were built up even on rock surfaces as well as on uncultivated moorland. Animal dung, old thatch compost, seaweed and shell sand were then added to the beds to provide enrichment. When prepared by the *cas-chrom*, the lazy beds could produce even higher grain yields than horse-drawn ploughing, but at the cost of a very great deal of human effort. Yet in a society where labour was plentiful and arable scarce, this was a rational trade-off.

3

The clan, *A' Chlann*, literally means 'the children'. Therefore, at the heart of clanship was the belief that all clansmen were bound together by ties of common kinship and descended by origin from legendary patriarchs of antiquity. Yet, in reality, clans in the Highlands had not evolved from the very remote past but rather as a response to political turbulence and social dislocation in northern Scotland during the early Middle Ages. At that time, people sought protection from danger and threat by gathering in loyalty to great men of influence, power and prestige as the crown itself could not guarantee law and order throughout the entire realm of Scotland. In particular, the hill country of the north and west mainland, the Western Isles and the Scottish Borders were semi-autonomous entities, mainly beyond royal control, from the thirteenth through to the seventeenth centuries.

The nature of clanship has long been shrouded in myth, song, story and romance. Only in recent years has modern scholarship started to unlock some of its secrets and begun to reveal a more convincing and authentic narrative of its origins, structure and complexity. Clanship was not unique to the Highlands. Until the seventeenth century other parts of Scotland had also been based on kin-based societies where the power and influence of great men and family networks commanded ultimate authority. The Borders, another region of recalcitrance in the face of royal authority, was in this sense entirely comparable to the western Highlands. In 1587, when the Scottish Parliament discussed the problem of regional disorder throughout the realm, it was both Border and Highland élites who were directed to impose more control over their people. In the north-eastern Lowlands, too, there were also some vestiges of similar social and cultural patterns.

There can be little doubt as well that claims of blood connection both in and beyond Gaeldom survived into the eighteenth century, albeit not for the purposes of making war. Lowland magnates at that time were very conscious of the need to provide support to kinfolk who sought careers, posts and opportunities in Scotland, Britain and the Empire. But clanship in the Highlands, in large part because of its martial imperative, became much more embedded in Gaelic culture through bardic genealogies, songs, stories and traditions. Even in the later eighteenth century and beyond, travellers to the Highlands who were appalled by the squalor and poverty which they witnessed were also mightily impressed by the rich culture of poetry and music of the people which they experienced.

More than any other part of Scotland, the Highlands and Islands were able to resist for longer the encroachment of royal power, because geography presented formidable barriers to the enforcement of state authority. In that sense, the distinguishing feature of the Highland clan was not so much its antiquity, social structure or family connections, but its longevity, surviving into the eighteenth century long after other kin-based regional societies in Scotland and Britain as a whole had passed into history.

The clans which can be documented during the Middle Ages had a range of ethnic and territorial origins. Anglo-Norman, Celtic, Norse, Gaelic, Anglian and Flemish families can be counted among their founding dynasties, a truly multinational inheritance. Over time, dominant tribal élites legitimized their status and power by tracing bloodlines to some prestigious figure in the distant past who could provide the commons of the clan with a sense of identity and historical meaning. Most of these pedigrees were created and re-created with the scantest of concern for historical or chronological accuracy. The invention of tradition was pragmatic and expedient in order to enhance family status, accommodate changing alliances and absorb other clans into the greater whole. It comes as little surprise, therefore, to learn that among the founding ancestors claimed by the MacGregors was Pope Gregory the Great, while ClanCampbell was wont to include the legendary but elusive King Arthur among its 'name-fathers'.

The realities were, of course, more prosaic. The Grants, for instance, who were probably of Anglo-Norman stock, did not become prominent until after the marriage in the fifteenth century of Iain Ruadh (Red John) to Matilda, the heiress of Glencairnie, which allowed the acquisition of extensive lands in Moray and Inverness. Thereafter, their rise to prominence depended above all on their close association with the Gordons, earls of Huntly, which allowed consolidation and extension of their landed interest and power in the central Highlands. The McKenzies became important only after they provided military support to the Scottish crown in the attempt to subdue the Lords of the Isles. After forfeiture of the Lords, the head of the McKenzies received a crown charter in 1476 for the lands of Strathconnan and Strathgarve in central Ross-shire. Thereafter, they ruthlessly expanded their domains until by the later seventeenth century the fiefdom of the McKenzies was second only to the mighty imperium of ClanCampbell.

The McNeills had a pedigree which went back to Niall, a Knapdale warlord of the eleventh century, but they seem only to have emerged as an important kindred in the turmoil which followed the Norwegian ceding of the Western Isles to the Scottish crown in 1246 and was then followed by the beginning of the Wars of Independence with England. It was at this time that they became established on their principal territory on the island of Barra. Then, through association with Alexander MacDonald, Lord of the Isles, the McNeills were awarded Boisdale in South Uist by charter. By the middle decades of the fifteenth century they were also ensconced on the isle of Gigha and in parts of Knapdale on the Argyll mainland.

The chief, as tribal patriarch or *ceann-cinnidh,* and the *fine,* or leading gentlemen of the clan, could be reasonably confident for the most part in their kinship connections to the ruling families of past generations as the relationships were recorded and embellished in the epics, eulogies and elegies of the bards and genealogists. Whether the mass of clansmen had inherited similar blood relationships to their chiefs is much more doubtful. The *belief* that they had done so, however, was what mattered, because that exclusive family bond was a critical factor in the development of cohesion across the different strata of clan society. One of the best insights into its central importance came not from a Gael, but from an outsider, Edmund Burt, the English officer of engineers, in his letters written in the 1720s and 1730s from the Highlands to a friend in London. The period is important because, as suggested in the next chapter, clanship was already in decay at that point. Despite this, the mindset of the clansmen whom Burt encountered seems to have remained cast in stone:

> The ordinary Highlanders esteem it the most sublime degree of virtue to love their chief and pay him a blind obedience, although it be in opposition to the Government, the laws of the Kingdom, or even to the law of God. He is their idol; and they profess to know no king but him.
>
> This power of the chiefs is not supported by interest as they are landlords, but as really descended from the old patriarchs or fathers of the families; for they hold the same authority when they have lost their estates . . .
>
> . . . as the meanest among them pretend to be his relations by consanguinity, they insist upon the privilege of taking him by the hand wherever they meet him.[7]

The chiefs personified their clans and were identified by patronymics which often went back several generations to the formative period of the evolution of the kindred, so providing the crucial legitimacy of myth, history and longevity. Thus the chief of ClanCampbells of Argyll was *MacCaileinMor,* the big son of Colin, and the chief of the Macdonalds of Clanranald was addressed as *Mac vic Ailean*, grandson of Allan.

Despite these ties of affection, however, the realities of history were in conflict with beliefs of consanguinity across the entire clan community. As the larger clans relentlessly augmented their territory through conquest, marriage and the acquisition of crown charters, effective control of the new lands became more difficult. This was especially the case when districts had to be annexed rapidly and effectively in times of conflict across difficult and broken terrain. A case in point was the challenge of command and control which confronted the MacLeods of Dunvegan. Their sprawling territories at the peak of possession included a number of small islands in the Outer Hebrides, such as Pabbay, Ensay, Berneray, Taransa and St Kilda, in addition to the main island of Harris, and the districts of Bracadale, Waternish, Duirnish and Minginish in Skye.

The strategic response to the challenge of governance within the context of kin-based society was to lease or make life-grants to junior members of the ruling family and so establish new lines of descent and cadet branches of the main clan. These cadres then became identified by the name of the district over which they held lordship and authority. Once consolidated, these kin groups would then infiltrate the existing landed hierarchy of the newly acquired territories and steadily replace the native élites with their own kindred. This practice was commonplace among such imperialistic clans as the Mac-Donalds in the heyday of the medieval Lordship of the Isles and then even more aggressively with the Campbells and McKenzies in the seventeenth century.

As ClanDonald reinforced territories in the Western Isles, so members of its *fine* were settled in different districts across the insular districts of the region. Eventually no fewer than seventeen different branches, or *sliochden*, had emerged to assume landed control. Each was linked with a particular part of the ClanDonald empire, such as Glencoe, Ardnamurchan, Sleat and Knoydart. Even these sub-hierarchies could split into further *septs*, or divisions, possessing even smaller areas. From the MacDonalds of Clanranald, for example, there developed the cadet families of Knoydart, Glengarry, Morar and Kinlochmoidart. There was a similar dynamic in other clans. Five branches of the Frasers were documented in 1650, but by 1745 the number had risen to over thirty. The ClanDonachy, or Robert-son, is noted as being in possession of lands in Strowan in Perthshire, in 1451. Each of the twenty-four branches of the clan had established authority over multiple sub-areas within the broader domain by the eighteenth century.

This evidence of evolution and aggrandisement makes nonsense therefore of any claim that clans were united through ties of blood.

The possessions of many of them were often in a state of flux as small kinship groups were overwhelmed and absorbed into the territorial empires of more powerful rivals through conflict or intermarriage. In such cases, changes of allegiance were commonplace as families adopted the identity of other locally dominant clans for sound reasons of security and survival. In addition, it was common for weaker units to develop close alliances with stronger kindreds. For instance, the MacRaes and MacLennans became loyal allies and followers of the MacKenzies, as did the MacColls in their long association with the Stewarts of Appin. The blood ties between the ruling families and the ordinary clansmen were therefore largely mythical, but the belief in consanguinity, suggested by the very term *clann*, or children, gave, as suggested above, a deep emotional bond which did much to cement social cohesion within clanship. Essentially, therefore, the clan did not consist of those of the same blood kindred but rather those who followed the same chief and ruling family whatever their own blood lineage or ancestral connections.

As noted earlier, clan-type social structures had been common in other parts of Scotland in earlier periods but lasted longer in the Highlands and Islands than elsewhere. A key factor was the topography of the region. Dr Johnson, during his travels, reflected on the advantages possessed by the people of 'mountainous countries' when presented with the threat of the imposition of control by a distant central authority:

> they are not easily conquered because they must be entered by narrow ways, exposed to every power of mischief from those who occupy the heights; and every new ridge is a new fortress where the defendants have again the same advantage. If the war be not soon concluded, the invaders are dislodged by hunger . . . The wealth of mountains is cattle, which, while the men stand in the passes, the women drive away.[8]

In the medieval period, feudalism had become the key strategy designed to integrate the kingdom of Scotland under royal authority. The crown in feudal theory exercised superiority over all men and land and the major lords held their domains directly from the monarch in return for military service. David I (1084–1153) did much to feudalize Scotland, including the southern and eastern frontiers of the Highlands. Even further west in the region, leading families often formally accepted royal authority and in return were granted feudal charters from the monarchy which guaranteed legal title to the possession of their lands. The status of the clan chiefs was therefore hybrid. On the one hand they were tribal leaders; on the other, thanks to the dictates of feudalism, they were also landowners in law, in the same way as their peers in Lowland society, and with the royal charters confirmed by the monarch to prove their legal authority over every square inch of their domain.

But allegiance to the crown did not necessarily follow on from these formal legal decisions and agreements. As Johnson observed in the later eighteenth century, the kind of medieval warfare pursued by forces of heavily armoured knights was unsuited to the Highlands since the terrain was incapable of providing for the heavy maintenance costs of that martial élite. The levies of the crown could live off the land in the arable districts of south and east Scotland but that was much more challenging in Gaeldom, where harvests were usually meagre and more at risk from climatic hazards. Moreover, unlike most of the Lowlands, those two important ancillary agencies for the enforcement of state control, the church and the towns, were much less influential in the north-west than elsewhere in the kingdom during the early modern period. It might also have been the case that the contemporary Lowland perception of the Highlands as a barbarous, primitive and poverty-stricken region would not have encouraged the Scottish monarchy to spend scarce resources in attempts to seek full incorporation of the recalcitrant *Gaidhealtachd* into the Scottish state.

The power vacuum which inevitably followed was filled by the larger clans, most of whom were in violent competition, one with the other, until the seventeenth century. The ensuing age of turbulence can be seen in the remarkable increase in formidable stone castles and other fortified dwellings which were built by the Gaelic aristocracy. Today the grandeur of their crumbling ruins, as at Tioram, Sween, Urquhart, Dunstaffnage and many other sites, are striking monuments to the age of medieval clan power. These great edifices also served another purpose in addition to their function of places of protection and defence. The mass of the population in the Highlands and

Islands lived in poor smoke-filled turf huts, and the castles in their sheer physicality and towering walls manifested in stone the authority and prestige of the ruling family to the ordinary clansmen, as well as projecting military strength and unyielding power to potential enemies and rivals.

For nearly 150 years in the fourteenth and fifteenth centuries, the Lordship of the Isles ruled by ClanDonald, a Gaelic kingdom within a Scottish kingdom, provided a degree of order and authority to a sea empire which stretched from the island of Islay in the south to the Butt of Lewis in the far north-west. The collapse of the Lordship after 1496, as a consequence of fratricidal conflict within the ruling Mac-Donald family, triggered decades of violence in the sixteenth century as the clans of the west warred for dominance. This time of chronic warfare cemented their internal loyalties as never before and further embedded the status of chiefs and *fine* as the supreme guarantors of protection to the people of their lands. It was against this background of endemic insecurity and constant rivalry, often punctuated by episodes of uninhibited killing, that some key aspects of clan society can best be understood.

Military preparedness was a *sine qua non*. Martin Martin, or Màrtainn MacGilleMhátainn (1669?–1719), a native of Skye, writing in the later seventeenth century, recalled how courage and prowess in war were the vital qualities of a chief. In the Western Isles, he described how it was necessary for young heirs to chiefdoms to demonstrate a 'publick specimen of their valour' before they could be accepted by the clan. Because of this, the chief and other members of the *fine* of the clan were wont to take part in 'a desperate Incursion upon some Neighbour or other that they were in Feud with' and to 'bring by open force the Cattle they found in the Lands they attack'd or to die in the Attempt'.[9] The intense militarism of the western clans at this juncture was also illustrated by the widespread practice of *sorning*, or the extraction by fighting men of food and hospitality from tenants within the clan territory or, indeed, on the lands of other clans with whom a feud existed. *Sorning* suggested the existence of a parasitic warrior class which was not engaged in labouring the land but in preparing for or making war.

In turn, the effective deployment of martial resources for battle depended on the depth and integrity of the connection between clan élites and followers. The levels of cohesion drew on a number of influences. The bards, genealogists and orators did much to embed the historical identity of the clan and enhance the prestige of the chief by recounting the epic deeds of his ancestors. The custom of fostering reinforced real or fictive ties of kinship within the clan élites as the children of the chief were brought up over a period of seven years or more in the households of leading clan gentry. They in turn would foster their own children in the same way among satellite families positioned below them in the social hierarchy.

Distribution of land by means of these networks also bound the subordinate gentry to their chiefs. Prominent among the clan gentry were the *fir-tacsa*, or tacksmen. As an earnest of kinship they were granted tacks (leases) to the townships, or settlements, of the clansmen. They lived as quasi-landlords among these tenants on the difference between the rents they gathered and the payments made to the chiefs. Tacksmen were the recognized organizers of their subordinate clansmen in time of war. But they also had important economic functions to ensure their subtenants carried out labour services for the ruling house and to order the fair distribution of land in the townships for which they had responsibility. The *fir-tacsa* were also key to the trade in cattle to the Lowlands. They not only organized the round-up of the beasts and gathering them into droves, but were also responsible for offsetting their sale value against township rental payments.

In addition, rentals in kind of cattle, sheep, meal, cheese, hens and geese, which were paid to the chief by clansmen in their role as tenants, were sometimes converted back into the provision of subsistence support in seasons of shortage. In this way, the clan élites were able to provide a form of social insurance in a volatile environment. It was an expected obligation which endured as an expectation among the people long after the ethic of clanship itself had passed into history. Feasting at the behest of the leading families also had a vital social purpose. As well as demonstrating the chief's capacities for generosity and hospitality, collective eating and drinking also generated a sense of communal harmony for all clan families no matter their rank. The feasts of the medieval period were often lavish affairs with the consumption of enormous amounts of food and drink. Even in the early seventeenth century, some of the old traditions survived and were reported in somewhat exaggerated terms. It was said that when the daughter of MacLeod married the heir of Clanranald, some of those present boasted that the feasting went on for six days and nights. They dimly recollected that 'we were twenty times drunk every day, to which we had no more objection than he had'.[10] These celebrations in a society where scarcity of basic food was common did much to enhance the status and prestige of the chief and his household. They were only made possible by the prevalence of rentals in kind in this period and their limited sale to markets outside the Highlands.

Ultimately of even more significance than support in times of crisis and the provision of hospitality was the provision of land to clansmen. As feudal lords the clan élites had the same absolute rights of ownership over their property as proprietors anywhere else in Scotland. Yet, within the kin-based society, the territory of the clan was governed by a quite different set of assumptions potentially in conflict with the legal realities of private landownership. The areas settled by each clan were regarded as its collective heritage, or *duthchas*, and the *fine* were seen, not as the sole masters of these lands, but as the current guardians, protectors and trustees of the people who lived on them. Real or nominal kinsmen within them felt they possessed a prior claim to clan holdings as a result of their loyalty to and connection with the ruling family. One instance of this comes from a Clanranald rental of 1718 for the Isle of Eigg which shows the Captain of Clanranald asserting his 'power of keeping in his own Kinsmen and tenents on this Isle'.[11]

The strong belief existed that the chief should provide land for his clansmen even if they did not have rights to specific individual holdings in perpetuity. Edmund Burt in the 1730s noted how chiefs commonly packed townships with tenants and subtenants for this purpose. This was a reflection of the subsistence needs of the people on the one hand and the military imperative to establish a large following on the other. Nevertheless, some chiefs apparently moved clansmen about their lands as circumstances required. When Sir James MacDonald was attempting to make peace with the crown in the early seventeenth century, he at first offered to remove elements of

ClanDonald South from Kintyre to Islay. Subsequently, he went further and undertook to move them anywhere the state wished.

Commonly, as a result of inter-clan feuds and fear of annexation, entire townships were abandoned and lay unoccupied for many years, the people who had lived there having gone elsewhere. Surviving estate papers record a considerable turnover of tenants, even in those townships under continuous settlement. The local mobility of tenants and cottars was often part and parcel of the old way of life and did not simply emerge during the era of clearance. For instance, a series of rentals for Kintyre, a relatively fertile district, between 1502 and 1605 reveals that no family held the annual lease of a township over the whole period. But, this evidence notwithstanding, the cultural force of *duthchas* seems to have pervaded Gaeldom and was central to clan identity. It articulated the expectations of the people that the ruling families had the responsibility to act as protectors to guarantee secure possession of some land in return for allegiance, military service, tribute and rental. It was a powerful and enduring belief which endured long after the rationale of clanship itself had vanished and when élites had shed ancient responsibilities and metamorphosed into commercial landlords.

2

The Long Death of Clanship

I

It used to be thought that Highland clanship died on the fateful battlefield of Culloden Moor in April 1746 and was then buried by a combination of punitive legislation and state terror. But the demise of clan society was much more protracted than that. Indeed, the roots of decay can be traced back to the early decades of the seventeenth century and the more effective imposition of crown authority throughout the Highlands during the reign of James VI and I (1567–1625). The Scottish government and, after the Regal Union of 1603, the British monarchy, began to enforce its writ in Gaeldom with more determination and success then than at any time in the past. As state power started to guarantee law and order in the north and west, the kin-based networks of chiefs, clan gentry and followers, which had evolved over generations for the purposes of mutual defence and protection in times of chronic instability, were bound to come under pressure as the practical rationale of clanship was steadily undermined. Decline, however, was very slow, piecemeal and varied in extent between the more stable eastern and southern Lowland fringes and the traditionally more turbulent western mainland and the islands of the Inner and Outer Hebrides. Also, as the history of the '45 Rising confirmed, even by the early eighteenth century the martial ethos of several clans, whether Hanoverian or Jacobite in sympathy, had not entirely died.

From the later sixteenth century, the government of James VI set out to impose more political and administrative control on the Highlands by employing the same tactics which were already delivering success in the Scottish Borders, that other recalcitrant region of feuding and lawlessness. New thinking was emerging within the counsels of the state that 'civility', stability and order should be established throughout the entire realm of Scotland. To this was added a concern that crown revenues from some of the semi-autonomous Highland districts were unacceptably low. At the same time, the old assumptions that the north was only a region of irredeemable poverty and devoid of resources were steadily being superseded by more optimistic ideas about the possibilities of unexploited potential for development from both the seas and the lands of Gaeldom. As a first step, from the 1580s, the crown demanded that some leading clan chiefs had to find sureties ranging from £2,000 to £20,000 Scots to guarantee the good behaviour of their clansmen. More-decisive initiatives were adopted after 1603, when James occupied the thrones of both Scotland and England. Now the western clans could be confronted by the full naval and military force of a unified and expansionist British state intent. The availability of English naval resources after 1603 was crucial because in the western Highlands it was the sea which united the bases of clan power and the land which usually divided them.

Equally critical in the drive for more control was the ruthlessly efficient annexation of native lands in six counties of the north of Ireland, which was then followed by the establishment of the Plantation of Ulster. This naked use of coercion and the forced displacement of the Catholic population brought home to the élites of the clans in the western Highlands, who had many kinship links with landed families in the north of Ireland, the present and future danger of resisting the authority of an increasingly aggressive and powerful British state. More directly, the conquest of Gaelic Ireland, associated with 'The Flight of the Earls' in 1607, after their earlier defeat at the Battle of Kinsale in 1601, finally eliminated the traditional opportunities for mercenary service in Ireland by the Highland *buannachan*, or household men. This specialist warrior class within clanship had long flourished on booty, plunder and violent employment across the Irish Sea. However, an Anglo-Saxon Protestant wedge had now been driven between the two territories of Gaelic/Catholic civilization. As a result, the old seaborne commercial and military ties between the northern counties of Ireland and *A'Gaidhealtachd* soon began to wither. Indeed, from the 1620s, the now redundant *buannachan* began to be shipped in large numbers by their own *fine* to Europe, where they first served in British expeditionary forces and then as mercenaries in Swedish and Dutch service during the Thirty Years War. Their fate was eloquent testimony to the fact that the militarized nature of Highland society was now in decay.

However, the government of James VI and I did not undertake the same draconian policy of wholesale territorial annexation in the Highlands of the kind which was imposed in Ireland. Instead, a range of strategies were adopted, including partial expropriation of the lands of those clans considered to be especially delinquent. The main targets for this approach were ClanDonald South, the ClanLeod of Lewis, the Maclains of Ardnamurchan and ClanGregor. A related policy of colonization was also designed to drive another *cordon sanitaire* between Gaelic Ireland and Scotland with plans to set up colonies of 'answerable inland subjects' (i.e. Lowland Protestants) in Lewis, Lochaber and Kintyre. Only the last of these settlements, however, was even partially successful. Much more effective was the launching of punitive expeditions along the western seaboard in 1596, 1599, 1605, 1607 and 1608. These violent incursions were paralleled by the award of judicial commissions to loyal lieutenants, drawn mainly from trusted magnate families on the Highland–Lowland frontier. The Gordons, earls of Huntly and the even more ambitiously imperialistic Campbells, earls of Argyll, were enjoined by the crown to extract surety for good conduct from neighbouring clans which were judged to be more prone to truculent disloyalty to the crown.

These were all conventional tactics long employed successfully in the unruly districts of the Borders. But the state also embarked on a novel attempt to produce a comprehensive solution to the Highland problem by tackling what were seen as the social roots of disorder. This was the policy of 'planting civilitie', which James himself had outlined in his book *Basilikon Doran*. It was first embodied in the Statutes of Iona of 1609 to which all major chiefs in the Hebrides had to give their consent. The Statutes ranged from the suppression of beggars and vagabonds, to the control of wine and whisky, from limits on the household retinues of the *fine* to the strengthening of the reformed church, from sending the heirs of men of substance to the

Lowlands to be schooled to the prohibition of ordinary clansmen carrying arms. Not only were the chiefs bound to observe these rulings, but they were also ordered to appear personally before the Privy Council in Edinburgh at stated intervals as proof of their good conduct within the terms of the Iona agreements in the present and also in the future. The Statutes were indeed a comprehensive programme designed to impose Lowland values on the *fine*, promote their assimilation with the mores of the 'civilized' Lowlands and eliminate what was seen as the chronic excesses of clanship.

There has been considerable historical debate about the practical impact of these initiatives. But whatever their short-term effect, they did have a potent influence on the clan élites over time. One scholar has suggested that 'central government's main priority was to educate the *fine* about their responsibilities as members of the Scottish landed classes, *not* to denigrate their status'.[1] Indeed as confirmation of their acknowledged social position, the clan gentry were permitted to carry arms and wear armour and also given monopoly licences to bring wines and spirits to the Western Isles. In return for these privileges, clan gentries were expected to become partners with the state in the maintenance of order and to be held to account for the conduct of their clansmen. This was to be ensured through the exaction of substantial sureties and the annual appearance of chiefs before the Privy Council in Edinburgh. These attendances were rigorously enforced until the outbreak of the Scottish Revolution in 1638.

Political control soon started to cause substantial changes within clanship. Severe financial burdens of surety were now imposed on the *fine*, varying in the 1610s from £3,000 to £18,000 Scots. The costs of regularly appearing before the Privy Council were also considerable and those who attended could often find themselves detained in the capital for up to six months at a time and even longer. Sir Rory MacLeod of Dunvegan complained to James VI in 1622 that his annual appearances meant that he was away from his estates for more than half the year, making it difficult for him to manage them effectively. Sojourns in Edinburgh would also lead to expenditure on legal fees, housing and the many pleasures of the capital. The accounts of seventeenth-century Highland families, such as the MacDonalds of Clanranald and the MacLeods of Dunvegan, show increasing outlays on expensive clothing, furnishings and exotic foods as they gradually became integrated into Scottish landed society with all the cost implications for the maintenance of personal status through material display which that implied.

The outbreak of civil war in Britain in 1638 brought these compulsory annual visitations to Edinburgh temporarily to an end. But that bitter conflict imposed even greater stresses through the devastation of lands and economic dislocation throughout the country. The bloodiest fighting took place during the Wars of the Covenanters in the central and south-western Highlands, especially after the incursions of Alasdair MacColla with his Irish-Catholic troops from Ulster in 1644. Entire districts were despoiled and numerous townships laid waste through the marching and counter-marching of royalist and Covenanting forces, all of whom lived off the land. One effect was to reinforce the militarism of the clans for a time and so postpone the decay of martial society. During the Cromwellian Union of 1652–60, further systematic destruction was inflicted on several districts, stretching from Lochaber to Wester Ross, by General George Monck during his suppression of the rebellion led by the Earl of Glencairn in 1653–4. The long-term economic impact of hostilities on some localities is vividly illustrated from the McLean estates in Mull, Morvern and Tiree. Sir Hector McLean of Duart fell with around 700 of his clansmen at the Battle of Inverkeithing in 1651. One thousand men had originally been raised and the losses were so great that the estate economy of the McLeans did not fully recover until several years afterwards. A rental of 1674 listed thirty-two out of 140 McLean townships still lying waste at that date, more than two decades after the slaughter which was suffered at the battle. The restoration of the Stuart monarchy of Charles II from 1660 brought little respite. The new fiscal regime which came into force then had an impact on landowners in the Highlands as well as the rest of Scotland. The excise (1661), the land tax (1665) and the cess (1667) were exacting burdens. Moreover, from 1661, chiefs were once again compelled to attend Edinburgh to account to the authorities for the conduct of their clansmen.

The fifty years after the Statutes of Iona saw a massive increase in the indebtedness of the Highland élites as a result of the combined forces of state action, absenteeism and conspicuous consumption.

The debts of the MacLeods of Dunvegan rose to £66,700 Scots in 1649 and climbed again to £129,000 by 1663, while in 1700 an account of Clanranald's debts to his kinsman MacDonald of Sleat stood at £64,000. Two decades before, fourteen leading members of the *fine* of that clan had put their names to a document, 'The Oath of the Friends', designed to protect the finances of their chief from inevitable ruin. In fact, indebtedness had become a structural problem and now plagued most of the ruling families of Gaeldom. Various responses to financial difficulties were adopted, including a huge increase in wadsetting (giving a pledge of lands, often to family members of the clan élite, in security for debt), growing dependence on Edinburgh and Glasgow merchants for bonded loans, and, not least, a more businesslike approach to the management of land in order to make estates yield more revenue. It was the last response which was likely to be of profound significance for the future of clanship. At some point, the new determination of chiefs and leading gentry to extract additional income from their tenants was likely to conflict directly with their patriarchal responsibilities to the clan. The long transition from tribal chiefs to commercial landlords was now in train, many decades before Bonnie Prince Charlie's historic defeat on Culloden Moor.

It is significant, for instance, that the old traditions of feasting, heroic drinking and collective hospitality seem to have been falling away throughout the seventeenth century. By the 1690s, Martin Martin reported this to be the case even in the far Outer Hebrides.[2] Rentals in kind, or 'victual' rents, were also gradually being converted to cash values, which meant that food rentals were now being increasingly marketed outside the Highlands for commercial gain. On the MacLeod estates in Harris and Skye, rents were mainly paid in kind until the 1640s. By the 1680s, however, money rents made up half the value of the total and by the 1740s over three quarters. The most lucrative export trade was the rearing of black cattle, which reflected the comparative advantage of the hill country economy for pastoral development. The beasts went to market on the hoof without any additional investment needed for transportation. Overheads in general were therefore relatively low. Tacksmen rounded up the cattle from the townships under their management, and once they had been taken to collection points on the mainland, the remaining costs were born by Lowland drovers and merchants until the droves were sold on at the trysts of Crieff and Falkirk. The needs of a massively expanded Royal Navy for salt beef during the Wars of the Spanish Succession, growing demand in the urban areas of Scotland, northern England and, especially, in London, the impact of the new common market between the two countries after 1707, and late-seventeenth-century prohibitions on cattle imports from Ireland were all significant factors in this golden age of the Highland cattle trade. By the 1720s it was reckoned that as many as 30,000 beasts were being driven south annually to the Lowlands. Estate incomes were also being augmented by sales of timber, fish, slate, linen and other produce as part of the drive to reduce debt and at the same time support the growing absenteeism and consumerism of the élites. The impact was especially marked in the southern and eastern fringes of the Highlands. Long before the era of clearances, the lands of great chiefs such as the Campbells of Argyll and Breadalbane and the Murrays, earls of Atholl, in Highland Perthshire were already locked into the demands of the Lowland economy.

By the early eighteenth century, therefore, the Highlands was a society in transition. The resolution of clan differences by force of arms had begun to die out. The last major clan battle, a bloody affair between elements of ClanChattan and ClanDonald South, was fought at Mulroy in the Braes of Lochaber in August 1688. The fact that the times were becoming more peaceful is one explanation for the horrified contemporary reaction to the infamous Massacre of Glencoe in 1692. Crown forces killed nearly thirty men, women and children of the MacDonalds of Glencoe, a small sept addicted to banditry and also loyal to the exiled House of Stuart. The episode has gone down through the ages in story, legend and song. Glencoe is remembered for several reasons, but partly because acts of collective violence which were commonplace in the sixteenth century and earlier had become exceptional a hundred years later.

In the same way, clans like the MacGregors were denounced as barbaric in the early eighteenth century for their thievery and cattle rieving. They now stood out as dangerous and threatening in a world that was moving on. For the most part cattle raiding and protection rackets were now confined to a few districts, such as the Highland/ Lowland peripheries and the more inaccessible parts of the Lochaber region. The growing costs of warfare in the age of gunpowder also made chiefs less willing or less able to arm their clansmen properly with muskets, pistols and shot. Indeed, probably only a minority of those who fought under John Grahame of Claverhouse, Viscount Dundee, in the Jacobite Rising of 1688–9 had seen action in the past. Before his famous victory at Killiecrankie, he was concerned how his mainly raw clansmen would perform under fire. Daniel Defoe, in his *Tour through the Whole Island of Great Britain*, in the early eighteenth century was impressed by the social changes which he saw for himself. While noting that the people of the central Highlands were considered in the past 'a fierce, fighting and furious kind of men', he added that they were also 'by the good conduct of their chiefs and heads of clans, much more civilized than they were in former times'.[3] The remarkable expansion of cattle droving, and the profits accruing to the *fine* from its success, tended to encourage most clans to act more within the law as banditry and cattle rustling were a threat to more lucrative peaceful commerce.

This argument, however, should not be taken too far. Military capability remained across the Highlands because many clan gentry and their rank and file often served as mercenaries in Dutch and French armies at the time. The presence of a pool of clan gentlemen who had held command rank in the European military explains why it was possible to regiment the clans as infantry formations during the later Jacobite risings. The establishment of the independent companies by the state in and after 1725 also allowed some chiefs to give their clansmen experience of modern military tactics even if inter-clan conflict itself was already a thing of the past before the Union of 1707.

The old social cohesion of the clans also came under stress as the new emphasis on economy imposed increasing strains. The bards lamented the habits of chiefs spending longer periods in Edinburgh and even London and criticized the upward spiral of rising debts which took place because of chronic absenteeism. For the people of the Highlands these were ominous signs. Rent rises started to become more common in some areas, especially in the southern and eastern Highlands. One laird, Archibald Campbell of Knockbuy in Argyll, for instance, raised his rental fourfold between 1728 and the 1780s on the profits from the booming cattle trade.

Firstly in Kintyre, about 1710, and then elsewhere on his properties in 1737, John Campbell, second Duke of Argyll, offered tenant leases to the highest bidder, thus substituting competition for clanship on the largest Highland estate. This was a radical strategy since it also involved the removal of the tacksmen, the *fir-tacsa*, from their centuries-old functions as military lieutenants in the clan structure and managers of the township economies. Land was now rented directly to tenants and the margins formerly creamed off by tacksmen went directly into the coffers of the Duke. Also under the new system of competitive bidding, rents were increased by averages of 60 per cent between 1720 and 1740 in the islands of Mull and Tiree, in part because inter-clan rivalry between incoming Campbells and subjugated McLeans for leases pushed them to higher levels. Even more dramatic changes were being enforced on the neighbouring and extensive estates of Argyll's kinsman, John Campbell, second Earl of Breadalbane from the early 1700s. As well as rent increases, rigorous controls over subdivision of tenancies were put in place, as was the selective removal of tenants who were in arrears of rent. The Breadalbane estate papers confirm that some 'warnings off' or evictions were taking place on the Braes of Lorn and Netherlorn in the 1720s and 1730s, a generation or more before major clearances began elsewhere in the Highlands.

Not surprisingly, therefore, in the 1730s, there came the first significant emigrations in response to these new ways. Small parties left from Argyll, Sutherland and the central Highlands to Georgia and the Carolinas across the Atlantic. Around the same time Norman MacLeod of Dunvegan and Sir Alexander MacDonald of Sleat, the two most powerful chiefs in Skye, devised an extraordinary but ultimately unsuccessful scheme to deport some of their clansmen, wives and children to the American colonies, there to be sold as indentured labour for the plantations. In the resulting scandal both MacLeod and MacDonald were threatened with judicial prosecution. The notorious case seemed to confirm as no other could that for some chiefs at least the ethic of clanship was already being subordinated to the pursuit of profit.

Yet care should be taken not to exaggerate the scale and extent of social change in the Highlands at this stage. Commercial values were indeed developing but were not yet dominant. Tenancies on most estates were still allocated on the basis of long kin connection and traditional affiliation. Significant agrarian improvements were still largely confined to the estates of the Argyll and Breadalbane Campbells and a few other lairds in the southern and eastern Highlands. Ironically, the new cultural, economic and political connections with the south, while influencing the decay of clanship in the long run, may have delayed the final demise of the old order in the short run because from the time of the Civil Wars in the 1640s the military capabilities of the clans became recognized by opposing forces in the Lowlands. The Revolution of 1688–9 and the exile of the royal House of Stuart led from that time to five attempts at counter-revolution by Jacobite loyalists over the following fifty years in 1689–90, 1708, 1715, 1719 and 1745. In all these episodes the fighting prowess of the clans was a major factor in the Jacobite and, to a lesser extent, anti-Jacobite forces. This factor served to perpetuate clan cohesion to some extent and for a time probably tempered the forces of commercialization. But the need for more cash resources did indeed powerfully influence the clan gentry before the '45, which explains their rapid and energetic exploitation of even greater economic opportunities after that final Rising was crushed. But though the process of conversion to commercial landlordism may have been advanced before 1750 among the *fine*, the commons of the clans were still by and large insulated from the transition. It was the tacksmen and the clan gentry rather than ordinary clansmen who undertook most of the business of selling cattle and other produce to Lowland markets. It seems clear, therefore, that while the élites were indeed undergoing a profound metamorphosis, most of their followers maintained traditionalist expectations. These values were not yet directly or generally challenged, however, because the nature of commercialization before the 1760s meant most chiefs were still able to extract more income from the land without entirely compromising their hereditary functions as protectors and guardians of the people. That uneasy equilibrium was unlikely to last for much longer.

2

It is against this background that the significance of Jacobitism for Highland society can be considered. In a sense, military force drawn from the Highlands became almost as important as diplomatic support from France for the cause of the exiled Stuart dynasty after 1688. The clan regiments provided the cutting edge of the Jacobite armies and were employed as the front-line troops in all major battles of each Rising from 1688 until the final disaster of 1746. In the early eighteenth century it was reckoned that a great host of 30,000 clansmen could potentially be raised for the Stuarts, though nothing like that number ever took the field. Charles Edward Stuart reached Derby in 1745 with fewer than 5,000 followers, not all of whom were Gaels. But only in the Highlands by the early eighteenth century in Britain could a force of lightly armed irregulars be quickly mobilized for military action. Indeed, given the absence of a large standing army in Britain and the recurrent need to despatch regular troops to the European theatre, even a small and determined force could have a dramatic domestic impact in the short term. This was evidenced during the '45. In a bloody affair lasting only around fifteen minutes at Prestonpans, south of Edinburgh, the Jacobite force, numbering a few thousand men, crushed Sir John Cope's Hanoverian army of regulars and instantly became the military masters of Scotland. As the Earl of Islay, future Duke of Argyll, wrote early in the Rising, the clans:

> are the only source of any real danger that can attend the disaffection of the Enemies to the Protestant Succession. Several thousand men armed and used to arms, ready upon a few weeks call is what might disturb any government. The Captain of Clanranald . . . has not £500 a year and yet has 600 men with him.[4]

English officers were less complimentary, contemptuously dismissing the Highlanders as a barbaric rabble exclusively bent on plunder. But that view underestimated the martial élan of the lightly armed clansmen who were able to endure greater hardship and were more mobile than troops of the line, especially in the kind of rough terrains where many had grown up and lived most of their lives. The better-armed clan gentry were usually in the vanguard of an attack and in the right conditions the famous Highland Charge could pulverize the opposition if launched effectively from hillsides with firearms followed up by close-quarter intense violence with broadsword, axe, dagger and targe. As already noted, the clan hosts were also organized into regiments and officered by gentlemen, some of whom were veterans of service in the armies of France, the Holy Roman Empire and Russia and were well acquainted with modern military technique. Lord George Murray, a younger brother of the Duke of Atholl and the leading commander of the Jacobite forces in the '45, was acknowledged to be one of the outstanding military tacticians of his day, but eventually fell foul of the inept amateur Bonnie Prince Charlie, and his role was marginalized in the weeks before Culloden. However, with Murray in command, his army won virtually every skirmish and battle against regular troops in 1745–6 except, of course, for the final resounding defeat in 1746 when his place was taken by Charles Edward Stuart as field commander. Indeed one reason for the decision to stand and fight south of Inverness on that day in April 1746 was Charles's belief in the invincibility of his clansmen when opposing regular forces. The ensuing disaster was largely caused by the incompetence of his leadership, the unsuitable nature of the ground for the traditional assault of the clans and the hungry and exhausted condition of the Jacobite forces, most of whom had taken part in a failed pre-emptive strike during the previous night on the camp of the Hanoverian army at Nairn a few miles to the south.

The support of many Highland clans for Jacobitism therefore gave the cause a degree of military credibility in the same way that the French connection boosted its political and diplomatic standing. Not all clans were Jacobite in sympathy, especially in those areas where Presbyterianism had made a deep impact by the eighteenth century, as in the counties of Argyll, Sutherland and Caithness, and in Wester Ross. It was said that Presbyterianism in A' Gaidhealtachd was essentially nothing other than the Whig/Hanoverian interest at prayer. Most of the Campbells, MacKays, Munros, Rosses and Gunns were usually likely to favour the established order. The Mackenzies, earls of Seaforth, were also loyal Hanoverians. But 'government clans'

were always a small minority, probably less than ten of the fifty principal clans, and their main effect was to divide family allegiances and
encourage those of wavering Jacobite loyalty not to come out in the
Risings.

Again, even if there was latent sympathy, active support for the
Risings in the Highlands varied very significantly over time and space
and within clanship. Some families were split on points of political
and religious principle and few clans were committed to either side in
their entirety, if only because it was prudent to keep a foot in both
camps to try to ensure that family lands would remain secure whatever the final outcome might be. Thus, the first Duke of Atholl was a
staunch supporter of the revolution of 1688–9 but three of his sons
fought for the Jacobites under the Earl of Mar in 1715. Over time
militant Jacobitism in the Highlands came to focus mainly on the
Grampian region and parts of western Inverness-shire; the clans of
the inner and outer Hebrides played little part in the '45 on either
side. The refusal of the chiefs of the MacDonalds and MacLeods in
Skye to take part was a particularly bitter blow for the Stuarts, but
the insular clans were likely to be cautious as it was they who would
have to face the formidable firepower of marauding squadrons of the
British navy.

Indeed, the grave risk of coming out in the '45 made even some
committed Jacobites opt for prudent neutrality. Charles had landed
in the Outer Hebrides in the summer of that year with only seven
companions, some arms and 4,000 French gold coins. The Jacobite
leadership in Scotland reckoned that he needed to bring with him a
war chest of 30,000 French gold pieces, supplies for 10,000 men and
a force of 6,000 French soldiers if he was to have any reasonable
chance of military success. Not surprisingly, therefore, many found it
difficult to reconcile Jacobite allegiance with hard political realities.
The uncertainties also explain why several families had members of
kin on both sides. One extraordinary illustration of this was the
experience of the Chisholms. The youngest son of Roderick Chisholm
of Chisholm led the clan for Prince Charles and perished at Culloden.
His father stayed at home and had two other sons fighting in the
Royal Scots Fusiliers on the Hanoverian side in the same battle.
Entire clans were also divided. William Mackintosh of that Ilk tried

to raise his men for the government, but all except nine deserted to join the 600 clansmen recruited by his wife, Lady Anne Mackintosh, for the Jacobites. Ewen MacPherson of Cluny, one of the most gifted Jacobite regimental commanders of the '45, was unable to bring out his entire clan in 1745 as its most powerful cadet branch, the MacPhersons of Invereshie, remained neutral throughout the Rising. In addition, but particularly in the '45, some chiefs had to resort to threats and strong-arm tactics to force out their clansmen. Sending around the 'fiery cross', the traditional call to arms, was no longer always enough.

However, the complex nature of shifting loyalties and divided responses does not answer the key question why so many clans remained loyal to the Stuarts and supported their restoration from the Revolution of 1688 until the 1750s. To some extent their allegiance was a dynastic extension of clan commitment to the concept of kinship:

> The royal house of Stuart was the rightful trustee of Scotland in the same way that clan chiefs were the customary protectors of their followers. Dynastic legitimacy was seen as the source of justice, the basis of government. But the lawful exercise of government and the maintenance of justice were imperilled by the sundering of genealogical continuity, first by the replacement of James VII and II by his son-in-law William of Orange in 1689, and then by the succession of the House of Hanover under George I in 1714.[5]

The religious factor was also fundamental. The victory of vengeful Presbyterianism in the revolution of 1688 swung Episcopalians and Roman Catholics in favour of the Catholic Stuarts in the Highlands and north-east Lowlands. Only through the removal of the revolutionary regime of 1688 and, after 1714, the House of Hanover could the full rights of the 'non-jurors' (those refusing to take the oath of allegiance to the new monarchy of William and Mary and their successors) be restored. Episcopalian clans like the Camerons and Stewarts of Appin were therefore Jacobite by nature, as were the small Catholic populations of Barra, South Uist, Morvern, Moidart, Arisaig, Morar and Knoydart. The tiny Catholic enclave on the western mainland was not only loyal, but remoteness also left it virtually immune from Hanoverian depredation until after the failure of the '45. It was no coincidence that it was here at Loch nan Uamh, between Arisaig and Moidart, that the Young Pretender (or claimant to the throne) made his first landing on the Scottish mainland at the start of his ill-fated expedition in the summer of 1745.

Catholics, denied full citizenship under the penal laws, usually owed allegiance without equivocation to their co-religionaries, the Stuarts. But they made up no more than a fifth of the fighting men in all the Risings. The overwhelming majority, around 75 per cent, were in fact Protestant but Episcopalian (from the Latin *episcopus*, bishop), whose commitment to the rule of hierarchy in the church was in direct conflict with the Presbyterian regime of kirk session and church elders established after 1688. Indeed, the refusal of the vast majority of Episcopalians, despite offers of toleration, to take the oath of allegiance to William and Mary and their successors and abjure the House of Stuart meant they, as 'non-jurors', were subjected to the penal laws in the same way as those of the Catholic faith. But the religious factor was not always decisive. The Protestant Mackenzies came out on the Jacobite side during the 1715 rebellion, as did the Campbells of Glenorchy and the Earl of Breadalbane. In that rising there were plenty of Protestant Campbells in the Jacobite camp. Religious faith did not always ensure clan unity, as the example of the Chisholms, a nominally Catholic clan discussed above, illustrates.

Religion gave a stiffening and a sense of moral purpose to Highland Jacobitism, but its roots also lay in the political and economic realities of seventeenth-century Scotland. It is possible to trace the identification of some clans with the House of Stuart back to the 1640s, when they had fought under Alasdair MacColla and the Marquess of Montrose on the King's side against the Presbyterian Covenanters during the civil wars. This was a connection which was also in large part based on the hostility of many western clans to the threatening expansion of the notoriously imperialistic ClanCampbell, which during that conflict was bitterly hostile to the Stuart king, Charles I, and his successor, Charles II. These were alliances and hostilities which were to become an integral part of the later struggle between Jacobites and Hanoverians but were already in place from a much earlier time. As one scholar has put it: 'If Highland Jacobitism was born in the 1680s it had been conceived in the 1640s.'[6]

At one level, the appeal of the cause for the clans may also have been because, as already argued, they could readily identify with the values of kinship and hereditary right which were shared in the traditions of both monarchy and clanship. James VII, when Duke of York in the 1670s, did much to enhance this relationship and build a bridge between the older Stuart policy of repression and a fresh strategy of co-operation with the clan chiefs. What almost certainly endeared James even more to clans such as the Camerons, McLeans and some branches of ClanDonald was that, during his short period of rule in Scotland, Archibald Campbell, the ninth Earl of Argyll and chief of ClanCampbell, was executed in 1685 for treason after his abortive rebellion against the monarchy, leaving his family's previously dominant position temporarily in complete disarray. The monarchy generally, and James and the Stuarts in particular, therefore came to be seen as the most effective checks on the rampant expansionism of ClanCampbell. Those clans along the western seaboard and in the islands who were steadily losing both lands and feudal superiorities to the earls of Argyll had often little choice but to support the crown because only it had the legitimacy and resources to counter Campbell power. As the Marquis of Hamilton remarked to Charles I in 1638, the western Gaels were likely to join the royalist forces during the civil war, 'not for anie greatt affection they cyrie to your Majestie bot because of ther splene to Lorne (i.e. Campbell) and will dou if they durst just contrarie to whatt his men doueth'.[7]

Inevitably in 1688–9 the removal of the Stuarts was quickly followed by the restoration of the Campbells to full power. Indeed, the tenth Earl of Argyll personally administered the coronation oath to William and Mary at Westminster and his family was soon rewarded with a dukedom for his faithful service to the new regime. In the western Highlands the revolution of 1688–9 became associated with the renewal of Campbell hegemony and so support for the exiled Stuarts was the only realistic response to the threat which that presented in the region. The link between Jacobitism and anti-Campbell sentiment became powerful and enduring. However, even here there was complexity. The huge Campbell empire itself contained political diversity and its Breadalbane and Glenlyon branches, for instance, had been sympathetic to the Stuarts in the Rising of 1715. Marital relationships between Cameron and Campbell and MacDonald and Campbell existed alongside clan and political divisions. But, overall, the enthusiastic support of the earls of Argyll for the Protestant succession in 1688, and later, for the house of Hanover, helped to swing their traditional rivals and mortal enemies in favour of Stuart counter-revolution.

The economic origins of Highland Jacobitism are more difficult to determine. Some writers have suggested that the risings were at root an epic conflict between the forces of ancient tribalism and the dynamic of modern capitalism. In this view, the archaic clan society of Gaeldom was confronted by the commercial vibrancy of the Lowlands in a long-drawn-out struggle which ended with Gaelic society defeated in the '45 and finally crushed in its punitive aftermath. There are, however, several objections to this superficially seductive thesis. For a start, Jacobite sympathies traversed the Highland/Lowland frontier. The Stuarts attracted support from most areas, both Lowland and Highland, north of the River Tay, including several towns in that region, which could not be considered as 'tribal' in any sense. In addition, throughout Gaeldom, though Jacobite clans were in a majority, others were loyal to the Hanoverians. More fundamentally, the image of a backward region, mainly insulated from commercial forces, is in conflict with the evidence presented earlier in the chapter of growing tensions within clanship as a result of trade developments taking place in the seventeenth century and early eighteenth. The expansion of droving was one of the most important growth points in the early modern Scottish economy and could not have lifted off if there had not been pools of enterprise within clanship. Some Jacobite chiefs were also noted for their entrepreneurial activities and were more than the tribal patriarchs or warrior leaders of popular legend. The *fine* of ClanCameron, one of the most committed to Jacobitism, had growing interests in American land, timber exportation, Caribbean plantations and the Edinburgh money market. MacDonnell of Glengarry was heavily involved in the provision of timber from his estate for charcoal for the production of iron. On his Lowland estates, the Earl of Mar, the incompetent leader of the 1715 rising, had a range of industrial investments, including coal-mining and glass manufacture. Robertson of Struan ran an extensive commercial forestry operation and timber from his estate around Loch Rannoch was floated down to the rivers Tummel and Tay and from there to Lowland markets. The Duke of Perth, who was prominent in the '45, was a noted early improver who was actively engaged in agricultural innovation on his estate in Highland Perthshire in the early 1740s.

At the same time, however, there was indeed some evidence of a close correlation between political disaffection and financial difficulty. During the '45 it was estimated that twenty-two clans were 'out' for the Stuarts and only eight for the government. However, overall, the Hanoverians had the more prosperous clans on their side. Three Jacobite clans, the MacDonnells of Keppoch, the MacGregors, and the MacDonalds of Glencoe, either were landless or possessed only marginal property. They mainly made ends meet by cattle 'lifting' and the running of protection rackets. A number of other chiefs who committed themselves to Prince Charles in 1745 were in acute financial difficulty, much of it as a result of the attempt to live in the style of eighteenth-century gentlemen on the meagre revenues of a Highland estate. One contemporary, doubtless of Hanoverian sympathy, claimed in the *Caledonian Mercury* that the annual total income of the clans which fought in the Jacobite army did not exceed £1,500, which if divided equally among the estimated 4,000 rebels came to only 7s 6d a year each and less than a farthing a day!

In addition, in the years between the failure of the '15 Rising and the '45 the state had effectively created a power vacuum in Gaeldom. For the most part, the rebels of 1715 had been treated relatively leniently, even if some forfeitures of property did take place. This was mainly on the grounds that Jacobitism in Scotland at the time was far too common for draconian action to be taken across the board against those disaffected to the state. The Disarming Act of 1725, passed after the abortive rising of 1719 and rumours of further clandestine plotting, may have indeed have had more impact on the government clans than on the Jacobites. Around the same time, General George Wade came north to supervise an ambitious programme of road, bridge and fort construction to reduce the inaccessibility of the clans and assist the movement of crown forces in the event of another rising. Between 1725 and his departure from Scotland in 1740 he claimed to have built 250 miles of road to facilitate the marches of government troops throughout the disaffected districts. These were also designed to link Fort William, Fort Augustus and small garrisons at Bernera and Ruthven which were to act as the government's eyes and ears in the Jacobite districts. The whole basis of Wade's strategy, however, was undermined from the later 1730s, when the government stripped the forts of adequate forces in order to increase the supply of troops for European service. Wade's roads did eventually prove to be useful, but only in expediting the march south of the Young Pretender's army in 1745.

3

The early phase of the '45 culminating in the victory at Prestonpans was followed by the invasion of England which on the face of it was a remarkable triumph for the small Jacobite force of a few thousand men. To a significant extent, however, Charles's early success not only reflected the martial élan of the clans but also the weaknesses of the Scottish state and its virtual paralysis in the summer of 1745. After the Union, the abolition of the Scottish Privy Council in 1708 had removed the only effective government executive as well as the main agency for intelligence gathering. When the Stuart standard was raised at Glenfinnan at the head of Loch Sheil in August 1745, the government commander in Scotland, Sir John Cope, had a mere 3,000 troops at his disposal throughout the entire country. Even ClanCampbell, traditionally the crucial military bulwark of the Hanoverian state in the western Highlands, had been weakened as a fighting formation by the second Duke of Argyll's estate reforms after 1737 described earlier in the chapter. They had not only eroded the position of the *fir-tacsa*, a key link in the chain of military command in the clan structure, but also made competition rather than clan loyalty the main factor in the granting of tenancies.

Yet the very potency of the threat posed by the advancing Jacobites ensured that the British state soon responded with determination and vigour as battle-hardened regiments were speedily withdrawn home from the European theatre. The retreat of the Prince's army from Derby was a reaction of Charles's Council of War to the intelligence that the Brigade of Guards now stood between them and London and that three Hanoverian armies were also massing to advance. There was also a recognition that the Rising had failed to attract any significant support in the north of England, thus making the retreat home the most prudent option. The return to Scotland, outnumbered by the enemy and marching through hostile territory, was itself an outstanding exploit. However, after a further partial victory at Falkirk, the Jacobite forces retreated again into the Highlands, so ensuring that they were no longer able to extract funds through levies and taxation on the richer Lowland counties and towns. Indeed, the central, and especially the western, Lowlands, the economic heart of Scotland, had always been vehemently hostile. The Presbyterian church wielded more power and had greater influence in the parishes of Scotland than a distant national authority and had always been stridently opposed to Jacobitism as the satanic ideology of a threatened Papist counter-revolution.

Sources of revenue now inevitably dried up, a problem compounded by the failure of the French treasure ships, especially *Le Prince Charles*, to make it through Scottish waters with vital financial support. The Young Pretender decided to turn and fight at Culloden on ground which favoured regular infantry and artillery and put the clan regiments at acute disadvantage, because his cause was by then, quite literally, bankrupt. It was not only fatigue, after the abortive night attack on the Duke of Cumberland's army at Nairn, which weakened the Jacobites on that fateful day in April 1746. Hunger also played an important part. A significant proportion of the army was away foraging for food and took no part in the battle.

The rout of the Jacobites on Culloden Moor became the prelude to a massive military, judicial and political assault on clan society which the government assumed had spawned subversion. The rock-solid belief of the state was that the martial nature of clanship was at the heart of the problem of chronic disaffection. The fact that Lowland formations from the north-east counties fought in the Jacobite army and that several important clans remained loyal to the Hanoverian state seems to have been of little consequence to London. The relative leniency shown the rebels after the 1715 rising was not to be repeated since there were two key differences from the aftermath of the '15. First, a great regular army, supported by naval units, had been drawn into the very heart of the Highlands and could be employed there in effective combination to wage a campaign of terror and destruction against the clans. Second, the '45 had come too dangerously close to final success and so the social system which was thought to have incubated disaffection had to be totally rooted out.

The Duke of Cumberland, the Hanoverian commander, contended that there had been a missed opportunity after the '15 to destroy clanship. He was determined that error was not to be repeated in 1746. Underpinning the eventual ferocity of the government's response was the belief that the Gaels were akin to a deadly poison threatening the body politic which only radical surgery could remove. Six years before the Rising, the following had appeared in a London magazine:

> In this great Extent of Country [the Highlands], Ignorance and Superstition greatly prevail; In some Places the Remains even of Paganism are still to be found, and in many others the Reformation from Popery has never yet obtained. The Parishes where Ministers are settled, are commonly of very great Extent, some 30, 40, 50 Miles long, and generally divided by unpassable Mountains and Lakes; so that most of the Inhabitants being destitute of all Means of Knowledge, and without any Schools to educate their Children, are entirely ignorant of the Principles of Religion and Virtue, live in Idleness and Poverty, have no Notion of Industry, or Sense of Liberty, are subject to the Will and Command of their Popish disaffected Chieftains, who have always opposed the propagating of Christian Knowledge, and the English Tongue, that they might with less difficulty keep their miserable Vassals in a slavish Dependance. The poorer sort have only the Irish Tongue, and little Correspondence with the civilized arts of the Nation, and only come among them to pillage the more industrious Inhabitants; they are brought up in Principles of Tyranny and Arbitrary Government, depend upon foreign Papists as their main Support, and the native Irish as their best Correspondents and Allies. This has been the Source of all the Rebellions and Insurrections, in the Country, since the Revolution.[8]

The onslaught began with the systematic pillage of western mainland Inverness-shire and the adjacent islands by Hanoverian forces before they marched across much of the rest of Gaeldom. Even Highland communities loyal to the crown during the '45 were not spared by the avenging juggernaut. This was a direct consequence of the prevailing Scotophobia in London government circles where Scotland as a whole was judged to be a disloyal country despite the majority opposition to Jacobitism north of the border. The terrorism of the state caused extensive depredations, the burning and laying waste of numerous townships, and the rounding up of cattle, the essential capital assets of the clansmen, for sale on government account in the markets of Fort Augustus, Inverness and elsewhere. In due course, the military road system was considerably extended until by 1767 over a thousand miles had been built. Between 1748 and 1769 one of the greatest bastion artillery fortresses in Europe was constructed at Ardersier, east of Inverness, and named Fort George. It was a permanent physical demonstration of the absolute determination of the British state that the clans would never again rise in arms to menace the Protestant Succession.

Through the passage of a series of Acts of Parliament, a comprehensive attack was also launched on the culture of the Gael and the system of clanship: tartans and kilts were proscribed as the sartorial symbols of rebel militarism; heritable jurisdictions, the private courts of landowners, were abolished; the carrying of weapons was forbidden; and rebel estates were declared forfeit to the crown. Forty-one properties were taken but significantly, in the light of earlier discussion about the financial pressures which fuelled disaffection, the vast majority had to be sold off by the Barons of Exchequer to pay off creditors. Thirteen, however, were inalienably annexed and managed by the crown between 1752 and 1784 through a Commission to promote 'the Protestant Religion, good Government, Industry and Manufactures, and the Principles of Duty and Loyalty to His Majesty'. The thinking was that Protestantism would induce ideological conformity while prosperity might draw the teeth of the causes of disaffection.

It is tempting to view this huge military and legislative programme as a major turning point in Highland history, especially since the second half of the eighteenth century did indeed see the rapid collapse of clanship. But the idea of a clear cause-and-effect relationship between the two developments should be resisted. As one historian has put it: 'The fact that there never was another Jacobite after 1745 owed more to a disinclination to rebel than to the government's repressive measures'.[9] The savagery of the Hanoverian forces seems to have shocked but then inspired stubborn defiance in a population long inured to hard times. Indeed, in the short run, there were more disturbances than usual in the Jacobite areas. William Anne Keppel, the second Earl of Albemarle, and Cumberland's successor, became so frustrated by the lawlessness that he came round to the view that the only effective way to ensure permanent stability was to utterly devastate the recalcitrant districts and then deport all their inhabitants to the colonies. Equally significantly, his intelligence reports ominously suggested that despite brutal suppression there was still the hope and expectation that the long-hoped-for French invasion might yet come about and provide some succour to the embattled Jacobite Gaels.

The proscription of wardship, or military land tenures, and heritable jurisdictions would probably have had little effect on clan loyalties because these were founded on beliefs in the emotional ties of blood and kin rather than legal regulation. Military land tenures in the Highlands had also already been rendered obsolete due to the commercial developments of the seventeenth and early eighteenth centuries already surveyed. The Commission for Annexed and Forfeited Estates strove to improve agriculture, establish industry and develop communications in territories it managed. Not all the effort was in vain. Significant improvement was made in communications, but there was no evidence that a social and economic revolution of the kind planned to inculcate Hanoverian loyalty or assimilation to the mores of the rest of Britain was achieved. The profound constraints of poor land endowment, distance from markets and hostility of the people proved hard to overcome. One Commissioner, Lord Kames, a distinguished figure of the Scottish Enlightenment and pioneering agricultural 'improver' on his Lowland estate, admitted that the resources poured into the Highlands had been 'no better than water spilt on the ground'.[10]

But Gaeldom unquestionably did change profoundly in the decades after Culloden. Samuel Johnson, during his tour of the Western Isles in 1773, famously proclaimed the last rites of clanship: 'the clans retain little now of their original character. Their ferocity of temper is softened, their military ardour is extinguished, their dignity of independence is depressed, their contempt for government subdued, and their reverence for their chiefs abated'.[11] But whether all this was due, as Johnson asserted, to 'the late conquest and subsequent laws' is unclear. Highland society had been in the throes of a long transition from clanship to commercialism many decades before the '45. More and more, the gentry of the clans were exhibiting the characteristics of landlords rather than chieftains. The traditions of *duthchas*, that the *fine* were obliged by the centuries-old duties of protection and guardianship, lived on among the people of their lands. The 'pacification' of Gaeldom by the forces of the crown was the final factor encouraging many of the élite entirely to throw off this historic responsibility in favour of the material advantages of proprietorship, so completing the transformation to landlordism.

3

Before Improvement

I

On the whole the rural Lowlands of Scotland were blessed with a much more favourable natural environment for arable agriculture than the Highlands. It was a fundamental advantage which went a long way to explain the different histories of the two regions during the era of removals from land. Of course, not everywhere south of the Highland line was flat and fertile. The terrain of the Southern Uplands, for instance, bordering England, often consisted of a moorland plateau, traversed by rolling hills and broken by mountainous outcrops which fashioned a rugged landscape not unlike parts of the southern and eastern Highlands. Like them it was a region in the central and western districts more broadly suited to pastoral than arable farming. Pockets of gentler hill country could also be found in other areas of the central Lowlands, notably the Ochils near Stirling, the Campsie Fells not far from Glasgow, and the Lomonds in Fife. These examples apart, however, comparing the geography of the Lowlands and Highlands at a general level does reveal deep contrasts between the two regions which had been fashioned over millennia by differences in geology, geography and climate.

Today, much of eastern Scotland receives less than 871 mm (34.3 in) of rain annually. The town of Dunbar, to the south-east of Edinburgh, has an annual rainfall of only 560.18 mm (22.05 in), less than Barcelona in north-east Spain. Further north, the eastern coastal strip is partly protected from storm clouds by the Highland massif to the west. In contrast, the western Highlands is one of the wettest areas of the UK, with an annual rainfall of 4,577 mm (180.2 in).

Sunshine in the Highlands and north-west coastlands reaches only 711–1,140 hours annually, but it reaches 1,471–1,540 hours on the eastern and south-west Lowlands. The north and west of the country are also the windiest parts of Scotland when the autumn and winter depressions sweep in from the Atlantic. Orkney, Shetland and the Outer Hebrides can experience more than thirty days of severe gales over the period of a year. These climatic differences have obvious implications for the agrarian economies of the Highlands and Lowlands and their historical development.

Of even greater consequence than climate is the extent of rich soil to be found in a number of Lowland districts. East Lothian, Berwickshire and eastern Roxburgh, lying to the north and east of the English border, are fertile plains with a climate which, unusually for Scotland, allows in some parts the widespread cultivation of wheat. Extensive stretches of alluvial soil, the 'carse' lands, also can be found across the estuaries of the rivers Forth and Tay, while the coastlands of the northeast lowlands of Aberdeen, Banff and Kincardine today contain the most extensive areas of continuous arable in the whole of Scotland.

Even in the sixteenth century, long before the age of improvement from the 1760s, some of those places already had high reputations for their fertility. In 1582, for example, George Buchanan enthusiastically praised the Carse of Gowrie as 'a noble corn country' and, for William Lithgow, it was 'the diamond plot of Tay'. Buchanan thought the Moray district, further north, so 'abundant in corn and pasturage . . . that it may truly be pronounced the first country in Scotland'. According, however, to the leading historian of that time, Hector Boece, the Lothians were 'the most plentuus ground of Scotland'. It was no coincidence that each of the hinterlands described as 'plentiful of corne' were close to the four major towns of Scotland, Edinburgh, Dundee, Perth and Aberdeen in the medieval and early-modern periods.[1]

Despite these advantages, however, which were to become even more evident over time, there was still a great deal of similarity in the seventeenth century between the landscape and farming techniques of the Highlands and Lowlands. The rural Lowlands of today with their vistas of separated and compact farm steadings, trim fields and neat hedgerows would have been completely unrecognizable to Scots of the centuries before the 1750s. Indeed, most contemporary descriptions portray a landscape at that time which was not unlike that of the inhabited localities of the Highlands considered in Chapter 1. As late as 1780, the Rev. John Mitchell, in his *Memories of Ayrshire*, provided a bleak picture of an older rural world already beginning to pass into history:

> The face of the country was far from being cultivated or inviting. On the contrary, it appeared rough and dank, consisting greatly of heath moss, patches of struggling wood and rudely cultivated grounds. The roads, made entirely by statute labour irregular in their line, and far from being level to their track.
>
> The ditches which bounded them were seldom cleared out. Young trees were rarely planted . . . , the country presented upon the whole a repulsive appearance.[2]

As in the Highlands, small clusters of houses, or *fermetouns,* spread at intervals across the countryside. Their dwellings were not much better than the turf huts of the Highland *baile*: 'pitiful cots, built of stone and covered with turves, having in them but one room, many of them no chimneys, the windows very small holes, and not glazed'.[3] Narrow strips of cultivated land linked by tracks or *loanings* crossed a landscape which was covered for the most part by bog and moor. As in the Highland townships, these small islands of cultivation were worked in the runrig system, each tenant or group of farmers with their shares of infield, outfield and rough grazing. The land was ploughed into ridges by the cumbersome old Scots plough pulled by several oxen, which was often jointly owned by the farmers of the *touns*. The plans of late-eighteenth-century surveyors, who were employed to advise landowners on improvement in the second half of the eighteenth century, convey a vivid picture of the old farming landscape. The cultivated areas were patches of unenclosed ground of irregular shape and size with the tiny holdings of tenants dispersed throughout the whole rather than set in compact, individual blocks. Many essential seasonal tasks, like ploughing, harvesting, peat-cutting and thatching, were carried out by collective effort. It also made economic sense that necessaries, such as wood and iron tools which had to be purchased from outside, should also be acquired through the pooling of the scarce resources of these small communities.

But, as elsewhere in the peasant society of Scotland at the time, most raw materials came from the land worked by the people: flax and wool for clothing; timber (where available in a country mainly bereft of woodland) for building; charcoal used in a number of manufactures; animal fats for soap and candle making; hides for tanners, boot and shoe makers, and saddlers; horn for cutlers; ponies, oxen and horses for transport and carriage; straw and heather to pack goods and thatch houses; and sour milk as a bleaching agent. Manufacturing was to some extent urban-based, but a striking feature of the period was that much industry was to be found in the countryside, with spinning, weaving, salt burning and mining especially commonplace. By the early eighteenth century, the plain-linen trade to England had become even more valuable than the traditional export of cattle across the border, while the removal of tariffs after the Union of 1707 gave it stimulus which was just as likely to be felt in the cottages of the rural townships as in the craft workshops of the burghs.

There was, of course, a close symbiotic relationship between country and town. Over two thirds of the incomes of the urban labouring classes were spent on food, primarily oatmeal, milk and some salted fish. The eighteenth-century novelist Tobias Smollett described the typical diet of the Lowland Scot: 'Their breakfast is a kind of hasty pudding of oatmeal, or peasemeal eaten with milk. They have commonly pottage to dinner composed of cale (kail), leeks, barley or big (a form of barley) and this is reinforced with bread and cheese made of skimmed milk. At night they sup on sowens flummery of oatmeal.'[4] Modern historians reckon that in Scotland as a whole grain provided around 82 per cent of the average daily calorie intake of the population. Ale, made from malted barley, was the usual drink of the people. When Westminster tried to impose an increased tax on malt in 1725, the decision provoked a storm of national anger and violent backlash. A number of confrontations with officers of the excise in several customs precincts culminated in the famous Malt Tax Riots in Glasgow which have come to be seen as the most dangerous challenge to the authority of the British state in those years since the Jacobite Rising of 1715. Order was finally restored only after several troops of well-armed dragoons arrived in the city.

What, therefore, both Highland and Lowland Scotland still had in common was the dependence of most country people on the land and above all else on the yields of the annual grain harvests in August and September. The vulnerability of the north and west to partial harvest failure has already been noted in Chapter 1. But after the Restoration of the Stuart monarchy in 1660, the Lowlands seem to have had a happier experience than the Highlands in most years. Indeed, whereas in the later sixteenth century there had been partial dearth and high prices in around a third of the localities, the economic challenge in Lowland Scotland before 1695 came to be seen as a problem of falling prices for cereals. An annual surplus of home-produced grain, apart from the year 1674, had become the norm and was leading to saturation of supply in the domestic market.

This novel condition saw Scotland emerge for a number of years as a grain exporter, a role in international commerce which would have been unthinkable a century before. Meal from the eastern coastal estates was now traded as far afield as Scandinavia, the Low Countries and France, as well as to the north-east counties of England. In July 1695 the Scottish Privy Council even decided to grant subsidies for grain exports because of the persistence of stagnant prices at home. In an 'Act for Encouraging the Export of Victual', a twenty-shilling bounty was provided on each boll of grain traded out of the country. It was indeed ironic, however, that in the very year that law was passed, surplus changed abruptly to serious shortage in what soon became one of the worst series of harvest failures in Scottish history. What followed confirmed the continuing exposure of the populations in both Highlands and Lowlands to climatic changes. A society where subsistence agriculture was dominant in most areas still remained at great risk to adverse weather conditions during the three key phases of seeding, growing and harvest.

The crisis which engulfed Scotland in the later 1690s lasted from 1695 until 1700. Devastation of the crops centred mainly on the Highlands, the hill country of the Borders, Aberdeenshire, Angus and, more generally, in upland areas of marginal farming. Fertile low-lying districts in the eastern Lowlands were spared the worst. East Lothian and estates along the Cromarty Firth and in Easter Ross, for instance, were still able to send grain supplies at famine prices into Edinburgh.

The crisis came about because of exceptional weather deterioration during the late 'Maunder Minimum' at the lowest point of the Little Ice Age in the early modern period. Scotland's experience was far from exceptional in what was one of the coldest phases ever recorded in Western Europe and which resulted in an advance of the Alpine, Scandinavian and Icelandic glaciers. The main features of the period were harsh winters and very wet summers. The countries of northern Europe were hit especially hard. Finland lost an estimated one third of its population through famine-related disease and Estonia around one fifth. But France and the Low Countries also suffered extreme privation. Uniquely England was spared the worst, due partly to its well-developed Poor Law system which provided some sustenance for the most vulnerable and, more crucially, because of the tradition of sowing grains in both spring and winter, which provided a degree of protection whenever one crop failed. Scotland, which had always sown only once, during springtime, proved to be much less fortunate.

The run of poor harvests had devastating consequences. Current estimates suggest that the population of Scotland may have fallen by some 13 per cent due to a combination of famine-related diseases and extensive emigration in the 1690s. Mortality rates climbed as high as 20 per cent in Aberdeenshire and other parts of the north-east and were probably even greater in the Highlands, Hebrides and Northern Isles. Death stalked the countryside on a scale never seen before in living memory: 'Everyone may see Death on the face of the Poor that abound everywhere ... the Thinness of their Visage, their Ghostly Looks, their Feebleness, and their Fluxes threaten them with sudden Death.' The author of this lugubrious description, Sir Robert Sibbald, recounted how even 'Poor Sickning Babs' were starving, 'for want of Milk, which the empty Breasts of their Mothers cannot furnish'.[5] It was the lesser folk, the smaller tenants, cottars and servants, who were most at risk. Contemporary records show many from these classes wandering in large numbers on the roads in search of subsistence from more favoured areas which had vanished at home. Many, especially from Ayrshire, Argyll and Wigtownshire, fled the country altogether and took the short crossing from the south-western ports to the north of Ireland. The most recent estimates suggest that over 40,000 Scots probably became refugees in Ulster between 1695 and

1700. It was the largest single accession of Protestants to the Ulster Plantation since its origins in the early seventeenth century. They left behind unpaid rents, derelict townships and abandoned land. It is clear that even abatements, reductions and so-called 'eases' of rent were not enough to stem the outflow in many districts. The records of a number of estates in parts of the south-west, north-east and the Border counties show that rent arrears resulting from the crisis of the last decade of the seventeenth century were still being paid off two decades later.

2

The shared experience of human suffering during these 'Ill Years' might imply an economic convergence across Highland and Lowland Scotland in early modern times. But an examination of deeper trends from the later seventeenth century suggests rather that this was at root a crucial period of quickening divergence between the two regions.

The British civil wars of the 1640s and early 1650s, which triggered considerable Scottish involvement, had caused immense loss of treasure and profound dislocation on both sides of the Highland line. Yet there can be little doubt that the forces making for eventual long-term social stability were even at that stage much more potent in the Lowlands. The power of the state was already dominant in most of the region, with the sole exception of parts of the Border countryside. But after the Union of Crowns in 1603, the joint monarchy of James VI and I rapidly subdued the recalcitrant districts of southern Scotland. For a few years afterwards legislation continued to be enacted there against 'outlaws and broken men', but by the end of James's reign in 1625 the Border region had become effectively incorporated in the Scottish state. This was the political background to the expansion of the cross-Border livestock trade and the packhorse commerce in linen from the western Lowlands, centred on Glasgow, and its growing community of 'English merchants', selling yarn to the markets of the north of England.

Furthermore, two key sources of long-term support for stable governance, the burghs and the reformed church, had a much greater physical presence and hold in the Lowlands than the Highlands. While urban life was notable by its virtual absence in the western Highlands and Islands, both the four 'great towns of Scotland' and the sixty-odd medium- and smaller-sized towns which existed in the years before the Union were situated in the eastern and central Lowlands. Towns had always a strong vested interest in law and order as peace was good for trade. Similarly, the church had established a full network of parishes and kirk sessions throughout the region by the early decades of the seventeenth century. Indeed, by the 1660s it was the normal thing for the Lowlands not only to have an organized parish structure but a school and a functioning system of poor relief as well. This 'parish state' was a vital agency for the maintenance of law and order at the local level through the moral surveillance of the kirk session, control of schooling and regular administration of funds for the poor. The authority of the parishes was strikingly illustrated by the reach and influence of the 'testificat' system. By this, men and women could only move from one parish to another with a certificate of proven good conduct, or testificat, signed by the parish minister. Kirk session records confirm the widespread enforcement of the system with ministers conscientiously checking details to ensure accuracy and noting the absence of anyone who had not received official consent to leave their parish. In areas distant from the southern and eastern fringes of the Highlands the influence of the national church was much weaker and more erratic.

The development of stability in the Lowlands soon became fully confirmed in a visual sense by the transformation of the great houses of the landed classes. Even in the first quarter of the seventeenth century, the curtain-wall castle and the tower house, or fortalice, were giving way to the country house. The former were designed for defence and the physical projection of military authority and power, the latter more for comfort, display and material status. Commonly, hybrid buildings began to appear, in which the old fortified dwellings were not abandoned but remodelled to form the core of a more modern structure better suited to less turbulent times. Thus, in 1602–6, Glamis Castle, in Angus, underwent a programme of radical alteration under the aegis of the first Earl of Kinghorne when a more symmetrical façade and grand new circular staircase were added to the building. In 1677, his descendant, Patrick, first Earl of Strathmore, made further improvements. Soon the old castle had metamorphosed into a fashionable and classical baroque mansion. The building of Palladian-style country houses was also a feature of the later seventeenth century. The architectural doyens of the day were Sir William Bruce (1630–1710) and James Smith of Whitehill (c.1645–1731) who designed such striking creations as Hopetoun House, Kinross House and Hamilton Palace. Gardens, terraces, avenues, parterres, water features and statues became integral elements of the surroundings of these great houses in order to show them off to best advantage.

The architectural triumph of the country house over the ancient castle was a telling physical metaphor for more peaceful times in the Lowlands. But law and order also had key effects on the structure of rural society. Dependence on armed followings became a thing of the past at a much earlier stage than in the Highlands. Even in the formerly troubled Borders, the military basis of tenancy and landholding had gone by 1700, even if some old-style paternalism lingered on among some of the great Border families, like the Scotts and Kerrs. But for most Lowland aristocrats and lairds, their estates were now mainly seen as assets for the extraction of revenue to support ever-growing levels of personal consumption. The relationships with their tenants still involved labour services inherited from the old feudal order: 'bonnage' (literally 'bondage'), meaning work to be done on the landowner's home farms, especially at harvest; 'thirlage', which bound tenants to have their corn ground at the landlord's mill; and the custom of digging, drying and stacking his peat supplies in the spring and summer months. But these hangovers from the past could not conceal the fact that the social relationships in the Lowlands were becoming more embedded in impersonal economic contracts rather than old-style paternalistic relationships. The clauses of the new leases (or tacks) between landowner and tenant were now exclusively concerned with the economic responsibilities of rental payment, management of livestock and requirements of cultivation. In the long run this was to become a major source of divergence between the mores and expectations of the people of many parts of the Highlands and Lowlands, a growing differentiation eventually to have profound social consequences in later decades.

Contrasts in the internal social hierarchies of the Highland *baile* and the Lowland *fermetouns* were also visible before *c.*1750. As seen in Chapter 1, Highland townships contained large numbers of small tenants and cottars who carried on the daily toil with their families without the need for hired labour. Written leases remained uncommon below the level of the tacksmen and security of tenure depended in the final analysis on custom and the will of the chiefs and leading clan gentry. Much of the work on the land, in harvesting, peat cutting, house construction and herding was carried out by communal effort. By and large, therefore, the clansmen and their families remained locked within a subsistence regime. Direct contact with markets elsewhere, especially for the lucrative droving trade in cattle, was usually monopolized by the *fir-tacsa* and others in the clan élite.

These traditional social arrangements were mirrored in many parts of the Lowlands, more especially in the hill country of the Borders, parishes on the fringes of the Highlands in Aberdeen, Angus and Perth, and some of the counties in the south-west region. However, in favoured districts with more arable land, such as the coastal strip from eastern Aberdeenshire to Berwickshire, different structures were coming to the fore. Some townships in these areas had almost reached the size of small villages with consolidated and compact holdings of 100 acres or more and a single husbandman employing cottars, tradesmen, farm servants and day labourers. In effect, the tenants of these places had become an embryonic rural bourgeoisie who employed other people to work the farms on their behalf. These dependants no longer had any legal right to the occupation of land, and any security which they did possess was based on wage contracts (as servants or labourers) or tradition and custom (as in the case of the numerous cottar class). In the advanced areas of the eastern Lowlands, many rural dwellers and their families were now more proletarian than peasant in status and occupation, and this some time before the much more wide-ranging social changes of the second half of the eighteenth century.

Another distinction between the two regions was that some substantial farmers in parts of the Lowlands were now making direct connection with the grain and livestock markets of neighbouring Scottish towns and across the border to England. No longer did landowners and their agents have monopoly control of this commerce. These larger holdings produced supplies of meal, beef, cheese and butter well in excess of the needs of the families and dependants of the tenants. It was therefore inevitable that they had to sell into the market and break out of the constraint of subsistence culture. The substantial husbandmen also made decisions for themselves and were no longer prepared to be confined by inherited custom or communal traditionalism. In the northern and western Highlands, however, such pushing, richer and more enterprising individuals were usually notable by their virtual absence below the social rank of the *fir-tacsa*.

Even by the early decades of the eighteenth century, this small class of capitalist farmers was expanding and absorbing the smaller holdings of their neighbours. Multiple tenant farms were in retreat, not only in the progressive eastern Lowlands but also on several estates in the north-east and south-west. In the Douglas estate in Lanarkshire, for example, the proportion of multiple tenancies had fallen from 64 per cent in the 1730s to 16 per cent by the 1750s. Similarly, on the Morton lands in Fife, where 40 per cent of the holdings were in multiple possession in the 1710s, only 3 per cent were so described in the 1740s. On the Earl of Glasgow's properties in Ayrshire a mere 3 per cent of the tenancies were held in multiple possession by the 1750s.

Two examples of the new breed in the vanguard of these changes were George Leith of the parish of Tillinessell, Aberdeenshire, and William Nisbet of Crimond parish, also in Aberdeenshire. Leith's holding supported seven cottars and servants in addition to the labour of his own immediate family in the 1690s. By the end of the seventeenth century Nisbet had become the only tenant farmer in the Kirktoun of Crimond, which had comprised several other possessions in the past. But he had an impressively large labour team to support his activities consisting of three cottar families, six servants and herds and half a dozen tradesmen, including a weaver, tailor and shoemaker.

As the labour force of these enlarged single tenancies grew, so their masters invested in better living quarters and outbuildings. That led in turn to the steady replacement of the old long houses where beasts and people had shared the living space with the courtyard farm steading with byres, stables and more accommodation. It was followed by another key development, the use of lime mortar enabling the construction of houses with load-bearing walls without the need for the old roof-couples. Tenant houses with two or even three storeys started to be built, a form of construction hardly known in the Highlands, except occasionally among the clan gentry. The introduction of dwellings of this type implied a new commitment to longer-term investment. Rather than a house which might only stand over the term of a lease or even less, these new buildings were designed to last over several generations. Some may have been constructed by landowners as a means of attracting able tenants by offering them more congenial quarters. But others reflected the willingness of richer farmers to sink more of their own resources into holdings because extended tenures were guaranteed by the long-term tacks which were now more common.

These bigger and more elaborate dwellings for some tenants also suggested the development of a greater degree of social stratification within Lowland rural society, since little evidence has survived of any parallel improvement in the dwellings of the lesser folk. A survey of the barony of Lasswade near Edinburgh in 1694, a district recognized to be in the van of progressive agriculture, highlighted the significance of the new buildings:

> The houses of the larger tenants there, on holdings with 65–130 acres of arable land, were of two and in one case three stories, with lime-mortared walls.
>
> They had several rooms, with up to four on the first floor and glazed windows. Sketch plans of the farmsteads accompany the survey. They show that while traces of the long-house plan survived in the layout of the main block, some of the outbuildings were grouped into separate wings forming L-shaped steadings or in one instance a Z plan. It is significant that the best of these houses had been built as recently as 1693.
>
> It is also interesting to note that the descriptions of the cottar houses associated with these farms do not differ materially from those found elsewhere at the time.[6]

These house types may still have been uncommon outside favoured arable areas in the later seventeenth century. The tenants of Lasswade, for instance, had the benefit of proximity to the Edinburgh market and also worked rich and fertile land. Nonetheless, their steadings were the forerunners of the even more elaborate buildings which eventually became common in most parts of Lowland Scotland. These changing house types also demonstrate the social and economic gap which was opening up between much of the Highlands and the rural Lowlands. Stone-built houses did eventually become more common in Gaeldom by the early nineteenth century, but when the layout of deserted townships of the Victorian era are explored, the houses differ little from those which were already being abandoned in a few Lowland districts more than 150 years before.

More permanent housing both reflected and resulted from the proliferation of secure, longer leases which have been identified for many Lowland estates in the early eighteenth century. Nineteen-year tacks became standard after the 1760s but their origins lay further back in time. On the extensive Leven and Melville lands in Fife, 11 per cent of tacks were for nineteen years, while by 1700–1724 the proportion had risen to 40 per cent. Equally, of seventy extant tacks for the Duke of Hamilton's estate in Lanarkshire for the years 1710–50, all but two were for nineteen years. The pattern was repeated on the Earl of Eglinton's Ayrshire properties with all extant pre-1750 tacks being for nineteen years. Even on those estates where such especially long leases were uncommon, as in the Earl of Panmure's Angus lands, the mean tack length in the first two decades of the eighteenth century had already reached fifteen years.

This development was by no means universal throughout Scottish rural society. In pastoral areas, such as the Border counties and the Highlands, the granting of longer tacks to the lower peasantry was much less common, even if it was *de rigueur* among the gentlemen of the clans. One reason for this was that the cattle-droving trade was primarily vested in proprietors in the Borders and the *fine* in the Highlands. Tenants themselves did not deal directly with the markets; their function was rearing the livestock, not selling on the animals. It was, however, a different story in arable or mixed-farming areas. To increase grain outputs, the continued cooperation and commitment of tenants was essential during the year-round process of cultivation, preparation and adoption of new techniques. Therefore the provision of longer leases became more likely because landlords needed to attract and retain capable and enterprising tenants by offering them more secure conditions. The dichotomy was therefore not so much a Highland/Lowland social division, but rather one between pastoral and arable districts wherever they existed in Scotland. The problem for Gaeldom, however, was that large-scale arable agriculture of the Lowland type was impossible in many parts of the Highlands and Islands for reasons of geography and climate.

Such differentiation had great future importance. In areas of arable and mixed farming, long leases necessarily lapsed at greatly varying times, making it difficult for landlords to carry out sudden wholesale removal of small tenant communities in single acts of collective eviction. They were forced to act in a gradual and piecemeal fashion through attrition as tacks ended one by one over a period of years. In pastoral districts, on the other hand, large-scale removals proved much easier to achieve over relatively short periods of time. In the Highlands, as late as the middle decades of the nineteenth century, crofters held their smallholdings only on annual leases. That kind of short-term tenure left them much more at risk to the changing economic priorities of landlordism.

3

The people below tenant rank are much more difficult to document for the period before c.1750. Estate archives are abundant for many parts of the Lowlands, but they primarily record the rent-paying tenants who mattered most to proprietors. The majority of rural inhabitants rarely appear in the documentation and, for the most part, remain a shadow people. One unique source does, however, provide some important insights into their condition. The Scottish Parliament authorized three consecutive poll taxes in 1693, 1695 and 1698, and the record of allocations of payment contain details of the entire social pyramid of that decade from the most powerful aristocrats to the humblest servants. Since the sums levied depended on wealth and social position, the poll tax material gives a kind of surrogate outline of Scottish society at the end of the seventeenth century. Inevitably analysing it presents technical problems of interpretation; also the documentation has only survived for some areas in the Lowlands. The Aberdeenshire returns are comprehensive, and partial poll lists are also available for Renfrewshire, Midlothian, Berwick, West Lothian and Selkirk. They represent a fraction of the original records but can still provide useful coverage of areas with different economic and social profiles across the country. In all, it is possible to examine from these data the social position of 25,690 individuals from over sixty parishes in the north-east, south-east and south-west of Scotland.

The most striking feature of 'the people below' was the virtual ubiquity of the cottar class and its overall numerical significance throughout much of the Lowlands. Indeed, in most rural parishes, cottar families made up somewhere between a third and a half of the entire population. If Lowland Scots of today could trace their ancestry directly back to the seventeenth century, it is more than likely many of them would find they were descended from the cottar families who were so common across the countryside before the time of improvement. Cottars held small patches of land from tenants or subtenants in return for labour services and occasionally for small payments in rental. They possessed a few acres or lived in rows of cottages known as *cottouns* within the *fermetouns*. Many were also weavers, blacksmiths, carpenters and other artisans with a house and a 'yard' in the township. A typical set of cottar-tenant obligations is shown below in Table 1.

The poll tax data suggest that only in Renfrewshire and highland Aberdeenshire were the number of cottars significantly below the average. Tenancies in those counties were relatively small and had less need for additional manual labour other than that which could be furnished by the families of the farmers. Cottars, however, were much more common on the bigger market-orientated single holdings which had come about through early phases of farm consolidation. Thus, in the 1690s, two thirds of Midlothian parishes and over half of those in Berwickshire, both counties in the fertile south-east of labour-intensive arable husbandry, had significant cottar communities. Equally, high proportions were recorded in Lowland Aberdeenshire with cottars present in 67 per cent of parishes in the grain-producing Lowland coastal belt. However, throughout the hill country in the west of that county, which was dominated by stock rearing needing little labour, cottars were few and far between. As seen in Chapter 1, the same

Table 1 Cottar structure in a Fife *fermetoun*, 1714

–	Arch^d Myles in Craigburn posses a house yeard and one acre of Land Laboured by the Tennent
–	Alex^dr Miller in Knowhead 2 acres and a half Laboured and payes 3 bolls and 21 lib. of money
–	Jems Leslie ane hous yeard and ane acre Laboured
–	John Robison Sheepherd a hous yeard and ane acres in 2 divisions
–	David Reekie 2 acres with hous and yeard and land Laboured payes 5 bolls bear 1 shearer and—of money
6.	David Patie ane acre with hous and two years and land Laboured pays 2 shearers and seven lib. of money
7.	Willie Lanceman ane acre without hous or yeard to it 12 lib.
8. & 9.	The Whythons and yeard with 4 acres to it possest by Will: Patrick and Cristian Tullow in 2 Divisions
10.	Thom: Shipherds relict a hous yeard and 2 acres of Land
11.	Wm. Greig a hous and yeard without Land payes 7 lib.
12.	Janet Shipherd ane hous yeard and acre
13.	Andrew Baxter a hous yeard and payes 5 lib it has ane acre of land belonging to it but not possest by him
14.	Alex^dr Mackie in hillhead about ane—acre
15.	Alex^dr Paterson 3 acres whereof two are on the Westermost march above the highway

Source: NRA(S) 874, Berry Papers, Box 12/6, Ane Account of the Rinds and Parcells, Inverdovat, 1714

social pattern was typical of most Highland townships, where the tiny pockets of cultivable arable could be easily worked by families of tenants without support from hired workers.

Cottars were prevalent in the old society for a number of reasons. Much of the work in the *fermetouns* concentrated in a few periods of peak demand for ploughing, harvesting and fuel gathering, a cycle which combined short periods of maximum effort with much slacker times. Cottar families therefore provided a reserve supply of labour guaranteed to meet requirements in the busy times but could easily be laid off for much of the rest of the year. Again, by paying for labour in small patches of land, tenants saved on money outlay when the cash economy was underdeveloped. In the old-style farming, tenants were burdened with considerable services to their landlord and had to provide a number of days' work on the mains (or landowner's) farm, additional labour at harvest, and help with the carriage of the land-owner's grain, manure, lime and peat. Cottar families were the first option to go to for help with these tasks, which tended to be demanded at the busier times of the agricultural year.

Moreover, the labour routines of the period demanded abundant supplies of workers as almost everything depended on human effort and the use of hand tools. Therefore, as farm size increased in some places, the number of cottars and servants inevitably had to rise in turn. Enclosures were still few and far between, outside some areas of pastoral farming, and so children of the cottar families were widely used to herd cattle to prevent damage to crops on the arable as they neared maturity. Peat digging, gathering and drying was also an arduous task throughout the spring and summer months. Ploughing the land by the 'old Scots plough' needed several men not only in attendance but also to maintain and feed the animals. Some cottars within the townships were also skilled tradesmen whose small plots of land provided for their subsistence needs. The expansion of cottage industry in the rural communities was a notable feature of the pre-1750 period, with the spinning and weaving of woollens becoming especially significant in the Border region and the north-east, while the making and selling of linen cloth was a common pursuit across much of the rest of the Lowland countryside.

There might be a temptation to sentimentalize the way of life of the cottars. On the face of it, their possession of some land, though tiny in extent, could be said to give them more 'independence' than the mass of landless servants and labourers who in later decades were to become the working proletariat of the new agrarian system. But the extent of cottar freedom needs to be kept in perspective. They had no legal rights to the land and lived on it at the sole discretion of their masters, the tenant farmers. If tenants moved to other holdings or their leases were not renewed at the end of term, cottar families in turn had no choice but to go with them or even be abandoned altogether. Significantly, references to cottar evictions are rare in sheriff court records, which suggests that they could be turned off at the will of masters without any recourse to the cost of a formal legal process. In the final analysis, indeed, they might be more accurately described as 'labourers' who had a patch of land rather than 'possessors'. They can be seen as a kind of hybrid class combining characteristics of both peasants and proletarians. Some also were required to help pay for their holdings not only in labour but in rent. Before their large-scale removal took place in the later eighteenth century, contemporary comments on the lives of cottars were few and far between. However, one graphic account from the estate of Lord Douglas in Angus supports the view that some at least had to endure a life of poverty, hard toil and profound insecurity:

> A Tenant here for every plow has Two sometimes 3 or more Familys of Cottars and these have two or three acres of land each which are set so Dear as that they commonly pay the half and sometimes the whole of the Taxman's Rent: if your Graces estate here was set at the same Rate as the Cottars and Subtenants Possessions are, it would be Ten or perhaps twelve times the rent it now is.
>
> These cottars uphold their own houses and work all the land, for I hardly have observed a Tennant work here; the Cottars slavery is incredible and what is worse they are liable to be turned out at the Master's pleasure to whom they work . . .[7]

The poet Robert Burns, himself of Ayrshire farming stock and who also laboured on the land for much of his life, immortalized the cottars in his popular sentimental poem 'A Cottar's Saturday Night', first published in 1786. Writing in the rural dialect of his native county, Burns praises their stoic acceptance of poverty. In the first stanza, he describes the cottar wearily wending his way home to his cot house on a Saturday evening in the early winter at the end of a week of hard labour. As he walks, he looks forward to a day of rest on the Sabbath:

> November chill blaws
> Loud wi' angry sugh: The short'ning winter-

day is near a close;
The miry beasts
Retreated frae
The pleugh
The black'ning trains o'
craws to their repose
The toil-worn Cotter [sic]
Frae his labour goes,
This night his weekly
Moil is at an end,
Collects his spades, his
Mattocks, and his hoes,
Hoping the morn in
ease and rest to spend,
And weary, o'er the
moor, his course does
homeward bend

[*sugh* – rushing sound of wind; *moil* – toil; *mattocks* – shortened
version of pickaxes]

Most of the remainder of the 'people below' in the old order were
smaller numbers of landless male and female servants who were hired
into full-time employment. Married servants, who were common in
the south-eastern counties, had labour contracts for a year, were paid
mainly in kind and were provided with cottages attached and the
keep of a cow. Single male and female servants, who comprised the
vast majority of that class beyond Fife and the south-east, had no
such partial independence. They possessed no land, were paid partly
in money and kind, lived within the farmer's household and ate with
his family in the kitchen. The poll tax lists suggest that servants in a
few counties were already equal in number to cottars and their families, as in Berwick, Midlothian and Renfrewshire, but elsewhere
remained a minority. The existence of such a landless class in some
districts might seem to be in conflict with the argument above that
access to some land, however limited, was the firm cornerstone of the
old rural Lowlands before 1750. But the inconsistency was more
apparent than real.

One scholar explains:

Often they [the servants] came of cottar families and on marriage might set up as had their parents. Cottars and servants therefore formed a seamless group, in which, through life, the child of a cottar bound to give service for some days in the year, yet with that precious if insecure title to land, would move into full-time service for a period before marrying and returning finally to the cottar position.[8]

PART TWO

4

Forgotten History:
Dispossession in the Borders

Today travellers by train from Carlisle to the north crossing the Border countryside can look out at mile after mile of uninhabited but apparently fertile land. Only the occasional cottage or farm steading is seen as a rare sign of human habitation. Flocks of sheep graze almost everywhere. This is not a natural landscape but one formed by social and economic change in the seventeenth century and early eighteenth.

For, contrary to popular belief, the removal and abandonment of traditional rural communities in eighteenth-century Scotland did not start in the Highlands. Two generations or more before clearances began north of the Highland line, the dispossession of many tenants and cottars was already under way in the hill country of the Borders, many miles to the south, in a social revolution which has long been mainly ignored. The proximate cause was the expansion of large sheep farms, often with flocks averaging between 4,000 and 20,000, and the parallel growth in other districts of extensive cattle ranches. The specialist region for sheep was Roxburgh and Peebles in the central and eastern Borders, while cattle rearing and fattening was more dominant further west in Galloway and the surrounding districts. What happened in those areas eventually generated the model for the later and more familiar clearances in the Highlands. Indeed, it was Border-reared and -improved Cheviot breeds which from the last quarter of the eighteenth century began to stock numerous farms across the north-west and the islands in a seemingly inexorable white tide which led to the uprooting of many peasant communities. Moreover, some of the pioneering flockmasters and shepherds who managed the new sheep walks in the Highlands were often men who were Borders-born and -bred from Liddesdale and Eskdale, where they had first learned how to run large-scale pastoral farms in the early eighteenth century.

This chapter considers the reasons for the early onset of dispossession in the deep south of Scotland by pastoral specialization and expansion and tries to document its extent and significance. The analysis also explores the intriguing question of what became of the people who lost land during a historic transformation which within a few decades had brought to an end a traditional way of life which had existed in the Southern Uplands for centuries.

I

Sheep farming in the eastern and central Borders had a long lineage. As far back as the eleventh century, the abbeys of Melrose, Jedburgh and Kelso began to develop upland pastures in the Cheviot Hills, upper Teviotdale and Eskdale, and the hinterlands of the Yarrow and Ettrick Waters. When the monastic lands were expropriated during the Reformation of the sixteenth century, it was influential Border families, such as the Scotts, future dukes of Buccleuch, and the Kerrs, later dukes of Roxburgh, who took much of the former church land into their own possession. By that time, sheep farming was already carried out on such a scale that it gave rise to some contemporary comment. Thus, Bishop Leslie in 1578 could write of Tweeddale: 'in this contrie . . . evin as with other nychbouris [neighbours], that sum of thame are known to have four or fyve hundir [hundred] uthers agane aucht [eight], nyne hundir, and som tyme thay ar knawen to have a thousand scheip'.[1]

However, full commercialization was inhibited by continuing instability in the Border countryside, whether from marauding armies or endemic livestock rustling. Therefore the great families in the region, like their counterparts in the Highlands, still had to depend on large and loyal followings to provide defence for property and social position. The force of these kinship connections had not entirely disappeared by the last few decades of the seventeenth century, so that by that time land was not yet considered to be simply an economic asset to be exclusively used solely for profit. As one authority has commented: 'So long as the Borders remained a troubled area, then large estates would have been tolerant of a numerous tenantry.'[2] Rentals from the Buccleuch as well as the Roxburgh properties in this period confirm that both upland farms and those situated along the river valleys had large numbers of both tenants (often in multi-tenancy) and subtenants. Two detailed maps of Scotland, one published in 1654 and the other compiled between 1747 and 1755, provide a pictorial and visual complement to the documentary sources. The seventeenth-century *Blaeu Map of Scotland* is the first known atlas of the country. A section on Galloway depicts the large number of small townships in the region before the era of dispossession, most of which had vanished by 1800. The other map, the famous mid-eighteenth-century survey of Scotland under the direction of Major-General William Roy, has been considered by cartographers to be not entirely accurate but is nonetheless very useful for sites which interested the military such as settlements, manmade structures and cultivated land. The Roy survey therefore provides an invaluable bird's-eye view of population distribution and cultivated arable in the Border counties, confirming once again their much greater density before improvement.

It was only in the period following the Regal Union of 1603 that joint action by Scottish and English authorities began the process of bringing the Borders into a condition of final stability. Though old attitudes, traditions and loyalties still took many years to die out in their entirety, state-imposed pacification soon became the essential precondition for the rapid expansion of commercial pastoral economy in the region. Growing demand for wool and mutton was also influential, not least in the latter case from the mining villages of the north-east England coalfield. Table 2 gives an indication of the scale of the cross-Border trade in sheep which had developed even before the Union of 1707 established free trade between Scotland and England.

Table 2 Number of sheep driven across the Border to England, 1665–91

Customs precinct Customs year 1 Nov.–31 Oct.	Dumfries	South Borders (Alisonbank)	Castleton	Jedburgh	Kelso	Ayton and Duns	Minimum total for all precincts
1665–6	–	6,625	–	–	–	–	–
1672–3	–	–	–	170	112	–	–
1680–81	823	1,363	Inc. in S.B.	2,672+	234	1,419	6,511
1681–2	230	3,163	6,492	8,540	4,914	395	23,734
1682–3	692	4,850	7,600	11,870	7,178	–	32,190
1683–4	300	4,284	6,010	5,366	2,735	184	18,879
1684–5	160	12,552	Inc. in S.B.	1,988	909+	684	16,293
1685–6	–	6,616	6,160	10,864	3,740+	1,264	28,644
1688–9	340	4,907	–	4,280	671	609	10,807
1689–90	164	6,740	2,832+	4,092+	1,643	285	15,306
1690–91	20	7,398	–	6,375	80	65	13,938

Inc. in S.B. = Included in South Borders

Source: Ian Whyte, Agriculture and Society in Seventeenth Century Scotland (Edinburgh, 1979), p. 239.

Also becoming more important were town markets in the central Lowlands. While the population of Scotland as a whole remained overwhelmingly rural, the five counties of the south-east, in and around the valley of the River Forth, had a surprisingly high level of early urban development. The number of small towns and large villages in East Lothian, Midlothian, Fife and Clackmannan meant the area had more urban dwellers than any other part of Scotland. In addition, of course, Edinburgh was by far the largest concentrated market in Scotland. The population of the capital doubled in size between 1560 and the 1640s to over 30,000. Edinburgh was also the richest town in the country, alone paying around one third of the taxation raised from the royal burghs in the later seventeenth century. Scotland as a whole may not have been a nation of meat eaters at this time, but the affluent middle and upper classes of Edinburgh had long had an appetite for Border lamb and mutton. Indeed, on the growing sheep farms, profits from the sales of lamb, hogs and cast ewes to the butchers at this time far outweighed those from wool and skins.

By 1700, then, sheep farming was already impressive in extent and geared to servicing demand outside the Border region. However, the evidence of estate papers shows that alongside the big holdings which specialized in stock rearing there was a considerable subsistence sector of small tenants and their families clustered in adjacent *fermetouns*. For example, a 1718 survey of the vast Buccleuch estate, with 140 farms spread across Ettrick, Teviotdale, Liddesdale, Ewesdale and Eskdalemuir, shows holdings of 500–1,000 acres and above were dominant in the upper hill country, but on the lower ground tenancies of 30–50 acres remained common. Equally, the big sheep farms all paid rental in cash – a sign of their commercial orientation – while many smallholdings still adhered to a regime of rentals partly in kind, a reflection of their subsistence status. Significantly, too, late-eighteenth- and early-nineteenth-century commentators, looking back to earlier times, often noted that in a number of districts long abandoned to large-scale pastoral husbandry by that later period, 'the mark of the plough' was still visible across the landscape, testifying to the small communities which had once worked the arable land.

As the prosperity of sheep farming grew, so a conflict between the two sectors of pastoralism and subsistence became inevitable. If the former was to maintain its unrelenting progress, the ground possessed by the small tenants would have to be given up. This was because increases in stock depended in the final analysis on the number of sheep which could be over-wintered and that in turn demanded access to the low-lying arable ground occupied by the *fermetouns*.

By about 1700, it must have been apparent to the more commercially minded farmers that by reducing their arable the size of their flocks and lambing rates could be increased. But, in order to do this, the subsistence needs of the farm had to be reduced. This, in turn, meant that tenant numbers had to be cut back and larger, more commercially viable units established.[3]

Sheep farming demanded considerable space for effective management of large flocks. That requirement in turn meant that the squeezing out of the small tenant class in the areas of expansion of large holdings was likely to be only a matter of time. One contemporary improving theorist with experience of pastoral farming in the Borders explained why size mattered:

It is well known that sheep when kept by a herd never thrive in a confined pasture. The reason is obvious, they are too frequently checked in their motions and disturbed in their feeding. Land therefore that is adapted principally, or for the Sole purpose of Sheep pasture Should be Laid out in pretty Large farms.

There is another Reason for this; the different ages and kinds of Sheep do not agree with the same pasture, the Store Master therefore Divides them into Separate Hirsels each of which must have a herd; a compleat Store or Sheep farm has at least four Separate Hirsels, viz. a live Hirsell an Eald Sheep or Wedder Hirsell, or Drummkond Hirsel, and Lamb or Hog Hirsel, each of these Hirsels or flocks must be so Large as to give the Herd proper Employment.

To This quantity for Hay, and if possible to Induce the tennent to raise Turnip for winter feeding, and for Corn for the family. So that the extent of a Compleat Stores farm must appear very Considerable.

If possible every Store farm Should be of this kind, such a quantity of Land is indeed absolutely necessary to Carry on the whole process of breading and feeding Sheep to the best advantage and a Regard should be paid to this, in the manner of laying out the moor and pasture grounds, sometimes it happens that the different pastures proper for the Different kinds of Sheep do not Life so conveniently as to be put into the same farm.

Therefore the farmer must often submit to have only one or two of these kinds of Hirsels, in this Case. The farms may be proportionably less, but Still they ought to be of such an extent as to make the necessary experience of it sit Light upon the profites.[4]

[*hirsel* = flock of sheep under the management of one shepherd]

This was the economic background to the eventual dispossession of communities in the eastern borders during the decades which followed. There were signs, indeed, by the early years of the eighteenth century that some estates were already beginning to plan for the removal of tenants as part of a policy of building up larger holdings.

2

The thinning of the tenantry was under way before *c*.1750. Multiple tenancies disappeared first and these were then followed by the elimination of entire *fermetouns*, with their communities of tenants and cottars. The *First* or 'Old' *Statistical Account of Scotland* (*OSA*), published in the 1790s, contains much detail on this social transformation. The *OSA* was edited by Sir John Sinclair of Ulbster and was an enquiry into all parishes in Scotland at a time of wide-ranging economic change during the early stages of the Industrial and Agricultural Revolutions. In 1790, Sinclair circulated a structured questionnaire to over 900 parish ministers across Scotland. The 160 questions ranged over geography, population, antiquities, religion, agriculture and industry. Inevitably, the quality and length of responses varied greatly, but for all its weaknesses the *OSA* remains a unique historical compendium of contemporary life of the period unmatched for any other country in eighteenth-century Europe. Evidence derived from it can also be supplemented from the *Second* or *New Statistical Account* (*NSA*), which was mainly published in the 1840s.

Some of the individual parish accounts, such as those of Smailholm, Sprouston (both in Roxburgh) and Selkirk, provide valuable outlines of the time frame of dispossession. It seems to have begun on a relatively small scale in the later seventeenth century, became more common from the 1720s, and speeded up again from the 1750s. The evidence of the *NSA* reports suggests that the suppression of smaller farms and cottages was virtually complete by 1815. Documentation of the removals can be presented in both a qualitative and a numerical fashion. The series of extracts reproduced below from the *OSA* reports leave little doubt about the scale of clearance. These are then followed by enumeration of population in a number of Border parishes for the half-century between the mid-1750s and 1790s. The accounts vividly illustrate the reaction of the local clergy to the dramatic changes they had witnessed during their own lifetimes, together with other evidence reported to them by their predecessors before they themselves were appointed to parish ministry. The tone is factual but also elegiac, descriptions of an older world which has now vanished:

> There are no new houses built in the parish of late, nor cottages, but a great many cottages pulled down, the farmer finding more loss than profit from keeping cot-houses. The throwing down of cottages must be one principal reason of the decrease of population.

Parish of Broughton, County of Peebles

> From the best information, there is reason to believe that the parish about 40 years ago was double in population to what it is at present. There were then considerable *villages* [N.B. almost certainly these were farming townships] in it: the one is entirely gone; and a few straggling houses are all that remains of the other. Farms now possessed by one, were then in the hands of 2, 4 and even 5 farmers, and the number of cottagers, besides the inhabitants of little villages, even greater.

Parish of Traquair, County of Peebles

> The population of this parish has decreased considerably. About 70 years ago, the lands were occupied by 26 tenants, but the farms since that period have been gradually enlarged in extent, and of course diminished in number; even of the 15 to which they are now reduced, so many are engrossed in the hands of the same persons, and those

often settled in other parishes, that there are now only 3 farmers at present resident in the whole parish.

Parish of Tweedsmuir, County of Peebles

The great decrease of inhabitants, within the last 40 years, is evidently occasioned by the too general practice of letting the lands in great farms ... lands, 50 or 100 years ago, were parcelled out into at least four times the present number of farms. As late as the year 1740, five tenants, with large families, occupied a farm now rented by one tenant. There were also, about these times, several small but proud lairds [owner-occupiers] in the parish. Their lands are now lost in the large farms, their names extinguished, and their mansions totally destroyed.

Parish of Hownam, County of Roxburgh

The decrease of the population has been chiefly occasioned by the monopoly of farms ... in the village [farming township] of Oxnam, between 60 and 70 years ago, there were 22 tenants who kept above 16 ploughs drawn by oxen and horses; whereas now, 3 persons occupy the whole and have only 7 ploughs, drawn by horses.

Parish of Oxnam, County of Roxburgh

The aged people all agree in asserting that it [i.e. population] considerably exceeded the present and their testimony is corroborated from the numerous remains of old houses. Various causes may be assigned for this depopulation. One, undoubtedly, may be imputed to the monopoly of farms which diminishes the number of farmers' families. Another may be attributed to the aversion of the farmers to rebuild cot-houses.

Parish of Yarrow, County of Selkirk

These comments, and the demographic evidence which follows below and supports them, suggest a number of conclusions. The parish ministers in their commentaries reveal a scale of dispossession in the early-eighteenth-century eastern Borders which evokes comparison with the more familiar Highland experience of later decades. Those primarily involved in the decisions to remove entire communities were, like those in north and west Scotland, the landowners, their factors and their agents. But the new breed of élite tenants which emerged in the sheep-farming districts was also directly responsible for the widespread removal of the subordinate cottar class which in traditional society had possessed tiny portions of land in return for seasonal labour services. Their social position had always been insecure since they had no legally confirmed rights to their modest possessions. Whether they continued to live on them or not depended in the final analysis not on the estate proprietors but on the decisions of the tenantry who sublet to them the plots of land which were vital to their subsistence and to whom they were directly responsible. Unequivocal confirmation of their dependent status was that when their masters moved to another holding, so did they, together with the ploughs, tools and other equipment of the farm. Yet rarely, except perhaps in crisis years of famine or harvest failure, had their lowly position in the rural hierarchy ever been systematically challenged. But now the cottar class as a whole was soon to be on the verge of extinction throughout the eastern Borders. Clearly, as more and more arable land was annexed for pastoralism, the need for cottar families to help with cultivation of the soil for grain cropping was becoming superfluous.

Also of significance in this narrative is the question of the silence of the people who were displaced in such large numbers. The process could not have been painless or devoid of stress, threat and anxiety. Yet, if surviving rent rolls had not revealed the extent of tenant removal and local ministers in the OSA had not described the reality of extensive dispossession in their parishes, the clearances in the eastern Borders could well have been lost to history. There was no evidence of public disturbance or protest against loss of land of the kind which might have attracted interest and concern beyond the region and so left a deposit of evidence for later scholars to evaluate.

The silence is indeed remarkable in light of the age-old connections which the people had with the land and which were so basic to virtually all material aspects of their existence. Moreover, the reintegration of the displaced populations into the big sheep farms as landless servants and labourers was unlikely. This did take place in areas of labour-intensive mixed or arable agriculture elsewhere in the Lowlands, a process which is considered in Chapters 8 and 9. But large-scale pastoral husbandry was land- and capital-intensive and needed little in the way of labour apart from a few experienced shepherds and labourers. The conventional eighteenth-century belief was that one shepherd was needed to manage 600 sheep. In other words, a giant sheep farm of around 10,000 sheep required only sixteen shepherds.

As the figures below suggest, tenant and cottar displacement was often followed by sharp falls in the population of individual parishes. Yet, while many did experience absolute decline in numbers, small increases in others could disguise the real extent of haemorrhage either due to dispossession or caused by young folk moving to seek opportunities elsewhere. The population of Scotland rose by an estimated average of 20 per cent, or one fifth, between the 1750s and 1790s. Therefore parishes with significantly lower increases than that were likely to be experiencing net out-migration.

The progressive decline in the population of some parishes was accompanied by a contraction in the arable which had once been cultivated. There is evidence that on the estates of Roxburgh, Marchmont and Lothian, rising prices for wool and mutton were encouraging landowners to insist in the tacks issued to new tenants that more and more land on upland farms should be converted to grazing. Travellers in the region noted the shrinkage of cultivation. Thus Robert Heron in 1793 wrote of the parish of Robertson in upper Clydesdale: 'Everywhere as I proceeded up the vale, I could discover by certain marks, that it had anciently been a scene of agricultural industry and a seat of no inconsiderable population. The houses were only cottages. But in many instances, the walls of these cottages seemed of very ancient erection'. He wondered what had become of the people who once lived there and grew corn on the now empty and barren fields.[5] Evidence from the Lammermuirs suggests that 48 settlements were abandoned between 1600 and 1750. Over the following half-century, the figure was 21 and between 1800 and 1825 the rate increased to 54 over that twenty-year period.

However, there is little indication in the Poor Law figures in the OSA parish reports that thinning of the working population had led to significantly increased poverty or vagrancy. The numbers of supported poor in virtually all the registers were described as being at normal or even sometimes at lower levels. Indeed, several ministers

Table 3 Population of selected east and central
Border parishes, 1755 and 1790s

Parish	1755	1790s	County
Broughton	400	264	Peebles
Drumelzier	305	270	Peebles
Eddleston	679	710	Peebles
Glenholm	392	300	Peebles
Linton (1777)	1,003	928	Peebles
Lyne and Megget	265	152	Peebles
Manmer	320	229	Peebles
Skirling	335	234	Peebles
Traquair	651	446	Peebles
Tweedsmuir	397	227	Peebles
Ashkirk	629	539	Roxburgh
Bedrule	297	255	Roxburgh
Bowden	672	800	Roxburgh
Castletown	1,507	1,418	Roxburgh
Eckford	1,043	952	Roxburgh
Ednam	387	600	Roxburgh
Hownam	632	365	Roxburgh
Jedburgh	6,000	6324	Roxburgh
Kelso	2,781	4,324	Roxburgh
Lilliesleaf	521	630	Roxburgh
Oxnam	760	690	Roxburgh
Robertson	651	629	Roxburgh
Smalholm	551	357	Roxburgh
Sprouston	1,020	1,000	Roxburgh
Yetholm	699	976	Roxburgh
Ettrick	397	470	Selkirk
Galashiels	998	901	Selkirk
Selkirk	1,793	1,700	Selkirk

Sources: 1790s: *OSA* reports for the various parishes. 1755: 'Dr Alexander Webster's Account of the Population of Scotland in 1755', in J. G. Kyd, ed., *Scottish Population Statistics Including Webster's Analysis of Population 1755* (Edinburgh, 1952).

asserted that, far from causing immiseration, depopulation had led to sharp increases in money wages. Poverty, therefore, could have been exported through the emigration and migration of the dispossessed. Some *OSA* reports did indeed mention that movement to the American colonies occurred on an extensive scale from the region in the early 1770s. It was noted of Smallholm in Roxburghshire, for instance, that many young men from the parish had joined the army and navy during the American War of Independence and never came back home. Others were said to have left for the East Indies, the Americas, the Caribbean and above all for England. The parish minister was of the opinion that from the whole of Scotland '10,000 journeymen, wrights, carpenters, bakers, gardeners, and taylors [*sic*] go yearly to London'. He went on to suggest that 'Many of them emigrate from this part of the country, sailing from Berwick and Newcastle, where the passage is short and frequent, and the freight easy.'[6] Regrettably, however, little systematic evidence has survived about the specific extent of outward movement for this period. Between 1755 and 1801, the population of the rural parishes in the county of Roxburgh rose by 7 per cent, Peebles by 18 per cent, Dumfries by 19 per cent and Kirkcudbright by 24 per cent. The national average population figure for the same period was an increase of 20 per cent. Apart from Roxburgh, therefore, the numbers do not imply mass outward migration from the central and eastern Borders before the 1790s. On this evidence, the demographic impact of dispossession seems mainly to have been contained within the Border region itself.

On the other hand, there is compelling evidence that many of those removed from the land by the spread of large-scale sheep farming moved to towns and villages in the region where they managed to find some work in the developing cottage industries. The town populations of Kelso, Hawick, Galashiels, Selkirk and Jedburgh all showed significant increases in the later eighteenth century. These urban spaces were gaining people at the expense of the surrounding countryside, which was continuously shedding inhabitants. Of Kelso in the 1790s, for instance, it was said:

In 38 years the increase in people has been 1543. This great increase may, in part, be accounted for from the destruction of many villages (farm townships) in the neighbourhood, occupied by small farms. From the enlargement of the farms, many were obliged to follow other trades, and Kelso, being the metropolis of the district, they flocked there for habitations and employment; and in proportion as labourers and mechanics have become fewer in the country, Kelso increased in population.[7]

Another case in point was the village of Yetholm in Roxburgh. In the second half of the eighteenth century, it more than doubled in numbers because many townships in the adjacent parishes of Hownam, Morbottle and Linton 'had been totally razed since the memory of people now living' and many of their inhabitants had moved to Yetholm.

The 'other trades' mentioned in the description of Kelso were mainly associated with textile work organized at the time on a domestic basis. Home-based spinning, weaving and knitting proved to be the salvation of many of the evicted families in the years immediately before the rise of factory-based woollen manufacturing in the Border towns. It is known that many of these skills had long been practised within the communities of the *fermetouns*. David Loch, in his tour of the region in 1778, noted the range of textile working in the closing decades of the eighteenth century which included the making of plaids, carpets, linen, stockings, napkins, serges and blankets and was centred on the towns of Hawick, Peebles, Melrose, Kelso, Jedburgh, Moffat, Carnwath, Sanquar and Dumfries. As the decay of the old rural society gathered pace, some alternative possibilities were beginning to emerge which provided a basic living for families who no longer had a place in the modernizing rural economy which had sustained their ancestors for generations in the past. That interaction between the growth of small-scale urban industry and the parallel process of dispossession on the land might go some way to explaining why this part of the Borders, unlike some parishes further west in Galloway, never erupted into violent peasant resistance.

3

While the great sheep runs concentrated in the centre and east, the heartland of cattle rearing in the Borders was the south-west. In the later seventeenth century more than nine out of ten of the cattle which

Table 4 Number of cattle driven across the Border to England, 1665–91

Customs precinct	Dumfries	South Borders (Alisonbank)	Castleton	Jedburgh	Kelso	Ayton and Duns	Minimum total for all precincts
Customs year 1 Nov.–31 Oct.							
1665–6		7,292 Irish 1,045 Scots					
1672–3				209	228		
1680–1	1,273	2,089	Inc. in S.B.	–	108	156	4,346
1681–2	9,053	4,641	1,784	330	261	267	16,336
1682–3	10,500	11,503	3,346	1,076	1,438	–	27,863
1683–4	4,865	4,480	1,993	532	607	87	12,564
1684–5	9,090	10,639	Inc. in S.B.	903	251+	282	21,065
1685–6	–	14,747	4,799	1,828	1,586+	1,122	24,082
1688–9	7,528	8,088	–	244	141	225	16,226
1689–90	4,569	5,554	–	199	60	9	10,391
1690–91	801	3,694	1,011	155	67	17	5,745

Inc. in S.B. = Included in South Borders

Source: Ian Whyte, *Agriculture and Society in Seventeenth Century Scotland* (Edinburgh, 1979), p. 239.

crossed the border for sale in England were accounted for by the three western customs precincts of Alisonbank, Castleton and Dumfries.

These figures confirm that the droving trade was already substantial before the Union of 1707. As with large-scale sheep farming, pacification of the Borders in the decades following the Regal Union had been a precondition for expansion. But other influences cannot be ignored. The rapid growth of English urban markets for meat during the second half of the seventeenth century was also very relevant. London's expansion, for instance, was little short of phenomenal. By 1660 it was second only in size to Paris and fifty years later had become the biggest city in Europe, dwarfing all others, with a population of some half a million people. The gargantuan size of the 'Great Wen' forced the suppliers and traders of the city to draw on the whole of Britain for essentials of foods, fuel and raw materials. After months of fattening in the fields of East Anglia, cattle from Scotland were driven on the hoof a short distance to the slaughterhouses of Smithfield in the capital. Many of these beasts had been bred in the Borders. Some had been reared in the Highlands counties and in addition cattle from the Buccleuch lands around Dalkeith were fattened for sale close to Edinburgh.

A critical factor in the emerging market for Border stock was the passage of the Irish Cattle Act by the English Parliament in 1666 prohibiting live imports from across the Irish Sea. Irish cattle were heavier and bigger than the Scottish breeds, which offered them little competition in the English market. By 1663 it was estimated that as many as 61,000 Irish cattle were imported annually into England, a volume of trade which completely dwarfed the Scottish enterprise. The prohibition of 1666 was therefore a precondition for the rise of Borders cattle ranching and its eventual success in the London market.

Droving was also encouraged by a successive lowering of customs duties at the Anglo-Scottish border. The Scottish Privy Council changed from a policy of preventing livestock exports to one of encouraging them with considerable enthusiasm. So, by the 1680s, the customs charge per beast had sunk to a twentieth of that levied at the start of the century. More than ever, the way was now open for Galloway landowners to enter the cattle trade across the border in a big way. By the end of the seventeenth century, some estates were each sending annually droves of 400–500 cattle to England. One estimate suggests an overall yearly average of 20,000–30,000 cattle were crossing the border. But this was based on official figures of stock passing through the customs precincts. As the frontier between the countries was very porous at the time, there is no way of knowing how many more came over by clandestine routes. Then came free trade after the Union of 1707; Border landowners were more than ready to profit from the anticipated bonanza of cattle sales to English markets.

In response to these increasingly favourable market opportunities, some of the south-west gentry began to develop cattle parks and extensive grazing grounds. One of the leaders in the development was Sir David Dunbar. At Baldoon, south of Wigtown, he constructed a large grazing area in 1684. Estimated to be two and a half miles in length and one and a half in breadth, it was reckoned to be capable of providing wintering for 1,000 cattle in the mild climate of the Solway lowlands. Dunbar bought cattle from neighbouring tenants and landowners in late summer, wintered them in the park and then drove the fattened animals to markets in England in August and September.

His enterprise drew most attention at the time – it was described as 'the mother of all the rest' – but other Border landlords, such as the Stair family and Lord Bargany, were also active in the same way.[8] Enclosed pasture had several advantages over open-field grazing because it permitted segregation of livestock and better management of herds. Now it became possible to prevent inbreeding of sick and healthy animals and improve the quality of the animals. Selective breeding of beasts took place on what was usually the best land on an estate, while the pasture ground was enriched further by liming and cattle manure. The result was improved livestock with higher sales value at market.

Even before the Anglo-Scottish Union then, what the local people calling 'parking' was a familiar trend in some western districts of the Borders. It was inevitable, however, that at some point there conflict would arise between the subsistence way of life of the small tenants and cottars and the continued spread of the cattle ranches into contested areas of good grazing land. This was likely to be the equivalent for Galloway of the depopulating effects of commercialized sheep farming in the central and eastern estates of the Borders . Evidence soon began to emerge of the clearance of townships and the annexation of

THE SCOTTISH CLEARANCES

common grazing lands which were essential to the functioning of the peasant livestock economy. Travellers in the region saw the impact. In 1723, Sir John Clerk of Penicuik noted in his journal: 'The inhabitants of Galloway [Wigtownshire] are much lessened since the custom of inclosing their grounds took place, for there are certainly above 20,000 acres laid waste on that account.' He described 'the inclosures for black cattle' with 'diks [dykes] of stone without mortar, very thinly built' and 'had occasion to compute that they bring in ten thousand guineas to their country, for the price of their cattle is commonly paid in gold'.[9] Another source noted how 'the very little town of Minnigaff belonging to Mr. Heron [Patrick Heron, Laird of Kirroughtree] is only a nest of beggars since he inclosed all the ground about'. It was also reported that 'Evry year several tenants are exposed to the mountains, and know not where to get any place', and alleged that there were instances of peasant suicides about the Whitsun term time 'when they were obliged to go away and did not know where to go'.[10]

The plight of the dispossessed was described in a vitriolic, anti-landlord ballad, *Lamentation of the People of Galloway by the Pairking Lairds*, composed by James Charters of the Kirkland of Dalry. Charters was a tenant of the Gordons of Earlston and there is some evidence he was associated with the 'levelling' of cattle dykes in protest against the removals. Originally circulated in manuscript, the ballad was then printed in Glasgow for wider distribution:

A generation like to this
Did never man behold,
I mean over great and might men
Who covetous are of gold.
Solomon could not well approve
The practice of their lives
To oppress and to keep down the poor,
Their actions cut like knives.

Among great men where shall ye find
a godly man like Job,
He made the widow's heart to sing
But our lairds make them sob.
It is the duty of great men

The poor folks to defend,
But worldly interest moves our lairds,
Their mind another end

The lords and lairds may drive us out from mailings
    [tenant farms] where we dwell
The poor man says: 'Where shall we go?'
The rich says: 'Go to Hell.'
These words they spoke in jests and mocks
That if they have their herds and flocks,
They care not where to go

Against the poor they will prevail
with all their wicked words,
And will inclose both moor and dale
And turn cornfield into parks.[11]

The enclosures soon led to a loss of people. Of the fourteen parishes in Kirkcudbrightshire which showed a fall in population below
the Scottish average in the later period 1755–1801, the six which
experienced absolute decline were situated in the remote hill country.
They included Carsphairn, Dalry and Kells. The adjoining parish of
Balmaclellan registered a rise of only 3.7 per cent, though the national
average increase was over 20 per cent in the second half of the eighteenth century. But there was one dramatic difference between the
clearances for sheep farming in the northerly parishes of the Borders
and those which facilitated the expansion of large-scale cattle ranching in Galloway. As noted above, in the sheep-farming districts the
removals took place in silence with little evidence of any social disturbance. But in 1724 Galloway was convulsed by a major peasant
revolt against the 'parking' of land and the evictions which were said
to cause much distress among the people of the region.

5

Resistance

The 1724 Galloway disturbances have come down in history as the 'Levellers' Revolt' since the aim of the protesters was to 'level' the dykes of the large cattle parks which had been developing in the region since the late seventeenth century. The disturbances were unique in scale and intensity. Armed gangs of small tenants and cottars, sometimes over 1,000 strong, roamed the countryside at night breaking up the dykes of enclosed parks and fields which were believed to have resulted in the eviction of peasant families. So alarmed were the local landowners that they had to call for six troops of dragoons from Edinburgh. But even their arrival did not immediately bring peace and stability to the affected parishes.

The disturbances came to national attention. They were condemned by the General Assembly of the Church of Scotland, attracted the attention of the Duke of Roxburgh, the Secretary for Scotland, and even came to the notice of King George I himself. The national press brought the story to a wider audience. Indeed, it was the leading Edinburgh newspaper, the *Caledonian Mercury*, which first reported on outbreaks of levelling in April 1724:

> We are credibly informed from Galloway and other places in the West that a certain Mountain Preacher, in a discourse he had in that District not many days ago, among other Things, so bitterly inveighed against the Heritors [landowners] and others of that County, for their laudable Frugality in Inclosures etc. and (as he term'd it) making Commonty [common grazing land] Property, that next Morning several hundred arm'd Devotees, big with that ancient <u>Levelling</u> Tenet, in a few Hours rid themselves of that Grievance, to the great Detriment of the Gentlemen in the Neighbourhood.[1]

I

Kelton Hill Fair, near Castle Douglas, was the location of the great annual summer gathering for the people of Galloway in the early eighteenth century. It was one of many held throughout the Scottish countryside where, in a society of humdrum routine and few entertainments, they provided a release for the country population. Many were notorious for drunkenness and sexual excess and regularly condemned by the church and local authorities alike for 'riot and dissipation'. In June 1723, Kelton Hill was the usual scene of cattle and horse trading, stalls selling food and liquor, dancing and carousing:

> Here are assembled from Ireland, from England and from the more distant parts of North Britain, horse-dealers, cattle dealers, sellers of sweetmeats and of spirituous liquors, gypsies, pick-pockets, and smugglers ... The roads are for a day or two before crowded with comers to the fair. On the hill where it is held tents are erected, and through the whole fair day one tumultuous scene is here exhibited of bustling backwards and forwards, bargaining, wooing, carousing, quarrelling amidst horses, cattle, carriages, mountebanks, the stalls of chapmen, and the tents of the sellers of liquors and cold victuals.[2]

It was at Kelton that some disaffected tenants first came together to discuss a response to the displacement of families caused by the continued expansion of enclosures and cattle parks. Notices to quit tenancies at Whitsun had already been served on sixteen households in the area and rumours were rife that up to 300 farmers would also face eviction later. Documentation is scarce but so far as is known future tactics and a campaign of resistance against the evictions were discussed. No action was taken at that point, however, and the area continued to remain quiet until early 1724. By then the parishes around Kelton Hill became the centre of the disturbances. All of the levelling activity which occurred in the Stewartry of Kirkcudbright in the period between March and June 1724 took place within a twelve-mile radius. Fourteen of the twenty-eight parishes in the Stewartry lay within this area, which occupied over 330 square miles and contained around 50 per cent of the population of the district in the early eighteenth century. The Levellers especially drew on the communities of the parishes of Twynholm, Tongland, Kelton and Crossmichael in their attacks on the dykes which took place in the spring, summer and autumn of 1724.

It was not until January or February of that year that a secret bond was drawn up and widely circulated to those prepared to resist further evictions. It is clear that considerable planning and preparations for the levelling had taken place. The organization of the groups of dyke breakers was to be managed by 'captains' in each parish. This practice of recruitment in the area dated back as far as the early 1640s, when 'captains' were appointed to supervise the raising of volunteers to resist the monarchy of Charles I during the Wars of the Covenant. At a later date, anti-Jacobite cadres had been raised in the same way during the Rising of 1715.

Moreover, the Levellers sought to gain sympathy for their cause by posting several manifestos, justifying their actions, on the doors of churches in Tongland, Borgue and Twynholm parishes in April 1724:

> Therefore in order to prevent such a chain of miseries as are likely to be the consequences of this unhappy parking we earnestly entreat the assistance and aid of you the loyal parish of Borgue in order to suppress these calamities and that we may either live or die in this land of our nativity. We beg your assistance which will tend to your own advantage in order to which we desire you to meet at David Low's in Woodhead of Tongland where we expect the concurrence of Tongland and Twynholm [parishes] upon Tuesday morning, an hour after the sun rise which will gratify us and oblige yourselves.[3]

The manifesto was composed in English rather than Scots. The writer was probably a local clergyman who was most likely sympathetic to the Levellers' cause.

It is clear from other evidence that the Levellers were not simply conservative supporters of the status quo and hostile to all agricultural innovation. Their opposition was to the large-scale enclosing of cattle parks and the effect this had on the common grazing ground and arable lands of the small tenants. Thus, in their *Account of the Reasons of Some People in Galloway, their meetings anent Public Grievances through Inclosures*, the Levellers stated their willingness 'to take up the lands which were parked as they were set formerly, and further to pay the interest on the money laid out in enclosing the ground'.[4] They were far from being a mindless mob intent on opposing all improvements. Again, in their 'Letter to Major Du Cary', the Levellers asserted:

> The Gentlemen should enclose their grounds in such parcels that each may be sufficient for a good tenant and that the Heritors lay as much rent on each of these enclosures as will give him double the interest of the money laid out on the enclosures. If he cannot get this enclosure set to a tenant whom he may judge sufficient, he may then lawfully keep that ground in his own hand till he finds a sufficient tenant taking care that the tenant's house be kept up and that it may be let with the first opportunity and that a lease of twenty-one years be offered. This will considerably augment the yearly rent of the lands and the tenant will hereby be capable and encouraged to improve the breed of sheep and black cattle and the ground, which without enclosures is impossible.[5]

Dyke breaking first occurred on 17 March 1723 at Netherlaw near Kirkcudbright. Significantly, the cattle park there was not new but had been established some decades before, in 1688. This suggests that the attacks were meant to form a collective resistance to the entire development of parking and enclosures since the later seventeenth century and not simply to the new additions which threatened evictions in the 1720s. By the beginning of May the disturbances had achieved considerable momentum. Large bands of 500, 1,000 and even up to 2,000 strong roamed Galloway during the spring and summer nights. After the loose stones were pulled down, poles between six and eight feet long were pushed into the foundations of the dykes until they were levered to the ground. Tools which were used to build them were also removed or destroyed. Another common practice was cutting the hamstrings ('houghing') of the cattle which were grazing on the parks, especially if they were suspected of having been imported illegally from Ireland.

James Clerk gave a memorable eyewitness account of what happened in a letter to his brother, Sir John Clerk of Penicuik, dated 13 May 1724:

On Sunday 10th instant they caused public proclamation to be made at doors of eight Parish Churches, ordering all men and women upward of 15 to repair to the Main of Bomby.

I saw them yesterday between the hours of 8 and 12 in the morning coming in bodies from all quarters . . . making in all a body upwards of 2000, half of which were armed with good effective firelocks upwards of 400, and pitchforks and clubs; the other half being the workmen had long poles for prizing up the seams of the dykes for quick despatch.

About 12 of the clock Mr Basil Hamilton's [a local landowner accused of being a 'parking laird'] servants with about two or three of this town, advanced to them in order to make a Treaty. They were quickly enclosed, dismounted and taken prisoner, and instead of coming to any agreement they were with much difficulty dismissed. The mob fired three shots upon them in retreat then gave the word 'Down with the Dykes' upon which they fell vigorously to work to Mr Hamilton's large dyke, for the space of three hours they levelled to the ground seven miles of stone dyke in length.

. . . there were a great many lusty young women among them who performed greater wonders than the men. It cannot be well doubted that perhaps there were several venereal conjunctions among the lads and lasses, which appears being transacted in the proper posture dykewards might very much contribute to the carrying on in throwing down the work. I left them still at work about 5 in the afternoon.[6]

If accurate, several points of interest emerge from this account, apart entirely from the evidence that levelling seems to have provided opportunities for amorous activity among 'the lads and lasses'. Clearly the gang was armed to the teeth, not only with clubs and scythes, but also with firearms. However, apart from a few shots being fired the confrontation with the servants of a landowner did not end in violence. Indeed, attacks against persons seems not to have been employed by the Levellers. The targets were the property of the landowners in general and their cattle parks in particular. The numbers involved in this example of levelling were impressive, as was the boldness of those who took part. This was not a clandestine or midnight operation but one carried out in broad daylight, with several witnesses present who observed what took place. Also worthy of note is that levelling had become a collective act undertaken by entire communities. The menfolk were joined by women, young adults and, as some other sources pointed out, also by children.

Other methods were employed in combination with physical destruction of the dykes in order to encourage support for the ultimate objective of bringing 'parking' to an end. A propaganda war was launched with public declarations and pamphlets outlining grievances and calling for support. One example was the *Account of the Reasons* ... , cited above. Another anonymous polemic acknowledged the legal right of the landowners to carry out improvements to their estates but condemned the destructive effect that some of them were having on society. Using evidence from the scriptures at length, the author contended that wholesale dispossession threatened not only public order but the ruin of God's creatures. The religious theme ran through several of the printed protests. The oppressed tenants and cottars, it was argued, had a God-given right to be supported by the fruits of the earth.

Even after only a few weeks of disturbances and agitation, some members of the landed élite in Galloway feared that the local structures of law and order were under acute pressure and increasingly unable to cope with the excesses of the Levellers. The sheriff and baron courts and Justices of the Peace were usually enough to suppress and punish petty criminality. But they had difficulty confronting what was, in some parishes of Galloway, a revolt driven by entire communities. What made matters worse was the position of the Church of Scotland and that of individual ministers. Arguably, the church was the main bastion of moral and civil order in the eighteenth-century countryside. Its hierarchy of church courts, ranging from the General Assembly, through synods and presbyteries, down to local kirk sessions, made it a powerful force for stability and influence. In this structure, the parish sessions were the most crucial. The minister and his elders could be counted on to maintain disciplined surveillance over most aspects of the lives of the parishioners.

The General Assembly in Edinburgh and the Presbytery of Galloway did denounce the levelling in no uncertain terms. An Act of the Assembly was passed in May 1724, vigorously condemning those who levelled the dykes for their sinfulness. All ministers in the Synods of Dumfries and Galloway were enjoined to warn the people from their pulpits about the threat to their eternal salvation caused by such criminal behaviour. But at the local level the church was far from united against the Levellers. Some ministers refused to read out the Assembly proclamation while others were accused of actively supporting the destruction of the dykes and siding with the plight of the dispossessed. Indeed, at least one Church of Scotland minister, the Reverend William Falconer, was arrested in July 1724 and sent to Edinburgh for trial with another man, having 'unlawfully convocated themselves with other accomplices, demolished several enclosures in the Stewartry [of Kirkcudbright], and continued to the number of twelve or more in a riotous manner after Proclamation against riots had been read to them'.[7] Clearly, even the reading of the Riot Act was having little effect.

It now seemed that only the forces of the crown brought in from outside Galloway could control these serious disturbances. Thus did the Earl of Galloway write to his brother-in-law, Sir John Clerk, in May 1724, in somewhat alarmist terms, urging government action:

> you would hear the insolences of ane sett of people that have drauen together and destroyed the whole encloasures in the Stewartrie, and if we have not the protection of the Govert by allowing troops to march in the countrie for our assistance, I doe relie believe the whole gentlemen of Galloway will be ruined.[8]

2

The concern about the continued breaking of the law, combined with an expression of sympathy for the plight of the evicted, prompted the Duke of Roxburgh, himself a leading Border magnate, and Secretary for Scotland, to authorize a public enquiry into the grievances of the Levellers. This met in August 1724 and was chaired by John McDowall, Steward Depute of Kirkcudbright. No trace has survived either of its proceedings or conclusions. Earlier in the summer, troops, mainly drawn from the Earl of Stair's Dragoons, had intervened in the disturbed region for the first time. Eventually, in June, a further six troops of dragoons were reported to have left from Edinburgh, 'the better to level the Levellers'.[9] A combined force was then brought together under the command of Major Du Cary. Even before that, several of the leaders of the protesters had been tracked down and arrested and committed to prison in Edinburgh. Despite this early success the military did not entirely intimidate the Levellers or cause them to end their campaign against the hated cattle parks. Indeed on 12 and 26 May, after the arrests had been made, large bands of dyke breakers, reckoned to be up to 2,000 in number, confronted the authorities on Bombie Moor and Kelton Hill. They then dispersed from these gatherings to mount successful levelling raids across the neighbouring countryside.

On 2 June two troops of horse and four of dragoons, under Du Cary, in addition to several local landowners and their servants, came face to face with a tiny group of Levellers, a mere fifty strong, at Steps of Tarf. They were easily dispersed and several were taken prisoner. But, despite this reverse, there was still no end to the dyke breaking in Galloway. The local people knew the hills and valleys of the area intimately and when confronted by the forces of law and order were able to disperse from the incident and fell the dykes elsewhere by night. As the *Caledonian Mercury* reported on 16 June:

> We hear the Levellers began again to peep out since the Forces are retir'd to their Quarters; and lest the work should not be regularly carried on, they in the Night-time detach some *chosen ones* into the Country, who soon remove all Objects of Offence, and bring all to a beloved Party.
>
> We see here handed about a very scriptural printed Three-halfpenny Apology for these Men, pretending to justice this their Procedure with the Square of the Sacred Texts.[10]

The references to support from Holy Scriptures for the Levellers' cause is significant. Earlier, in May, proclamations had been read out twice in some parish churches seeking the support of the people for the Levellers. On the first occasion this was done in eight parishes, and on the second twelve. This suggests a degree of sympathy, if not support, from some local ministers. Since the traditional sources of authority were not always on the side of the 'parking lairds', officers of the crown, such as Du Cary, had to deal with the Levellers with some sensitivity rather than draconian force. There is also evidence of a degree of sympathy for the dyke breakers among some merchants and lesser landowners not directly involved in the creation of the large cattle parks.

The rising had not been finally crushed by the end of the summer months. Incidents of levelling continued to be reported well into the autumn in both Kirkcudbright and Wigtown. Even after the last stand of the Levellers took place at Duchrae in Balmaghie parish, which was followed by many arrests, sporadic disturbances still went on. Brigadier Tom Stewart of Sorbie could report as late as mid-November that 'they have not been soe violent upon the dicks [dykes] in genll'. Nevertheless, as he went on:

> but the spirett keeps upp amongst them. They one Wednesday night last, mett in a considerable body near Whithorne with sythes, pitf-forks and other weapons, killed and houghed Wig's cattle in the inclosure they lately throen doun, but being advertised from the town that the dragoons were mounting to march upon them they dispersed and severall of them threw away their wepons which have been since found. They have broke to pieces severall of my brother's big yetts [gates] upon highways, leading through his inclosures to Whithorne, and they breack and destroyed almos all the carriages and tools Broughton had for making up his inclosures.
>
> They have likewise a practice in sending their emissaries in the night time to the country people houses, threatening them that iff they doe not join them to burn their houses and meal stacks.[11]

The tenants and cottars who had been imprisoned stood trial at the Tolbooth of Kirkcudbright for their offences in January 1725. Facing them on the bench were the representatives of local landowners sitting in judgement upon the malefactors who had destroyed their own enclosures or those of their friends and kindred.

The accused had in their favour that, although large-scale depredations against property had occurred, no one had been killed or seriously injured during the disturbances. The acknowledged sympathy on the part of some leaders of Border society had also to be acknowledged and taken into consideration. In addition, the attitudes of the eighteenth-century judiciary towards plebeian riot and disturbance were frequently complex. There was often a tendency towards leniency in order to restore good relations within the local community as quickly as possible. Heavy sentences imposed on the accused in such circumstances might simply lead to more unrest. It is significant, for instance, that in October 1724, when over 200 Levellers confronted a force of dragoons at Duchrae, the troops were ordered to use minimum force. In response, the Levellers put up only minimal resistance. Many were arrested but almost all were allowed to escape on the march back to the town of Kirkcudbright. For those who were eventually tried, no capital sentences were passed, or of transportation across the seas to the colonies. Significantly, also, those who were arraigned were tried under civil rather than criminal law. Instead, large fines and compensation payments were levied on those found guilty of damage to property. Even then the punishments might seem harsh. Yet, from another perspective, they could be seen as merely symbolic. Impoverished small tenants and cottars would simply be unable to pay the fines handed down by the court.

3

The history of the Levellers is well documented in some respects but in several others the evidence about them is patchy and obscure. This is especially the case when trying to answer the most intriguing question of all: why did these disturbances actually occur in south-west Scotland in the 1720s? On first consideration the answer might seem obvious. They were triggered by the reality or the threat of peasant dispossession in Galloway because of the onward expansion of cattle ranching leading to the annexation of small farms. On the surface, that explanation appears plausible and convincing. After all, the tactics of the people in levelling the dykes surrounding the large cattle parks seemed to confirm an absolute connection between initial cause and final effect of their actions. Yet, arguably, though indeed a necessary part of an overall explanation, this in itself is insufficient, as elsewhere in the Borders at the time, and later throughout the Lowlands, the removal of small tenants and cottars was a commonplace. But only in some parishes of Galloway in 1724 was eighteenth-century landlordism confronted by a popular revolt of such threatening magnitude that it could be eventually subdued only by military force. Moreover, the timing of levelling is puzzling. 'Parking' had been going on since the 1680s, a quarter of a century before the disturbances began. Why only in the 1720s did the anger of the peasantry boil over into violent and armed resistance?

Part of the answer might be found in the economic sphere. By the early eighteenth century the big cattle farms were beginning to encroach on, and enclose, open or common grazing grounds, the 'commonties' referred to earlier in the chapter. That process would have proven a serious threat to peasant communities which were not subject to direct eviction. They would have experienced profound problems from strategies which menaced the tight margins of their household economies. The slender balance between subsistence and shortage might have been squeezed by the annexation of common lands. Again, there is evidence that not only landowners but tenant farmers had tried to exploit the new post-Union market opportunities in the cattle trade. Some had invested in more stock because of those possibilities. Now, however, as 'parking' intensified, they stood to lose the vitally important access to the common grazings for the livestock they had purchased at great risk. For them and their families, descent into penury and beggary might follow.

There was also the economic context of the Galloway clearances to be considered. As argued in Chapter 4, in parts of the central and eastern Borders, the dispossession of small tenants and cottars to make way for larger sheep runs was paralleled by the growth of cottage industry and employment opportunities for the displaced in the towns of Kelso, Hawick, Selkirk and Jedburgh. But these alternatives were not available to anything like the same extent in Galloway, where woollen working and other manufactures were much less developed. It is likely, therefore, that the poorer rural communities in the western Borders were faced with a much narrower set of options: acceptance of 'parking' and eventual likely eviction, or violent resistance in an attempt to reverse the transformation of the old agrarian society.

By May 1724 it was reckoned by James Clerk, Collector of Customs at Kirkcudbright, that the Levellers 'have already thrown down 12 or 14 gentlemen's inclosures and are still going on'.[12] But a new development had occurred. They were also systematically slaughtering any cattle illegally imported from Ireland in contravention of the Act of Parliament of 1666. They alleged that this illicit trade in the bigger and more valuable Irish stock was a prime influence on the larger-scale development of the cattle parks in the early 1720s. Undeniably, there were some close personal and family links between landlords in the western Borders and Ulster. Nonetheless, the allegations remain unproven, though they must have further angered the local people in Galloway. In a missive addressed to Major Du Cary, the commander of the troops sent to subdue the Levellers, they asserted:

> understanding that there were a considerable number of Irish cattle in the Parks of Netherlaw, we did, in obedience to the law, legally seize and slaughter them to deter the gentlemen from the like practice of importing or bringing Irish cattle, to the great loss of this poor country as well as the breeders in England, too much the practice of the gentlemen here.[13]

By such allegations, they were able to maintain pressure on the authorities' attempt to unite the landed classes and occupy the moral high ground as defenders of the law.

In addition, however, we also need to probe the complex world of west Border political and religious history in order to provide a comprehensive explanation for the Levellers' Revolt. Arguably it is there that the distinctive origins of the disturbances can be found. Several aspects of the recent Galloway past are relevant to the analysis. The long Covenanting tradition of south-west Scotland was important. The restoration of King Charles II in 1660 led once again to the rule of bishops in the Presbyterian church. This action was thought heretical and oppressive by many pious communities and their ministers, and in open conflict with the sacred Covenants between Christ and his church established during the civil wars of the 1640s. As a result, many clergymen left their parishes and held alternative open-air services or conventicles. These were soon outlawed by the state as treason and the army then enforced the will of the King, often in a particularly brutal fashion. This period, known as the 'Killing Times', is still marked in the countryside around Wigtown, Kirkcudbright and Dumfries by the many memorials to the martyrs who defied the civil authorities and faithfully clung to their ideals despite savage state oppression. Galloway remained a hotbed of Covenanting activity despite the draconian policies of the monarchy.

Not surprisingly, the majority of the population were therefore enthusiastic about the removal of the Stuart king, James VII and II, in the 'Glorious Revolution' of 1688–9. But then the Jacobite Rising of 1715 rekindled the old fears of a Stuart counter-revolution. Bitter memories were revived, not simply of the Killing Times, but also of the many years of Presbyterian struggle between the signing of the National Covenant in 1638 and the Revolution of 1688. Old wounds were reopened especially because of the class fissures in the local communities. The people may have been overwhelmingly anti-Jacobite but several of the landowners were not only sympathetic to the Stuart cause but joined the Jacobite forces of the Earl of Marr in 1715. There were also Roman Catholic lairds in the parishes of Pantien, Kirkpatrick, Durham and Buitlle, including the Maxwells, earls of Nithsdale. Another prominent figure with similar loyalties was Sir Basil Hamilton, the largest single landowner in the Stewartry of Kirkcudbright.

During the disturbances, the estates of these families became prime targets of the Levellers. Rumours abounded in 1724 of an Irish-inspired Jacobite rebellion and that the enclosures were part of a Jacobite plot. In their public statements the Levellers were wont to stress their absolute loyalty to King George and the House of Hanover. Thus did old grievances and memories add fuel to the fire of economic discontent. These political and religious factors were specific to the western Borders in the 1720s and they help to explain why protest on the scale of the actions of the Levellers did not take place in later decades. They, as well as the impact of enclosure, were the catalyst for the disturbances and they were not replicated in any other locality in the second half of the eighteenth century.

The story of the Galloway Levellers lived on in local tradition over several generations. In 1838, a century and more after the dykes were levelled, John Nicholson wrote a play about the disturbances.

S. R. Crockett, the Victorian Scottish novelist, himself born in Duchrae, parish of Balmaghie, in the shire of Kirkudbright, used tales from his birthplace to write *The Dark o' the Moon* (1902) about the Levellers. It was a sequel to his most famous novel, *The Raiders* (1894). Yet, by that time no trace remained of the runrig fields of the small tenants and cottars of the 1720s, or indeed of the large cattle parks which had caused them to rise in protest. By the later eighteenth century the agricultural revolution in Galloway had taken a different course. By then the region was exporting grain from arable farms as well as selling cattle. Not unlike the pattern in some parts of the Highlands, clearances in the Borders seem not to have left a legacy of bitterness or an enduring folk memory of dispossession.

Some scholars argue that the Galloway landed élites had been given a real fright by the depredations of the Levellers and that the expansion of 'parking' slowed for a time as a result. Others contend that what happened in the south-west of Scotland helped to shape the agricultural revolution throughout the Lowlands. It is argued that one of the reasons why there were fewer disturbances later in the eighteenth century was partly because the Galloway levelling activities had so alarmed the authorities that they took care to ensure that popular resistance would be avoided in future. Landowners in the second half of the eighteenth century are also said to have implemented policies designed to prevent opposition by the people as agrarian change gathered pace.

Perhaps, but no evidence has so far come to light in landed archives or contemporary comments of any such causal connection in later decades between the nature of the agrarian revolution in the Lowlands in the second half of the eighteenth century and events in Galloway in 1724. As will be argued later, the displacement and redeployment of small tenants and cottars was dictated by a nexus of economic and demographic factors at the time and not by any lingering awareness of events nearly half a century before in the south-west Borders.[14]

> The Fields That Once were Homes
> On Airieland Farm's a field called Meadow Isle
> enclosed by fat, well-fed dykes of local stone.
> Who'd guess that once this field was home

to saddler, cobbler, cutler, chandler, horner,
that Galloway teemed with such living fields
of cottars? Their names are all but lost
to OS maps and local deeds, preserved
occasionally as woodland, little hills
or streams, not in anything so crudely, surely human as ferm
    toun or croft.

Records show Meadow Isle long abandoned
by 1800, a new farmhouse built
that year, the failing gable ends a camp
for dykers hoying up brand new enclosures,
longer, higher, wider. Their final act –
demolishing its walls for use as stones
to build the last new stretch of dyke.
From out this field that once was home and more
80 years before walked John McKnaught armed
with gavelock, intent on levelling
the future. What he left behind's
lush pasture now, a ready grazing ground
for cattle, archaeologists and those
we've built the longest, highest, widest dykes around.

[*gavelock* – iron crowbar]

Stuart A. Paterson, *Looking South* (Indigo Dreams Publications, 2017)

6

Transformation and Landlordism

It has become fashionable in recent years for some historians of English society in the eighteenth century to argue that economic growth and social change were much slower and more protracted than suggested in earlier accounts of the Industrial Revolution. In this view the modernization of England was more evolutionary than revolutionary. Already, by *c*.1700, the industrial, trade and urban sectors in England were well developed and both structural change and economic advance in agriculture were widespread. Growth, therefore, on this model was cumulative, modest and undramatic, though punctuated by phases of faster and more radical change.

The Scottish route to modernization differed from this pattern. By the middle decades of the nineteenth century both countries had become integral parts of the 'Workshop of the World', twin pioneers of the new industrial society, with remarkably high numbers employed in manufacturing and mining and living in cities and towns. But Scotland reached that condition over a shorter timescale than England. From the later eighteenth century, the break with the past north of the border seems to have been more decisive and social transformation therefore more disruptive.

Indeed, the Scottish experience in such key areas as demographic growth, urbanization and agrarian change was so distinctive that any uncritical attempt to combine the two in an analysis of *British* social change runs the risk of distorting the historical process. This is not to suggest that before the middle decades of the eighteenth century Scottish society was inert and static; nor is it to argue that the old order was swept away within a few decades. The commercialization of agriculture was advancing in some Scottish regions before

1760, urban growth was in place, and mercantile activity becoming more significant both at home and overseas. In a few areas in the Lowlands, farm organization was more recognizably 'modern', with larger compact holdings under the control of single tenants who were committed to servicing the market. As already shown in Chapters 4 and 5, dispossession of some rural communities in the Border counties had already occurred before the middle decades of the eighteenth century.

However, by the standards of England, one of the most advanced economies in Western Europe in the seventeenth century, Scotland still remained poor and laggard. Crises of mortality triggered by famine occurred as late as the 1690s in Scotland though they had disappeared from England from the 1620s. Food shortages were also acute in the early 1740s. Average rates of mortality were also higher in Scotland than in England before c.1760. This helps to explain why Scottish population increase in the later eighteenth century seems to have been more associated with a sharp fall in death rates, whereas in England it was primarily linked to a significant rise in fertility. The structures of the two societies reflected their respective stages of economic and social development. In most of England, a three-tier rural social system of landlords, tenant farmers and landless wage labourers was already established. But before 1760 there were few entirely landless people in the Scottish countryside. Even rural tradesmen normally had a patch of land, much of the farm labour force was recruited from cottar families with access to some land, and even landless farm servants were often born into cottar households, with some of them then taking on a smallholding at marriage. Therefore, on the eve of the agrarian revolution the vast majority of rural dwellers in Scotland depended to a greater or lesser extent on a stake in the land to make ends meet. In broad terms, therefore, this remained a peasant society which bore a closer similarity to many countries in mainland Europe than to the big neighbour in the south.

A considerable contrast in the scale of urban development should also be noted. Town growth did take place in Scotland, but as late as c.1700 only an estimated 5 per cent of the national population lived in towns of 10,000 inhabitants or more compared to a figure of 14 per cent in England and Wales. This difference partly reflected the much greater commercialization of English society. In the seventeenth century Scottish overseas trade was less varied than England's, with exports dominated by unprocessed or partly processed primary products and imports by luxuries, manufactures and essential raw materials such as timber, and grain in years of harvest shortage. In the eighteenth century increasing market activity spread to the core of the rural economy as village and small town growth brought many more than ever before into the nexus of commercial exchange. But, relative to England, Scotland was still behind. One telling indicator was the very late survival of 'archaic' controls associated with traditional societies, where the market enclave was relatively weak. The regulation of bread prices and artisan wages lingered on in Scotland into the period of the Napoleonic Wars. This partly explains why, in the later eighteenth century, the incidence of meal rioting in periods of high grain prices was much less common than in England. Intervention either by local authorities or the judiciary until c.1800 to some extent helped to cushion the impact of market forces.

However, by 1830 Scotland had become a different kind of society from that of c.1760, although not all links had been severed with the old world which was now passing into history. Most Scots by 1830 still lived and worked in the countryside as their forefathers had done. The position of the traditional governing class, the great landowners, was not undermined in this period and may actually have been temporarily strengthened. Traditional religious affiliations were disturbed by increases in the number of dissenting congregations and Irish Catholic immigration, but religion remained a vital element in social life. The process of industrialization was also far from complete in 1830 and the great nineteenth-century staples of coal, iron, engineering and shipbuilding were all underdeveloped and only came to maturity after the 1840s. Fast industrial expansion was primarily concentrated in linen, cotton and wool before 1830, and the metal manufactures, the giants of the later period, were only managing to achieve modest growth.

Yet too much stress on continuities obscures the real significance of the unprecedented social changes from the 1760s. It is true that as late as the 1830s as many as two Scots in three still worked on the farm, or the croft, or in the country village or the small rural town.

But their way of life differed radically from those who had gone before. In the Lowlands most of the rural population had already become a landless proletariat who hired their labour power in the market to employers. Their lives were now just as much subject to labour discipline, the drive for more productivity and cyclical levels of employment as those who toiled in manufacturing and mining. In the western Highlands a 'peasant' society remained but differed radically from that of the age of clanship before c.1750. Indeed, social transformation in Gaeldom was more traumatic and cataclysmic than anywhere else in Scotland. The Highlands moved from tribalism to capitalism over less than two generations. The communal *bailes* had been broken up by c.1820 and replaced by single crofts (individual smallholdings), or in the south and east Highlands by small compact farms under single masters. Everywhere, large-scale pastoral farming was in the ascendant. Crofters were in fact a quasi-industrial class whose tenure of smallholdings depended in the final analysis on working at tasks to supply the burgeoning markets for fish, kelp, whisky, military manpower and cattle. Their crofts were meant to be small in order to ensure they could not provide a full living for their families and pay rents only from work on the land but had to be fisherman or kelp burners as well. Crofters were to be labourers first and peasant farmers only second. Lingering customary relationships and traditional connections between clan élites and followers soon disintegrated as the entire fabric of society was recast in response to landlord demands, ideological theory and, above all, the overwhelming force of market pressures. The most dramatic and controversial exemplars of transformation were the partial or full clearance of several communities, as an empire of sheep farming eventually extended to all of the Highlands and Islands.

Also, studies of comparative urban development in Europe suggest that the rate of growth in Scotland at this time was the fastest of any region either in Britain or on the Continent. By 1850, Scotland was second only to England and Wales in a league table of 'urbanized societies', a position achieved over a much shorter time scale than the rest of mainland Britain. Town growth at such a speed suggests a remarkably high level of labour mobility because the urban areas grew primarily through inward migration. In many areas of Ireland, rural France and

Germany before 1830, substantial proportions of the population often lived and died in the same parish. This was not the case in most areas of Lowland Scotland. Population mobility was already noteworthy before the eighteenth century, but then became much more rapid as the squeezing out of small tenants and cottars together with the lure of the towns combined to cause high levels of internal permanent and temporary migration. It was within this transforming environment that the landed class planned and implemented wideranging schemes of agrarian modernization on their estates. The next section focuses on the powers and influence which underpinned their dominant role in land improvement.

I

The role of Sir John Sinclair as editor of the multi-volume *Statistical Account of Scotland*, published in the 1790s, established his reputation as the leading authority on Scottish rural society in the second half of the eighteenth century. Therefore, his opinion that 'In no country in Europe are the rights of proprietors so well defined and so carefully protected as in Scotland' merits serious consideration.[1]

This section begins by examining the real extent of landlord authority and then turns to a consideration of those factors which led the landed classes to embark on a set of radical strategies of improvement which eventually had enormous consequences for those who worked the land and lived in the age-old communities of the countryside. It was the decision and the will of the proprietors which initially drove forward the historic transformation of rural society in the second half of the eighteenth century, with the objectives then worked out in detail and introduced on their estates by surveyors, factors, superintendents, chamberlains, managers and other subordinate functionaries.

As in any pre-industrial society, land was the primary unit of resource and those who possessed that asset, especially if their ownership ran to thousands of acres, had immense economic, political and social authority. There is a case for saying that the grandees of Scotland could be placed near the top of any comparative European hierarchy of power when judged by social position and political influence. For a start, landownership in Scotland was confined to a small élite class, reckoned at just over 2 per cent of all adult males in the population. By comparison, 12 per cent in England and 20 per cent of the population of Sweden had landed status. Ever since feudal tenure was introduced in the eleventh century, the land of Scotland had been possessed by fewer than 1,500 owners. Even that figure underestimated the extent of concentrated control by a very small number of aristocratic grandees, like the eighteenth-century ducal families of Buccleuch, Hamilton, Sutherland, Argyll, Atholl and a few other major owners. There were 7,500 landlords by 1800 but 90 per cent of Scotland was owned by only 1,500 of them. The ranks of the smaller lairds were in decline as the greater families absorbed their estates through marriage and purchase.

This degree of control over land was matched by a virtual monopoly of political power. After 1707 there were thirty seats in the Scottish counties and fifteen from the burghs in the Westminster House of Commons. So great was the dominance of the magnates in the political sphere that even most smaller landowners below aristocratic rank were effectively excluded from a franchise which was the tiniest of all the British nations. A mere 3,100 men, or 0.2 per cent of the Scottish population, had the right to vote. The Irish capital, Dublin, could boast more electors than in all of Scotland in the eighteenth century. But oligarchical control was even more exclusive than this would suggest. In the countryside it was generally feudal superiors rather than landed proprietors *per se* who had voting rights. By splitting superiorities among kinsmen, associates and clients, the greater men manufactured fictitious or 'faggot' votes which both helped them to control elections in the local constituencies and extend their personal influence. The noble houses of Argyll, Sutherland, Buccleuch and Atholl orchestrated a system of unequalled electoral manipulation which reinforced the hegemony of their families both on their own lands and further afield.

Two legal instruments further embedded magnate power. Primogeniture ensured that landed estates were inherited by single heirs under impartible process, so preventing the kind of territorial fragmentation which impoverished those European gentry families who practised partible inheritance. Entail was formally established by an

Act of the Scottish Parliament in 1685 with a public record of entails introduced at the same time. This meant that inheritance was confined to a definite series of heirs and a succeeding owner could not break the line. Selling the estate was also prohibited, as was contracting debts that might threaten ownership. By 1825 at least half of all land in Scotland was under entail, with the majority of deeds registered after 1780. This legal device afforded protection and security but was also potentially a constraint on development of land. An Act of Parliament was passed therefore in 1770 permitting investment in the improvement of an estate through the owner becoming a creditor to his heirs for up to the value of four years' rental income. Some degree of financial flexibility was therefore introduced into the system precisely at the time when considerable resources were needed for costly programmes of agricultural investment.

Across most of Western and Eastern Europe peasant proprietorship was widespread and well entrenched, and curbed the capacity of seigneurs to change customary structures and practices. Peasants were not only considered to be inherently conservative, but were also able to impede élite schemes of improvement, because in many regions of the Continent they were the legal owners of their own smallholdings. In Scotland, however, as in England, the balance of power and authority was much more in the landlord's favour. Peasant proprietorship in Scotland was uncommon except in a narrow stretch of land from Ayrshire in the west to Fife in the east occupied by so-called 'bonnet lairds'. Elsewhere the lease, or 'tack', alone gave legal access to land. Becoming the tenant of a farm therefore depended in the final analysis on the will of the proprietor, who also determined the length of occupation for each holding.

The system was vital to the perpetuation of landlord authority. Since farmers held land at the discretion of the owner, they were in a subordinate position in competition with others for a scarce and vital resource. The proliferation of written leases, a feature of seventeenth-century agrarian development in the Lowlands, made the dependent relationship more explicit. It also gave the landed class even more legal muscle, which, through detailed clauses in the contractual agreement, were infinitely adaptable to encourage and nurture enterprising husbandmen, insist on the adoption of improving methods, and, above all, provide an instrument of control to shape the number and size of tenancies when leases expired at term. The next chapter will illustrate how removal of tenants most commonly took place through the decision of a proprietor not to extend the period of an individual lease when it lapsed. Numbers were perforce thinned in a staged and gradual fashion as part of the normal routine for leasing and re-letting farms.

The Union of 1707 not only maintained these traditional powers of the landed classes but also provided them, their kinsmen and associates with easier access to the rich stream of patronage and career opportunities in London and throughout the British Empire, as well as the benefit of free trade with England for the products of their estates, like coal, salt, linen, cattle, wool and grain. Three developments after 1707 were also important. First, the decisive defeat of Jacobitism in 1746 finally removed the possibilities of a Catholic counter-revolution and the danger of any return to absolute monarchy. Second, the Patronage Act of 1712 gave landowners (in their role as heritors) the legal right to appoint to vacant church offices in each parish of Scotland, including who succeeded to the important and influential post of kirk minister. In later years this privilege was often bitterly contested by local communities whose role in appointments had been brought to an end by the legislation. Third, the thinkers of the eighteenth-century Scottish Enlightenment helped to give intellectual credibility to a system of government dominated by a tiny propertied oligarchy. The great men of the time, Adam Smith, David Hume, Adam Ferguson, William Robertson and others, were innovative thinkers on philosophical and social matters but never questioned an established order founded on the belief that only those with a firm and secure stake in landed property could be trusted to govern the country with prudence. Whereas the *philosophes* in France may have helped to arouse radical fervour, the writings of the *literati* in Scotland served to legitimize existing political structures.

In reality, however, there was no deep conflict on the issue of governance between the intellectuals of the two countries. The first phase of the French Revolution was dominated by the ideas of Montesquieu, notably those expounded in his masterpiece, *L'Esprit des lois*, of 1753. He favoured exactly the system which prevailed in both

England and Scotland at the time: a liberal, constitutional monarchy with sovereignty shared between crown, Parliament and the law courts, together with a major role for the landed aristocracy in government. The great French philosopher did not therefore differ fundamentally from his Scottish contemporaries. He was revolutionary in the French context, but Scotland like England had already achieved many decades before the 'ideal' government on which he bestowed so much praise. The Scottish thinkers were therefore 'conservative' in the sense that they too agreed about the merits of a property-based regime.

The main material threat to landed dominance might have come from the new age of industrialization and urbanization and with it the emergence of a powerful new class of city and town élites. Ironically, however, the economic revolution, far from undermining the hegemony of the old ruling class, helped to give it further material resilience. One mark of enduring magnate power was the evidence that the larger estates were still growing in size at the expense of smaller properties throughout this period. Urban and industrial growth was indeed striking, but Scotland remained an overwhelmingly rural society until well into the nineteenth century. Urbanization led to a significant rise in the number of families who did not grow their own food but instead had to buy in the market place the meal, potatoes and milk produced by the farmers of the landed estates who as a result were able to pay higher rents to proprietors. Industrialization and agrarian change in the early stages were interrelated because much weaving, spinning and mining still took place in small villages set in the countryside rather than large towns. Many landed gentlemen were at the very cutting edge of market-driven capitalism, which is confirmed by their energetic role as agricultural 'improvers', founders of industrial villages, partners in coal pits, ironworks and banks, and in the construction of roads, canals and ports. They were stubbornly conservative in political terms but revolutionaries in the economic sphere who made a major contribution to the shaping of the new order.

As a result, the 'unreformed' political system which the magnates controlled was entirely capable of passing and implementing legislation for the advance of capitalism. The system of bounties on linen exports, which was crucial to the expansion of that strategic sector in the mid-eighteenth century, the establishment of the Board of Trustees for Manufactures and Fisheries, and the abolition of 'serfdom' in the collieries and saltworks in 1775 and 1799, designed to attract more labour to those industries, were only a few examples of parliamentary measures devised to boost economic development. Such innovative legislation in the economic sphere arguably also helped defuse potential discontent among the leaders of the new urban society who might otherwise have felt aggrieved at their continued exclusion from political authority. The 'unreformed' state might have been politically archaic, and even perhaps reactionary, but was demonstrably proactive in economic affairs. Ironically many of the emerging class of merchants and manufacturers also helped to consolidate the power of the traditional élites, by themselves buying into landed status. But that did not lead to a bourgeois conquest of the old landed interest. Those who managed to move into land were small in number and even the wealthiest from the towns, such as Glasgow's tobacco lords and sugar princes, found it difficult to move beyond the ranks of the lesser gentry as the cost of land was great and increasing in the later eighteenth century. The territorial hegemony of the aristocracy was therefore not in the least impaired and a potential class of critics was successfully absorbed within the existing system.

In the early 1790s the regime controlled by landed magnates and their kindred in the law was challenged for a time by the development of political radicalism. But the threat was weak and ephemeral as, after a scare from 1790 to 1792, the challenge from reform alliances like the Friends of the People Associations petered out. The war with France made it possible for the state to brand all radicals as traitors, which helped to legitimize the use of coercion against them. The excesses of the French Revolution, with the onset of the Reign of Terror, seemed also to confirm the validity of the conservative position that popular democracy would lead inevitably to bloody anarchy. In Scotland, this prompted a closing of the ranks of the propertied classes, especially after the third Convention of the Friends of the People, because its proletarian composition and overtly radical demands posed a threat not only to the magnate-controlled oligarchies but also the entire propertied hierarchy of the time. The new spirit of political conformity was displayed in the widespread popular enthusiasm to join the volunteer regiments by both the professional and commercial classes, and in the sweeping success of the governing party in the elections of 1796.

Another key foundation of the structure of power was the distribution of patronage. Posts, pensions and promotions within the army, navy, civil service and legal system were dispensed by figures of influence and the government in return for loyalty and conformity. The favour of the great was essential for any gentleman who aspired to a position of significance. If sources of patronage had contracted in relation to demand, the régime might possibly have been destabilized. For instance, there is some evidence from Ireland that shortage of opportunity for younger sons of the gentry and 'middleman' class in the 1790s helped to produce the 'restless spirits' who played a significant role in the extensive social disturbances of that decade and which eventually led to the great rebellion of 1798. There was little danger, however, of this occurring in Scotland. Economic growth at home and the expansion of the British colonies in North America, the Caribbean and India in the eighteenth century had released jobs and posts for the sons of the middle classes and the gentry. Furthermore, Henry Dundas, the government's political manager in Scotland, achieved an even more influential role in the dispensation of patronage when he became Secretary for War and then the leading figure in the new Board of Control of the East India Company. The huge expansion of the army and navy after 1793 funded by the financial resources of the 'fiscal-military state' produced numerous new opportunities to strengthen government support and buttress the stability of the prevailing social order. India became, in Sir Walter Scott's words, the 'corn chest for Scotland', as a host of young Scots made their careers in the civil and military administrations of the subcontinent.[2]

In France, economic crisis, harvest failure and high grain prices were at the very heart of the revolution. In Scotland, too, there seemed abundant reasons for popular discontent. Meal prices rose sharply in the final two decades of the century, and increased again from 1795. As will be seen, the way of life of countless communities in the countryside changed dramatically as consolidation of land and dispersal of people intensified in the wake of the agricultural revolution. Town workers also were exposed to new insecurities, demands and pressures, as industrial development became increasingly linked to the rise and fall of international markets. But, given the scale of the upheaval, what is striking is the *relative* social stability of Scotland. There was little of the angry peasant rebellions or of the great surges of collective unrest which characterized Ireland or France at this time. Food riots did occur in years of particularly high grain prices but they were much less common and frequently less violent than those in France, and far fewer even than the outbreaks which occurred in England. Closer connections than hitherto realized have recently been identified between the anti-Militia Act rioters of 1797 and the radical United Scotsmen in parts of the eastern Lowlands. But, on the whole, there was little effective fusion in the 1790s between the episodes of popular unrest and the overtly political movements which sought constitutional change.

Examination of the social history of the later eighteenth century reveals why popular protest was sporadic, and in the event posed little threat to the governing grip of the landed classes. In the period, many communities throughout the length and breadth of Scotland suffered loss of land, and customary rights were challenged as never before. The experience must have inflicted pain and anxiety. But in the same decades there was a modest rise in living standards for the majority of people, especially between *c*.1780 and *c*.1800. Surveys of occupational groups as varied as male farm servants, urban masons and rural handloom weavers have found that while grain prices were indeed rising, money wages were rising faster still. Only from the second decade of the nineteenth century was there a clear break in this upward trend. The cushion of moderately improving living standards in the short-term for the majority may have alleviated some of the harsher effects of social disruption and reduced one possible cause of widespread popular disturbance.

This was a distinctively Scottish experience and not paralleled in most areas of Western Europe, or even of England, where, in the 1780s and 1790s, prices did outstrip money incomes. Peculiarly Scottish factors help to explain the trend north of the Border. So much of the economic expansion depended on labour-intensive methods that it led to a huge increase in demand for such major groups as handloom weavers and farm servants. At the same time, Scotland contributed disproportionate numbers of soldiers and seamen to the war effort between 1793 and 1815. Added to that was the relatively slow pace of national population increase, significantly lower than that of Ireland, France and England in the later eighteenth century, which ensured that the labour markets were rarely in danger of being glutted with a flood of additional workers. The general result was that employers, whether in country or town, had to bid higher to ensure regular supplies of labour.

Potential unrest was also defused by the widespread opportunities for both emigration and migration. Population mobility in this rapidly changing society was unusually high by the standards of many Western European countries. Transatlantic emigration was undoubtedly one alternative to physical protest against the onward march of agrarian capitalism in the western and central Highlands. But the 'safety valve' of migration worked also very effectively in Lowland Scotland, where the close proximity of 'improving' areas of agriculture, the foundation and extension of planned villages and new towns, and the rapidly expanding cities of Glasgow and Edinburgh facilitated and encouraged temporary and permanent movement of people in large numbers. Losing a stake in the land, therefore, did not present as grave a threat to survival when alternatives not only existed but were close and accessible to many.

In the final analysis, however, the survival of the old régime depended ultimately on the role and responses of the landed class itself. In a hierarchical society, the legitimate right to govern was based not only on the inherited privileges of rank, but also on the expectation of the performance of traditional obligations. The tenant, for example, paid his rental in good years on the assumption that his landlord might be a source of support in bad times. There is considerable evidence that, before 1800 at least, some among the Scottish landed classes had not entirely shed paternalistic values. Indeed, they intervened in two key areas to reduce the worst aspects of social distress. The first was by purchasing grain in years of scarcity and making it available at subsidized prices to local communities. The second, and more recent, development was the willingness of landowners to allow themselves to be rated for poor relief. It was at this time that local assessments became common in several districts of the Lowlands. In the later eighteenth century also no clear distinction was yet made between the 'impotent poor', entitled to relief, and the able-bodied unemployed, who were not. Only in the nineteenth century did the system become more rigorous and discriminating. In earlier decades, however, poor relief was much more flexible and less parsimonious, and helped to provide a basic safety net in years of economic crisis such as 1782–3, 1792–3 and 1799–1800. It was not uncommon for tradesmen to petition Justices of the Peace and the Court of Session in wage disputes with their masters, and the judiciary in return was sometimes prepared to use its powers to adjust wage levels in order to take account of rising prices.

A free market in prices or in wages was therefore not yet a complete reality. Regulations were mainly jettisoned in the years after the end of the Napoleonic Wars, and the removal of the old controls then did much to intensify the deeper social tensions of that later period. But in the 1790s lingering paternalism, through the provision of food subsidies, a more responsive poor law and intervention in wage bargaining had not yet disappeared. This helped to give the old régime a degree of social acceptance and a legitimacy which enabled it to come through even the challenging decade of the French Revolution remarkably unscathed.

2

Yet, despite their overwhelming authority, landowners were not omnipotent monarchs in their domains. The later eighteenth century was indeed a time of rising rent rolls for many gentry families but also one of strain and anxiety for others. An increase in the number of surviving children among landed families was a new and challenging feature of the period. More financial support was now needed for younger sons and tochers (dowries) for daughters, as well as maintaining annuities for widows, spinsters and other ageing relatives, costs which were all bound by family duty and obligation. More than a few landlords coming into their inheritance were soon confronted by the harsh realities of the many financial obligations to kinfolk. The women of gentry households had taken part in the work of the estates in the past. By the Victorian era they had become leisured wives and daughters, consumers not producers and dependent on the support of their families. The young men flocked in large numbers to become officers in the British military from the 1750s and in doing so, in the words of one authority, 'were exposed to the most luxurious, individualistic, fashionable and reckless profession of the age'.[3]

Landlords in the western Highlands and Islands were especially constrained. A challenging and volatile climate, precious little workable soil for grain cultivation, and distance from urban markets in the Lowlands, hugely compressed their available options, compared at least to proprietors with estates situated south and east of the Highland line. The basic contradiction at the heart of Highland landlordism soon became crystal clear: a vain attempt to emulate the levels of display and consumerism of their peers elsewhere in Britain on the meagre surpluses of a poor peasantry. Most of the Highland gentry began to live outside the region from the later eighteenth century, and in their search for gentlemanly status among their peers in the south soon fell into what has been termed 'the luxury trap'. David Stewart of Garth suggested that misadventure was not inevitable and there was a choice to be made:

> If unable to vie with their southern neighbours in luxury and splendour, might not gentlemen have possessed in their mountains a more honourable distinction – that of commanding respect without the aid of wealth, by making a grateful people happy, and thus uniting true dignity with humanity.[4]

However, the scholar who has looked in most detail at this key issue argues that Stewart's suggestion was unrealistic:

> Family and land had been the main source of identity and status in the pre-modern Highlands, and although these factors retained a disproportionate role within the Highland psyche, in the modern metropolitan context it was individual wealth and possession, education, employment and personal behaviour that were more important for identity and social regard.[5]

During the Napoleonic Wars, despite increasing revenue streams from cattle, kelp and military recruitment, pressures were already intense.

Loans and credit formerly readily available in the market were being drained away by the higher returns now offered from government stocks and bonds in order to pay for the costs of the conflict and support allies in the struggle against France. Also, the creditors of the landowners were no longer in the main the loyal clan gentry of old, but banks and insurance companies based in the cities which had a much more rigorous approach to unpaid debts than faithful kinsmen. So acute did the strains eventually become in the decades of price collapse in the 1820s and 1830s that almost all families descended from hereditary clan chiefs were forced to surrender lands in bankruptcy which had been possessed by their families for centuries. They had been irrevocably caught in a contracting vice of stubbornly high costs and falling levels of income from which in the end there was no escape.

Few, apart from the great ducal families of Atholl, Argyll and Sutherland, were able to survive the financial tempest. The Malcolms of Poltalloch in Argyllshire, for instance, were a rare example of traditional Highland lairds who were able to prosper throughout the period while most of the rest lost their estates. But the Malcolms survived because they possessed immense sources of external income through multiple investments in Atlantic trade and slave plantations in the Caribbean. Some properties came to be managed by trustees for the creditors of the insolvent but most were sold off to affluent merchants, bankers, industrial tycoons and lawyers from outside the Highlands, who often had little rapport with, or sympathy for, the hordes of impoverished crofters and cottars whom they found crowded into their estates after purchases were completed. By the middle decades of the nineteenth century over two thirds of Highland estates had changed hands. All of the Outer Hebrides, from Barra to Lewis, and extensive districts in the islands of Skye and Mull, together with Knoydart, Moidart, Glengarry, Glensheil, Arisaig, Kintail and Morvern on the western mainland, had been acquired by a new wealthy élite, few of whom had any traditional or family connections with the Highlands.

Also, as was to become painfully obvious once the market economy had successfully colonized all corners of Scotland, the comparative advantage of the west Highlands in the longer term lay almost exclusively in the development of large-scale pastoral husbandry. Such a land- and capital-intensive economy offered few possibilities for the people of the region, apart from the hiring of a small number of shepherds and ancillary labourers. But sheep ranching was to have more lethal social consequences for the local populations than its limited impact on employment. Large-scale pastoral farming and subsistence peasant agriculture were fundamentally incompatible in the long run. In return for paying inflated rentals, the flockmasters demanded access to the low-lying patches of arable on which the people of the small townships lived and scratched a poor living from a few acres of land. Only the dispossession of small tenants and their families eventually resolved that conflict as peasant traditionalism succumbed to the power of agrarian capitalism. The history of dispossession in the Border counties many decades before had already demonstrated that harsh reality. Soon it would be illustrated again on an even bigger scale in the Highlands and upland districts of the Lowlands on the fringes of the hill country.

Because of richer land and a more benign climate, however, the Lowland landed classes in general had more options and greater flexibility than their Highland counterparts. Yet, even for improving lairds in mixed farming areas, modernization of estates was not always a straightforward business. Landlords and their managers did not labour on the land. It was tenant farmers, their families, cottars and servants who made the improved regime work in districts of grain or mixed farming and which led to radical increases in crop yields and so to higher rents. In that context draconian imposition from above to force change was likely to prove counter-productive. Instead, the embryonic capitalist farming class had to be nursed to maturity by a combination of cajoling, reward, careful management of rentals and, when necessary, the threat of removal if improving clauses in leases were broken or not implemented. The stick was used but more often it was the carrot. The process of negotiation ensured that social relations between proprietors and tenants in most of the Lowlands tended to be more cooperative than in many parts of the Highlands, where the two sides were often driven apart in bitter dispute over absolute rights to land between sheep and people.

There were also serious tensions between the old élite obligations for the people of their properties and the imperatives and attractions of the new market economy. Certainly, the profit motive now became much more influential than it had been in the past. But both Highland and Lowland landowners sometimes agonized over the conflict between maximizing estate revenues and maintaining traditional responsibilities to the people of their estates as their forebears had done. When the removal of families from the land was judged the most 'rational' economic option, these dilemmas rose to the surface and became especially acute.

Two examples can be offered for illustrative purposes. Francis Humberston Mackenzie of Seaforth possessed ancestral lands in Kintail in Wester Ross, with Brahan Castle in Easter Ross the main family seat. He also owned the island of Lewis in the Outer Hebrides and tried for a time to play the role of clan chief while at the same time enjoying the material rewards of commercial management of his estates. He served as MP for Ross-shire from 1784 to 1790 and again between 1794 and 1796. Seaforth owned houses in fashionable areas of both London and Edinburgh. He had inherited large debts and these continued to increase as a direct consequence of the demands of his lifestyle in the cities. Deep anxieties about finances now started to surface in the Seaforth correspondence. Higher rentals from sheep farming were an obvious option to offer some temporary respite from the pressures, but Seaforth persistently refused very attractive offers from flockmasters to rent his lands in Glenshiel because he believed sheep runs would inevitably lead to widespread evictions of the people:

> In the years 1784 and 1787 while I was labouring under the most cruel distress and doubtful if I could keep even a remnant of my lands, I was so anxious to keep together the people I looked on as hereditably attached to my family that in spite of all wishes and better advice I refused to deal at all with the sheep farmers who offered double and treble their rents.[6]

This decision was against the strong advice of his factor, Colin Mackenzie, who saw large-scale pastoral husbandry as the only financial panacea for the encumbered estate.

Seaforth was not the only Highland laird caught in this dilemma. Sir John Sinclair wrote of him: 'Col. Mackenzie of Seaforth . . . and other proprietors of Highland estates . . . who may be desirous of having full value of their property but cannot think of parting with their people.' Another adviser also recommended in 1800 that the island of Lewis be turned over mainly to sheep but thought the proprietor would not be willing 'to break the strong line of affection which unite ten thousand people to the place of their nativity'.[7] Only in 1802, nearly two decades after the first approaches to turn Seaforth's lands over to pastoralism, was a sheep farm finally established on Lewis. The lucrative offers of inflated cash rents and his continued struggle with large debts had finally made Seaforth surrender to harsh realities in what had been a vain attempt to save the patrimony of his family from forced sales. As time passed, more and more of the Mackenzie lands had to be sold off to meet debt payments. When Seaforth's own heir died in 1862, most of the old estate was already in the hands of new owners.

The other example comes from the improvements of the third Duke of Buccleuch on the great Border estates amassed by his family, the Scotts, over several centuries. These were reckoned in 1781 to extend to 193,530 acres over immense areas of eastern Dumfriesshire, southern Roxburghshire and south-west Selkirkshire. From the 1770s a major programme of agricultural reform on these territories was launched under the direction of the Duke's 'overseer of improvements', William Keir. The rich diversity and extent of the Buccleuch lands allowed for greater flexibility of action than Lord Seaforth had in Wester Ross and Lewis. But, in the same way, Buccleuch was determined to avoid dispossession of the tenants. He therefore ordered Keir to draw up a list of all families living on his estates and to report back to him on the best way of ensuring how they could be resettled after the boundaries of the traditional holdings were altered. It is clear from the Duke's correspondence that this objective was of major concern to him and it had to take priority over the planning of new farms judged by the sole criterion of economic efficiency. However, evidence from many other estate papers suggests that the Duke of Buccleuch was unusually magnanimous in his concerns for the people of his estates, perhaps because his great wealth allowed him more scope to provide for them in a more benevolent fashion than was the case among more impecunious lairds.

The incidence of dispute and protest over the rights of local land-lords as patrons of appointments to vacant church offices also confirms some of the limitations of élite authority. Lay patronage had been abolished at the time of the Presbyterian settlement of 1690 and replaced by a system whereby the parish elders selected new ministers. Amid great controversy in Scotland, patronage was restored by the Westminster Parliament in 1712 in defiance of the Act of Union, a decision which came into practical effect after 1729 when the General Assembly finally ceased to veto the selections of patrons. Thereafter, patronage often led to confrontation between landed patrons and con-gregations. The system was abhorred as a process which placed the superiority of secular over spiritual authority and also smacked of the post-Union anglicization of the Church of Scotland. It is reck-oned that opposition to appointment of ministers by lay patrons occurred in one third to one half of Scotland's parishes between 1712 and 1874, the date when patronage was finally abolished.

Protests often took the form of collective acts of violence against the decisions of landed patrons, which could result in intervention by the military to restore order. Not all the rioters were from the lower levels of rural society. Affluent tenant farmers, professional families and even smaller landowners also came together to try and defeat the authority of greater magnates, who controlled most rights of patron-age. The bitter complaint was that they were usurping the popular rights of the people to decide on who should be the representative of Jesus Christ among them in their Sabbath worship. These disputes became the most common form of popular protest in rural Scotland in the eighteenth century. When the objectors failed in their objective to overturn the decision of the patron, it was not uncommon for entire congregations to secede from the church and join the ranks of dissenters. Indeed, patronage stirred such deep feelings that it event-ually led to the Great Disruption of 1843, which split the Presbyterian establishment in Scotland down the middle between the Auld Estab-lished Kirk and the Free Church.

In John Galt's novel *Annals of the Parish* (1821) his main character, the parish minister, the Rev. Micah Balwhidder, was appointed to his office by the local patron in 1760. This triggered 'a mad and vicious protest' by the people and a 'guard of soldiers' had to be summoned to protect the presbytery. As Balwhidder approached his new charge to address the congregation for the first time on the Sabbath:

> Dirt was flung as we passed, and reviled us all, and held out the finger of scorn at me ... Poor old Mr Kilfuddy of the Braehill got such a clash of glar [soft mud] on the side of his face, that his eye was almost extinguished.
>
> When we got to the kirk door, it was found to be nailed up, so as by no possibility to be opened. The sergeant of the soldiers wanted to break it, but I was afraid that the heritors [landowners of the parish] would grudge and complain of the expense of a new door, and I supplicated him to let it be as it was: we were, therefore, obligated to go in by a window, and the crowd followed us making the most unreverent manner, making the Lord's house like an inn on a fair day with all their grievous yellyhooing.

We should not therefore assume that the people were automatically submissive to landed authority. The Levellers' Revolt in Galloway, described in the previous chapter, demonstrated that power had to be employed with some care to avoid inciting a violent reaction. Robert Burns's great poem and song on the dignity of labour and poverty, 'A Man's a Man for a' That', published in the radical decade of the 1790s, contains some irreverent verses written by one Ayrshire ploughman about those who had dominion in his district. Burns's feelings derived in part from the Calvinist tradition in Scotland of the equality of all souls before God, whatever the earthly rank of social classes:

> Gie fools their silks, and knaves their wine;
> A Man's a Man for a' that:
> For a' that, and a' that,
> Their tinsel show, an a' that:
> The honest man, tho' e'er sae poor,
> Is king o' men for a' that.
>
> Ye see yon birkie, ca'd a lord,
> Wha struts, an' stares, an' a' that:
> Tho' hundreds worship at his word
> He's but a coof for a' that:

For a' that, an' a' that,
His ribband, star, an' a' that:
The man o' independent mind,
He looks an' laughs at a' that

[*birkie* – conceited fellow; *coof* – silly or stupid person]

Even landlords in the Highlands did not always have it their own way. Public protest did take place, but probably much more common was covert opposition to landowner plans. An example of this took place on the Tiree estate of the improving grandee, John, fifth Duke of Argyll, in the late eighteenth century and early nineteenth. The island of Tiree was blessed with fertile land and for the Hebrides a relatively benign climate. In an almost identical strategy to improvers in the Lowlands, the Duke and his advisers determined on a policy of establishing medium-sized compact farms under single husbandmen, breaking up the traditional townships and decanting the displaced population into villages, there to work in fishing and textile manufacture. The numbers required to move were considerable because the settlements were populated not just by tenants but also by colonies of cottars, who were often kinfolk of the rent-paying peasants.

For over four decades, with some intermittent gaps, the Argyll estate battled against refractory tenants in the runrig townships who stubbornly refused to participate in schemes of improvement despite a largely benevolent approach. All the time, the population of the island was continuing to rise while the Duke's need for higher rents from the improved farms became ever greater. But his grand plans ultimately depended on the cooperation of the people, and this was not forthcoming. In 1803 he conceded defeat, gave up the idea of larger single farms and ordered that the townships be divided into small croft holdings for not only the tenants but also for cottars and their families. He was swayed as well in this decision by rising prices for kelp and the need for a large seasonal labour force on the coast, for the gathering and burning of the seaweed.

In any society as grossly unequal as eighteenth-century Scotland, there were bound to be tensions below the surface which might become more visible and sometimes violent when stirred by high food prices, rises in taxation or threats to popular rights. Meal mobs could gather in seasons of spiralling grain prices and attacks on the hated excisemen and customs houses were so routine as to be regarded as something of a national sport. However, as the patronage disputes confirmed, it was in the sphere of religion that direct conflict between élites and the people was probably most common and enduring.

3

The impetus for landlord-driven improvement in rural society from the 1760s came in large part as a response to the steep rise in demand for agricultural produce and raw materials caused by Scottish industrialization and urbanization in the second half of the eighteenth century and thereafter. It was these booming markets in most years which fundamentally lowered the threshold of risk for both large-scale investment in infrastructure and widespread changes in agrarian organization. One informed contemporary, writing in 1815, noted the remarkable pace of Scottish rural transformation in earlier decades:

> there never were greater agricultural improvements carried on in any country than there have been in Scotland during the last thirty years; that the progress of the most correct systems of husbandry has been rapid and extensive beyond what the most sanguine could have anticipated; and that in short, when we compare the present state of agriculture in the south-eastern counties with what must have been its state about the middle of last century, the efforts of several centuries would seem to have been concentrated in the intermediate period.[8]

Scottish exports rose ninefold in volume between 1785 and 1835 with manufactured goods the main driving force in that colossal rate of expansion. By the census of 1851, Scotland had become even more industrialized than the rest of Britain as measured by the proportion of the male labour force employed in industry and mining: 43.2 per cent for Scotland compared to the national figure of 40.9 per cent. City and town growth was equally explosive. As suggested earlier, urbanization in Scotland in the century between 1750 and 1850 was the fastest of any country in Europe. In 1750, Scotland was seventh

THE SCOTTISH CLEARANCES

in the league table of 'urbanized societies', as measured by the ratio of national populations living in towns of 10,000 inhabitants or above. By 1800 it was fourth, and second only to England and Wales by 1850. Even that figure underestimates the full extent of urban development because it fails to take into account the smaller towns and larger villages, which started to spread from the later eighteenth century. In the 1790s there were sixteen towns with populations over 5,000; thirty-three with between 2,000 and 5,000; and, below 2,000, as many as seventy others. Overwhelmingly, this small-scale urbanism was concentrated in the Lowlands, with only marginal town and village growth north of the Highland line.

The entire process greatly multiplied the number of those who had to depend on the market for food, drink and raw materials rather than on their own labours on the farm or smallholding. Grain prices soared on trend with a significant spike during the Napoleonic Wars, except for a few years of slump before and immediately after 1800. In the Kingdom of Fife, for example, average prices for oats between 1765 and 1760 were 56 per cent higher than in the years 1725–60. But between 1805 and 1810 they averaged more than 300 per cent greater than the 1760s. Landowners creamed off much of the profits of their tenants by raising rents, and that stream of income fuelled in turn even more estate investment. In the same period, Lowland and English consumption of Highland beef, wool, mutton, timber, slate, fish, kelp and illicit whisky went up. Prices for black cattle alone quadrupled between 1740 and 1800, while some commentators suggested that during the Napoleonic Wars Highland lairds could increase their rentals fivefold simply by converting land to sheep runs. Commercial forces were now so overwhelming that radical social change in Gaeldom seemed inevitable.

But it is important to recognize that material factors alone did not drive landlord strategies. The power of ideas was also decisive, especially those derived from the Scottish and European Enlightenments on the optimistic possibilities for progress in both the human and natural spheres. The common eighteenth-century collective term for all this was 'improvement'. Improvement was by no means a uniquely Scottish phenomenon. Similar ideas were influential in the rest of the British Isles and Europe, but they seemed to have been introduced in

Scotland with unusual force and vigour, not only in terms of agrarian change but also in the rebuilding of urban spaces. Partly this may have been because of the growing consciousness among the Scottish ruling classes of the material inferiority of their country in relation not only to England but also to other more advanced and prosperous nations. Closer political association with England after the Union of 1707 only made these patriotic feelings more palpable and pressing. For the optimists it seemed that the propitious economic conditions of the middle decades of the eighteenth century had finally made it possible for the laggard northern kingdom to catch up with its greater southern neighbour.

Another factor may have been the early and widespread dissemination of enlightened ideas among the Scottish educated classes. Enlightenment thought in Scotland most often emerged in full flow from the lecture halls of the country's five universities. It has become almost a cliché to say that some of the key works of Adam Smith, Francis Hutcheson, Adam Ferguson, William Robertson, John Millar and others first saw the light of day as teaching notes. Their students left university and went on to careers in the church, the legal profession, teaching and civil administration, armed with the benefit of the new learning and its emphatic belief in human progress. It is striking, for instance, how the local parish ministers of the 1790s, virtually to a man, welcomed and praised the new ethic of agricultural improvement in their reports published in that decade in the OSA. The estate factors and surveyors who carried out the practical business of agrarian reform were also educated professionals who would have been aware of the innovative ideas. It is striking, for instance, that William Keir, 'overseer of improvements' on the Duke of Buccleuch's lands in the Borders, for thirty-eight years from 1772, had certainly read and reflected on some of the writings of Adam Smith and other luminaries of the Enlightenment. Keir's major report to the Duke in 1791 was shot through with Smithian ideas and principles.

Several common precepts emerged from the improving literature and the practical programmes of the estate managers. Virtually all aspects of the traditional rural social and economic structure were vigorously condemned for irrationality and inefficiency. Uncritical intellectual legitimacy and credibility were afforded instead to virtually everything that was novel and innovative. Communal holdings and traditional patterns of work were especially damned because they were thought to inhibit individual freedom of enterprise and the natural aspiration of man to strive for profit and reward. Common lands were also unacceptable and they should be taken over, put under the plough and worked by industrious husbandmen. Nature was not preordained but could be changed for the better by rational and ordered human intervention. Indeed, the enthusiasts for improvement sometimes seem like religious zealots determined not only to take more profit from the land but to do so as an essential part of an ideological mission to modernize Scottish society.

7

Clearance by Stealth

As late as the 1750s most people in the rural Lowlands had a stake in the land, however small, as single or multiple tenants, subtenants or cottars. The truly landless, such as farm servants and day labourers, were but a small minority in the Scottish countryside. Half a century later that time-honoured social order had all but vanished. Multiple tenancy had virtually gone and the numbers of rent-paying tenants, already in decline from the later seventeenth century, had contracted much further. Cottar families, once universal in the old world, hardly existed at all within the new farm holdings by 1815 and their disappearance became the source of much contemporary comment. By the end of the Napoleonic Wars, landless servants and labourers, housed in the new farm steadings, and tradesmen, plying their crafts in villages and small country towns, were now in the majority.

The population of Scotland rose by more than a fifth between the 1750s and the census of 1801. That increase, coupled with the narrowing opportunities for land, further grew the proportion of the landless in Scottish society. This was nothing less than a social revolution, but it was also an economic revolution. By the 1820s, Lowland Scotland was starting to attract international praise for the excellence of its agronomy. The new farming had produced formidable figures like Hugh Watson of Keillor in Forfarshire, who pioneered the Aberdeen-Angus breed; Amos Cruikshank, who did the same for Shorthorn cattle; and James Kilpatrick of Kilmarnock, who brought the Clydesdale strain of draught horses to perfection. James Small introduced the improved light plough, and Andrew Meikle built the first successful threshing mill, in 1788. 'Lothians farming' soon became a byword across Europe and beyond for 'state of the art' arable agriculture. George Hope's 600-acre holding at Fenton Barns in East Lothian became so renowned that English farmers came across the border to learn the new ways. The physical world of agriculture was also becoming more familiar to modern eyes. An old landscape of runrig cultivation, township clusters, scattered arable, bogs and moors had taken on a new face: enclosed fields, compact farms with the attached labour force of ploughmen, servants and labourers, radically higher grain yields, because of improved rotations, and the mushrooming expansion of neighbouring rural villages.

Remarkably, too, it was a silent revolution. Loss of land and old rights must have caused pain and anxiety for many but collective protest of the kind seen in the western Borders in the 1720s and later in the bitter disturbances across parts of the Highlands were notable by their absence. Even when the famous 'Captain Swing' riots almost brought the agricultural parishes of southern and eastern England to the brink of social war in the 1820s and 1830s, the rural Lowlands of Scotland remained quiet. Furthermore, in the longer term, there was little evidence of folk memory of dispossession in song, verse or story among the communities, another stark and dramatic contrast with the social history of many parts of the Highlands and Islands. The verses of the national bard, Robert Burns, were composed in the later eighteenth century as the social revolution gathered pace, but there is no mention in them of any social trauma which the rural population might have suffered as a result.

The English radical William Cobbett saw for himself the social consequences of displacement and land consolidation during his tour of Scotland in autumn 1832. As he crossed the border into Berwick and then on to the Lothians he noted the contrasts with the countryside of his native England, which he had described previously in his *Rural Rides* of 1830. He was certainly mightily impressed by the productivity of the agriculture and described the big arable farms of the region as '*factories* for making corn and meat'. But to him these remarkable achievements had come at a human cost: 'Everything is abundant here but people, who have been studiously swept from the land.' He came across one district, more extensive than the English county of Suffolk, which had only three towns and a few villages. Cobbett reckoned that in Suffolk there were nearly forty market towns and 490 villages. Of richly fertile East Lothian, he remarked on 'such a total absence of dwelling houses as, never, surely were before seen in any country on earth', and then added: 'in this country of the finest land that ever was seen, all the elements seem to have been pressed into the amiable task of sweeping the people from the face of the earth.'[1]

I

The practitioners of landlord-inspired improvement in the Lowlands were an élite group of surveyors and factors who planned the changes and managed both their introduction and development. Sometimes described as 'superintendents of improvements', they were function-aries of professional standing and wide experience – men such as William Keir, John Burrell and Robert Ainslie, who respectively served the dukes of Buccleuch, Hamilton and Douglas in the 1760s and 1770s. They reported to these magnates at regular intervals on the conduct of their duties, which they performed only with the tacit consent of their aristocratic employers. But some were also afforded considerable latitude and discretion in their management and so had enormous influence over the shaping of the new social order on some of the great landed estates of Scotland.

It becomes clear, when their papers and diaries are compared, that they shared a common set of precepts and principles.[2] The report presented by Robert Ainslie to the Duke of Douglas in 1769 can serve as an exemplar of their approach to improvement. The Douglas fam-ily owned considerable acreage in the four counties of Lanarkshire, Renfrewshire, Angus and Berwick. Ainslie laid out a scheme of improvement for the Lanarkshire estate which stretched across nine parishes in the south of the county. He described the lands as 'mostly run-rig and Rundale amongst the Tenants who generally occupied their pastures amongst them in common . . . no place admitted of more Improvement'.[3] The key precondition for reform was to be the abolition of communal holdings, contraction in tenant numbers, and the building up of compact arable farms to a size which should be determined by the work rate of the improved horse-driven plough teams. Pastoral husbandry, however, demanded much more extensive holdings: 'Land therefore that is adapted principally or for the Sole purpose of Sheep pasture Should be Laid out in pretty, large farms.' But none should contain less land than was sufficient for the working of one plough team. Fifty acres in 'a good climate and middling soil' were recommended. However, in the improved regime, about half of all land should ideally be in grass and the remainder in arable. Therefore, Ainslie claimed, the actual optimum size for a viable holding was likely to be around 100 acres, which was considerably in excess of the size of most pre-improvement tenancies.

These bigger farms also had another purpose:

> In every Business which requires money and skill there must be an object Sufficient to attract the attention of the man possessed of these.
>
> Very small farms present no such object and therefore where they prevail improvements are not to be expected.

For Ainslie, then, the removal of many small tenants was a necessary preliminary to the advance of improvement and in time higher rentals for the landlord. But, crucially, he judged that equally vital to success was the need to avoid large-scale displacement of the existing tenantry. Mass clearance was in his view, 'a dangerous and most destructive experiment'. He shared the eighteenth-century belief in the causal connection between a large population and the wealth of a nation. Therefore he condemned in the strongest possible terms the policies of clearance which he understood were being introduced on some Highland estates at the time and were leading to loss of people through emigration. But Ainslie also had a specific and practical reason for hostility to depopulation. He recognized that improvement in mixed farming was a labour-intensive process: 'improvements cannot be carried on without hands and therefore the present inhabitants of a country instead of being forced from it, should on the contrary be preserved with great care'. In a single sentence, Ainslie had gone far to explain a critical distinction between the process of agrarian change in most of the arable Lowlands on the one hand and the hill country of the Borders and much of the western Highlands on the other. On lands more suited only to pastoralism, the availability of labour was of much less concern to both farmers and proprietors.

But while Ainslie opposed loss of people, he was also fully aware that the enlargement of farms would lead to a great many being turned off the land. A decline in the number of rent-paying tenants was inevitable but he took the view that since improvement in its initial stages needed more people, not fewer, many of the dispossessed could be redeployed as servants and labourers under the new régime. He estimated that they would even enjoy more regular work and hence higher incomes in improved agriculture. However, the basic key to his policy of maintaining those who lost their holdings was to relocate them in rural villages: 'a parcel of houses together where people might be accommodated with houses and a few acres of land each, barely to maintain a cow and a horse or two, which they will employ in driving carriages and be hired by the proprietor in his works, or as is common by the carrying on with rapidity their necessary improvements of inclosing, liming, etc'. Significantly, too, Ainslie envisaged that the new hamlets would be built within the bounds of the old townships from which smaller tenants and cottars had been removed in order to minimize disruption and maintain some links with the past. Today, the names of many villages and small towns in the Lowlands end with the suffix '-ton', such as Lamington, Newton and Abington in Lanarkshire, recalling their origins as the sites of once traditional townships. In addition, labourers, wrights, masons, ditchers and hedgers, together with shoemakers, weavers and tailors, would be needed to service the needs of the larger population. They too should be housed in the new villages. Indeed, Ainslie took the view that the transformation of landed estates would bring lasting benefits not only to landlords but also to the people who laboured in them. In this he may well have been drawing on one optimistic strand of Scottish Enlightenment thought which stressed the possibilities of progress for all. Indeed, his concluding remarks were almost utopian in aspiration:

> By preserving the people on the lands, inducing more to come thereto; promoting their propagation By encouragement to many and Giving them Examples of proper Industry. In short, By Defusing honest Industry amongst the people every thing will prosper; peace; plenty; and Smiling Facility; will run through the whole, with that Blessing their worthy Patron, will have Joy and Comfort in his permanent profits;

But fleeting and Comfortless are the sums squeezed from the Bowels of the Poor.

To Attempt to force more will ruin the whole design, and to expect it, and be disappointed is freight [*sic*] with the worst Consequences.

In the words of one scholar, writing about the Lowlands in the later eighteenth century, 'the overwhelming tenor of the evidence in every county, is of holdings thrown together to make larger farms and of tenants evicted'.[4] On the Morton estate in Fife, the proportion of multiple tenants fell from 20 per cent of the total in 1735 to 8 per cent by 1811. In the Lanarkshire lands of the Duke of Hamilton, the number of multiple tenants declined by 61 per cent between 1762 and 1809. Ruthven parish in Forfarshire had forty tenants in 1750 but the number had shrunk to twelve by the early 1790s. There were ninety-one in 1750 and fifty-one forty years later. The table below presents data from eleven estates across the Lowlands and confirms the widespread nature of tenant removal throughout the region.

But there was little uniformity in the extent of consolidation. Agricultural specialization, topography, soil type and climate all dictated a range of outcomes. The biggest arable holdings, averaging over 300 acres or more, were to be found in the rich lands of East Lothian and Berwickshire. Some of the parishes there contained fewer than a dozen farms *c.*1800, a significant decline from the pattern of the past. In the parish of Athelstaneford, East Lothian, for example, in 1794 only sixteen holdings were recorded, mostly between 100 and 200 acres; three were over 300 acres, but only one under 100. In the same county, the number of farms in the parish of Spott had fallen by two thirds over sixty years. Elsewhere, in the carse lands of the rivers Forth and Tay and the dairy-farming regions of the south-west Lowlands, holdings were usually smaller, with farms in Ayrshire and Lanarkshire worked mainly by families without much in the way of hired help. The introduction of big sheep walks in the hill country on the fringes of the Highlands and upland parishes of southern Lanarkshire, Aberdeenshire and Angus could lead to a more rapid collapse in small-tenant numbers, not unlike the experience of the central, western and northern Highlands. For instance, in the south Lanarkshire parish of Carmichael, population fell by 13 per cent between 1755 and the early

Table 5 Tenant numbers on eleven Lowland estates, 1735–1850

Estate	Period	Change in tenant numbers	Percentage change
Bertram of Nisbet	1769–1850	42 → 31	−26
*Crawford	1771–2	38 → 32	−16
Douglas	1774–1815	99 → 72	−27
Hamilton	1758–98	142 → 123	−13
Glasgow (Shewalton)	1761–1806	25 → 19	−24
Cavens	1741–82	27 → 22	−18
Balbirnie	1770–1818	46 → 38	−17
Leven & Melville (Balgonie & Melville)	1750–80	114 → 131	+15
Morton (Aberdour)	1735–1811	50 → 38	−24
Panmure	1758–1826	177 → 176	−1
Airlie	1790–1821	122 → 103	−16
Eglinton (Coilsfield)	1757–1800	38 → 34	−11

* The estate of Crawford figure only covers two years because it is derived from the original survey of farm reorganization to be implemented in subsequent years.

A bracketed reference is to a barony of the estate.

Sources: NRS, Bertram of Nisbet Papers, GD5/1/497–8; HPL, John Burrell's Journals, 631/1, Journal, 1771–2, 8 July 1771; NRA(S), Douglas-Home Papers, 859/62, 174, vols. 74–8; NRA(S), Hamilton Muniments, 2177/778. EI.32, 33, 59, 73, 78, 65, 70, 89; NRA(S), Earl of Glasgow Papers, 0094/4, 8–9; NRS, Oswald of Auchincruive Papers, GD213/22/54; NRS, Balfour of Balbirnie Muniments, GD288/4/122; NRS, Morton Papers, GD150/2061; NRS, Leven and Melville Papers, GD26/5/251–95; NRS, Dalhousie Muniments, GD45/18/506–1091; NRS, Airlie Muniments, GD16/30A, vols. 2–111; NRS, Eglinton Muniments, GD3/8360, 8361, 8359.

1790s, when numbers on average rose by 20 per cent throughout Scotland. In the same upland area of the county, numbers in the district of Douglas declined by 15 per cent and in that of Roberton by more than a third in the second half of the eighteenth century. The parish minister reported of Libberton in south Lanarkshire that 'the ruins of demolished cottages are to be seen in every corner, the number of inhabitants had fallen by a half since the 1750s due to the letting of the lands in large farms'.[5] In nearby Crawford, a report from 1771 suggested 'the present plan of turning the whole farms into large store farms had so reduced the numbers of consumers and consequently the quantity of corn needed to maintain them'.[6] Similar trends were described in Lamington, where the congregation of the local church had gone from 400 to 200 in the space of a few decades. It was alleged that this was caused by the 'union of farms in the district of Wandell where 4000 out of 5000 acres were now devoted to sheep pasture'.[7] In the hill country of the adjacent county of Ayrshire, where large grazing farms had also replaced numerous arable tenancies, 'in consequence whole baronies and large tracts of land, formerly planted thick with families were thrown together to make way for the new mode of management'.[8]

It is plain from the evidence that social dislocation on this scale was not typical of most of the Lowlands but was more likely to take place in the upland fringes of the region where both topography and climate dictated the dominance of pastoral husbandry. The papers of the principal landlord in Ayrshire, the Earl of Eglinton, show that extensive displacement of people was uncommon in Lowland districts in the later eighteenth century and mainly confined to the hilly parts of his estates. Indeed, throughout the Lowlands the general pattern of tenant reduction, movement to compact holdings and larger farms, was a gradual, step-wise process which might often take several decades to accomplish until the old settlements traditionally occupied by many multiple tenants eventually came to be controlled by single husbandmen. This was clearance by stealth and attrition but in the end had the same long-term effect as the dramatic episodes of collective eviction: many fewer people at the end of the process with a stake in the land. On the whole, tenancies contracted and disappeared through the patient 'weeding out' of possessors until the end result was achieved of holdings, which were essentially modern farms, leased to single individuals.

Three brief examples show how this was achieved. First, the *ferme-toun* of Letham on the Fife estate of Lord Melville had eight tenants in the 1670s and six in 1694 who shared the rental payments. But the overall population of the township was significantly greater than the families of the main husbandman as it was also much subdivided among cottars and their kinfolk. By 1740 four tenants remained and ten years later only two. By 1755 the old well-populated township had become a single farm with just one tenant and his family. To get to that final stage, however, had taken over eight decades from the 1670s.

Secondly, there is the case of the township of Carngillan on the estate of the Earl of Eglinton in Ayrshire. In 1747 it was farmed by eight tenants together with cottars and servants. The thinning of the inhabitants began in 1757, when tenant numbers declined by one. The lease of another was terminated in 1777, followed by four more in 1797. By 1815 Carngillan was occupied by a single farmer, named Alexander Morton. He eventually had the single lease of a holding which had once supported eight families and their cottars in the 1740s. The Mortons were not listed in the original rental of 1747 and only appeared for the first time in 1757, when John Morton took a share in the township. From then until 1815 he and his descendants slowly absorbed more and more land as leases lapsed over the years until the goal of sole possession was attained.

The third illustration comes from the township of Drumglary on the Earl of Strathmore's estate in Angus. In 1690 it was held in runrig by five families. One tenant had one third of the land and the others shares of a sixth each. The first attempt at reorganization came in 1771 with an agreement between the Earl and three of the tenants as leases of the other two had already expired earlier that year. The estate was about to undertake an ambitious programme of improve-ment, so Strathmore's factor offered a deal to the two remaining tenants whose leases would not lapse until 1777. In return for sur-rendering them in advance, each was promised preferential treatment when the new, improved holdings became available. The promise was kept. In 1784 the names of both tenants remained on the rent books of the estate.

Of course, austere figures cannot begin to convey anything of the human story of displacement and the pain of losing a secure liveli-hood. It should be recognized that clearance by attrition did not simply affect single husbandmen or heads of households. When a lease was not renewed, wives, children, aged family dependants, cottar families and servants also lost their homes. The casualties of trans-formation must have been very considerable indeed.

The basic legislation governing eviction had been introduced as early as 1555, when an Act of the Scottish Parliament 'Anent [con-cerning] the Warning of Tenants' was passed and then clarified by an Act of Sederunt of the Lords of Council and Session of 1756. Consent to a landlord's request to remove a tenant could only be given in a sheriff court through an application submitted at least forty days before Whitsun. (See Annex D for the text of a 'summons of remov-ing [or removal].) If the sheriff agreed, the decision 'shall be held as equal to a warning executed in terms of the Act of Parliament'. This was a much simpler and speedier procedure than the processes which took place when enclosures were being established in England. Also obliged to 'flit' (move) would be the tenant's family, his servants, cot-tars, subtenants and other dependants. If those listed in the writ of removal refused to comply, they would be 'held as violent possessors and compelled to pay the violent profits of the same, conform to law in all rigour'. Continuing disobedience meant officers of the court were entitled to use force and physically eject the offending parties. By analysing the summonses preserved in sheriff court records, it is therefore possible to compile rough 'indexes of coercion' during the era of improvement.

The data for four courts throughout the Lowlands at Cupar, Dun-blane, Peebles and Linlithgow are set out in Annex C, and below for a fifth, Hamilton sheriff court in Lanarkshire.

According to this evidence the threat or reality of eviction was rare. Even during the peak years of improvement, summons of removal were employed only infrequently. The average for the five courts surveyed in Annex B was a mere 16.8 writs per annum in the last four decades of the eighteenth century. These figures can be con-trasted with the hundreds of summonses of removal granted in some years to west Highland and Hebridean estates. Moreover, most sum-monses granted by these Lowland courts seem only to have been

Table 6 Summonses of Removal, Hamilton sheriff court,
1763–84 (available years)

| Year | Cause of summons | | | |
	End of tack	Arrears	Breach of tack regulations	Others
1763	8	4	2	2
1764	60	4	1	–
1765	4	3	1	–
1766	23	7	2	–
1767	58	–	1	–
1768	19	18	2	–
1779	–	14	1	–
1781	5	8	2	–
1782–4	9	13	2	–
Totals				
1763–84	186 (68%)	71 (26%)	14 (5%)	2 (0.7%)
1768–84	33 (35%)	53 (57%)	7 (8%)	–

Source: NRS, Sheriff Court Processes (Hamilton), SC37/8/7–20.

granted to provide legal recognition of the end of leases and formal notice to tenants to leave their farms by the date specified in the original agreement with the proprietors. Actions for arrears of rent or breaches of contract were few and far between.

Gradual dispossession rather than mass clearance within short time frames was therefore favoured in most of the Lowland regions with the exception of districts more suited to large-scale sheep farming. One critical factor influencing the pace of change was the cost of improvement in mixed-farming economies. Sheep walks needed little more than the construction of miles of drystone dykes and the building of a few shepherds' cottages. In most of the arable districts in the Lowlands, however, the depletion of tenant numbers was only one part of the comprehensive improvement of estates designed to deliver the financial holy grail of a massive augmentation in rental income. That rents did eventually climb to unprecedented levels is not in question. On the Douglas estate in Lanarkshire, for example, average rents rose eightfold between 1737 and 1815. The Earl of Morton's annual rental in Fife spiralled from £377 in 1742 to nearly £4,000 in 1815. On the Earl of Eglinton's Ayrshire lands the annual rental had risen to £11,084 by 1797, then more than doubled to £25,992 by 1815. The greatest gains in landlord incomes took place during the Napoleonic Wars. Even then, however, it was reckoned that at least four to five years from the initial investment in schemes of improvement had to pass before rewards of this order of magnitude could be realized.

Improving theorists assumed that independent farmers, liberated from the chains of archaic communal agriculture, were alone capable of introducing and developing the new husbandry successfully. However, once this élite cadre was in place, the opportunities of the market could only be exploited with the support of substantial landlord investment in enclosure, farm steadings and roads. None of this came cheaply. The conventional wisdom, for instance, was that enclosure by hedge and ditch cost £2 per acre (£148 at 2017 values). Overall expenditures were even more costly. From 1771 to 1776, the Earl of Strathmore invested £22,233 in his Angus estate on a large-scale programme of improvement on enclosure, drainage, roads, bridge construction and the building of new farm steadings. It was estimated that enclosing only a quarter of the tenancies on the Duke of Hamilton's lands in Lanarkshire would cost £2.65 per acre in the 1760s and £4,659 overall. It was perhaps inevitable, given the considerable financial demands of improvement, that even the wealthiest magnates were forced to pace the consolidation of farms and decline in tenant numbers.

Also, these high expenditures are suggestive of a partnership type of relationship between Lowland landlords and tenants. The proprietors during improvement did not simply cream off unearned incomes via increased rents. They invested heavily in the process and it was this in collaboration with the work and skill of the farmers which eventually produced higher returns. Some Highland magnates also spent on fishing enterprises and on unsuccessful attempts to establish manufactories. But the general programmes of letting crofts to those who laboured on the kelp shores or in unreclaimed moorland required little investment. The income derived from those activities was unearned and the process more exploitative than collaborative.

A harvest crisis could also influence the speed of development. Many estates began to implement programmes of improvement in the 1760s. But several of these stalled for a time in the following two decades during the years 1772–4 and 1782–3 because of a sharp deterioration in weather conditions. Between 1757 and the later 1760s the weather was benign and this, together with rising grain prices, helps to explain the first dynamic phase of improvement. Then, in 1772, in the western Lowlands at least, 'shakening winds' were accompanied by 'Rotting Rains' and followed by 'parching Drought' in 1773.[9] One factor noted that 'the whole spirit of Improvement is knocked on the head' as a result.[10] Arrears of rent mounted and some tenants even had to surrender leases because of harvest failure. A similar crisis occurred in 1782–3. As a result, on the Duke of Hamilton's Lanarkshire estate, for example, the consolidation of tenancies virtually came to a halt, with only 2.5 per cent of farms between 1782 and 1785 involved at that time.

The rate of displacement may have been influenced in part by a concern to maintain social stability. The agricultural reporter for Fife, John Thomson, argued that there were dangers as well as opportunities in 'the uniting of farms'. Concentrating the management of the land in the hands of a few might make economic sense, but equally it could pose a grave danger to social order and even threaten the political stability of the nation. Thomson was writing during the long wars with France and pointed to events across the Channel to reinforce his point that economic discontent could lead to revolution and anarchy. How far these arguments were in the minds of the landed classes at this time cannot be easily known. Such concerns did not seem to have inhibited some Highland lairds from enforcing clearances before 1815. Equally, however, there was a recognition that the potential for tenant truculence had to be taken into account when plans of improvement were being prepared. Thus the Earl of Strathmore's factor in Angus wrote anxiously to his master in 1754 that 'he had enough to do for some time past to keep proper order in the [Baron Court]', which was still functioning at that date.

The disputed issue was the reclamation of the mosses in one part of the estate which had disturbed traditional rights of access.[11] In Ayrshire, apparently, tensions were also quite widespread. The agricultural reporter for the county commented in 1793 that 'Near some towns where the notions of manufacturers predominate' some farmers had formed themselves into 'associations'. It was said of these that members 'find themselves, under severe penalties, never to offer any mark of civility to any person in the character of a gentleman'. The reporter considered these groups so threatening that he advised proprietors to retaliate by forming counter-associations in order to prevent the recalcitrants being offered long-term leases to farms.[12] On the Hamilton estates in Lanarkshire in the later eighteenth century it was apparently not uncommon for the tenants of a particular neighbourhood to form a 'secret combination' to ensure that sitting tenants would triumph when farms were put up for public bidding at the termination of leases.[13] So effective were these that the Duke's factor counselled against 'public roups' (auctions), where collective action could develop, and argued in favour of letting land, wherever possible, through private bargains:

> it is my opinion that roups for farms in this country are the same with all the other places I have yet the experience of. That is, whatever the private offerer may intend by a private bargain, his mouth is entirely shut up from offering at a publick roup by a Secret Combination which is as Common to them as the Flame of Fire flies upwards, which establishes that solid oppinnion [sic] of mine never to get farms by any other method than private offers . . . [14]

A survey of sheriff court and other legal records confirms that some tenants, and especially the more substantial men, were more than capable of taking action to protect their interests by going to law. Summons of removal could be and were challenged in the courts and landlords who pursued eviction by those means had to be punctilious in following the formal process with great care if they were not to attract objections on technical grounds.[15] The legal representative of the Duke of Gordon in 1770 concluded: 'A Process of Removing which requires the most summary dispatch and from its nature must be extremely simple and plain, has of late years become quite a labyrinth in the law; and any heritor may sooner be dispossessed of his estate by a judicial sale than it is practicable to have a litigious tenant removed from a farm.'[16] In addition, among Court of Session papers, documentation of legal actions taken by tenant farmers against their landlords sometimes surface. These included cases of compensation demanded for building on lands during the tenure of a lease, resisting landlord claims of broken leases, opposing summonses of removal, protesting against the levying of feudal dues and the like.[17]

2

Increasingly the country population, and especially those with some means, had a choice. In the second half of the eighteenth century, emigration across the Atlantic, where land was cheap and abundant, offered an alternative to those who feared rack renting, dispossession and the loss of social status.

The end of the Seven Years War in 1763 with victory over France was decisive in this respect. Many thousands of acres in North America were won from the defeated enemy and became available for purchase and speculation. However, those who bought territory were conscious that land without settlers to farm it was useless. Before too long, therefore, a publicity campaign in the Scottish press began to attract emigrants. Emigration had rarely been regarded as a positive choice in the past but the offer of cheap land was likely to be more tempting when the opportunities even to rent it were narrowing in the homeland. Further, the emigrant trade was becoming more secure and efficient. Some Glasgow merchant houses engaged in the Atlantic trades began to become involved, partly because tonnages outwards to the colonies were never as great as their inward cargoes of tobacco, timber and rice. Emigration was becoming a specialist business with advertisements publicizing the 'comforts' which could be enjoyed during the long voyage and the competence of captains and crew.

Between 1700 and 1815 around 90,000–100,000 Scots left for North America, the majority going between c.1763 and c.1775. The Highland exodus has attracted most attention but emigration was taking place from all parts of the country. So great was it from the western Lowlands in the early 1770s that in the summer of 1774 the *Scots Magazine* observed with some alarm and exaggeration that emigration threatened to transform the west into a great grass park only suitable for grazing cattle and sheep. The *Register of Emigrants* for the years 1773–6 allows the scale, social composition and geographical spread of the movement to be explored in some detail. Forty per cent of the nearly 10,000 enumerated in the *Register* were from Scotland. It was not a migration of the rootless poor or of unskilled labourers. The vast majority were farmers or artisans in the textile trades, which were then experiencing a serious depression. Twenty-five per cent of 'independent' or 'semi-independent' individuals came from agricultural occupations. A striking feature of the migration was the role of tenant groups which came together to plan the voyages across the Atlantic and then organize settlement of migrants on American land. One such was the 'United Company of Farmers' based in the counties of Stirling and Perth. It sent agents across the Atlantic to search for good land, gathered funds to purchase territory and commissioned a vessel for the voyage, and eventually settled the emigrants in 7,000 acres along the Connecticut River in the colony of New York.

Another was the Scots–American Company of Farmers, which comprised over 138 tenants from Renfrewshire, Lanarkshire and Dumbartonshire. The ambitious objective was to gather enough funds to enable them to purchase 100,000 acres in North America. They complained of high rents and the threat of dispossession on the west of Scotland estates of Lord Blantyre and the Duke of Douglas. The Company sent two of their number across the Atlantic to survey lands on the frontier, and their travels there became a veritable odyssey. In four months they covered more than 2,700 miles from up-country New York to North Carolina, before deciding to purchase 20,000 acres at Ryegate, far up the west bank of the Connecticut River in New York colony.

But emigration did not lead to rural depopulation. The migration data assembled in Table 7 suggest the key feature was more *internal* mobility within the countryside rather than any mass exodus of people from the land. Some parishes were indeed losing numbers, but others were gaining population through the interaction of village and town development, agrarian specialization, and the spread of rural manufacturing and mining communities.

Table 7 Parishes gaining and losing population in the
counties of Angus, Fife, Lanarkshire and Ayrshire, 1790s

	Parishes losing		Parishes gaining		Totals
	>30%	>0–29%	>0–29%	>30%	
Angus:					
No. of parishes	15	17	16	5	53
% of total	28.3	32.1	30.2	9.4	100.0
Fife:					
No. of parishes	17	28	9	5	59
% of total	28.8	47.5	15.3	8.5	100.1
Lanarkshire:					
No. of parishes	12	13	7	6	38
% of total	31.6	34.2	18.4	15.8	100.0
Ayrshire:					
No. of parishes	12	10	11	12	45
% of total	26.7	22.2	24.4	26.7	100.0

Note: For methods of calculating net out-migration, see T. M. Devine, *The Transformation of Rural Scotland* (Edinburgh, 1999), pp. 146–7.

Source: OSA.

As Robert Ainslie argued in his treatise on improvement considered earlier, there was a positive advantage within the mixed-farming economy in retaining rather than expelling those who had lost tenancies through the reorganization of holdings. Several strategies were employed with the objective of absorbing the displaced and so benefiting from their labour. The most common was the foundation of village settlements. Several were planned, others seemed to have grown more organically. By the 1790s there were villages in 43 per cent of parishes in Fife, plus 83 per cent, 35 per cent and 44 per cent respectively in parishes of Ayrshire, Angus and Lanarkshire. Table 8 provides

Table 8 New and extended settlements, villages and towns in four Scottish Lowland counties, 1790s

County	Settlements		Villages		Towns		Percentage of parishes with additions
	New	Extended	New	Extended	New	Extended	
Ayrshire	1	0	8	7	0	11	47.8
Lanark	1	1	4	10	0	6	56.4
Fife	7	0	1	12	0	8	38.3
Angus	5	0	2	0	0	6	22.2
Totals	14	1	15	29	0	31	41.17 (average)

Notes: 'Settlements': this was the category used when the other two were not indicated. Such developments as a few houses built where the site was not specified and where land was feued for buildings were recorded here; perhaps generally where the scale, form or name did not suggest at least a small village.

'Village': recorded as such when the settlement was noted in the OSA as such.

'Town': again, recorded as such when so indicated in the accounts. Though in one or two cases a 'toun' could perhaps have been implied, there was by and large no doubt about this category.

more detail on those and on the small rural towns which also saw growth in the number of their inhabitants.

Displaced tenants could be absorbed by other means. In the north-east Lowlands, farms were being thrown together with as much enthusiasm as elsewhere. But the emerging pattern in the counties of Aberdeen, Kincardine, Banff, Moray and Nairn differed from other areas. New smallholdings were being created even as larger holdings were being established. The reason was that there was a good deal of unimproved moorland and mosses in the region. Landowners hit on a scheme to reclaim these areas. They settled them with crofters or smallholders, often evicted tenants or cottars, who were given tracts of moor and encouraged to cultivate them while having only to pay minimum or zero rents until the land furnished steady returns. Thus, in one parish of Old Deer in Aberdeenshire in 1840, there were 140 extended compact farms but also 401 crofts and smallholdings. These strategies were very successful, with most parishes reporting considerable expansion of their available acreage by the 1840s.[18]

The same approach was adopted on a much lesser scale on poor land elsewhere outside the north-east:

> In the more fertile and better cultivated portions of Buchan, a system had prevailed of augmenting the number of large farms; and in consequence diminishing that of the small. By the operation of this system, many of the small holders, deprived of their possessions, were forced to betake themselves to the improvement and cultivation of a piece of wasteland on the side of a hill, or on the margin of a moor or moss, given them by one proprietor at a nominal rent for a stipulated number of years, seldom exceeding seven, and afterwards to be paid for at value.
>
> At the same time the active spirit of improvement . . . led to the removal of cottars and subtenants . . . those also had no other resource left them but that of the crofters.[19]

Also elsewhere, irregular patches of nutrient-poor soil which had been part of the pre-improvement landscape were rented out to colonies of smallholders for the purposes of reclamation. It was a cheap form of land improvement which substituted human labour for capital investment. More land became available as the commonties were privatized. Commonties of waste land were shared between different estates and varied in size between several thousand and a few acres. They could be divided into private ownership under legislation of the pre-1707 Scottish Parliament simply by one landowner pursuing a claim in the Court of Session whether other parties in the neighbourhood agreed or not. The peak years of these divisions were from 1760 to 1815, when 45 per cent out of all actions undertaken from 1600 to 1914 were recorded. Some of the commonty land was simply added to adjacent farms but in other cases it was split up into small lots to provide for those displaced by tenant reduction, which helped to preserve some of the human capital of the estates.

3

A paradox remains to be resolved. Many tenants and cottars were dislodged from the land in the second half of the eighteenth century. Concurrently, the population of Scotland was rising, an increase which was not only sustained after 1800, but became even faster in the following decades. Nevertheless, there was little evidence of structural unemployment in the countryside and wage levels there were not only stable but started to increase from the 1760s to 1812 in most years. That cycle goes a long way to explain the silence and absence of disturbance associated with the Lowland removals.

In part the rural labour market remained uncongested for the reasons given earlier in this chapter: the need for many hands to be employed in the infrastructure of the new agriculture during the primary phase of improvement and the simultaneous spread of textile work and other manufactures in the country parishes. But it is also important to recognize that some of the rural population were being drawn from the land to the expanding cities and towns by the hope of higher wages and fresh opportunities. Some of the tenant class must have also felt the pinch of high rents, especially in years of poor harvests such as 1772–4 and 1783–4. Others, and in particular the lesser folk, had lost their tiny holdings completely and been forced to work as landless labourers. Serious deprivation might have been unusual but a sense of falling status would have been common. And, as will be shown in Chapter 9, once the mould of the improved structure had taken shape, the mechanisms of labour recruitment in the Lowlands effectively squeezed out those who were surplus to the work of the farms. The rigour of the lease system also meant that any attempt by farmers to subdivide their holdings, which might have anchored families to the land, would have been met by landlords starting legal proceedings against them for breach of contract followed by summary eviction. Subletting to kinfolk or others was universally opposed by landlords in the Lowlands, while it was enthusiastically encouraged in the western Highlands and Islands until the 1820s. As one scholar has put it: 'Any increase in population tightened the screw, with increasing numbers struggling for a diminished number of tenancies or for employment in a tightly organized labour market. The pressure or temptation to flee the land was intense'.[20]

There is a final issue to consider. As population rose, proportionately fewer Scots worked the land as their forefathers had done to provide food and shelter for their families. Many more than before now had jobs in industry, mining and a host of other urban employments. They had to pay in the market for the houses where they lived and the food and drink they consumed. Without the huge increase in the yields of grain crops and higher levels of labour productivity resulting from agricultural improvement, many of this growing army of non-food producers would soon have faced intolerable prices for bread and drink and even perhaps the threat of starvation. It was the reformed agricultural system which delivered the enhanced supply of food and, together with some foreign imports, helped to avoid such a disaster. Thus the agrarian transformation was of vital human benefit, but it also came with some social costs and one of them was the dispossession of numerous families whose ancestors had lived and worked on the land since time immemorial.

8

Whatever Happened to the Cottars?

Before the later eighteenth century cottar families were very numerous across the Lowland countryside. Indeed, as the surviving poll tax returns of the 1690s surveyed in Chapter 3 confirmed, they and their families probably accounted for between a quarter and a third of the rural population in many areas. Cottars were provided with smallholdings in return for supplying labour to main tenants at busy times of the farming year. As already shown, while the consolidation of direct tenancies and the eradication of multiple tenure took place relatively gradually, the removal of the cottars was carried out more rapidly in most counties during the last few decades of the eighteenth century and was virtually complete by the early years of the nineteenth. Their dispossession was compressed in time and carried out in a systematic and comprehensive fashion.

I

An abundance of contemporary evidence confirms that the cottar system was under widespread attack from the 1770s. In Lanarkshire 28 per cent of parishes reporting in the *OSA* described their extensive removal. For Angus, the figure was 22 per cent and in Fife 33 per cent. But these data almost certainly underestimate the sheer scale of dispossession because most parishes in the *OSA* returns made no specific mention of cottars at all. For instance, of sixty Ayrshire parish reports, only twenty-four contained details on cottars. Of those which did, however, nearly all described clearance and dispersal. The testimony of observers at the time adds further weight to the numerical conclusions. The agricultural reporter for Lanarkshire commented in 1798 that 'It is vain to see anything of the ancient cottages . . . the former nurseries of field labourers, for they may be said to be now no more.' He went on to add that 'the few scattered ones which still remain can scarcely be called an exception'.[1] Similarly, in Fife the reporter described an identical process in the northern parishes of the county. The witnesses were at pains to emphasize the radical nature of the removals by their colourful use of language. The minister of Kilmany in Fife referred to 'the annihilation of the little cottagers'.[2] His colleague in Marrikie, Angus, described how 'many of the cottagers are exterminated'.[3] Other observers noted the existence of numerous dwellings in their parishes, formerly the huts of cottar families, which were gradually falling into ruins. Elsewhere, cottar houses were being demolished and the stone used for drystone dykes and walls for field and farm enclosures.

Ironically, however, while the scale of this social transformation has been virtually ignored by scholars until recent times, it did attract a great deal of comment and concern in the late eighteenth century. Some contemporaries thought the removals were to blame for the increase in the overall wage costs of farm labour. The critics pointed out that the attack on the cottar system was eliminating the traditional 'nursery of servants' because it was the sons and daughters of cottar families who provided the main source of these farm workers. But recruiting them had now become much more difficult because so many cottar families had been forced off the land. This, together with the lure of more and better-paid opportunities in industry and the towns, had led to the possibilities of a crisis in the agricultural labour market. Other commentators, perhaps less convincingly, saw a relationship between the clearance of the cottars and the rising costs of the Poor Law in some of the larger towns as the disinherited were having to move there in the search for work.

Perhaps, however, it is only by focusing on the local experience that we can gain specific insight to the cottar removals. Thus, in the district of Inverdovat on the Tayfield estate in Fife in 1707, ten 'cotteries' had existed. A few years later, the number had risen to thirteen. As late as 1733, several cottars remained in the township, though evidence for some decades after that is meagre. By 1813, however, when the social structure of the district can be documented once again, no cottar holdings remained. Again, in the parish of Colmonell in Ayrshire, the cottar class was still numerous in the 1760s: 'there was hardly a tenant who had not one or more cottagers on his farm'. By the 1790s it was acknowledged there were 'very few' in the entire parish'.[4] Similarly in Kilwinning, in the same county, cottars were virtually omnipresent in the farms of the early eighteenth century. But by 1790 'the cottages are, in great measure, demolished'.[5] Virtually identical patterns were described in several areas of Angus at the other end of the Lowlands. A general decline in population was reported in the parish of St Vigeans because of holdings being united into one. But the fall in the number of cottars was even more extensive than the decline of tenants. Of one farm, for instance, it was reported that there had been eighteen of them in 1754. By 1790 only a single solitary family remained.

Eradication did not take place at the same pace or on the same scale in all parts of the Lowlands. In the later eighteenth century, for instance, the cottar system was still relatively undisturbed in much of the north-east region. Of seventy-eight parishes in the *OSA* which made reference to cottars in the counties of Angus, Ayrshire, Fife and Lanarkshire, twenty-seven (or 34 per cent) noted their existence without suggesting removals. Nevertheless, the long-term trend was plain as evictions accelerated into the early decades of the nineteenth century. The clearance of the cottars was a remarkable change in the entire structure of rural society. It became a fundamental factor in the growth of a predominantly landless wage-earning labour force, a rise in local migrations in the countryside and a revolution in traditional patterns of human settlement. In essence, an entire social tier of the old order had been eliminated in many areas over the space of a few decades.

One factor which speeded up clearance, though did not in itself cause it to happen, was the nature of the legal process. Unlike tenants and subtenants, cottars, in the sense defined here, had no legal rights to land. In addition, they do not appear to have been protected by the legislation of 1555 and 1756 which laid down the formal procedures to be taken to enforce removal of tenants, especially the requirement to issue legal warnings forty days before Whitsun in order to allow writs to be challenged at law. There are only a few instances in court records of notices of removal being issued against cottars. Thus, at Hamilton sheriff court in 1779, John Crawford of Aikerfin obtained a 'Lybell of Removing' against William Young and James Young, 'who possess a cothouse and two cows grass in Aikenfin'.[6] A similar decision was made in favour of Matthew Baillie of Carnbroe in Lanarkshire against five 'cottars in Carnbroe village with houses and yards'.[7] But these cases were unusual and probably related to cottar families who opposed removal. The paucity of references to such cases in court records tends to suggest that cottars were usually evicted at the will of individual tenant farmers.

As noted earlier, several observers took the view that the destruction of the cottar system had led to a number of adverse effects. In the opinion of some it made the recruitment of the next generation of unmarried farm servants more difficult. The cottar families had also provided essential labour for ploughing, sowing, herding, shearing, grain harvesting and peat cutting in return for a cot house, a few rigs within the lands of the township, and the right to graze a cow or a few sheep. Widespread forcing out of cottars must have meant for most farmers the possible risks of losing a secure supply of labour. Yet these drawbacks seem to have been considerably outweighed by the potential long-term advantages of mass removal. In fact, when the displacements are examined in detail, their rationale can be seen to have been entirely consistent with the nature of the improved agrarian economy. When farms were united and the number of tenants fell, a decline in cottar numbers could also be expected, especially where arable farms were being replaced by pastoral holdings with more limited needs for labour.

The division of commonties and the intaking of mosses and muirs, described in Chapter 7, also weakened their way of life. These marginal lands had long been crucial to cottar subsistence support. They provided many of the basic needs of families at no cost other than their own labour. Building materials, like stone, wood, heather and bracken, came from these sources. They also afforded peat and turf for fuel while commonties were also a key resource for grazing a few stock. In the second half of the eighteenth century, however, all of these traditional sources of subsistence were being removed or drastically reduced as the division of commonties grew apace. The process was part of a broader strategy which led landowners to exploit all the territory of their estates 'at proper value'. Thus, on some properties bogs were drained, and in others marginal land was absorbed into regular cultivation and new rent-paying smallholdings were created. Moreover, just as proprietors laid claim to all the minerals on their lands, they also increasingly sought to control access to former 'common' resources like peat and wood. There is plenty of evidence of a drive to cut back or even eliminate traditional rights of access to moorland and peat bogs. One example, from the Earl of Panmure's estate in Angus, illustrates the process:

> The Estate of Edzel and Newar is now mostly sett and the boundaries of the several possessions settled, and there is reserved the Moss of Mergie as is thought of about 800 or 1000 acres . . . the muir of Slateford ought to be enclosed and planted and the thing should be set about immediately. It will be a most beautiful thing and in time will come to be of great value.
>
> For many years past this muir has been grossly abused by casting of turf in it. No less than thirty stacks or thereby yearly have the inhabitants taken out of it besides what the adjacent tenants and cottars take. The factor has prohibited these practices for the future under the severest penalty and has taken the tenants bound in the Minutes of Tack granted them not to cast turf themselves nor suffer others to do so, so far as they can hinder it.[8]

[*cast* – cut]

Cottars were also being squeezed out by other forces as the system was now seen to impose unacceptable costs on tenant farmers. Plots of land and grazing rights provided in return for labour had been acceptable when there were plenty of under-utilized areas within the *fermetouns*. It was less tolerated when outfields were being taken into the infields and worked intensively by regular sequences of crop rotation. The higher rents farmers had to pay in the later eighteenth century forced them to look more critically at the real costs of cottar holdings. In Colmonell parish in Ayrshire, for instance, cottars had possessed a house, a yard, a small piece of land and enough grass for one or more cows. Their value was 'thought to be trifling while rents were low' and markets limited.[9] But the balance of advantage in the new agriculture meant that it was more profitable to absorb the land of the cottars in order to produce more grain and stock for the market. The resulting savings could be considerable. In one estimate for the Rossie estate in Fife, cottars were said to have occupied a fifth of the infield land. As grain prices rose, there was a powerful incentive to remove these families and add their possessions to the full cultivation regime of the improved farms.

Increasingly, also, other observers argued that cottars might place a burden on the Poor Law. The fear was not in itself new. Cothouses had long been seen as repositories of the poor, the aged and infirm, and of landless vagrants coming from elsewhere. Thus the kirk session of Wiston in Lanarkshire proclaimed in 1752 that 'all persons who have coattages [sic] to set to beware that they bring no persons or families from other parishes who are not able to maintain themselves'.[10] Those who did so would be obliged to support them without any assistance from the kirk session. But concerns became more common in later decades with the greater mobility of population then. Certainly, in some rural parishes, there was growing alarm about higher levels of vagrancy in the last quarter of the eighteenth century. In Douglas in Lanarkshire, for example, reference was made in 1764 to 'the great number of vagrant persons and sturdy beggars' who were now in the parish.[11] Again, in 1788, the poor lists for Douglas increased as a result of the influx of strangers who were attempting to take possession of deserted cothouses. Demolition of these dwellings now became commonplace. As one commentator put it, those who still kept cottars had 'to submit to the risk of being burdened with a heavier poor's rate'.[12] Several of the *OSA* reports described how empty cottar dwellings were no longer allowed to moulder away but were being pulled down and completely levelled.

In essence, therefore, the cottar structure was in conflict with key aspects of new agrarian order. Cottars fitted well with a regime where demand for labour tended to concentrate in brief periods of the year around tasks like grain harvesting and fuel gathering. It was an advantage for tenants then to have a reliable pool of labour which could be called upon in the busy seasons and then laid off without any cash cost until needed again. However, the needs of improved agriculture were radically different from the old. Intensive cultivation of land, by regular ploughing, adoption of new crops – such as sown grasses, turnips and potatoes – and of innovative rotations, ensured that the working year started to lengthen. There was, on the whole, an evening out rather than an accentuation of seasonal labour needs within mixed farming. The regime favoured the hiring of full-time workers on wage contracts who laboured throughout the entire farming year.

The number of labourers needed in the new system did not fall. Indeed, for a time it rose considerably because of the making of enclosures, building of farm steadings and construction of roads. The key change was, therefore, in the way labour was contracted, not in the amount of labour needed. Therefore the traditional stake in the land was stripped out of the contract and instead full-time landless servants and day labourers became the norm throughout the Lowlands. Married servants hired by the year were most common in the intensive arable districts of the south-east, but elsewhere single male and female servants employed for periods of six months predominated. Ironically, the hinds, or married servants, bore some similarity to the cottars of old. They too were provided with a house, garden, fuel, the keep of a cow and other privileges as part of the wage reward. The crucial difference, however, was that they were full-time workers, entirely under the masters' control during the one-year term of employment, and could be dismissed at the end of it.

This position of subordination was crucial. While the independence of the cottars can be exaggerated – they did possess land but only in mere fragments and they had to obtain work in larger holdings in order to make ends meet – they were obviously less dependent on the will of the masters, because their smallholdings provided their families with meal and milk. But the new agriculture demanded much higher levels of labour control as tenants were coming under added pressures. Not only were rents going up, but the wages of agricultural workers were also rising from the 1770s, and especially from the 1790s, as industrial and urban expansion lured many away from the country districts to the towns. There was therefore an incentive for tenants to introduce ways of improving the productivity of labour.

The clearance of the cottars can be seen in this context. In the most improved districts, where the old Scots plough was being replaced by James Small's much lighter version, eventually using a team of just one man and two horses, the clearest effect is evident. Gradually the whole work routine centred around raising the efficiency of the horses. Hours of labour and number of workers became closely related to the horse teams and their work rate. Ploughmen took responsibility for a particular pair and their entire routine from early morning to evening was devoted to the preparation, working and final grooming of their animals. The system meant that the horsemen had to be permanent servants, boarded within the farm steading or in a cottage adjacent or close to the stables of their horses. The part-time labours of the cottars were now redundant. It also became possible to tailor labour requirements to the numbers actually required for specific farm tasks. Since farmers who hired servants had fixed, certain, and clear wage and housing obligations to their workforce for periods of either one year or six months, they began to tailor their needs exactly to the labour required for the proper running of the farm. In addition, there was an urge to ensure that the work team was organized in such a way that it was fully employed when at work.

There were, therefore, clear incentives to evict cottars. Yet there was one important constraint on such action. Cottar families had been the main source of seasonal labour, especially at the key times of grain harvesting, gathering and processing. Harvest labour had not only to be available, but vitally it also had to be reliable at the most crucial time of the agricultural year. To risk eliminating a traditional source of harvest workers without secure alternatives was to court disaster. This was especially so in those counties outside the south-east region and parts of Fife, where farmers were increasingly dependent on unmarried servants. In western and central districts, single servants were in the majority. There were few families to lend a hand at busy times. Not surprisingly, it was principally from these areas that the complaints came that the attack on the cottar structure was causing difficulties of labour supply. Eviction of the cottars therefore depended on finding a secure alternative source of seasonal labour.

There were three possibilities. First, in the 1780s and 1790s, seasonal migration by young men and women from the southern and eastern Highlands had already become established on a considerable scale. Second, migrants from Ireland were also recruited in large numbers during the grain harvest season throughout the counties of the south-west and western Borders. Third, and crucially, the dissolution of the cottouns was paralleled by a growth in rural settlements and villages, a subject which will be treated in more detail later in this chapter. This small-scale urbanism was primarily, though not solely, driven by the spread of the textile industry in many Lowland counties in the later eighteenth century and the concentration of services and trades ancillary to agriculture. Increasingly, therefore, the gap left by the cottars in the supply of seasonal labour was filled by the dependants of weavers, miners, iron-workers, day labourers and tradesmen hired from neighbouring rural villages and small towns. The clearance of the cottars could therefore progress with little economic impediment or disadvantage.

2

A major question is what became of them and their families after they lost their smallholdings. The numbers displaced must have been considerable and for that reason there was considerable contemporary interest in their fate. John Naismith, the agricultural reporter for Lanarkshire, noted how in that county in the 1790s the cottars had mainly gone and been replaced by unmarried servants boarded in the houses of the farmers. But, while the cottars had vanished from the steadings, he also went on to describe the presence of 'a new set of cottages':

> The county . . . is supplied with a new set of cottages. Several landholders partly perhaps to prevent the depopulation of the country, and partly for their own emolument, have let out, either in feu or long leases, spots of ground, for houses and little gardens, generally upon the sides of the public roads. Upon these, many little handsome cabins have been erected, which accompanied with neatly dressed gardens, supplied with pot-herbs, and frequently ornamented with a few flours [sic], have a very pleasant effect. These are mostly clustered into villages, some of which are pretty and populous.[13]

Crucially, therefore, Naismith seems to be reporting not the dispersal of the cottars but rather their relocation. An almost identical development was described in one district of Fife at the same time. There, in the parish of Ferry, a parallel was drawn between the decline of population in the rural districts and an increase in numbers in the local village. Farmers were 'Not inclining to keep such large cottaries [*sic*] as formerly', so several cottar families therefore moved into Ferry village, 'where they hire small houses and support themselves by their industry, either as tradesmen or day labourers'.[14] The parish minister of Sorn in Ayrshire noted a similar connection between clearance of cottars in the country districts and village growth. He commented on the settlement of Dalgain, which lay beside the water cotton-spinning complex of Catrine and had been founded in 1781 by a Dr Stevenson from Glasgow. He feued out small lots of land and by 1797 the population of the settlement had risen to more than fifty families. Significantly, the minister added that the majority of these 'formerly lived in cothouses, which are now in ruins. Most of these families are provided with gardens of various dimensions behind their houses.'[15]

These observations, describing contraction in the country population and associated increases in village and town numbers in the neighbourhood, were repeated in several other areas. In Stonehouse in Lanarkshire, the 'country' population in 1696 was 600, the 'village' total 272. By 1792, a mere 467 resided in the rural area and 593 in the village. Similarly, in Dalmellington in Ayrshire, total parish numbers declined from 739 in 1755 to 681 in 1792. However, the general trend concealed dramatic changes within the local demographic structure. It was observed that in the country area population had 'considerably diminished' due to cottar removal but had risen 'in proportion' in the village of Dalmellington, which by 1792 contained over 500 inhabitants, or almost three quarters of the total parish population at that date. In Dalry numbers in the parish had increased by around one third from Webster's census in 1755 to 2,000 in 1792. But the country part had fallen while the population of the village had almost doubled to 814, or 41 per cent of the total. It would appear therefore that the key to an understanding of what happened to the cottars after their displacement lies in village and small-town expansion in rural areas which was taking place at the same time.

Historians have long been aware of the proliferation of planned villages in this period. But perhaps insufficient attention has been paid to the function of these settlements and others in suppressing potential social discontent which might have arisen from cottar removal and also in maintaining the labour supply vital to the completion of the improvement process. Partly this may be because the sheer scale of small-settlement development in this period might not have been wholly appreciated. The 'planned' villages were significant but they seem to have been only a part and, in some areas, only a fairly minor proportion of settlement building and extension. The rise in the population of rural small towns and existing villages was also significant. The numbers gathering in unplanned settlements, several of them no bigger than clusters of a few dozen houses, also need to be noted. For instance, one published list of planned villages describes only seven being founded in a sample of four Lowland counties between c.1760 and c.1800. When the analysis is extended to include all references to villages, both planned and unplanned, in these counties, the pattern changes. By that measure, 48 per cent of parishes in Fife, 83 per cent in Ayrshire, 35 per cent in Angus and 44 per cent in Lanarkshire contained settlements of that kind.

A substantial population increase in some of the individual settlements should also be noted. The village of Larkhall in Lanarkshire rose in numbers by 44 per cent between 1755 and 1792. In the parish of Glassford in the same county, population was rapidly concentrating in 'three small but thriving villages'.[16] One of them had 14 houses and 83 inhabitants in 1771. By 1791 the number of houses had risen to 44 and the population to 196. Small hamlets were growing throughout the county. Six existed in the parish of Cambuslang and were in flourishing condition in the 1790s. It was also common to find houses being built along main roads and at important junctions. The expansion of industrial and mining towns set in rural settings was especially fast. Airdrie increased its population sixfold in the second half of the eighteenth century. In Fife the town of Dysart and associated villages rose in numbers to 2,699 in 1792, a 62 per cent increase from the 1750s. The pattern was repeated in the south-west Lowlands. Girvan in Ayrshire had no more than a couple of dozen houses and 100 people in the 1750s. By the 1790s this figure had swollen to over 1,000 inhabitants. The parish minister was convinced that the town's growth was in large part linked to 'the almost total exclusion of cottagers from the farms'.

The above is not intended to be an exhaustive account of settlement development. Nevertheless, the evidence seems conclusive: cottar eviction was paralleled by a striking expansion and foundation of villages. This seems to suggest that many displaced cottars must have managed to find alternative jobs and homes within the modernizing rural Lowlands. Chapter 3 showed that cottar families endured a hard life of deep poverty and heavy toil in the traditional townships. Hence, while many may have abandoned their few acres because they had little choice but to do so, others might well have been positively attracted by the thought of better prospects and higher earnings in these new villages which were spreading across the countryside.

The major determinant of village development was the enhanced labour needs of the agrarian and industrial economies of the rural districts. But an additional factor was landlord strategy. The proprietors of many estates showed a keen interest in the foundation or extension of these settlements. There was an awareness that laying down farmland in smallholdings close to a town or village could be highly profitable. It might attract artisans and 'manufacturers' who could pay high rentals and also extend local markets for agricultural produce. In addition, there was a general concern among many magnates about depopulation and losses of human capital. Villages were able to take in some of those displaced by improvement, and so helped to maintain social stability and, by attracting industry, absorbed the dispossessed as an economically valuable population.

At the same time, however, the village system was fundamental to the progress of improvement itself. It was recognized that the new agriculture needed other workers as well as those who actually cultivated the land. The building of enclosures, digging numerous ditches, the taking in of waste, construction and extension of roads, bridges, farmhouses and mansions for the gentry were all going on apace in late-eighteenth-century Scotland. Tables 9–11 below give an idea of the range of works in progress. The labour needed to undertake them was considerable. On the Hamilton estate in May 1772, the 'putting out' of enclosure on the 131-acre farm of Over Abbington needed twenty-seven labourers, or an average of nearly five workers per acre. Gangs of contracted labourers had to be brought in to build the enclosures. On the estate of Lord Dumfries in the Borders, for example, one Robert Patrick, 'dyker', was employed with sixty men and twenty-four horses, constructing dykes and planting hedges. His services and those of his men were available for hire to other proprietors in the district.

It is against this background that the growth of small settlements, linked to the labour requirements of the new farms, can best be understood. Small lots with a house and garden were divided up within the villages to accommodate casual labourers and their families. They paid rents for the plots and sold their labour by the day to farmers in the neighbourhood. They could be hired and laid off when necessary. This new class was an adjunct to the improvement process, a reserve army of labour which no longer had traditional rights to land of the kind possessed by the cottars, but were still available for hire on a casual basis. Waged connections had replaced customary relationships.

Table 9 Intended improvements on the estate of
the Earl of Eglinton in Ayrshire, 1771

–	to repair Mansion House and Castle and improve gardens etc.
–	to compleate enclosure and subdivide Over, Mid and Laigh Moncurs, Chapple, Weirstoun, Ladyhall, Milnburn, Banrsleys and Auchinwinsey [Kilwinning] 'with ditches and Clapt Earth Quickset Hedges'.
(iii)	Same to Meikle and Little Stones, Stonemoor and Stone Castle, Bowhouse and Lawthorn [Stone Barony].
(iv)	New steading on Stonecastle and Little Stone 'which are quite fallen to ruin with lying waste several years'.
(v)	To enclose a subdivide in Ardrossan barony 'partly with snap stone dykes and partly with ditches and Clap quickset dykes'. Blackstone (stone dyke), Holmbyres, Towerleanhead, Yonderhouses, Gaithill (?), Burnhouse and Ittington (all with ditch and hedge). Meikle Busbie, Little Busbie (stone snap dykes), Ardrossan miln and Chappelhill (stone and ditches). Also to enclose and subdivide Sorbie, Darleith, Coalhill Mains and Stanley Burn with ditches and quickset dykes.

(vi)   Steading of houses on Knockvivoch, Coalhill and Chappelhill, north end of Little Busbie – 'all of which farm houses are gone to ruin' and little steading in Saltcoats lands.

(vii)   In Roberton to enclose and subdivide properly with ditches and quickset dykes: Milntoun, Milnlands, Mnurehouse, Gatehead, East and West Murelands, Corsehouse, Annanhill and Knockentikes. To complete enclosures already begun and to subdivide Windyedge, Thornhill, Greenhills and Fordalhills (with ditches and quickset dykes).

(viii)   In Dreghorn to enclose and subdivide with ditches and quickset dykes in the 2 Towend farms possessed by Jas. Orr and Hugh Galt and lands possessed about Kirktoun by Robt. Wilson, Jas. Cockburn, Jas. Mure, Hugh Bankhead, Andrew Fulton, David Dale and Hugh Dunlop and John Barnet. Also lands of Corsehill and Lowhill possessed by Gavin Ralston, Poundstone by Jas. Auld and Kirklands by Jas. Boyd.

(ix)   To build steading of houses on lands of Jas. Auld, Hugh Dunlop, And. Fulton (about 60 acres) 'whereon no house ever was'.

(x)   Also steading of houses on Corselees, Sclates, Cleugh 'which were let down and gone to ruin the last nineteen years'.

(xi)   In Eastwood to complete the enclosure and subdivision on Giffnook, Hillhead, Henry's Croft (all with hedges and ditches) and to complete manor house in Eaglesham.

(xii)   A steading of houses on High Craigs, Temples, Stonebyres, Stepends, Walkers. And to enclose and subdivide these farms partly with stone dykes and partly with ditches and hedges.

(xiii)   In Eaglesham to complete the enclosure and subdivision of Threepland, Nethercraigs, Polnoon, Mains, Kirklands, Hole, and the sundry inclosures marked out and begun about the Kirktoun of Eaglesham and also the farms of Brackenrigg, Borlands, Windhill, Rossmiln, Floors, Boggside, Tofts, Corselees, Picketlaw, Hills, Upper and Nether Braidflat, Over and Nether Kirkland Moore, Kirktoun Moors, Bonnytoun, Blackhouse, North Moorhouse, Langlee.

Source: NRS Sheriff Court Records (Ayr), SC6/72/1, Register of Improvement on Entailed Estates.

Table 10 References to improvements on Richard A. Oswald's possessions in Ayrshire, 1803

Total expenditure: 14 May–31 Dec. 1803 - £2,624.12.8d

Places where some improvements took place	Work undertaken	Approximate number of mentions
Auchencruive	Draining (lawn)	2
Craighall	Repairing coachhouse	2
Gibsyears	Repairing stables	2
Brocklehill Meadow	Altering dining-room	1
Mount Hamilton	Repairing cattle sheds	4
Little Ladykirk	Dyking	14
Ladykirk	Roofing	7
Barclaugh	Cutting & cleaning drains	5
Barquhay	Bridge work	3
Mainholm	Barn repair	2
Newdykes	Plastering	4
Raith	Sundry repairs	3
Orangefield	Building walls	6
Kerse	Carthouse work	5
Kersmine?	Hedging & ditching	8
Loanhouse	Roads – making & repairing	4
Mount Oliphant	Masonwork	12
	Poultry house building	1
	Pigsty building	1
	Wrightwork	5
	Repairing houses	5
	Paving	1

Source: NRS Sheriff Court Records, SC6/71/1, Register of Improvement on Entailed Estates (Ayrshire), 1771–1804.

In the old social order, many cottars were also tradesmen. Improved agriculture had, if anything, even greater need for wrights, masons and ditchers than the traditional system. These craftsmen, too, increasingly congregated in villages and small rural towns, but their disappearance from the farms should not necessarily be seen as the consequence of coercion. The need for their skills was increasing to such an extent that they too could become detached from the land and pursue their trades on a full-time basis in a different setting. It was not simply farm servants who were becoming more specialized. Others, such as day labourers and tradesmen, who had been integral parts of the cottar communities, were now able to work for longer periods in the year because of agricultural transformation.

Table 11 Men employed in enclosing and planting Hamilton estates, Lanarkshire lands, March 1774

Numbers employed	Farm	Purpose (if specified)
7	Merryton	–
6	One of Merryton field farms	Belt of planting
6	Field land of Over Dalserf	–
9	Cornhills	Belt of planting and hedge round farm
4	Field land of Carscallen	–
2	On coach road	Planting sweet briars
2	On Strathaven road	Belt of planting
2	Between Larkhall and Bottoms Gate	Belt of planting
2	Round South Garten	Hedge
*9	Carscallen	Enclosing farm
*4	Darngaber	Enclosing farm
*3	Green	Enclosing farm
*6	Newhouse	Enclosing farm
62		

* = employed by tenants; others employed by the estate.

Source: HPL, 631/1, John Burrell's Journals, vol. 2, 1773–8, 17 Mar. 1774.

3

In the decades after *c.*1760 there was little evidence in Lowland Scotland of the angry peasant revolts or the great surges of collective disturbances which characterized much of French and Irish rural society at that time. The relative stability of the Lowland countryside was especially striking in light of the social dislocation and the systematic attack on customary rights and privileges documented earlier in this chapter and in those which follow. Pain and anxiety must have been inflicted, but anguish and bitterness rarely surfaced above the relative calm of rural life.

Most scholars would accept that no hidden popular uprisings on the scale of the Galloway Levellers in this later period remain to be uncovered by more research. As one historian has remarked: 'it is highly unlikely that there exists a seam of undiscovered public rural violence in eighteenth-century Scotland'.[17] At the same time, however, some writers have criticized the orthodoxy of uniform stability, asserting that public protest was pointless and would inevitably have led to swift retribution by the authorities, so other means had to be employed to defend traditional rights. These would be subtle and clandestine and include sabotage, theft, arson and pilfering.

Rural protest was indeed common in the Scottish Lowlands, but instead of attacks on landlords and farmers it was channelled into collective religious dissent. One scholar has asserted that patronage disputes, caused by opposition to the system whereby a hereditary patron had the right to 'present' (or select) the minister of a parish church, represented 'the most significant Scottish equivalent to rural protest in the rest of the British Isles'.[18] The first of these contentions can be tested against a mass of sheriff court records and estate archives. One suggestion is made that 'indirect' protest is 'harder for the historian to discern'.[19] In part this may be true. But as earlier chapters in this book have shown, factors and ground officers maintained very close surveillance on their estates and the people who lived on them. It is highly unlikely that serious or systematic destruction of property, physical assault or widespread pilfering would have gone unrecorded in their correspondence, reports, memoranda and journals. The same can be said of the records for seven sheriff courts throughout the Lowlands which have been the subject of close research for this book. These local jurisdictions dealt with petty theft, grazing disputes and right of way, mobbing, assault and enclosing disputes and breaking into private lands, as well as some more serious criminality.

A scrutiny of both sets of material provides little support for the notion that 'everyday forms of peasant resistance' were at all common. Only four cases were discovered, among the hundreds of removal actions examined, of refusal to leave land, so that 'letters of ejection' had to be issued to enforce eviction. In the court material only one instance came to light of dyke breaking. Those brought to justice were described as 'White Boys or Levellers', which had connotations both with peasant gangs in Ireland and the events in Galloway during the 1720s examined in Chapter 5. But this was no agrarian protest. Those prosecuted were all colliers from Ceres in Fife who had broken down part of an enclosure, formerly an open field, so they could walk to the village kirk. A handful of cases of pilfering of wood also came to light. One court process alleged that stealing wood was caused by new landlord controls over common lands. Thus, at the Dunblane court in 1790, seven women were charged with 'having broken down, leapt over, destroyed fences surrounding the enclosures of William Stirling of Keir, and carried away pailings [sic] of these fences'.[20] Two of the women denied the charge but admitted carrying away 'two small burdens of rotten sticks'. Another went further, questioning 'If it was or is a Crime to carry off rotten Whins or Broom from any Gentleman's ground in the neighbourhood without ever being challenged.'[21]

But, according to the records, incidents like these were uncommon. Indeed, in such a grossly unequal society, undergoing dislocating economic change, the small number of petty misdemeanours which came before the courts is remarkable. The fundamental historical significance, therefore, of this period is not the evidence, slight as it is, of scattered acts of hostility. Rather, it was the extraordinary imbalance between the unprecedented transformation of rural society in the Lowlands on the one hand and the virtual absence of any overt popular opposition to it on the other. Even if future research discovers more incidents of routine resentment, the meaningful question will still remain, not why there were some incidents, but, on the contrary, why there were so few.[22]

It has been acknowledged earlier in the book that disturbances caused by disputed elections to church offices were common in the Lowlands. One argument is that they reflected not only strong feelings on ecclesiastical governance but also opposition to agrarian improvement. Yet whether that was indeed the case is debatable. The contention places two social trends, agrarian improvement and religious dissent, together and assumes rather than demonstrates a causal link between them. Religious protest encompassed all types of community and took place in virtually every district of Scotland. It cannot be associated solely or mainly with those rural parishes of the Lowlands where cottar removal and tenant reduction occurred.

Equally, the implicit assumption that those who protested over patronage were driven by economic stress and class bitterness hardly convinces. The growth of religious dissent in the eighteenth century was a European phenomenon which took place across a great range of economic and social contexts. By 1826 around one third of Lowland Scots belonged to Presbyterian dissenting congregations and by 1850 nearly 60 per cent of Protestant worshippers no longer belonged to the established church, in large part because of the emergence of the Free Church of Scotland in 1843 and increases in Irish Catholic immigration. At the same date, 47 per cent of English churchgoers were also to be found in Nonconformist congregations. The fracturing of the national churches was based ultimately on changing popular beliefs, the growing appeal of evangelical religion and a broader transformation of British society. It did not reflect developments peculiar to the rural Lowlands of Scotland.

The limited available evidence of the social composition of the dissenting congregations also suggests that a crude class-based analysis of religious dissent and opposition is difficult to accept. Thus in West Calder in West Lothian, one third of the population were Presbyterian dissenters. But they included four landowners, 40 per cent of the tenant farmers and 21 per cent of cottars and day labourers. At Strathaven Burgher church, between 1767 and 1789, 58 per cent of the members' names on the baptismal role were those of tenants. The sketchy evidence for other areas suggests similar patterns. Dissent drew heavily on the middle ranks of rural society and even a few landowners. It was not a movement exclusively of the poor and dispossessed.

The curious silence of the rural population does not necessarily mean the absence of pain, anxiety, insecurity or misery. But the public tranquillity of the time does demand some explanation. After all, rural society was not naturally peaceful. Food rioting broke out in many parts of the country in 1709–10, 1720, 1740, 1756–7, 1763, 1767, 1771–4, 1778, 1783 and 1794–6. On occasion these eruptions could pose a strong challenge to local forces of law and order. Attacks on custom officials by mob violence were commonplace. The scale and extent of patronage disputes and religious dissent, already discussed, are also revealing. They all show that the Scottish people were not instinctively deferential or submissive to established authority. The fragmentation of Lowland Presbyterianism suggests rather a society with a robust independence of mind and spirit derived from the Calvinist inheritance of the 'equality of souls' before God. It was a tradition which helps to explain the social and political radicalism of Scottish Presbyterians in Ulster, most of whom were the descendants of small tenants, cottars and servants who had migrated across the Irish Sea from the western Lowlands in the seventeenth century. The Scottish Militia Riots of 1797 which engulfed several Lowland rural communities were an angry response to the legislation which brought in a form of conscription by ballot for the Scottish militia. For a time also, in the early 1790s, the reform societies incorporated as the Friends of the People briefly threatened the hegemony of the landed political establishment. These illustrations of popular discontent confirm that the people of the Lowlands were not naturally apathetic when customary rights were challenged. It seems likely, therefore, that social stability would indeed have been gravely threatened if the removal of people from the land had caused widespread hardship and destroyed traditional status as in parts of the Highlands. There was indeed a precedent for such disturbance in the Levellers' Revolt in Galloway described earlier in the book. That the countryside remained quiet in the later decades of dispossession might be explained by the nature of the cottar function, the relocation of cottar families in the expanding villages, small country towns and other settlements, and the buoyant labour market of the rural Lowlands at the height of the removals.

By the later eighteenth century cottars can be described more as proletarians than peasants whose links with land had become very tenuous. They did possess small patches but had to provide labour on neighbouring larger holdings to secure a living. Both pronouncements by Justices of the Peace and sheriff court records suggest that, in law, servants and cottars were defined collectively as dependent labourers and not independent possessors of land. Some information extracted from the records of Cupar sheriff court in Fife confirms the point. Normally the cottars are a shadowy and elusive group in the historical documentation. But depositions given in a legal case of 1758 cast light on some aspects of their way of life. This evidence is presented below. The short biographies in Table 12 illustrate how cottars had both servant and labouring experience, that their families included both cottar and labouring children, and that there was considerable lateral and vertical mobility among them. On the face of it, the distinction between them and the servant class seems very blurred.

Moreover, dissolution of the cottar system coincided with rising employment opportunities as a result of agrarian improvement and the first phase of industrialization. Inevitably there were years of crisis in each of the last three decades of the eighteenth century, notably in 1772–4, 1782–4 and 1795–6. But in most years the rural labour market in the later eighteenth century remained buoyant for both farm and industrial workers. Parish ministers commented on the fact that there were usually jobs in most districts for those who wanted them. Crucial to the future employment of the cottars was the dynamic development of the linen and cotton manufactures. Many cottar families had textile skills and were likely to take advantage of the new opportunities. An examination of the social structure of six rapidly expanding small towns spread across the countryside of Cambuslang, Carstairs, Larkhall, Balmerino, Galston and Kirriemuir confirms the overwhelming importance of textile spinning and weaving in the household, not only for adult males but also for women and girls. Previous discussion has not only stressed that textile industrialization was in many ways a rural phenomenon but that employment in

Table 12 Life histories of six cottars, Monthrive, Fife, 1758

Henry Reickie: 'in Pratis'; married; 52 years = born 1706
History: herded for 1 summer in Monthrive 38 years ago (c.1720) and was
a cottar and had beasts pasturing there 3 years sometime after his herding
and had lived in Pratis (which adjoins Monthrive) ever since.

William Morgan: 'In Pratis Cottoun'; married; 55 years = born 1703
History: Born and raised in Monthrive, his father being a cottar there.
Herded therein 1715 then sent to Nether Pratis and other places, returning
in 1721 to herd for one year at Monthrive. Then 2 years in Baliarmo.
Then a fewar [tenant of a feu] in different places till 10 years ago when he
returned to Nether Pratis, has been a workman at Balbirny's Cuarry at
Clutty Den, for last 7 years.

David Dowie: 'in Lethem Cottoun'; married; 44 years = born 1714
History: Born and raised in Monthrive; 1722–5 herded his father's beasts;
lived at Monthrive till 1727 when he went to Over Pratis for 2½ years;
then returned to live with his father for 5 years who was a cottar at
Monthrive; has been at Lethem ever since.

William Lindsay: 'in Skelpie Cottoun'; married; 36 years old, thus born
in 1722
History: 1739–51 – herd and servant in 'The Room of Monthrive'.

Thomas Honeyman: 'Cottar in Carskerdo'; married; 56 years – born 1702.
History: 1715–16 – herd in West Quarter of Monthrive; 1726–32 – servant
in ditto.

Thomas Braid: 'Cottar in Muirhead'; married; 56 years = born 1692
History: c.1713–14 – Herd in Muirhead; c.1714–15 – 'in the Keam in the
neighbourhood . . .'; c.1715–20 – servant in Monthrive; then ½ year in
Cairny as servant; following all as servant: 2½ years Clatto; 2½ years
Greenside; ½ year Waltoun; 6 years Cassindilly; 5 years Muirhead;
6 years Tarritmiln; 11 years Scotstarvit; since then in Muirhead.

Source: NRS, Sheriff Court Records (Cupar), SC20/5/12.

country districts rose as the economic transformation gathered pace. The removal of cottar families was, with clearances in the pastoral districts of the Borders and Lowland hill country, the closest numerical parallel with the level of displacement which took place in the Highlands and Islands. But the cottars were fortunate that eviction did not necessarily mean destitution because of the opportunities which prevailed in the Lowland labour market until the end of the Napoleonic Wars.

9

The Lowlands after Dispossession

The dispossession of people in the Highlands has always had a high historical profile. In the Lowlands it is low to the point of virtual non-existence. It is ironic, therefore, that landlessness in relation to overall population of each region was considerably greater among the people of the Lowland countryside at the end of clearance than in the western Highlands and Islands. As the next chapter will show, the number of those with some stake in land, however tiny, as crofters and cottars, continued to grow in the north-west region throughout the entire cycle of mass clearance until the evictions mainly came to an end in the years after the potato famine of the later 1840s. The numerical and political significance of the crofters became clear in the 1880s when government set up a Royal Commission to investigate their conditions and then passed legislation in 1886 to protect their interests. Long before that time, however, the vast majority of rural Lowlanders were already bereft of land. Only in one region did the age-old connections survive. In the north-eastern counties of Aberdeen, Banff and Kincardine, as has been seen, landlords divided wastes, moors and hillsides above the line of cultivation into small crofts at no rental until economic returns were achieved. The lives of these crofting families was one of unremitting drudgery and hard toil for meagre returns. Some of them might well have been tenants and cottars who had lost land when dispossession gathered pace. It was said of some parishes in upper Banffshire, for example, that at first the new colonies of crofters were 'mere specs of cultivated land in the midst of the great waste'. Eventually, however, whole areas came under regular cultivation without, so it was said, 'costing the proprietor a penny'.[1]

In Aberdeenshire, by the 1880s, 43 per cent of holdings were at or under 100 acres; in Banff the figure was 49 per cent and in Moray and Nairn 40 per cent. Elsewhere in most of the south, especially across the eastern plain, the big farms reigned supreme. Only 4 per cent of holdings in Berwick, 5 per cent in East Lothian and 12 per cent in Fife and Kinross were less than 100 acres. The old world of subsistence husbandmen, multi-tenants and cottars had passed away into history in these districts to be replaced by enlarged compact farms, where full-time waged servants and labourers lived and worked. Landless tradesmen, formerly living in the *fermetouns*, with a few rigs of land, were now gathered in rural villages and country towns. Everywhere single blocks of land of varying size had taken the place of the traditional township clusters. These improved holdings were under the authority of one master with his family house, out-buildings for tools and storage, together with living space of different kinds for his workers, all within the same steading.

I

However, it would be wrong to conclude that these far-reaching changes atomized rural society and left it arid and devoid of human colour. The age-old institutions of kirk and school maintained their social centrality and connection with the past, as did the inns and howffs where the menfolk from different farms would gather for evenings of conviviality. As Robert Burns memorably recorded of one watering hole in Ayrshire in the late eighteenth century:

> While we sit boozing at the nappy,
> And getting fou and unco happy,
> We think na on the lang Scots miles,
> The mosses, waters, slaps and styles,
> That lie between us and our hame,
> Where sits our sulky sullen dame,
> Gathering her brows like gathering storm,
>   Nursing her wrath to keep it warm.

[*nappy* – strong ale; *fou* – drunk; *unco* – very; *mosses* – marshes; *slaps* – steps; *dame* – wife]

Robert Burns, *Tam O'Shanter*, published 1791.

Also, the larger farm steadings were communities of families, ploughmen, labourers, foremen and single women, working both in the house and in the fields, which replicated something of the life of the *fermetouns*, though the people who laboured in them were now engaged as hired employees rather than landholding cottars or small independent husbandmen. Lewis Grassic Gibbon's *A Scots Quair* (1932–4), his great trilogy of rural life set in the north-east Lowlands before and after the Great War, describes a society where neighbourliness remained very much part of the weft and woof of the countryside. Weddings, christenings and funerals were all collective events which drew in many people from far and wide. Neighbouring tenants and crofters supported one another when some were stricken by the misfortunes of bereavement, disability or financial loss. As the sons and daughters of the large families of the small tenants grew to adulthood they would take service as ploughmen and maid servants in other districts, so extending family networks far and wide. Gossip, good or bad, and plenty of it, was a popular source of news and rumour which helped bond the people together as well as sometimes fracturing relationships if the reputation of a family was shamed in the telling. In the long winter evenings in the kitchen or the bothy after a day's work, there were stories and jokes to be told, singing to be enjoyed, making music with fiddle, bagpipe or melodeon, playing games and cards and 'speeran guesses' (posing riddles). Books were generally too expensive for the farm servant community until the later nineteenth century. But broadsheets and chapbooks were widely read, as was the remarkably popular *People's Journal*, the biggest-selling periodical in Scotland among the working classes both in country and town for most of the nineteenth century.

The new rural world also had a rich popular culture. Many of the rituals and festivities of days gone by survived but also meshed with others which emerged in response to the different patterns of living and work after improvement. By the early nineteenth century, the twice-yearly hiring fairs were firmly established in the small towns and villages of the countryside. Apart from the serious business of gaining a fee for the next term, the fairs were great social occasions, a time to renew acquaintance with old friends from isolated farm steadings, enjoy the *craic* (good banter and chat), partake of a drink or two, and perhaps meet a new lad or lass. The ending of one year and the beginning of the next on 31 December and 1 January was a special time in rural and urban Scotland since it combined an inebriated wake for what had gone before with hopeful celebration of what was yet to come. Thanksgiving Sunday for a successful harvest, or *hairst*, usually took place in October and was also an important date in the farming calendar. Another event of great antiquity was the harvest home, or *kirn*, when the fields had all been shorn and grain stored for the year. The centrepiece of the *kirn* supper was the preparation of a distinctive concoction known as meal-and-ale. One recipe advised: 'A bottle of stout, half a bottle of whisky and two bottles of brisk ale were poured into a large milk plate, and a bowlful of sugar stirred into it. The oatmeal was strown into the mess gently, till it was of the consistency of not too thin porridge'.[2] Beef, fowl and plum-duff often followed until the tables were redded (cleared) and the dancing started, usually lasting into the wee small hours: 'with many folk far from sober, and some of them under the table. Neighbours were invited, of course, and every farm had its meal-and-ale in turn. Once upon a day you could be worn out by the time they were all of them put past.'[3]

The daily lives of the farm servants, whether at work or leisure, took place under the watchful eye of the farmer or of his grieve (foreman), the so-called 'iron men' of the new agriculture. The working day for the horsemen began at 5 a.m. and, with hurried meal breaks, lasted until 6 p.m., or until darkness fell. In the larger farms the labour force resembled military regiments with their hierarchies, rules, predictable monotonies, set working hours and barrack-like living quarters: 'there was a tyranny about the great touns; their men were as firmly shackled by the cry of a hungry beast or a week of fine weather as any modern factory hand to the punch-clock at the plant gate'.[4] It was said that the unrelenting manual work in all weathers bred men who were hard and dour.

The daily cycle of their labours was well captured in one of the most famous 'bothy ballads' of the time, 'Drumdelgie':

> Oh ken ye o' Drumdelgie toon
> Where a' the crack lads go?
> Sra'bogie braw in a' her bouns
> A bigger canna show
>
> At five o'clock we quickly rise
> And hurry doon the stair
> It's there to dorn oor horses,
> Likewise to straik their hair
>
> Syne, after workin' half an hour,
> To the kitchen each one goes;
> It's there to get oor breakfast
> Which is generally brose
>
> We've scarcely got our brose well supt
> And g'en oor pints a tie
> When the foreman cries, 'Hullo, my lads
> The hour is drawin' nigh.'
>
> At sax o'clock the mull's put on,
> To gie us a strait wark;
> It tak's four o' us to mak' to her,
> Till we could wring oor sark
>
> And when the water is put aff,
> We hurry doon the stair,
> To get some quarters through the fan,
> Till daylicht does appear
>
> When daylicht it begins to peep,
> and the sky begins to clear,
> The foreman he cries oot, 'My lads,
> Ye'll stay nae langer here!
>
> There's sax o' you'll gae to the ploo,
> And twa can ca' the neeps;

And the owsen they'll be aifter you,
Wi strae raips roon their queets.'

But when that we gyaun furth
And turnin' oot tae yoke,
The snaw dang on sae thick and fast
That we were like to choke

The frost had been so very hard,
The ploo she widna go;
And sae oor cairtin' days commenced
Among the frost and snaw.

Oor horses being but young and sma,
The shafts they didna fill,
And often needed the saiddler lad
To help them up the hill
But we will sing oor horses' praise,
Though they be young and sma';
For they outshine the neiper anes
That tip the road sae braw

Sae fare ye weel, Drumdelgie,
For I maun gang awa';
Sae fare ye weel, Drumdelgie,
Your weety weather an a'.

Fare ye weel, Drumdelgie,
I bid ye a' adieu;
I leave ye as I got ye –
A maist unceevil crew.

[*ken* – know; *toun* – farm steading; *braw* – fine; *boun* – bounds;
corn – feed oats; *straik* – stroke; *brose* – oatmeal and water dish;
pints – laces; *mull* – threshing or meal mill; *wark* – work;
sark – shirt; *oot* – out; *ploo* – plough; *sax* – six; *ca'* – carry;
neeps – turnips; *owsen* – oxen; *raips* – ropes; *queets* – ankles;
cairtin' – carting; *saidler lad* – lad with a whip; *neiper* –
neighbouring farm; *maun* – must; *gang awa* – go away;
unceevil – uncivil; *weety* – wet; *crew* – work force of a farm]

The ballad vividly brings out the continuous round of hard toil from before dawn until dusk. Dressing and then eating a meagre breakfast was done in a hurry ('pints', or boot laces, not even being tied in the rush) under the watchful eye of the foreman. Even before dawn broke, the hour when labour in the fields usually started, there was still strenuous work to be done beforehand manning the barn-mill. The frost was so deep that the ploughs could not turn the earth but there were plenty of other outdoor tasks to be carried out while the snow storm lasted. It is hardly surprising given the unrelenting daily round that the ballad ends on a sour note which is very typical of the genre. Only the bond between the ploughman and his pair of 'young and sma'' horses gives more of a glimmer of pleasure and contentment among the daily grind. The horses were fed and groomed before the ploughman had his own breakfast and though they might need the whip to climb the hill, he still proudly sings their praises as a better pair than any in the neighbouring farm.

Cottar families, the dominant social formation in the countryside before c.1750, had been entirely stripped out of the system by the early nineteenth century. Wage-earning married servants, hired for a year, and single male and female servants contracted for six months, now comprised the vast majority of the farm labour force. There had always been some landless servants in the *fermetouns* but their numbers now swelled into a great rural army which outnumbered all other workers. In the rich arable lands of the south-east region they were married men for the most part who lived with their families in small cottages within the farm steadings. The same class could also be found in other districts, but in most parts married horsemen were vastly outnumbered by the young bachelors who had come to their first jobs on the farms in their early teens. As men of skill and reputation, the ploughmen, fully trained after two years of apprenticeship, would doubtless have had a greater sense of pride in their work and status than Highland crofters scratching a living from poor land or toiling in the gathering and burning of seaware to make kelp in the islands and coasts of the north-west region. The ballads sing of their skills and reputation, as in 'The Praise of Ploughmen':

> Ye lads and lasses a' draw near,
> I'm sure it will delight your ear

And as for me I'll no be sweir
Tae sing the praise o' ploughmen
The very King that wears the crown
The brethren of the sacred gown,
The Dukes and Lords of high renown,
Depend upon the ploughman.

The gardener he cries out wi' speed
I'm sure I was the first man made,
And I was learned the gardener trade
Before there was a ploughman.

Oh gardener, lad, it's true you say;
But how long gardener did you stay?
I'm sure it was just scarce a day
Ere y became a ploughman.

The standing of the horsemen in rural communities was burnished at the ploughing matches which became popular in the localities after improvement. Judges 'would be looking for furrows as neat and as regularly set together as the pages of a book' if they were to award a prize.[5] A champion ploughman was a figure of high repute in his local area who could earn more than his fellows and be offered a higher fee at the next hiring fair. A ploughman also had a strong sense of craft pride, which was fortified and protected by initiation as a brother of the Horseman's Word, a fraternal secret society based on Masonic ritual open only to those who worked with horses on the farm. The society originated in north-east Scotland, then spread throughout the Lowlands and eventually into England. At the conclusion of the ceremony of initiation, which took place at dead of night, the novice was given a secret word which, it was said, when merely whispered to a horse would make the animal compliant. Rumour also had it that the word was likely to have the same effect on young women. The penalties for those who revealed the secret to anyone outside the society were self-inflicted and awesome. The initiate promised:

So help me Lord to keep my secrets and perform my duties as a horseman. If I break any of them – even the last of them – I wish no less than to be done to me than my heart be torn from my breast by two wild horses, and my body quartered in four and swung on chains, and the wild birds of the air left to pick my bones, and these then taken down and buried in the sands of the sea, where the tide ebbs and flows twice every twenty four hours to show I am a deceiver of their faith. Amen.[6]

The horsemen might have seen themselves as the princes of the farm, but they could not function without the support of many other hands. Of crucial importance were women workers. By 1871 over a quarter of all permanent farm servants in Scotland were women, and they also formed the majority of the seasonal labour force at the busy times. The reliance on female labour was distinctively Scottish as nothing like the same dependency existed in the southern and Mid-land counties of England. By custom females were paid half the male wage. They carried out all the work of the farm except those which directly involved the management of horses: sowing, reaping, weed-ing, hoeing, singling and pulling turnips, gathering in the potato crop and spreading manure. Women had also a monopoly of milking and cheese making. Small family-run farms in the south-west region esp-ecially depended on the labour of wives and daughters. The lives of these women were likened by some observers to those of black slaves, so all-consuming were the hours of work and so tiny the pittance paid by fathers to unmarried daughters under the 'tyranny of family labour'. It was said that women were such a significant part of the workforce because the heavy industries in Scotland of iron, steel, engineering and shipbuilding drew off so many men from the country-side to better-paid jobs in the towns and cities.

The 'orra man', or 'other man', was a master of all trades. He could plough, manage cattle and put his hand to the repair of the farm tools. During the busy season of grain and potato harvests, all the permanent servants were joined by day labourers from the villages, together with Irish and Highland migrants who came annually from much further afield. Then there were the shepherds, the 'lonely men of the glens and the hills'. They were highly paid, their status and wages equalling those of the farm grieves, but they lived a life of lonely isolation for most of the year, and, if single, usually had only their faithful collies for com-pany or perhaps from time to time a boy apprentice. The job was monotonous outside the busy times of lambing, dipping, shearing and the arduous task of smearing the sheep to protect them from parasites. But during harsh Scottish winters shepherding could become a dangerous occupation, when the men risked their own lives for the safety of their flocks. It was reported that on one fateful Sunday in the town of Moffat in the Borders, twelve shepherds who had died during severe blizzards were buried in the kirkyard on the same day. Being apart from society over many years could also take its toll: 'In time he could take to drink, and his teeth blackened by long years of tobacco usage and a reliance on primitive hygiene; in his hill bothy he made his porridge once a week in the big bothy pot and then poured it into the drawer of a chest, it was said – there to be cut in cold slices when he needed it.'[7]

The first half of the nineteenth century was lotus time for the country tradesmen who were now detached from the steadings and lived in villages or plied their crafts in the neighbourhood of the farms. There had always been trades in the old style farming like millers, weavers and smiths. But improvement revolutionized demand for skilled men. First, iron replaced wood in countless small details, such as household utensils, hinges, locks and much more. The supply of timber also became more abundant. Wood sawn in straight angles and shapes was essential for the joiners who helped construct the new steadings and farm houses. Wooden fitments transformed house interiors with a *hallan* (partition or screen) at the door to reduce drafts, box beds, benches, seats, shelves, dressers. Iron-framed ploughs also hugely increased repair and construction work for country *smiddies* (blacksmith workshops). In this period, they became akin to small social centres to which the menfolk would gravitate to gossip and hear the latest local news. The cultivation of land by the work horses was an additional boon for the smiths as iron shoes had to be replaced at regular intervals. Following in the train of improvement was also a great rebuilding of the countryside. To function to best effect the steadings on the larger farms needed adequate barns, milkhouses, grain lofts, stabling and cart sheds. These works led to an unprecedented demand for masons and joiners as well as the supplying trades of sawmilling, brick and tile making, and quarrying. Only later in the nineteenth century did the good times tail off as transport development of road and rail helped businesses in the urban areas to colonize the countryside and undercut many small rural enterprises.

2

At the end of the Napoleonic Wars, the long boom which had sustained the huge wartime profits of British agriculture came to an
abrupt end. After c.1812 there was a downward trend in grain prices,
a marked fall in the wage levels of farm labourers and a visible
increase in the numbers out of work on the land. Unemployment, initially caused by a temporary decline in the fortunes of the farming
class, was then exacerbated by the postwar demobilization of large
numbers of soldiers and sailors and a persistent natural increase in
rural population. In some parts of the British countryside the labour
markets rapidly became saturated, triggering desperate and violent
disturbances of the labouring poor. The most threatening outbreaks
were in the southern and eastern counties of England. Angry risings
by farm labourers took place in East Anglia in 1816, again in the same
region in 1822, all over the south and east of England in the famous
'Captain Swing' riots of 1830, and again, though more scattered, in
1831–4. Furthermore, these spectacular episodes were paralleled by
the more common incidence of casual violence, of stacks being fired,
of animals maimed and fences destroyed.

Protest also took place in a few parts of the Scottish Highlands, in
rural Ireland and in Wales, but not in Lowland Scotland. The tranquillity of the region was noted by contemporary observers, who drew
a contrast with overt unrest in other parts of Britain and also with the
spirit of revolt coming to the surface in some of the towns and cities of
the industrial west of Scotland which finally erupted in the 'Radical
War' of 1820. As one East Lothian farmer commented in 1812:

> during this season of scarcity and distress, when part of the labouring
> classes in other districts of the Kingdom, almost driven to desperation
> and madness by the want of employment and the high price of prov-
> isions have committed the greatest outrages against individuals and
> property, the lower orders in this district have sustained the pressures
> and hardships of the times with a degree of patience and regularity of
> conduct which entitle them to the highest confidence and respect from
> their superiors in rank and fortune.[8]

Again, during the difficult winter of 1817–18, the Justices of the Peace in the south-eastern Lowlands, after the most careful enquiry, found no evidence of any rise in social tension and agreed that there was therefore no need to appoint a single special constable. Kincardine magistrates reported somewhat smugly in 1820, the year of the disturbances by weavers and other workers in the south-west, that 'there was scarcely a murmur to be heard, and our "little community" is too much of an agricultural cast for the spirit of radicalism to take root in it'.[9] In the year 1830, William Cobbett, the English radical, came north to find out why the Scots were quiet while the English burnt the ricks. It was a good question and trying to answer it helps to bring out some of the distinctive features of rural Lowland society after the era of dispossession.

One salient contrast between the two regions was their differing systems of recruiting labour. By the end of the Napoleonic Wars, farm workers in the southern and eastern counties of England were paid and hired in a variety of ways depending on local custom and agrarian specialization. In general, however, the old system of long-hires and the tradition of boarding labourers within farms and paying them in kind had been abandoned. Instead, most workers by the early nineteenth century took their earnings on a daily or weekly basis. They had become a casualized labour force likely to be at risk from both short- and long-term unemployment. Furthermore, they were in the main hired from neighbouring local villages rather than boarded within the farm steadings. Increasingly these labourers were paid in money with only vestigial remains of traditional allowances in kind. In sum, a very significant number of farm workers in the south of England were accustomed to volatility in money wage-levels and to the direct impact of price changes on their material condition. Since they lived in villages with their fellows rather than in the farm steadings supervised by the masters they were also likely to be less amenable to the social discipline of the farming class.

In the Lowlands of Scotland the structure of labour payment and recruitment differed markedly. Payments in kind, though they varied in detail, still formed a very substantial part of the wage reward for most workers. In the south-eastern Lowlands and parts of the east-central district, as noted earlier, most permanent farm workers were married ploughmen, or *hinds*. As far as life's necessities were concerned, they were insulated from the market when fee'd. The allowances of the *hind* included stipulated measures of oats, barley and pease, the keep of a cow and ground for planting potatoes. The rental of the cottage was paid for by the labour of his wife and daughters during harvest. Fuel was carted from town at the master's expense and, by law, he was also obliged to provide for the *hind* for six weeks when he was unable to work because of ill-health. Single men and women servants, who were most common in the north-east and south-west Lowlands but were also important elsewhere, obtained board and lodging within the steading in addition to a cash wage. The system undeniably provided Scottish farm servants with an enviable security compared to their counterparts in southern England. They were guaranteed food and shelter according to familiar and acknowledged standards. But, crucially, these advantages were only provided for those who were employed.

The contract of service was also different north of the Border, with most farm workers hired for periods of a year or six months. This was caused in part by contrasts in the labour markets and agrarian structures of the two regions. Labour was in surplus by the end of the eighteenth century in southern England. The region had become an area of cereal monoculture and, as the acreage under the grain crops grew as a result of the wartime rise in prices, large fluctuations in the seasonal demand for labour developed in parallel. On the one hand, more workers than ever before were required at harvest; on the other, the widespread adoption of the threshing machine from the early nineteenth century took away a traditional winter task from men on the farm. Therefore, because of the marked differences in labour needs at different seasons, masters in the south and east had an incentive to eliminate the principle of the long-hire and instead take on men only when they needed them.

In the Scottish Lowlands, however, the tradition of long-hires was perpetuated because it fitted in so well with farmers' needs. From the late eighteenth century, agriculture came into direct competition with manufacturing and mining for labour. Industrial and agrarian change proceeded simultaneously and, more importantly, often in close geographical proximity in the Lowlands. Indeed, most spinning and weaving of textiles took place in the countryside, while before the 1830s industrial and agricultural work were rarely wholly separate activities. But ironically it was precisely at this time that improved agriculture demanded a more specialist and dedicated labour force. Yet, because of the elimination of the cottars and the counter-attraction of the towns, the farming class found it increasingly difficult to maintain the necessary pool of extra workers. These varied pressures, therefore, not only forced a marked increase in agricultural money wages but also embedded the long-hire, at least in part, as a means of securing labour.

Shortage of workers, however, could not have been the only factor, because after 1815, when they became more plentiful, there was still no incentive to move towards casualization. An additional influence, therefore, was the impact of land and climate. Few areas in Scotland had either the soil conditions or the favourable weather of the great grain-growing districts of south-east England. Apart from commercial pastoralism in the hill country, mixed agriculture, fusing both cultivation and stock breeding, was the norm throughout most of the Lowlands. The regime needed abundant acreage under turnips and artificial grasses to feed cattle and sheep, and that in turn led to an extension in the working year because of the multiple tasks of weeding, dunging, singling and, most importantly, of intensive and regular ploughing associated with this crop sequence. In essence, then, the social effects of agrarian change in a mixed-farming region were almost the reverse of those in a specialist cereal zone. Since work was spread evenly throughout the year, farmers had a vested interest in recruiting labour over long periods.

This was vital anyway because of the crucial position of the horseman in the agricultural workforce in Scotland. As already shown, the key to the Scottish farmer's policy of hiring was the need to use his work horses as economically as possible. Horses cost much in both feed and maintenance whether they were at work in the fields or unoccupied in the stables. It became essential, therefore, to spread work for the horses throughout the day and the year and to ensure they functioned as efficiently as possible when at work. Thus, each ploughman assumed responsibility for a pair and his entire routine from the early morning to evening was concerned with their preparation, working and final grooming. Experienced ploughmen had therefore to be permanent servants living in the farm steading near their horses and engaged on the long-hire. Furthermore, while giving security to the worker when in employment, these contracts also helped to reinforce the farmer's powers of labour discipline. The hired servant was entirely dependent on his master during the period of contract and it was also suggested that the very personal interaction of bargaining between each of them at the feeing (hiring) markets made for an individualized relationship which weakened collective solidarity among farm workers. Doubtless, also, the custom of boarding unmarried servants in the steading and often feeding them in the farm kitchen made it much easier for the farmer to impose surveillance on them.

Only the bothymen were said to be less amenable to social control. They slept, ate, drank and passed their time off work in the evenings in rough and spartan barracks, or bothies. They had the reputation of being more detached from their employers than other workers and, so it was said, likely to be more restless and easily discontented. For instance, while Chartism in the 1830s seems to have had little appeal for Scottish farm workers in general, it did attract some adherents from the bothy districts. Also, in the same areas attempts had been made earlier to pursue action over grievances. In 1805, for example, an organization of farm servants in the Carse of Gowrie was suppressed under the Combination Acts. In 1830 the same area was agitated again. A meeting at Inchture, near Dundee, brought together around 600 ploughmen to be addressed by trade unionists from the city. A committee was elected to extend the movement throughout Perthshire and to press demands for an 8–10 hour day and payment of overtime. But the bothy system was not common in most farming regions in the Lowlands. It was virtually unknown in the south-east, and in the north-east bothies were rare outside the old red sandstone areas of southern Kincardine and parts of the coastal plain of Moray and Nairn. In the Carse of Gowrie in Perthshire, bothies were more numerous because there was a good deal of stiff, clay land requiring large numbers of horses and ploughmen to work the land and an obvious incentive therefore to build basic accommodation for single men.

Because the ploughmen were the specialist horsemen of the new agriculture, general labourers had to be brought in for other tasks such as harvesting or to carry out draining and ditching work, which became a rural obsession from the 1840s. Superficially, they bore a resemblance to the labourers of southern England; both were hired on a short-term basis and both were paid mainly in cash. Yet their intrinsic differences were more important than their apparent similarities. Day labourers in Scotland formed only a minor part of the workforce. In the 1790s, 20 per cent of agricultural workers in Dalmeny parish, Fife, were day labourers; 10 per cent in Gask, Perthshire; 7 per cent in Oldhamstocks, Berwick; 1 per cent in Auchentoul, Fife; 5 per cent in Barmie, Elgin; 11 per cent in Edzell, Forfar. Indeed, many of them were actually the wives and children of married male servants. In the south-east, for example, the cash wages of dependants formed a useful addition to the income of households paid in kind. Scottish farmers therefore did not have to keep a large pool of underemployed labourers in the fashion of southern England in order to meet the exceptional requirements of harvest time. The Highlands and Ireland provided a large and growing reserve army of seasonal workers, and the rest could usually be hired from neighbouring villages.

3

Most farm workers were therefore largely insulated from the volatility of the labour market because of the long-hire system, and this might help to explain the stability of the rural Lowlands in this period. However, this rests on the assumption that most workers on the land continued to find jobs in these years. Measurement of employment at any time before the late nineteenth century is difficult since there is little possibility of quantifying numbers in or out of work in precise terms because of the absence of suitable data. Nevertheless, some insights from the contemporary press and in parliamentary papers can help to provide a general profile of the labour market. An invaluable source until the later 1820s is the *Farmer's Magazine*, which published very detailed quarterly reports on each agricultural region in Scotland. These not only provide full comment on prices and products, but also describe conditions of employment among various grades of farm labour.

From this evidence it would seem that after 1815 short-term unemployment was reported in 1817–18, 1821 and 1827, but little indication of the problem of structural unemployment which caused such misery in the rural areas of the south of England. Also, the severity of unemployment in these exceptional years varied both regionally and between different groups of workers. In the crisis years, in the south-east it was single servants hired on six-monthly contracts who usually went without a fee. That experience was much less common among married ploughmen, who formed a majority on most farms there. But the south-east was likely to be most vulnerable when grain prices collapsed from the wartime peaks because of its emphasis on cereal cultivation. Most other areas were in a more fortunate position. In the central district, which included the counties of Fife, Perth and Stirling, there was a more nuanced response. Few complaints were recorded that agricultural workers had much difficulty in finding jobs.

The contrast was even more striking between the pattern in the south-east and the north-eastern counties of Banff, Kincardine and Aberdeen. Here the more balanced agrarian structure and the development of land reclamation projects after 1815 ensured a greater vigour in the labour market than elsewhere. In 1816–17, for example, the north-east began to shed farm workers later than the south-east and to take on additional hands at an earlier stage, when the temporary crisis had begun to pass. Again, 1821 was a bad year in the south-east but hardly at all in Aberdeen and Banff. Throughout the period, indeed, half-yearly money wages for single male ploughmen in these latter counties were consistently 15–20 per cent higher than those offered in the Lothians and Berwickshire. Crucially, no evidence was recorded of the growth of a significant surplus of labour of the kind which caused social instability in southern England and, as will be seen in the next chapter, was also starting to emerge in the western Highlands and Islands as the bi-employments of military service, kelp burning and fishing during the Napoleonic Wars suffered protracted decline.

One of the reasons for the favourable equilibrium of jobs and labour in the rural Lowlands was the buoyancy of industry. The decline of linen spinning and stocking knitting in the countryside was compensated by a sustained expansion in linen weaving in the east-central districts. Weaving increasingly became a specialized activity, carried on mainly in rural villages rather than farm cottages, and so became a real alternative to agricultural work, since wages, although they fell after 1815, proved more resilient than in the cotton-weaving districts of the west. But probably even more important was the response of Scottish agriculture to the postwar depression in grain prices.

Lowland farming was better placed than the specialist wheat-producing regions of southern England. The range of crops grown, the significance of animal rearing and fattening, and the relative unimportance of wheat cultivation, except in the south-east, lent the agrarian system a versatility which regions of grain monoculture manifestly lacked. The grains commonly grown in the north, oats and barley, were notably less affected by the slump in prices than wheat. Between 1805 and 1812 the average annual price for wheat in the south-east zone, according to the Haddington fiars (annual grain price averages used to determine clerical stipends), was 85/- per quarter. Between 1813 and 1820 it fell by 7 per cent to 5/- per quarter. On the other hand, the decline in barley and oat prices was much less acute. Barley fell by about 9 per cent between 1813 and 1820 in relation to the average of 1805–12; oats by 1 per cent.

Scottish farmers had another basic advantage. Some of the money costs of agriculture were less onerous north of the border. There was no payment of tithes in kind: they could be valued and, when valued, did not afterwards increase. Poor Law assessments were still only a marginal and indirect burden on Scottish tenant farmers compared to southern England; landlords paid half the amount directly, and the remainder was passed on to their tenants. But as late as 1839 only 236 out of 900-odd parishes had assessments and the majority of these were to be found either in the south-east or in the growing towns and cities of the central belt. A more important cost, however, was labour, and here the continuation of payment in kind as an integral part of the total wage was again of considerable significance. When grain prices were depressed and pressures on cash resources increasing, it made economic sense to maintain in-kind rewards and so cut down on money outlays.

The resilience of the labour market, however, is still surprising. True, it was only much later in the nineteenth century that mechanical reapers and other key innovations started to replace some workers.

Nonetheless, even earlier, improved agriculture did undeniably bring savings in labour costs. Ploughing was now carried out by single men and two horses. The threshing machine and the import of coal, instead of peat dug and dried on the farm, released many from old tasks. With the removal of the cottars, farmers also secured much more control over labourers and were able to force their concentration exclusively on farm work and so boost their productivity.

But while fewer hands might be needed for some tasks, in other aspects demand for workers continued to increase because of the more intensive cultivation of potatoes and barley. For the first time, from 1821–2 a major export trade developed in potatoes from the counties of Perth, Stirling, Angus and Kinross. The real agricultural potential of the north-east as a cattle-fattening region was also unlocked from the later 1820s as a result of the growth of steamship connections with London. Previously beasts destined for the southern market had had to be sold lean and under-priced. The Lothians and Berwick, where grain farming had always been of most significance, also began to move at this time towards a more closely integrated regime of arable cultivation and stock fattening.

All those developments, to a greater or lesser extent, soon led to an increased intensity of work on a given area of land. Employment expanded in the north-east because more acres were absorbed into cultivation by the draining of stiff, clay land and the extension of turnip husbandry. The impact of this development is clearly evident in wage rates. Money wages for single male servants in Aberdeenshire had reached a wartime peak of eight guineas per half year in 1810. By 1816 this figure had been sharply reduced to just over £4. Thereafter, however, the recovery became obvious. Rates rose to £6 in 1820, steadied around that figure until 1823, reached £7 by 1825 and remained at about that level until the early 1830s.

In the south-east, agrarian adjustment resulted in heavy investment in drainage schemes and generous additions of rape and bone dust to boost turnip yields. These advances had a visible impact on the job prospects of single female servants and day labourers. Female money wages in East Lothian and Berwick showed an impressive stability in spring and summer from about 1819. Indeed, between 1819 and 1825, Whitsun wage rates for women were actually higher than those for men on three occasions. This, of course, was as much a reflection of the demand for women domestics in nearby Edinburgh as proof of the more vigorous labour market in agriculture. The same qualification could not, however, be applied to male day labourers. Between 1815 and 1817 unemployment was acute among this group as investment plans were abruptly curtailed. But in the following decade day labourers apparently only encountered similar problems in 1827.

In the same postwar decades of the 1820s and 1830s being considered here, the people of the north-west Highlands and Islands had been caught in a contracting vice of an inexorable increase in population on the one hand and the collapse of the economic activities which had sustained them for a time before 1815 on the other. The future looked increasingly desperate, since only sheep farming seemed likely to have any prospect of profit. Landowners were also starting to agonize about how they could manage to rid their estates of the growing 'surplus population' of destitute people. The contrast with the experience of the communities in the rural Lowlands had now become stark in the extreme.

4

As in the crofting districts of the Highlands, the root cause of the social crisis in southern England was the emergence of a gross imbalance between a rising population and limited employment opportunities. Indeed, fewer labourers were leaving the agricultural districts of East Anglia, Suffolk, Surrey, Sussex, Middlesex, Kent and Hampshire precisely at the time when grain farming was itself in acute difficulty after the Napoleonic Wars. There was thus increasing pressure on the regional Poor Law at a time when farmers and landlords were less able or less willing to raise their rate subsidies to provide support. Indeed, the attempts to cut the Poor Law dole was a major factor in the discontent which triggered the 'Captain Swing' riots all over the south and east of England in 1830.

The demographic experience of the Lowlands in Scotland was again different. In the later eighteenth century, migration from the rural counties, although it had already begun, was occurring at a relatively slow pace. The safety valve of migration and emigration then became of much greater consequence in the nineteenth century. Indeed, between 1801 and 1851 many parishes in the Lowlands showed a net decline in numbers as the movement from country to town began to accelerate. The vital fact was that Lowland counties were able to shed potential surplus numbers more effectively than the southern regions of England or the Highlands. For example, the way labour was housed in some Lowland regions influenced the movement of younger workers. In districts where there were few others then employing farmers and unmarried servants, ploughmen had to come from a distance at their first engagement, and when they married might have to move on again because of the scarcity of family cottages. So in Perthshire the dependence on unmarried men was great enough to cause a drain from agricultural labour at the age of marriage. In the mid-nineteenth century between a quarter and a third of the men in that county who had been servants or agricultural labourers were likely to leave for some other occupation by the time they were thirty.

The labour structure in Perthshire was, however, almost unique. Of general significance throughout the Lowlands in promoting migration was the generalized Scottish system of hiring farm servants. The long-hire did offer security of employment for a time, but when it lapsed the majority of workers, and single men especially, tended to discharge themselves and venture to the hiring fairs in search of a better master, attractive conditions and more experience. The Scottish single farm servant was therefore habitually mobile, even if his movements were usually confined to a particular neighbourhood. Furthermore, the feeing market was a uniquely effective medium for relating the number of places to the number of potential servants needed by farmers for periods of between six months and a year. Those not hired at Whitsun (May) or Martinmas (November) were confronted with the prospect of seeking work elsewhere, not having a job for six months until the next fair, or trusting to the chance of being hired as day labourers and accepting the fall in status that implied. Unlike the cottars in the western Highlands it was impossible for them to find any other place on the land, because the iron rule applied in all Lowland leases was that any farmer who dared to subdivide his tenancy would suffer immediate eviction by the authorities of the estate. Nor could the rural unemployed, unlike their counterparts in England, necessarily depend on the Poor Law, because in Scotland the rights of the able-bodied, or the unemployed, to relief were not officially recognized. Moving from the parish of origin, therefore, did not imply a loss of 'settlement' rights as it did in southern England and where it acted as a deterrent to migration from that region. Those without a hire had no choice therefore but to move on, either to a village, a town or overseas, because in Lowland farm service the place where they ate, lived and slept always went with the job. The mechanism did not involve any form of direct eviction but was nonetheless a subtly effective system for limiting population congestion on the land.

Nevertheless, as far as migration was concerned, the positive lure of the towns and the opportunities which came from moving overseas should also not be underestimated. Towns and industrial areas more generally provided a greater range of jobs and often better wages than the humdrum life of farm service. Here was another striking parallel between the Scottish Highlands and the English south. In both regions, non-agricultural employment was shrinking in the early nineteenth century as manufacturing in England increasingly retreated to the coalfields of the north, and in Scotland concentrated in the central Lowlands. There were therefore few local alternatives in these two regions to draw rising population off the land. It might also be that as farmers imposed more discipline on their workers, urban places offered lives of more freedom and independence, especially for young adult migrants. A key feature of the Lowlands, unlike the western Highlands, was that few rural parishes were far from towns. The four great city hubs of Aberdeen, Dundee, Edinburgh and Glasgow were set some distances apart across the region, and each had its own distinctive pulling power in the immediate hinterlands of the north-east, central, south-east and western regions. By the census of 1871 one in five Scots lived in these cities; by 1851 it was more like one in three. The urban areas could only have grown fast by immigration because of the lethal effect of their high rates of mortality on natural increase. The majority of the new urban dwellers therefore had to come from the farms and villages of the rural districts. In 1851, for instance, Glasgow took 53 per cent of those not born in the city from Lowland sources, Edinburgh 66 per cent, Dundee 60 per cent and Aberdeen 80 per cent.

In the last quarter of the nineteenth century migration moved up another gear. Now the movement really did become a flight from the land. Between 1871 and 1911 the number of ploughmen and shepherds fell by more than a third and the decline in women workers was even more. It was the young of the rural world who were leaving in greatest number. One early-twentieth-century estimate suggested that half of all workers had left agricultural employment by their twenty-fifth birthday. What had begun as a trickle at the beginning of the nineteenth century had become a flood by its end.

Some of this exodus was caused by the ebbing away of industry from the countryside in later Victorian times. It should be remembered that much industrial activity was still rural-based as late as 1830. In the central Lowlands, and in some other districts, handloom weaving remained an important rural activity even up to the 1850s. Moreover, as already noted, a multitude of skilled trades had grown up as essential supports of improved agriculture. Country blacksmiths were necessary for the making and repairing of the new iron-framed ploughs. Horses replaced oxen in the later eighteenth century and had to be shod regularly, on average every six to eight weeks. The building and rebuilding of farm steadings with houses, byres, milkhouses, barns and stables took place in two main phases during the 'High Farming' of the 1850s and again, to a lesser extent, in the 1870s. This created demand on a large scale not only for the building trades but also for skills in quarrying, stone breaking, brick making and sawmilling. In addition, the new-style farming could not have been carried on without millers, joiners, masons, ditchers and dykers. Tailors, shoemakers (or 'souters') and country weavers served the needs of the labouring population. The signal importance of this range of trades is often forgotten when writers focus simply on ploughmen, women workers and bothymen.

But these trades were being steadily undermined by urban competition in the second half of the nineteenth century. Already by the 1850s, the technology of power looms was destroying the textile economy in numerous villages in Perth, Fife and Angus and promoting large-scale migration as a result. The development of a myriad of railway branch lines enabled cheap factory goods to be sold far into the rural districts, and so threatening traditional markets for tailors, shoemakers and other tradesmen. This displacement of craftsmen and their families from the smaller country towns and villages became a familiar feature of the rural outflow by the end of the nineteenth century. While some, such as the country shoemaker, vanished into oblivion, others, such as the blacksmiths, continued to thrive as long as the horse economy survived, and in some cases even diversified into agricultural engineering.

Attitudes were also changing among the farm workers. The structure of service in Lowland Scotland resulted in high levels of internal mobility in the countryside. 'Flitting' (moving) to another farm, usually in the same parish or county, at the end of the six-month or annual term was part of the way of life. The contract of employment meant that in law servants had only one or two opportunities to move in the year and that focused minds at the crucial periods when there was always the temptation to seek a place elsewhere for better wages, more experience or a change of surroundings. But the reasons for mobility were legion. When asked, one Lothians farm worker between the wars in the twentieth century answered tersely: 'Possibly the neighbours, possibly the gaffer [foreman], possibly the farmer, possibly the horses. Maybe the horses came first if they didnae have a good pair of horse, or the harness wasn't up to scratch.'[10] For married men the costs of moving were low. A house came with the job and the new employer provided a few carts to move the family and their household belongings. Servants could carry their own locks with them when they flitted. An East Lothian writer noted in 1861 how one married ploughman's door 'was literally covered with keyholes, made to suit the size of the lock of each successive occupant'.[11] Almost all this habitual movement was localized and over short distances, but it accustomed farm servant families to levels of mobility that could in certain circumstances encourage them to leave the land altogether for a new life elsewhere.

The relationship between the system of employment and migration was even more clear-cut in the case of single servants, the majority of regular workers in the Lowlands. At marriage they faced a stark choice, because in many areas there was a distinct lack of family cottages.

Some could continue in agricultural employment as day labourers. In the north-east they might seek to return to the crofts from where many had originally come as young servants. But the number of smallholdings was too few to absorb those who left full-time employment on the farms in their mid-twenties, and anyway the possibility of such a move back to the land was mainly confined only to the north-east area of the Lowlands. Young ploughmen had also been accustomed to a nomadic life, regularly moving from one master to another. At marriage, therefore, many left the land altogether, went to the towns and tried other occupations.

This traditional exodus became a great haemorrhage from the later nineteenth century onwards. The towns and emigration overseas now exerted a magical appeal over the rural young. This was partly due to rising expectations as a result of better agricultural wage levels and the spread of urban values, following the construction of railway branch lines throughout the Lowlands. Life on the land had always been hard, but now many came to see it as intolerable when compared to the working conditions and social attractions of the towns. Before 1914 a ploughman would rise at 5 a.m. to feed and groom his horses, yoke them at 6 a.m. and work until six in the evening, with a break between 11 a.m. and 1 p.m. The only holidays were Sundays, New Year's Day and hiring days. The burden of work on the family farms of the south-west fell very heavily on women. One observer in 1820 called it 'the slavery of family work'. Dairying near the cities involved very early rising, at about 2 or 3 a.m., because of the popular prejudice in favour of warm milk. Similarly, dairy women in upland farms needed to milk early to ensure that milk could be despatched to town by early-morning trains. Where milk was made into cheese there was, in the words of one commentator:

> an enormous amount of continuous labouring, seven days a week during six to seven months in the year . . . I have seen the women folk on such farms at 3 o'clock in the afternoon in the same garb they had hurriedly donned between 3 and 4 o'clock in the morning, having been constantly toiling, one day succeeding another . . . it is usual for women on dairy farms to work sixteen hours per day, time for meals only being allowed for.[12]

Even the leisure activities of farm workers were dominated by work. The bothy ballads were mainly about work and the *kirns* that marked the end of the harvest season also celebrated work. Compared to the life of hard toil on the land, the town jobs of domestic servant, railway porter, policeman and carter seemed infinitely less demanding. Not only did they pay better than agricultural work in some instances, but they also had shorter hours, more leisure time, and freedom in the evenings and weekends from employers. In contrast, rural life had fewer social attractions. Scottish farm workers were dispersed in cottages, bothies and chaumers (sleeping quarters for single male farm servants, usually above the stables) in the steadings. Long hours and the habitual turnover of labour at the end of each term confined most social life to the occasional fair or agricultural show. The hunger for a more interesting life was confirmed when the Board of Agriculture helped to establish the Scottish Women's Rural Institutes. They were an immediate success, despite initial male opposition, and five years later had 242 branches and a total membership of 14,000. But for many, and especially the young, this hunger could be fully satisfied only by moving off the land altogether. As the Royal Commission on Labour concluded in 1893:

> there is much drudgery and very little excitement about the farm servant's daily duties, and I believe the young men dislike the former and long for the latter. By the labourers themselves slight importance is attached to the healthy character of country life in comparison with various branches of town labour. That phase of the question sinks into insignificance in their estimation, and only the shorter hours, numerous holidays and ever present busy bustle and excitement of town life or the neat uniform and genteel work of the police constable or railway porter, are present to the mind of our young farm servant.[13]

5

A life of hard labour of the farms also had to increasingly compete with the attractions of life overseas. There could be found what was craved by both masters and men – the ownership of land. For both classes, independent status and owning land was impossible in Scotland. But the opportunities were abundant in North America, Australia and New Zealand. European migration to the New World had been under way from the period of the Discoveries in early-modern times, but in the second half of the nineteenth century the age of mass emigration began. This was not simply because of the voracious demand for labour in North America as both the American and Canadian economies experienced unprecedented expansion into new land. It was also made possible by the crumbling of two of the great constraints that had restricted emigration in the past, distance and cost of travel, both of which normally meant that leaving Europe for the Americas was likely to end in permanent exile. Also, the New World had long been seen by most Europeans as alien, covered by densely forested wildernesses where the risks and dangers far outweighed the opportunities.

Emigration, like all other aspects of human existence, was transformed by the transportation revolution of the nineteenth century. Although the cost of steamship travel was actually about a third higher than crossing by sailing ships, the new vessels radically increased speed, comfort and safety. In the 1850s it took six weeks to cross the Atlantic from the Clyde. By 1910 the average voyage time had fallen to around seven days. In the early 1860s, 45 per cent of transatlantic emigrants still left under sail. By 1870 all but a tiny minority crossed the Atlantic in steamships. By drastically cutting voyage times the steamship removed one of the major costs of emigration: the time between embarkation and settlement during which there was no possibility of earning. That also explains the increasing scale of return emigration. By 1900 it is estimated that around one third of those Scots who left came back sooner or later. Going to North America was no longer a once in a lifetime decision.

The steamship was the most dramatic and decisive advance but it was paralleled by the railway, which made it possible for emigrants to be quickly and easily transported from all areas through the national network to the port of embarkation. Agreements were commonly made between shipping and railway companies, allowing emigrants to be transported free to their port of departure. The expansion of the railroad in North America brought similar benefits. By the 1850s the completion of the Canadian canal network and the associated railway development facilitated access to the western USA by allowing emigrants to book their passage to Quebec and Hamilton and then by rail to Chicago. The links between steamships and railways led to the provision of the highly popular through-booking system by which emigrants could obtain a complete package, with a ticket purchased in Europe allowing travel to the final destination in America. The *Chambers' Journal* in 1857 described it as a 'prodigious convenience' which would 'rob emigration of its terrors and must set hundreds of families wandering'.

Some of the leading railway companies in Canada played a vigorous proactive role in the emigrant business. They recognized that the railway was not simply an easy and rapid mode of transport for new arrivals from Europe, but was also the most effective way of opening up the wilderness and prairie territories to permanent settlement. The mighty Canadian Pacific Railway Company (CPR) vigorously promoted emigration because of this. In 1880 it had been allocated 25 million acres of land between Winnipeg and the Rocky Mountains by the Dominion government. In order to generate profit, the company had to increase traffic through expanding areas of settlement, and to achieve that goal embarked on an aggressive marketing campaign in Britain designed to stimulate emigration to the prairies. Scotland was specifically targeted and agents of the CPR toured the country areas, giving lectures and providing information. The CPR even sought to limit the hardships of pioneering by providing ready-made farms in southern Alberta, with housing, barns and fences included as part of the sale.

A veritable explosion in the quality and quantity of information available to potential emigrants took place. The Emigrants' Information Office opened in 1886 as a source of impartial advice and information on land grants, wages, living costs and passage rates. Circulars, handbooks and pamphlets were made available in greater volume and were valued because of their avowed objectivity. Even more important were local newspapers. The *Aberdeen Journal* was a significant vehicle for raising interest about emigration in the rural communities of the north-east. Advertisements for ships' sailings, information on assisted passages, numerous letters from emigrants and articles on North American life were very regular features as the country population was relentlessly bombarded with all the facts about the emigration experience. Overseas governments and land companies also became more aggressive, professional and sophisticated in promoting emigration. In 1892, for instance, the Canadian government appointed two full-time agents in Scotland who undertook tours of markets, hiring fairs, agricultural shows and village halls. The illustrated lecture, using the magic lantern, was a favourite device. W. G. Stuart, the agent for the north, was even able to deliver his presentation in Gaelic if the audience asked for it.

From the 1870s to the Great War, the Canadian government's aim was to settle the Prairie West with immigrants who would establish an agricultural foundation for the Dominion. The key influence on the strategy was Clifford Sifton, the Minister of the Interior from 1896 to 1905. He pioneered the first emigration communications strategy by flooding selected countries with appealing literature, advertisements in the press, tours for key journalists who then filed flattering copy on their return home, paying agents' fees on a commission basis for every immigrant who actually settled in Canada, and giving bonuses to steamship agents for promoting the country in the United Kingdom. The rural districts of Scotland were particularly targeted because of the historic links with Canada and their population of experienced farmers and skilled agricultural workers.

The Lowlands, as noted, had very high levels of internal mobility. That most rural parishes in the 1860s already experienced net outward movement of people is crucial to an explanation of the roots of emigration. The Scots were mobile abroad, in large part because they were also very mobile at home. There is now some evidence that from the later nineteenth century the volume of emigration varied inversely with that of internal migration. People in country farms and villages searching for opportunities elsewhere seem to have been able to weigh the attractions of the Scottish towns against those of overseas destinations and come to a decision on the basis of these comparisons. In the decades 1881–90 and 1901–10, for instance, there was heavy emigration, with 43 and 47 per cent respectively of the natural increase leaving the country. In the same twenty-year period, movement to Glasgow and the surrounding suburbs fell to low levels, while there was actual net movement out of the western Lowlands. On the other hand, during the 1870s and 1890s emigration declined but larger numbers moved to the cities and towns. The pattern suggests a sophisticated, literate and mobile population which had access to sources of information in newspapers, letters from relatives and intelligence from returned migrants that allowed informed judgements about emigration to be made. It also highlights once again the key importance of the transportation revolution which enabled the historic and habitual internal mobility of the rural Scots to be translated fully into international movement.

Lowland rural emigration was not induced so much by destitution or deprivation – as in the Highlands for long periods – as by the lure of opportunity. Throughout the nineteenth century and early twentieth, Canada was the great magnet for those who wished to work the land, while rural tradesmen and industrial workers tended to opt more for the USA. In his novel *Sunset Song* (1932), Lewis Grassic Gibbon wrote a memorable evocation of rural life in the Mearns district of north-east Scotland in the years before the Great War. He depicts the restlessness now affecting the young men who worked on the farms of the area. One of his characters, Will Guthrie, had decided, like others, to leave for North America: 'soon as he'd saved the silver, he was off to Canada, a man was his own master there'. From emigrant letters and newspaper articles one can piece together the attractions of emigration for both small tenants and farm servants. A primary incentive was the possibility of owning land for themselves which was impossible at home. Land was cheap to acquire and increasingly made available for purchase in developed form by land companies and by the Dominion and provincial governments. In Canada and Australia land was plentiful, whereas in Scotland even affluent farmers were dependent on their landlords, with tenure regulated by detailed leases enforceable at law and other sanctions. The Board of Agriculture in 1906 reviewed the reasons for the decline in the rural population and concluded with respect to Scotland that:

> Many correspondents refer to the absence of an incentive to remain on the land and of any reasonable prospect of advancement in life, and it is mentioned in some districts, particularly in Scotland, many of the

best men have been attracted to the colonies, where their energies may find wider scope and where the road to independence and a competency is broader and more easy to access.[14]

The last word should go to Joseph (Joe) Duncan, the able and shrewd secretary of the Farm Servants' Union, when he commented on the volume of emigration in the years before the Great War:

> There has been a fairly steady stream of emigration from the rural districts of Scotland, rising at times into something of a torrent, such as we have just had within the last three or four years.
>
> It is interesting to note the counties from which emigration has been the greatest. By far the greatest emigration has taken place from the counties of Elgin, Nairn, Banff and Aberdeen. This is probably accounted for by the fact that there are fewer industries in these districts and less chance for farm workers changing occupation within their own districts.
>
> It is in these counties too that the largest number of single men employed on the farms are to be found, while the fact that it is the custom there for the bulk of wages to be paid at the end of the six months, produces a system of involuntary saving which provides the young men with the necessary cash to pay for passage abroad . . .
>
> The emigration has been less in the counties south of this where the wages are higher and where the opportunities of entering other employment are greater. Emigration has generally been to Canada, Australia coming next, and increasingly, and then, much behind these, New Zealand and the United States.
>
> Emigration has helped to increase wages and has also contributed to the independence of the workers remaining. It is the case today all over Scotland that there is a scarcity of suitable men for the farms, and although there seems now to be a slackening in emigration it is not likely that any large increase in the number of competent men will take place.[15]

PART THREE

IO

More People, Less Land

I

A rapid and sustained increase in population was the critical and dominating factor in the social history of the Highlands in the century after c.1750, though often ignored in popular accounts of clearance. Numbers were rising, of course, all over Britain and Europe at the time, but the demographic revolution posed major challenges to those regions, like the Scottish Highlands, where their inhabitants had always lived close to the margins of subsistence. In the 1750s the population of Scotland was 1.265 million and by 1821 it reached 2 million. The retained population of the country between 1755 and 1820 had therefore grown by roughly two thirds in sixty-five years. The consensus among demographic historians is that the increase came about mainly because improved and more secure food supply had helped to cut to some extent the appalling levels of mortality among infants and the very young. To this amelioration in nutrition was added the impact of inoculation on smallpox from the 1760s, a disease which was by far the most lethal epidemic killer of the time.

A rise in numbers was evident across all four Highland counties, but two strikingly different regional profiles also became apparent throughout the period. In the southern districts of the county of Argyll and the eastern areas of the Highland plateau the increases were very moderate. Indeed, 41 out of 68 parishes there failed to show any actual growth at all between the 1750s and 1790s. It was a different story, however, in the far west and north, specifically along the seaboard from Morvern to Cape Wrath and including most of the islands of the Hebrides. Here, thirty-two of forty-three parishes showed a rise of more than 25 per cent, significantly above the average for Scotland as a whole.

The difference between the two zones became even more significant during the following half-century. Across the western districts between 1801 and 1841, the increase was of the order of 53 per cent, while in the south and east growth of a mere 7 per cent overall was recorded. At the local level the rise was sometimes more spectacular. On the island of Tiree, the population was 1,500 in the 1740s but had swollen to 4,453 by 1831. Throughout the Western Isles, growth was of the order of 80 per cent between 1755 and 1821. Even without clearances, increases of this order of magnitude would have posed massive challenges to a society which had always existed close to the very margins of subsistence. It was also a tragic irony that where arable was more available and a resilient agrarian regime had been introduced the rise in numbers was small, but it was significantly greater in those parts of the Highlands with the poorest land and the most fragile peasant economies.

The basic cause of this profound demographic differential, which was to profoundly shape the course of Highland history, was the variation in regional migration. In simple terms, many more people consistently left the parishes of the south and east than they did the north-west. Proximity to the booming centres of industry and urban development in the Lowlands was undeniably one explanation for this pattern. Studies of Highland migration to Greenock, Paisley, Glasgow and Dundee in the decades before 1851 show that the vast majority of those who settled in these cities and towns had been born in the southerly and easterly parishes which were close to them.

But the distinctive social structure of the region was also crucial. By c.1840 a moderate consolidation of traditional townships had taken place throughout the south and east which, as already noted for the Lowlands, led to a continuous decline in the numbers holding direct tenancies of land. The extent of contraction varied significantly within the area; it went furthest, for instance, in highland Perthshire and along the coastal plain north of Inverness. Nonetheless, across the entire region legal rights to land were being widely and inexorably reduced. Complete landlessness of the Lowland kind was not always common, since the *New Statistical Account* of the 1840s confirms that smallholdings and subtenancies clung on in most areas. But in the main they were effectively linked in with the labour needs of neighbouring larger farms and the people who lived on them were as much dependent on earning wages as on what they could grow on the land.

The attachment to land was further weakened by the development of work outside agriculture and the growth of small towns and villages. For instance, the prosperous fishing industry in southern Argyllshire, along the lochs of the Clyde estuary and Loch Fyne, provided secure income and steady employment. The fishery supported village populations with a commitment to the sea and only tenuous connection to the land. Several of the Argyll burghs, such as Campbeltown, Tarbert, Inveraray and Lochgilphead, had particularly heavy rates of migration to the Lowland towns, a pattern which reflected their capacity to pull in migrants from surrounding rural districts and then channel them south. This was therefore a regional society where a money economy was now in place which was likely to lead to an erosion of peasant culture and values. The local manufacture of necessities, such as clothing, was already in retreat and by the 1840s the import of foods, fuel and some luxuries like tea and sugar had become common. The southern and eastern Highlands were therefore being assimilated to the market economy of the Lowlands and in the process the age-old peasant attachments to land were starting to fray.

Some contemporaries argued that the spread of schooling in the region added to this social revolution by raising expectations and spreading literacy. In 1826 the Church of Scotland estimated that in the Hebrides and other western parts of Inverness-shire at least 70 per cent of the population were unable to read, but in Argyllshire and Highland Perthshire the figure fell to about 30 per cent. These data correspond with other evidence. In 1858, for instance, less than 20 per cent of migrants from Argyllshire to the town of Greenock signed marriage registers only by mark, compared to 8 per cent for Lowland migrants and 64 per cent for those who had come from Ireland. A number of experienced contemporary observers saw a close connection between literacy rates and migration trends, though there is no easy method of determining how accurate their opinions were. The Rev. Norman McLeod, minister of the Gaelic Church of St Columba in Glasgow, a man with intimate knowledge of the Highland community in the city, reckoned that 'from the places where there are good schools young men come to Glasgow and Paisley to look for employment'.[1] He also asserted that on the Isle of Tiree the density of population was 'lower in parts where schools are'. Charles Baird, Secretary to the Committee for Destitute Highlanders in 1837, was equally confident of the relationship between literacy and mobility: 'Highlanders when educated become migrants' was his simple aphorism.[2] It is not made explicit in these comments, but what might be implied by 'good' schools were those which favoured instruction in English.

The much greater increases in population in the northern, central and western Highlands bring into sharp focus an intriguing historical puzzle. This region was to become notorious as the centre of large-scale clearances to make way for extensive sheep runs. Yet, despite widespread dispossession, mass migration leading to depopulation did not automatically follow from the displacement of many communities. Only in parts of estates where removals hit particularly hard was there extensive evidence of abandoned dwellings and empty habitations. Indeed, in general, the population of the four main Highland counties increased decade by decade in this period. Argyll reached peak population first in 1831, because of the substantial outflows to the Lowlands already discussed. But Inverness did not do so until after 1841, Sutherland in the decade 1831–41 and Ross-shire only in the early 1850s. In fact, the loss of people had been proportionately heavier in parts of the Borders countryside of the eighteenth century, where the spread of pastoralism had also led to considerable levels of eviction. Indeed, many more Gaels left the Highlands for overseas or the Lowlands *after* mass clearance had come to an end in the later 1850s than during the era of the great removals in earlier decades.

The answer to the conundrum cannot lie in the possibility that the scale of Highland eviction has been exaggerated. On the contrary, the historical record confirms the evidence of a troubled trail of social convulsion as the sheep frontier steadily moved north. The introduction of cattle ranching was first to have an effect in parts of Argyll, Dumbartonshire and Perthshire as peasant communities were widely dislodged in its wake. One observer, John Walker, estimated that, as a result of the conversion of small farms into large cattle holdings, population had fallen in seventeen parishes in those counties over the space of three decades since 1750. Much more significant, however, was sheep farming. The new Blackface and Cheviot breeds from the Borders, *Na Caoraich Mora* (the big sheep), had much greater carcase weight and wool-carrying capacity than the native animals. They were also greedy for land and required different levels and types of terrain for the different ages and genders of the flocks. The Cheviots in particular had special needs. Initially they enabled sheep farmers to pay twice the rent than was usually possible on land grazed by Blackface, but they could not easily survive the Highland climate without access to low ground for wintering, which inevitably posed a threat to the arable of the traditional townships. At the same time, sheep competed for grazing with the black cattle of the tenants. Also at risk, therefore, were the sheilings in the hill country where livestock were driven during the summer months to allow the grain grown in the townships to mature and ripen. Sheep farming consequently undermined the basis of the old economy by other means than direct clearance. So, in two sheep-grazing parishes in Sutherland (Creich and Assynt) between 1790 and 1808 the numbers of cattle fell from 5,140 to 2,906, while sheep flocks grew from 7,840 to 21,000.

Much more cataclysmic, however, was the direct removal of peasant communities to make way for the big pastoral farms. The new order and the old economy were fundamentally incompatible, since not only was there intense competition for scarce land, but the rental return from sheep was many times higher than that from black cattle. This was not only because of price differences in the market caused by the new industrial demand for wool. Sheep used land more intensively *and* extensively than cattle as they could graze in areas which had been little worked in the older pastoral economy. In addition, landlords stood to gain from more secure returns. Sheep farms were normally managed by affluent graziers from outside the Highlands who could guarantee proprietors regular and rising incomes in single large sums, whereas large numbers of small tenants were much less reliable as their rent payments fluctuated with the weather and volatility in the markets for cattle.

Nor could many of the indigenous inhabitants hope to gain a

substantial share in the sheep economy. Pastoralism was most efficient when practised on a large scale, which built an insurmountable
financial barrier for most Highland tenants. There is evidence, for
example, on the estates of MacDonnell of Glengarry and Cameron of
Lochiel in Inverness-shire of some townships putting together small
flocks of Blackface in the 1770s. So-called 'club farms' with some
sheep were also organized by the peasantry in several other districts.
But by and large the landlords were too impatient for the huge profits
to be won from grazing in big holdings, especially since there was a
plentiful supply of ambitious and enterprising farmers coming in
from the pastoral districts of Ayrshire, the Borders and Northumber-
land eager to bid highly for Highland leases. Most landowners and
their managers seem to have taken the hard line that the unexploited
lands of the north had become too valuable to risk being let to in-
experienced peasant farmers.

As the sheep frontier advanced, so also therefore did clearance. The
most notorious and controversial removals took place on the Sutherland estate, at the time the largest landed property in private ownership
in Europe. Between 1807 and 1821 the factors of the Countess of
Sutherland and her husband, Lord Stafford, removed several thousand
people from the internal parishes to tiny crofts of no more than three
acres established on the inhospitable eastern coast. There they were to
labour to bring barren land into cultivation by spade husbandry and
at the same time take up fishing in a harbour-less maritime environment. One of the principal managers of the estate asserted that the
small size of the holdings would be sufficient 'for the maintenance of
an industrious family' but also 'pinched enough' to force crofters to
take up fishing as well.[3] Meanwhile the fertile inland straths where
their ancestors had lived since time immemorial were converted into
large holdings for sheep. In its scale and ambition the Sutherland strategy was the most extraordinary example of social engineering in
nineteenth-century Britain. Old men looking back from the 1880s,
giving evidence to the Royal Commission on the Highlands and
Islands in that decade, could name forty-eight cleared townships in
the parish of Assynt alone.

The plan to create a dual economy with different specializations on
the coast and in the interior might have some appeal in theory – such a

division of function had been successfully implemented on a number of Lowland estates – but had grave weaknesses in practice. On more than one occasion the new houses and allotments were not ready for occupation when the people were moved. Those who had worked the land and grazed cattle for a living could not suddenly become expert fishermen. The process of dispossession was also sometimes carried out with great harshness, notably when two agricultural experts from Moray who had been employed by the Sutherland family, William Young and Patrick Sellar, forced through large-scale clearances in 1812 and 1813 which pushed the people of the Strath of Kildonan to open revolt. Sellar was a lawyer by profession but also a zealot for agricultural improvement. Two years later, in neighbouring Strathnaver, he was alleged to have behaved with such brutality in enforcing some clearances that he was indicted for breaking the law and eventually stood trial at the High Court in Inverness for 'culpable homicide, oppression and real injury'. The indictment charged him with 'wickedly and maliciously' burning hill pastures, 'violently' turning out pregnant women, the aged and infirm from their homes and 'cruelly depriving' them of shelter. He and his henchmen were also accused of 'setting on fire, burning, pulling down and demolishing . . . dwelling houses, barns, kiln, mills and other buildings'.[4] Sellar was determined that, once cleared, the settlements would be rendered completely uninhabitable. Despite the weight of eyewitness evidence, however, he was eventually acquitted after trial of culpable homicide. Nonetheless, his name lived on in infamy as the most hated man in the Victorian Highlands.

The main objective of the Countess of Sutherland and the Marquess of Stafford was to substantially increase income from their vast estate through the creation of enormous sheep farms across the interior worked by farmers and shepherds from the Scottish Borders and northern England. But they were not unmindful of the needs of the people who were dispossessed from these areas as the large pastoral farms came into being. The aim was not dispersal or expulsion but relocation of the population. The estate invested many thousands, building from scratch a large planned village at Helmsdale on the coast at the mouth of the Strath of Kildonan, complete with a harbour, designed by John Rennie, the famous engineer, and facilities for fish curing. This was intended to be the hub of a new fishing industry which would provide work for those who had lost their land. In outline, the scheme bore a resemblance to the villages successfully developed on several Lowland estates in the later eighteenth century, described in previous chapters, as alternatives for the displaced populations. But the scheme was botched. The people were alienated by Sellar's reign of terror and little thought was given as to how peasant farmers with no fishing skills and little capital would adapt to a new and strange way of life. There was a striking contrast with the way in which many landowners south of the Highland line gradually nurtured their tenantry into the new practices of improvement. The Sutherland experiment, on the other hand, demanded instant transformation from the people. The Countess, but especially her estate managers, had apparently little understanding of the values and culture of the people and their attachment to a time-honoured way of life. To these non-Gaels, their attitudes were not only archaic but wholly irrational. Sellar, for example, had nothing but racialized contempt for the people, dismissing them scathingly on more than one occasion as primitives or 'aborigines'. The inevitable failure of the strategy soon led to significant levels of emigration to North America from the coastal crofting settlement, and in the longer term a tarnished reputation for the House of Sutherland from which it never recovered.

In the scale and ensuing controversy which they generated, no other set of clearances matched those of Sutherland. Indeed, the vast majority of removals probably only involved a few people at a time until the more draconian episodes of the 1840s and 1850s took place during the potato famine. Gradual and relentless displacement rather than mass eviction was the norm, but taken together the numbers involved were considerable and suggest a systematic process of enforced movement on an unprecedented scale. A pioneering modern historian of the Highlands summarized what happened:

> After 1800 in a more remote country and among a more stagnant population, sheep farms, individually much larger than the south, began to sweep over wide areas of the country; previously we hear of groups of families moved, and of remote glens cleared, but now of whole straths emptied from source to sea.

Where dispossessed families had been numbered in tens before, now there were hundreds. Kintail, Glenelg, Loch Arkaig, Balnagowan, Glencalvie, Greenyards, Strathglass and Glenstrathfarrar, names of bitter memory plot the movement of the sheep frontier.[5]

Press reports from external commentators on the evictions are not uncommon. But the reactions of the people who were actually cleared are rare indeed. One of them is presented below. It concerns the eviction from their homes of over fifty inhabitants of the settlement of Aoineadh Mor, or Inniemore, sometimes Unnimore, in Morvern, western Argyll, in 1824. Later surveys have found the remains of twenty-two buildings, fifteen of which were probably dwellings. Christina Stewart, a rich spinster from Edinburgh, bought the lands from the Argyll Estates in Morvern in 1824. Very soon after purchase, she evicted the smallholders of four townships, including Inniemore, a total of 135 people in all, in order to establish two large sheep farms. So far as is known Christina Stewart never visited Morvern.

The minister of Lochaline village in the parish had a son, Norman MacLeod, who later visited the Inniemore folk in their new homes in Glasgow and then published the Gaelic memories of Mary Cameron in his *Reminiscences of a Highland Parish* in 1863. The remains of the settlement had been long covered by forestry planted in the 1930s but they were rediscovered several years ago and the site is now open to public view.

Mary Cameron's account runs as follows:

That was the day of sadness to many – the day on which *MacCailein* [the Duke of Argyll] parted with the estate of his ancestors in the place where I was reared.

The people of Unnimore thought that 'flitting' would not come upon them while they lived. As long as they paid the rent, and that was not difficult to do, anxiety did not come near them; and a lease they asked not. It was there that the friendly neighbourhood was, though now only one smoke is to be seen, from the house of the Saxon shepherd.

When we got the 'summons to quit', we thought it was only for getting an increase of rent, and this we willingly offered to give; but permission to stay we got not. The small sheep were sold, and at length it became necessary to part with the one cow. When shall I forget the plaintive wailing of the children deprived of the milk which was no more for them? When shall I forget the last sight I got of my pretty *cluster* of goats bleating on the *lip* of the rock, as if inviting me to milk them? But it was not allowed me to put a *cuach* [pail] under them.

The day of 'flitting' came. The officers of the law came along with it, and the shelter of a house, even for one night more, was not to be got. It was necessary to depart. The hissing of the fire on the flag of the hearth as they were *drowning* it reached my heart. We could not get even a bothy in the country; therefore we had nothing for it but to face the *land of the strangers* [Lowlands]. The aged woman, the mother of my husband, was then alive, weak, and lame. James carried her on his back in a creel. I followed him with little John, an infant at my breast, and thou who art no more, Donald beloved, a little *toddler*, walking with thy sister by my side. Our neighbours carried the little furniture that remained to us, and showed every kindness which tender friendship could show.

On the day of our leaving Unnimore I thought my heart would rend. I would feel right if my tears would flow; but no relief thus did I find. We sat for a time on 'Knock-nan-Càrn' [Hill of Cairns], to take the last look at the place where we had been brought up. The houses were being already stripped. The bleat of the 'big sheep' was on the mountain. The whistle of the Lowland shepherd and the bark of his dogs were on the brae . . .

What have you of it, but that we reached Glasgow, and through the letter of the saintly man who is now no more, my beloved minister, (little did I think that I would not again behold his noble countenance), we got into a cotton work [mill] . . .[6]

But despite widespread eviction of this kind, the numbers living in the north-west Highlands and Islands continued to rise until the 1850s. It is therefore difficult to argue that sheep farming *per se* triggered a great exodus from the Highlands *as a whole*, although the loss of people in particular districts was undeniably grievous. Thus the aforementioned parish of Kildonan in Sutherland had 1,574 inhabitants in 1811 but only 257 two decades later, or less than a sixth of the earlier figure. But the scale of migration from the south and east Highlands suggests instead that proximity to the Lowlands and a regional social structure which prevented the splitting of land among heirs and kinfolk were in the long run more potent 'push' factors than episodes of clearance. When fourteen sample parishes in Argyllshire are examined for the 1790s, no clear pattern of population loss emerges from those which had more sheep than the county average. However, when the same parishes are arranged in two geographical groups, a much more coherent picture can be traced. In those closest to the Clyde estuary, eleven out of twelve showed a decline in population. On the other hand, only two out of fourteen in the more remote northern parts of the county showed a decrease.[7]

2

Why then were clearances before the potato famine of the 1840s not followed by depopulation in the north-west Highlands but by continued growth in the number of people? Unfortunately, there are no systematic data available to chart the extent of land taken over by sheep farming, though in some areas, notably on the Sutherland estate, it is plain that the land lost by the old tenants was very great. The same could be said of the small islands of Rum, Muck, Canna, Lismore and Ulva, which were swept of almost all their native inhabitants, as were some districts on the western mainland such as the Knoydart peninsula in Inverness-shire. Yet it has also to be remembered that much of the territory claimed by the big flockmasters had never been cultivated before as arable and lay in the hill country rather than in the lower areas where the townships of the people congregated. Also, clearance sometimes involved the piecemeal erosion or removal of some townships, while others, even in the neighbourhood of those which had been lost, were left untouched and managed to survive for many years afterwards. Local evidence can provide some useful insights into what happened at the micro-level.

On the Duke of Argyll's Ross of Mull estate in the 1840s and 1850s, there were eleven townships before 1840. As Table 13 below shows, the process of eviction was complex. Five townships – Kilvicuen,

Knocknafenaig, Tireregan, Shiaba and Ardalanish – were cleared, sometimes quickly but also over much longer periods of time. Crucially, many of the displaced were not expelled from the estate but resettled from the fertile districts of the southern Ross to the poorer lands of the north, centred on the township of Ardtun, which saw a considerable rise in population as a result. Six of the settlements survived into the post-clearance era after c.1860 in the southern Ross of Mull, though by the later twentieth century they were all abandoned and entirely bereft of inhabitants as a result of 'voluntary' migration from the later nineteenth century.

Table 13 The population of South Ross of Mull in mid-century: effects of clearance

| Township | Year of census | | | |
| | 1841 | 1861 | 1871 | 2001 |
	People (households)			
Shiaba	128 (23)	16 (4)	11 (2)	0
Scoor	38 (7)	34 (7)	32 (6)	
Saorphin	66 (12)	29 (16)	42 (17)	
Kilvicuen	35 (8)	0	0	0
Knocknafenaig	85 (13)	22 (6)	5 (2)	0
Uisken	85 (17)	83 (20)	83 (21)	
Ardchiavaig	165 (30)	149 (28)	81 (22)	
Ardachy	56 (10)	25 (5)	24 (3)	
Ardalanish	131 (25)	18 (8)	23 (6)	
Tireregan	75 (10)	0	0	0
Knockvologan	64 (12)	15 (3)	19 (4)	
Total	928 (167)			
Eilean Erraid	0 (0)	9 (1)	131 (29)	

Source: J. Stewart Cameron, *A History of the Ross of Mull* (Bunessan, 2013), p. 247.

The modern history of the parish of Morvern in west Argyll is probably the most thoroughly researched of any in the western Highlands to date. Phillip Gaskell's micro-history, *Morvern Transformed* (1968), drew on a great mass of estate papers and plans, personal correspondence and census returns, together with careful archaeological surveys of existing township remains. It is known that Morvern was the scene of ten clearances carried out by five local landowners between 1824 and 1868. In all, these proprietors evicted 150 families over a period of sixty-four years. Gaskell's meticulous scholarship provides an unusually comprehensive guide to what happened. Over 760 men, women and children were forced to move from their homes in the parish during the course of the century. The despair and distress of the people who were cleared are described. However, known evictions accounted for only 23 per cent of the estimated 3,250 people who left Morvern over the same period, most of whom moved away after *c*.1870 when no significant removals took place. The migration of the great majority was therefore 'voluntary', or at least was not triggered directly by eviction, though the estates had other means at their disposal to induce movement if they chose to deploy them.

The remains of forty-six settlements with three houses or more in each case were also analysed and yielded significant results when combined with appropriate documentary evidence. Ten survived into the twentieth century and sometimes beyond; one had been partially cleared, but some of the inhabitants lived on for some time afterwards before the settlement was finally abandoned; ten were fully cleared; and twenty-five were eventually abandoned, mainly in the later nineteenth century, but with no evidence of any evictions having taken place. In sum, of the forty-six settlements, 22 per cent were emptied by clearance alone.

The history of clearance on the Isle of Skye is different again. Unlike on Mull, there are few physical remains of townships abandoned because of eviction, although it is known that clearance did take place on some properties. Strathaird in 1849 had a population of over 600, most of whom according to the landowner, Alexander Macalister, had not paid any rents for several years. All were served with summonses of removal in that year and offered assistance to emigrate. The tenants petitioned Sir George Grey, the Secretary for Home

Affairs in London, calling on him to intervene and prevent this 'compulsory emigration':

> Your petitioners are utterly averse to emigrate to America, on considering their inability to do so arising from these distressed conditions of potato failure, low prices for cattle, together with the numerous privations to which they will be subjected by being cast pennyless and unprovided for on a foreign shore without any aid from the proprietor to convey them from the place of their landing to that part of the country where they could obtain farms.[8]

Grey refused to intervene, but pointed out that writs of ejectment were perfectly legal and that no landowner could compel the people of his estate to emigrate. The only further record of the Strathaird people came in May 1852 when 148 of them embarked for Australia under the auspices of the Highland and Island Emigration Society, with Macalister paying part of their passage.

The papers of the biggest landowner on the island, those of Lord Macdonald, suggest the estate tended to target the displacement of the cottar class and for the most part left the rent-paying tenantry undisturbed. That is one reason why the visitor of today sees a more populated island with many crofting communities compared to the empty glens and shores of much of the landscape in Mull. However, there was at least one well-documented and famous exception to this pattern. The clearance of the two townships of Boreraig and Suishnish in the parish of Strath in 1853 attracted considerable publicity and external comment. Boreraig had a population of 120 men, women and children living in 22 households before the removals took place. Eight of the families and nine from Suishnish were resettled in other townships on land left behind by those who had gone to Australia supported by the Highland and Island Emigration Society. Most of the remainder of the evicted also sailed later for the Antipodes in one of the ships chartered by the Society.

But in general tenant removals were unusual on the Macdonald estate. The surviving rentals suggest continuity rather than change. In 1848 there were 410 small tenancies paying rents of £10 per annum or less on the Macdonald lands in the parishes of Sleat and Strath. Ten years later 387 of them remained on the rental books, a marginal loss of 6 per cent.

One of the most extensive and best documented series of removals occurred on the Island of Lewis in three phases between 1851 and 1855. The wealthy owner, Sir James Matheson, the China opium magnate of Jardine, Matheson & Co., decided to 'emigrate' many of his destitute tenants and cottars through a huge programme of eviction and 'assisted' transportation to Canada. No fewer than 2,327 men, women and children were eventually given the bleak choice of being cleared and left destitute or of boarding the emigrant ships for supported passage across the Atlantic. This was the essence of compulsory emigration. In 1851, just before the evictions, the population of Lewis outside the town of Stornoway stood at 17,320 men, women and children. The proportion 'emigrated' accounted for just over 13 per cent of that total. By 1861, after the clearances and emigrations

Table 14 Summonses of Removal as proportion of number of households, parish of Barvas (Lewis), 1848–53

Area	1848 (1)	1848 (2) %	1849 (1)	1849 (2) %	1850 (1)	1850 (2) %	1851 (1)	1851 (2) %	1853 (1)	1853 (2) %
1	–	–	–	–	–	–	25	17.5	–	–
2	3	2.6	58	50.9	–	–	26	22.8	8	9.1
3	–	–	–	–	3	1.7	48	27.7	39	31.2
4	46	48.4	42	44.2	–	–	12	12.6	5	6.0
5	–	–	14	10.1	–	–	26	18.8	–	–
6	3	2.0	6	3.9	–	–	58	37.9	–	–
Total	52		120		3		195		52	

Source: NRS, Sheriff Court Processes, Stornoway, SC 33/17/26–33; GRO, Census Enumerator's Schedules, Barvas, 1851.

Notes: (a) Column (1): Number of Summonses of Removal issued per area. Column (2): Summonses of Removal as percentage of number of households per area.

(b) For areas, see Table 10.3.

had come to an end, there were still 1,125 more people in the land-ward parts of Lewis outside Stornoway than in 1851. The diary of the estate chamberlain, John Munro Mackenzie, makes it plain that his programme of eviction was based on clinical and rigorous selection, in which human feelings or concern played no part, of those families who had to go. Both within and between townships those not in heavy arrears and involved in successful fishing kept their crofts, while the poorest and those who had laboured in the declining manu-facture of kelp were scheduled for removal. As the tabulations below confirm, summonses of removal were targeted at specific parishes and areas, with Barvas and West Lewis coming off worst.

Table 15 Census areas and population,
parish of Barvas (Lewis), 1851

Area	Townships	Households	Male	Female	Total
1	S. Bragar, N. Bragar, Srnol	143	304	338	642
2	Bru, Lower and Upper Barvas	114	286	303	589
3	Upper and Lower Shader, Fivepenny and Mid Barve, Melbost, Barve	173	400	449	849
4	N. and S. Galton, S. Dell	95	250	264	514
5	N. Dell, Cross, Swanbost, Habost	138	411	375	786
6	Europie, Fivepenny Ness, Knockaird, Port Caligral, Lionel, Eurodale, Skigersta	153	430	379	809
	Total	816	2,081	2,108	4,189

Source: NRS, Census Enumerator's Schedules, Barvas, 1851.

Table 16 Summonses of Removal, island of Lewis, 1848–53

District	1848	1849	1850	1851	1853	Percentage of total, 1848–53
Barvas	52	120	3	195	52	30
Tolsta	12	–	–	74	27	8
Stornoway	19	84	–	34	8	10
Eye Peninsula	34	91	–	124	–	17
West Lewis	4	120	90	157	34	28
Lochs	–	11	–	79	5	7
Total	121	426	93	663	126	100

Source: NRS, Sheriff Court Processes, Stornoway, SC 33/17/26–33.

Table 17 Summonses of Removal in kelp parishes, Lewis, 1848–53

Parish	Summonses of removal as percentage of total summonses, Lewis, 1848–53	Kelp proceeds as percentage of land rental, Lewis estate, 1826
Lochs	7	11
Uig	28	42
Barvas	30	47

Source: NRS, Sheriff Court Processes, Stornoway, SC 33/17/26–33; NRS, Brown MSS (Temporary Deposit) TD 80/100–4, Statement of Account, Seaforth Estate, 1826.

Elsewhere, not all or even the majority of those who suffered eviction migrated to the Lowlands or emigrated, though some obviously did so. Others, as will be shown later, were forced to move to already-crowded settlements in other parts of the estates. Also, in the wake of the removals, the displaced often sank into the ranks of the semi-landless cottar class, with the dispossessed gathering in villages across the region. One contemporary description reported of them:

> The cottars possess nothing but the cottage which shelters them, and depend on the kindness of neighbours for a few patches of ground for potatoes, and supply their other wants by fishing, and such work as they may obtain at home or abroad.
>
> The latter class live at all times in a constant struggle for the means of bare subsistence, and do not rise above the lowest scale of living necessary for existence, not to talk of comfort. In some seasons they are frequently reduced to live upon such shellfish as they can collect, with a little milk etc.[9]

Colonies of impoverished cottars were to be found by the 1840s in Tobermory in Mull, Lochaline in Morvern, Arnisdale in Glenelg, Ullapool, Lochcarron and Scoraig in Wester Ross, and in other similar settlements.

On Lord Macdonald's Skye estates there were 1,300 families who did not pay rent, 'chiefly relatives of the tenants, such as sons and sons-in-law, sometimes two or three of them are on the lot'.[10] On Macleod of Macleod's property on the same island, it was estimated that for every tenant family there were two cottar families. In Harris 450 tenants paid rent but a further 400 families existed as cottars on the estates. Similarly, in Barra more than half of those who held some land were not recorded in the rental book. In Skye in the later 1840s there were 1,900 crofter families and 1,531 cottars. The majority of the inhabitants of Glenelg, North Morar and Knoydart were also nominally 'landless'. On the Duke of Argyll's estate in Mull cottars outnumbered tenants, with 1,455 belonging to tenant families and 1,533 cottar families. In Tiree 63 per cent of the population belonged to tenant families and 37 per cent (1,838) to cottar families. The number of cottars varied significantly between estates, but in many of the Hebridean islands they often comprised as much as half and sometimes more of the entire population.

Arguably, then, the real effect of clearance before the 1840s was not to depopulate the Highlands in the short run, but to increase the terrible poverty and congestion of those townships which were spared but forced to accept more and more of the evicted by the process known as 'crowding in'. This in turn intensified the splitting of holdings into ever smaller sizes in order to accommodate the displaced. As a result the north-west became ever more at risk to the impact of crop failure and volatility of markets for fish, cattle and kelp.

3

But for the remarkably rapid spread of the potato crop as a new source of food in the Highlands after c.1750 there would have been a much greater flight from the land, especially by the poorest tenants and cottars. The history of the potato as a food crop in the Scottish Highlands is well documented. The first specific reference occurs in Martin Martin's account of the Hebrides in 1695, although by 1750 cultivation of the crop was still relatively uncommon. The period of greatest expansion was probably the last quarter of the eighteenth and first few decades of the nineteenth century. By then potatoes were being grown widely as a subsistence crop. Their importance was highlighted during the grain harvest failures of 1782–3, when they helped to save several communities from near starvation. Potato cultivation seems also to have developed further after the end of the Napoleonic Wars. Dr John Macculloch, who travelled annually in the western Highlands between 1811 and 1821, was one of several observers to comment on its increasing significance. In 1811, James Macdonald claimed that potatoes by then constituted four fifths of the nourishment of Hebrideans.

Potatoes grow in virtually any soil, adjust to different climates, but flourish best where the weather is cool and moist. They also allow for a dramatic increase in food supply without the need for radical changes in traditional methods of cultivation, technology or social organization. In the western Highlands the crop was grown by the lazy-bed (*feannagan*) method. Soil was turned over with the *cas-chrom*, or foot-plough. Earth from ditches dug between different ridges was cast on top, seeds were broadcast and the ridges well covered with seaweed, of which there was usually an abundant supply in the maritime districts, as well as animal manure. Once dug up, potatoes were ready for the pot and unlike grains did not require any additional labour to make them edible. They were easy to store but quickly lost their nutritional content if kept over long periods. The calorific content of a given quantity of potatoes was considerably less than the same amount of grain, but since potatoes had a much greater yield, an acre under them gave as much as 3–5 times as many calories as an acre in grain. They can provide for all human nutritional needs.

But the widespread adoption of the potato in the Highlands was not only because it provided more food. Only in the crofting region of the north-west and islands did potatoes assume overall dominance in the diet of the majority of the population. This suggests that they suited not only the natural limitations of these districts but also met the social and economic needs of the people who lived there. In the eighteenth century, the inhabitants of the western Highlands and Islands lived close to the very margin of subsistence. Famine was always a threat and, in several years, a reality. Any food resource which would provide more security was a welcome addition. A significant factor was that oats tended to ripen later in the western Highlands than elsewhere in Scotland. The earliest potatoes, however, were available in August, two months earlier than the oat crop. They therefore helped to fill part of that key gap in the period between the consumption of the old grain harvest and the harvesting of the new. Grain crops were notoriously volatile in much of the Highlands and yields in most areas were relatively low. In 1814 it was estimated that oat yields in Scotland as a whole varied between ten and sixteen pecks per boll and in 'the best cultivated counties' from thirteen to eighteen pecks per boll. But in the western Highlands the average was a return of four to six pecks. In this respect, the potato had a crucial advantage. The produce of grain in the Hebrides was often no more than one third of land elsewhere in Scotland, but the return from the potato was equal or superior. The heavy rainfall and high winds which harassed grain farmers were often a positive advantage in potato cultivation. They provided a natural protection against the 'curl', the most destructive potato disease of the eighteenth century. It is now known that the greenfly which spreads the disease rarely moves from a host plant when the wind rises above eight miles per hour. Heavy rainfall washes plants clear of the parasite altogether. The potato was not invulnerable, but until the partial failure of 1836–7 the crop was only damaged by early frosts. In the first few decades of the nineteenth century at least it promised a much more secure return than grain.

Yet the major attraction of the potato lay not simply in the fact that it lowered the threshold of risk. It also had a remarkably high yield. In Mull a normal return would be twelve barrels for each one planted. In parts of Skye it was between eight and ten barrels and in Lochalsh six to eight. Sir John Sinclair estimated that four times as many people could be supported by an acre of potatoes as by an acre of oats. As the greatest yielder of food of any crop known in early-nineteenth-century Europe it therefore formed an integral part of the social and economic revolution which spread across the Highlands between 1750 and 1840. The cultivation of the potato expanded with such speed not simply because of its intrinsic merits but because the development of crofting, the movement of communities into areas of waste and marginal land and the subdivision of holdings could not have occurred on the same scale without widespread adoption of the new crop. It was almost a precondition of the social transformation which swept over the Scottish Highlands in this period.

Four factors were fundamental. First, the minuscule holdings formed to support kelp gatherers and burners, whisky distillers and fishermen were only able to provide a subsistence living because of the high yields derived from potato cultivation. Their work was seasonal, so potatoes provided food for much of the rest of the year and especially during the winter and spring months. Second, the fragmentation of lots among cottars depended on the adoption of the potato. The evidence suggests that the smaller the holding, the greater the reliance placed on the crop. Third, potatoes were well suited to the policies of clearance and relocation pursued by landlords as they could be grown in all soils except stiff clay. It was partly because of the potato that new communities could be established on narrow strips of land on coast, moorland and moss. One contemporary claimed that 'It is by the potato crop that all the wild land has hitherto been reclaimed.'[11] The capacity of the potato to support evicted people on small patches of land helps to explain why clearance in the western Highlands caused dispossession but not immediate or wholesale regional depopulation.

Fourth, the potato became even more vital after the Napoleonic Wars. Sir John Sinclair estimated that the typical crofter had to be able to obtain at least 200 days of additional work outside his holding to escape destitution. But external employment within the Highlands contracted in the 1820s and 1830s in some areas and vanished altogether in others. At the same time, there was a slump in cattle prices. The price of a three-year-old, which in 1810 had stood at about £6, had, by the 1830s, fallen to around £3.10/-. Black cattle had traditionally been the peasant's store of value and an important means of both paying rental and covering the costs of meal imports in seasons of scarcity. Cattle stocks were diminishing over time and many small tenants and cottars by the 1830s had only one or two beasts, or none at all. In a survey of holdings of stock in thirty-four tenancies, in a wide sample of areas, rented at £6 per annum or less, the average number of cattle ranged between 2.5 and 1.84 per holding. This was substantially less than was allowed for in rental agreements. Almost certainly these problems in the pastoral sector dictated a greater reliance on the arable patch than hitherto and hence on the potato as a primary source of food.

4

Like their counterparts elsewhere in Scotland, West Highland landowners in the eighteenth century remained convinced of the value of a large population as an economic resource. Their concern to maintain the people on their estates may have also reflected a lingering sense of patriarchal obligation to former clansmen who had served their families loyally for generations. But new economic incentives for large estate populations also emerged in the later eighteenth century as Lowland markets opened up even more for kelp, fishing, distilling and slate quarrying. As with the dispossession of the cottars in the Lowlands who were relocated in villages, so small tenants in the Highlands were moved to the coasts from the glens, where large grazing farms were taking over much of the land. Eighteenth-century theorists argued that the maritime resources of the western Highlands in both fish and kelp were richer by far than those of the soil. It therefore became common to emphasize the benefits of a division of labour, of a dual economy which would efficiently combine the pastoral potential of the interior and the quasi-industrial possibilities of the coast. The impoverished population of the inland districts should be resettled in the maritime areas, there to earn a living and generate rental income for the estates by working in the labour-intensive activities of fishing and kelping. The rich grazings of the inland straths would at the same time be laid down to sheep farming.

This programme of action had powerful economic attractions. In the 1790s and early 1800s demand for Highland kelp, an alkaline extract from seaweed, used in the chemical manufactures of the time, reached hitherto unprecedented levels as industrialization broadened markets and the Napoleonic Wars impeded the supply of cheaper Spanish barilla (soda ash produced from plant sources). The herring fishery also flourished as the shoals began to visit the western sea lochs on a more regular basis. Moreover, laying out land in individual crofts was in theory an attractive solution to the problem posed by an increasing population in an era of agrarian rationalization. It transformed communities likely to be made redundant by a more profitable form of pastoral husbandry into a productive resource and a significant source of revenue. There had been a few crofts in the old society but the idea of a crofting *system* was new. It was not in any way an archaic hangover from the past but judged by theorists to be just as innovative in its way as the steam engine and the textile mill.

Crofting had three particular attractions. First, like their counterparts in the north-eastern counties of Aberdeen and Banff and some other parts of Lowland Scotland, Highland landlords viewed the settlement of colonies of crofters, in the first instance at nominal rents, as an effective means of bringing into cultivation by spade husbandry the stretches of waste and moor land which dominated large areas of their estates. It was characteristic of late-eighteenth-century optimism that those barren tracts were thought ripe for profitable reclamation by presenting a major opportunity for a region rich in abundant and underemployed resources of labour but very poor in arable land. Expansion of smallholdings into waste land was likely anyway as numbers increased and areas of existing settlement no longer sufficed for all the additional numbers which had to be fed.

Second, the increasing prosperity of illicit whisky making in the later eighteenth century encouraged landlords in districts where it flourished to divide holdings in order to accommodate a larger population able to pay higher rents from these 'industrial' earnings. Third, during the wars of the later eighteenth century, there was a huge expansion in the recruitment of Gaels to regiments of the British army. Several proprietors became military entrepreneurs, raising family regiments from the men of their estates in return for payments from the state. It therefore became common for land to be allocated in return for service. For instance, one reason given for the proliferation of tiny holdings on the island of Tiree by the 1820s was that 'four fencible regiments of men' had been raised during the Napoleonic Wars by the Duke of Argyll. Plots were carved out of existing tenancies to accommodate those who had served in order to honour the obligations made by the ducal house.

Between the middle decades of the eighteenth and early nineteenth centuries, numerous communities were therefore displaced and moved to the crofting townships which have formed the characteristic settlement pattern of the western Highlands and Islands since that time. Since kelp manufacture, whisky making and fishing were highly seasonal, some land had to be made available to provide food and fuel for a part of the year. But too much land would act as a powerful distraction from other tasks. These crofters were to be labourers first and agriculturists only second. The townships in which they lived were essentially therefore quasi-industrial communities where rents were forced up beyond their limited potential in order to force dependence on the produce of the sea, loch and shore. The central weakness in the entire system was that most smallholdings were simply not designed to provide enough for the needs of a normal-sized family from subsistence cultivation alone. It was reckoned in the early 1850s that only crofts rented at £15 per annum could produce secure self-sufficiency from agricultural activity in average seasons. Yet the overwhelming majority of holdings in the western Highlands were valued at £10 per annum or less. Crucially, however, crofting helped to retain people in the region rather than induce the migration levels of the south and east districts of the Highlands, where controls over subdivision were much more rigorous.

Subdivision did not simply help to anchor many of the next generation on the land. The splitting of croft holdings among younger male kindred also created the possibilities for more marriages, new families and the birth of additional children. Partible inheritance, therefore, became a precondition not only for population retention, but also, in the longer term, for population increase. This was a process which would have more than compensated numerically for those lost to the western Highlands and Islands through clearance and emigration before the 1840s.

Some estimates suggest that, on average, west Highland mothers in mid-Victorian times each had around five surviving children. As one distinguished historical demographer has commented:

> On some rather big assumptions, I think it is reasonable to estimate the average family size of married women who stayed and lived to age 49 in Rosshire, and were not widowed before then, to be at about five children.
>
> Evidence at parish level for 1881 suggests that rates were higher in Skye and the Outer Isles, and in most of mainland Inverness-shire and a bit lower in mainland Rosshire.[12]

This perspective once again confirms how crucial the impact of population change was on the history of Gaeldom in the nineteenth century.

West Highland and insular landlords had embarked on an extraordinary collective gamble by completely restructuring their estates and transforming the lives of the people on them solely on the basis of high wartime prices for a few commodities which happened to be in great demand during the conflict with France. Some historians argue that the implacable influence of objective market forces made the policy inevitable. But what can easily be forgotten is that the decisions made at the time were subjective and consciously carried out by individual factors and owners, some of whom at least were aware that the rich harvest being reaped from kelp might prove transitory when hostilities inevitably came to an end. The potential dangers were spelt out by one of the most powerful Highland magnates of the age, the 5th Duke of Argyll, in 1794. He heavily criticized his factor on Tiree for allowing the agriculture of the island to be neglected for the sake of the kelp industry, so causing rental income to depend on a very risky enterprise:

> In place of recovering the rents from the *natural* [my italics] productions of the island as was done before kelp was known, you have allowed the tenants to drink their barley and squander the other productions of the land, and taught them to trust the payment of their rents to the price of kelp, and the consequence is that whenever a market for an article like that fails I am getting nothing for my land.[13]

There is little evidence either that the ephemeral flow of income from kelp and fishing led to social mobility, planned investment or the emergence of a richer peasant class which might have given the western Highlands a degree of social resilience in the hard times after 1815. Instead, landowners creamed off the earnings during the good times through higher rentals, which were absorbed in their own consumer expenditure and that of their families. At the same time, indebtedness on a large scale remained a serious and pressing problem, even on some of the best-run properties. The 5th Duke of Argyll, for example, had been a benevolent proprietor who was interested in improving his vast estate not only for his own benefit, but also for the people who lived on it. He was succeeded at his death in 1806 by his son, George, the sixth Duke. He was a dandy, spendthrift, gambler and familiar of the Prince of Wales. His estates soon went to rack and ruin and subdivision of land among crofting families was allowed to run out of control, so that by the 1840s widespread clearance had to be enforced to reduce the number of destitute small-tenant and cottar families. It is reckoned that the sixth Duke had personally reduced the Argyll fortune by something of the order of £2,000,000 during his lifetime.

By the 1820s the entire economic edifice on which the crofting system had been built was crumbling rapidly. The renewal of trade with Spain, allowing the importation of Spanish barilla, cheaper and richer in alkaline content than seaweed, and the repeal of the salt duties, leading to production refinements within the chemical industry, destroyed the prosperity of kelp manufacture. Illicit whisky making on a commercial scale had virtually disappeared in most areas by the

1830s as a result of changes in revenue legislation and more determined measures of enforcement by the excise service. Earnings from military employment fell away rapidly after 1815 and instead peace was followed by a considerable return migration of both demobbed soldiers and sailors, which added further to the demographic pressures becoming ever more evident in several districts. Although the herring fishery survived and in some years in the 1830s managed to equal the good times of the 1790s, it was much more sporadic, and the erratic shoals could vanish from several lochs for long periods. By the 1840s the fishing villages of Plockton, Dornie, Tobermory, Lochcarron and Shieldaig, the fruits of the era of high optimism in the later eighteenth century and the early nineteenth, were considered to be among the poorest communities on the west coast.

Nevertheless, there was still no mass desertion from the land during the economic crisis which followed the end of the wars. In 1841 there were 85,342 more people living in the west Highlands than the total recorded in the region in the 1750s, a rise of 74 per cent over the period. The growth in emigration was significant, but even in areas of substantial outward movement, such as Skye and parts of Wester Ross, the numbers continued to rise until the 1840s. The Sutherland removals achieved national notoriety, but during the decade of widespread clearance between 1811 and 1820 the population of the county continued to rise because, as described above, eviction was followed by attempted resettlement of the people rather than outright expulsion. Thus the estate records reveal that 3,331 men, women and children were removed in the year 1819. The managers reported that of those who could be traced afterwards, 2,304 (70 per cent) were relocated on the Sutherland estate and most of the remainder moved to other parts of the county. Just eighty-three were reckoned to have emigrated. It was only in later years, as the ambitious programme of transformation collapsed when the fishery stagnated and peasant families inevitably struggled to adapt to the challenges of eking out a living on the lotted marginal coastlands, that the real exodus of people began.

Actual decline in numbers therefore did not normally occur at a regional level, but instead was unusually confined to districts where landowners indulged in especially intense programmes of clearance and did not invest in schemes of resettlement. Thus, while the population of the Lochaber area in general rose into the 1850s, parishes such as Morvern, Ardgour and Ardnamurchan, and Sunart experienced a precipitous fall from the 1830s. In the half-century before the potato famine, the grip of most of the population on the land had not been completely broken. Eviction was more often than not followed by relocation in crofting settlements. Further, no entirely landless class of any magnitude emerged and the western Highlands remained a peasant society with the tenacious attachment to land characteristic of all such societies.

The productivity of the crofts did rise because of potato cultivation. As one contemporary noted: 'the potato has done more to prevent emigration than any device whatever'.[14] Temporary migration for work in the Lowlands also became increasingly important. It peaked during the months of summer and autumn, the period of greatest hardship in the Highlands, when the old grain and potato harvests had often been consumed and the new had yet to be gathered. While ensuring that there were fewer mouths to feed at this critical time, temporary migration also produced a flow of cash income into the north-west (since seasonal migrants had a very high propensity to save), which was used to buy meal and, to a lesser extent, defray rental payments. This support of the peasant way of life was, however, as insecure as any other and income from temporary migration fluctuated dramatically over time. Those who went south and east found jobs mainly in casual agricultural or industrial employment, the very sectors of the labour market which were most volatile.

The role of the landlord classes was also relevant. Their control over land was absolute and they were in a powerful position to promote the movement of people out of the region by eviction, assisted emigration and control of subdivision. If most landlords had been intent on maximizing their economic opportunities, the exodus of people would undoubtedly have been much more rapid and extensive, as it was only commercial pastoralism which could guarantee secure rentals in the 1820s and 1830s. If landowners had placed the profit motive above all else, the crofting sector would have been crushed to an even greater extent than it actually was in order to accommodate more sheep. Sheep farming would not simply have become dominant but, in theory, might have obtained a virtual monopoly of all Highland land. Emigration did not occur on a greater scale partly because landlords refused to exploit their economic opportunities to the full and settled instead for a muddled response of partial clearance, inaction, resettlement, indirect and direct subsidy to the people who lived on their estates, and desultory attempts to sponsor assisted emigration.

The reasons why the élites were unwilling before the 1840s to put into effect a strategy of fundamental economic rationalization varied. Some were reluctant for paternalistic and humanitarian reasons or simply discouraged by the unacceptable social costs and reputational damage of total clearance. Others could not afford to incur the expense of supporting emigration to North America. By c.1830 most hereditary estates in the western Highlands were burdened with heavy debts, and a process of massive transfer of ownership from the old proprietors to the new was already underway. Again, the crofting population had become less vital to the economic health of most properties. As the sheep economy flourished, so the small tenants furnished but a small and declining fraction of total rental. Even this minor contribution fell in real terms as arrears accumulated among them in times of hardship. Any real pressure to thin the population in order to reduce Poor Law rates in the western Highlands only became imperative after the Poor Law Amendment Act of 1845 and, even more so, during the potato famine a decade later.

In the event, therefore, some landlords became associated with policies which indirectly inhibited migration rather than promoted it, the very opposite of the stereotype in the popular literature. Three aspects merit comment. First, on several estates there was considerable tolerance of increasing rent arrears which was in effect an indirect subsidy to the small tenantry at the cost to them of more insecurity and indebtedness. In Ardnamurchan, in 1838, total arrears had reached £7,101, or £133 more than the annual book rental. In Coigach they ranged between 169 per cent and 121 per cent of total rental between 1834 and 1841, and had risen to £8,121 by 1839 on the Skye estates of Lord Macdonald. The widespread incidence of arrears suggests that a considerable part of the reduction in regional income after the Napoleonic Wars was being passed on to the landlord class by the small tenants. Their aspiration remained the traditional one of maintaining a basic level of subsistence on land and they were now quite unable to pay sums which could only have been justified during the wartime bonanza of high prices. Second, many landlords continued to provide grain in scarce years at cost price, which was initially credited against the rental account but eventually became submerged among the mass of arrears. Third, the decline in the profitability of kelp manufacture did not always have the expected demographic consequences because, despite falling returns, kelp continued to be made in several areas until the 1840s. In North Uist, in 1837, 400 families were still engaged in kelping, and in South Uist 1,872 persons. Production continued in Tiree, Harris and Lewis on a major scale until the later 1830s. One commentator explained:

> The price of Kelp bounded downwards; but the fall of price did not tell so rapidly upon the condition of the people as might have been expected, because considerable quantities were continued to be made long after it had ceased to afford a fair immediate profit. The employment enabled the labourer to pay his rent, that rent however consequently to be paid in work, and not in money. The circulating medium of exchange has become greatly diminished in the country; and in many cases the society is gradually going backwards into a state of barter.[15]

The maintenance of kelp production in some districts therefore restricted the outward mobility of the population, and probably also plagued estates through the perpetuation and intensification of subdivision. Since labour power paid the rent and kelping was highly labour-intensive, main tenants had a continued vested interest in providing a patch of land for kinfolk to augment the labour team. Landlords were indeed trying to exert some control of subdivision in Islay, parts of Skye, Coigach, Canna, Loch Broom and Barra by the 1830s, but it continued to flourish in many other areas of the Inner and Outer Hebrides, not least because kelp manufacture endured there in several districts. Elsewhere it was alleged that the fall in cattle prices encouraged many small tenants to break up their holdings in order to spread the burden of maintaining rent payments. In western Inverness-shire, 'when a man becomes unable to pay his rent or to manage his loss, he seeks to lighten his burden without parting

1 The ruins of Castle Tioram in Loch Moidart in the western Highlands, the traditional seat of the Clanranald (Clann Raghnaill) branch of Clan Donald.

2 The Cairn at Culloden Moor commemorating the decisive defeat there of Jacobite forces by the Hanoverian army on 17 April 1746, which is often seen as a major turning point in Highland history.

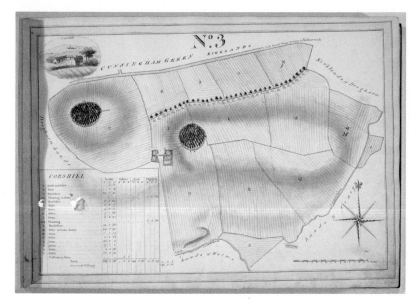

3 The runrigs of Corsehill, Eglinton estate, Ayrshire, 1789, depicted by John Ainslie, and showing the pre-improvement landscape of intermingled strips of land rented by different tenants.

4 A view of the Scottish Borders from Carter Bar. This was the first region in the country to experience substantial loss of population in the later seventeenth and eighteenth centuries, with the expansion of large cattle and sheep farms.

5 *Horsefair on Bruntfield Links, Edinburgh 1750*. It was at a country fair such as this that the Galloway Levellers first planned their campaign of resistance.

6 Culzean Castle, Ayrshire. Built in stages between 1772 and 1796 and designed by Robert Adam, this imposing edifice reflected the growing wealth of the Lowland Scottish aristocracy in the later eighteenth century.

7 An improved farmsteading of the later eighteenth century, Wester Kittochside, South Lanarkshire, built in 1782–4, probably on the site of a traditional longhouse.

8 The village of Tyninghame, East Lothian, built 1761. Numerous new settlements of this kind were established throughout the Lowlands in the eighteenth century, providing housing and employment for displaced small tenants and cottars.

9 Ploughman and horse team, later nineteenth century. Skilled horsemen were the key workers of the new agriculture.

10 Township of Ormsaigbeg, Ardnamurchan peninsula: a crofting settlement with individual strips of land running to the sea replacing the old system of communal agriculture.

The Scottish Highlander.   Un Montagnard d'Ecosse.

No. 10. G. Bickham ad viv. delin. & Sculp.   According to Act of Parliament April 3d

This Plate is most Humbly Inscribed to the Right Honourable the Lord Semple —
by his Lordships most Obedient Humble Servant W.m Meyer.

11 Private soldier of 42 Regiment of Foot in 1743, which was later to achieve fame as the Black Watch in the vanguard of British imperial expansion.

12 *The Last of the Clan* by Thomas Faed. This famous depiction of Highland emigration as tragedy does not fully capture the complex nature of the exodus.

13 The ruins of the township of Arichonan, Argyll, cleared in 1848 and the scene of a famous act of resistance to eviction.

14 The *Hercules*, which transported people from Skye, North Uist and Harris in 1852 to Australia at the time of the Highland potato famine. Many of the emigrants died of typhus or smallpox during the long voyage of 104 days.

15 Marines landing at Uig in Skye 1884. Such was the perceived breakdown of law and order during the 'Crofters War' that the authorities sent troops to the island to restore stability.

with all his interest and accordingly takes a partner into the concern. This is the way in which subdivision has mainly arisen.'[16] Proprietors therefore connived at a practice fraught with potential danger for the future in the hope of extracting a more favourable return from their tenants in the present. But by allowing many of the new generation with even a tenuous connection to land they helped to dissuade large numbers from permanently leaving the Highlands.

The inherent weakness in crofting society was brutally exposed in 1836 and 1837 when two partial but successive failures in the potato and grain crops pushed many of the population to the very edge of mass starvation. The deficiency in potatoes ranged from one quarter to one half of the normal crop, while oats failed from one half to two thirds throughout the region. This was a classic subsistence crisis reminiscent of pre-industrial times and entirely alien to the dynamic world of Victorian Britain, now proudly proclaiming itself the Workshop of the World. A concerned and alarmed government sent a special emissary to the north to report on the extent and causes of the disaster. Their agent was Robert Graham, Whig advocate and former Treasury Lord. Graham's detailed letters to the Treasury in London and his final report provide an authoritative guide to west Highland society in the later 1830s.

He reckoned that the total population of the distressed districts was around 105,000 people. Many communities faced the risk of starvation, though conditions varied markedly between areas and social groups. Sutherland had escaped relatively lightly, as had much of Wester Ross. The worst-affected localities were the island of Skye and the Outer Hebrides. The cottar classes were most vulnerable, but many small tenant families also suffered to a considerable extent.

However, Graham recognized that crop failure was simply the proximate cause of crisis. The more fundamental factors were long-term. The 'grand cause of the evil' was that 'the Population of this part of the country has been allowed to increase in a much greater ratio than the means of subsistence which it affords'.[17] Although emigration was a limited safety valve, numbers in some areas had continued to grow or did not decline rapidly enough in relation to the diminished job opportunities available in the 1820s and 1830s. The people depended on a narrow and fragile economic structure supported by the potato, subsistence fishing, temporary migration and occasional landlord assistance. It was a deeply precarious way of life which did not yield enough savings in good years to provide a margin of security in bad times. The whole system was likely to be threatened with total collapse if crop failure, even of a partial nature, took place. In times of shortage, the majority of the inhabitants of the distressed districts did not possess the purchasing power to buy supplies of food from other sources to avoid severe malnutrition. In the event, disaster was averted in 1836–7 by the combined efforts of government, landlords and Lowland charities. But that crisis was the harbinger of an even greater calamity which was to fall upon the region during the following decade.

II

Harvesting Men

In 1740 six independent companies of soldiers, established by General George Wade to police and watch disaffected areas of Jacobite loyalty in the Highlands, were regimented as the 43rd of Foot. The formation was soon renamed the 42nd of Foot, but became more celebrated in fame, myth and story as The Black Watch, *Am Freiceadan Dubh*, because of the dark colours of the regimental plaid which set the rank-and-file apart from the *Saighdearan Dearg*, the Red Soldiers, or Redcoats, of the rest of the British Army. It was an auspicious beginning to a saga of Highland militarism which helped to transform Gaeldom after the '45 and shaped the military history of the British Empire until the late twentieth century.

The recruitment of Gaels into the military during the three great wars of the period 1756–1815 is now a familiar story thanks to the recent publication of important research on the topic. Less well known, however, are the connections which can be drawn between the widespread nature of recruiting in the Highlands and the impact of that process on the development of crofting, dispossession and subdivision of land holdings in the region.

I

The Black Watch was the first of many regiments recruited from the Highlands into the armed forces of the crown between the 1750s and the early nineteenth century. The numbers were so remarkable that the Highlands quickly became the most militarized region in Britain with a bellicose tradition even greater than in the last years of clanship. Boom time for the Highland regiments began during the Seven Years War of 1756–63 and lasted throughout the American War of Independence and for much of the Napoleonic Wars. Six regiments of the line were mobilized between 1753 and 1763, including Fraser's and Montgomery's Highlanders. A further ten were recruited during the American War. Around 12,000 men were involved in the Seven Years War, almost the same number as the Highland army of the biggest rising, in 1715, and more than twice that of Prince Charles Edward Stuart's force of the '45. It was indeed a great irony that as clanship went into its death throes, the Highlands became even more militarized than in the recent past. By the French Wars the number of recruits was unprecedented. The most recent estimate suggests totals ranging from 37,000 to 48,000 men in regular, fencible and volunteer units. This was an extraordinary figure, given that the population of the Highlands was only around 250,000–300,000 during the second half of the eighteenth century. Not only had the region become the most intensely recruited region of the United Kingdom, but Scotland had the highest density of those famous retired veterans, the Chelsea Pensioners, within the British Isles, and the Highland counties had the largest proportion of all.

It was abundantly clear that in some districts recruitment had reached truly massive levels. Between the years 1793 and 1805, 3,680 men were under arms from the Skye estates of Lord Macdonald, MacLeod of MacLeod, and MacLeod of Raasay. From 1792 that number included no fewer than twenty-one lieutenant-generals or major-generals, forty-eight lieutenant-colonels, 600 other officers and 120 pipers. The parish of Gairloch in Wester Ross had been nearly stripped of all its menfolk by 1799. A survey for the Lord Lieutenant of Ross-shire arrived at the conclusion that hardly any adult males could be found there, and for the most part the population consisted mainly of children, women and old men because of the sheer scale of recruitment. Another estimate suggested that within the immense territories of the Earl of Breadalbane, straddling Argyllshire and Perthshire, as many as three farm tenancies out of every five had experienced some level of recruitment in the 1790s. Fort George at Ardersier, east of Inverness, the most formidable bastion fortress in Europe, built to control the clans after Culloden, now changed function. By the time of the American War after 1775 it had become 'the great drill square' where the Highland levies were trained and prepared for war overseas.

Clanship had metamorphosed into imperial service with the Gaels pioneering a role in the British military later to be assumed by other subjugated peoples of the Empire with renowned martial traditions, such as the Gurkhas, Sikhs and Pathans in Nepal and India. But the dramatic expansion of Highland recruitment was essentially short-lived. By c.1800 the manpower resources of the region had become virtually exhausted, not only because of over-recruitment, but also as a result of death in battle, disease, discharges, natural attrition and, not least, emigration. Even the most prestigious regiments were there-fore forced to extend the territorial range of their recruitment. At least a third of the Black Watch who fought at Waterloo were drawn from the Lowlands, the Border counties and even England. Later, some regiments were stripped of kilts and sporrans as their rank and file could no longer be considered authentically 'Highland' in social composition. By the late Victorian era, indeed, Highland regiments comprised only a minority of Highlanders as mass emigration took its toll on the region, especially after the potato famine of the 1840s, which preceded the Crimean War by only a few years.

It was perhaps surprising just a short time after Culloden that the British state determined to deploy Highlanders as a military spear-head of imperial expansion. Not only that, but the former rebels were to be regimented in distinctive and coherent units, officered by clan gentlemen, permitted to wear the banned Highland dress and encour-aged to develop their own ethnic esprit de corps. These were privileges not afforded the Irish (who vastly outnumbered Scots in the military service of empire) or battalions drawn from the Scottish Lowlands. In fact, the martial value of the Highlander was already being recog-nized some time before the Young Pretender landed in the Hebrides to launch his ill-fated adventure. Just before the '45, prominent Whig politicians in the Highlands, such as Duncan Forbes of Culloden and the Duke of Argyll, had suggested raising crown regiments from dis-affected clans. Officer posts in the British army for the clan gentry would, it was argued, help to cure them of their loyalty to the Stuarts. Again, in 1739, one prophetic commentator had observed:

They [the Highlanders] are a numerous and prolifick People; and, if reformed in their Principles, and Manners, and usefully employ'd, might be made a considerable Accession of Power and Wealth to Great Britain. Some Clans of Highlanders, well instructed in the Arts of War, and well affected to the Government, would make as able and formidable a body for their Country's Defence, as Great Britain, or Switzerland, or any part of Europe was able to produce.[1]

But vengeance, subjugation and punishment were at first the preferred responses after the failure of the '45. The Duke of Cumberland spoke for most of the victorious Hanoverians when he urged mass transportation of the rebels to the colonies rather than recruitment of the disaffected to the crown. The early history of the Black Watch, which had been recruited from clans loyal to the British state, also suggested caution. True, the regiment had distinguished itself at the Battle of Fontenoy, fought a few weeks after Culloden in May 1745, in what is now Belgian territory, during the War of the Austrian Succession. But the decision was still taken not to garrison it in Scotland but in England south of the Thames, and afterwards in Ireland between 1749 and 1755. Clearly even loyal Gaels were not to be fully trusted until long after the '45. But the idea of recruiting Highlanders did not fade away. The concept was advanced again in 1754 and 1755, only to falter against the express opposition of the King and Cumberland. However, attitudes then changed the following year. The arrival of a new Prime Minister, William Pitt, in 1756 signalled a more overt commitment to 'a blue-water policy' which advantaged colonial expansion over European commitment. An increased supply of fresh and reliable soldiers was thought vital, not least because of the outbreak of the Seven Years War with France in 1756, a conflict which more than any before was to be fought in the colonial theatre. The catastrophic defeat inflicted by the French and their Indian allies on the forces of General Edward Braddock on the Monongahela River in Pennsylvania, with the loss of two thirds of his command killed or wounded, did much to concentrate Pitt's mind. The 'Great War for Empire' was now going very badly and the Prime Minister was also known for his resolute opposition to the use of foreign mercenaries to strengthen the British military. The only realistic alternative, therefore, was to raise more troops from domestic sources. By early 1757 even the Duke of Cumberland had agreed to the employment of Highland levies. Two additional battalions were sanctioned, commanded by Simon Fraser, son of the executed Jacobite Lord Lovat, and Archibald Montgomery, later Earl of Eglinton. By the end of the war ten more Highland regiments were ready for action. They were the first of many which served not only during the Seven Years War but later in the American and Napoleonic campaigns. In 1766 Pitt looked back on the practice he had introduced in a famous speech:

> I sought for merit wherever it was to be found; it is my boast that I was the first minister who looked for it and found it in the mountains of the north. I called it forth and drew into your service a hardy and intrepid race of men, who, when left by your jealousy, became a prey to the artifice of your enemies, and had gone nigh to have overturned the state in the war before the last.
>
> These men in the last war were brought to combat on your side; they served with fidelity, as they fought with valour and conquered for you in every part of the world.[2]

Pitt had made the final executive decision but the mass recruitment of Highlanders was not his own idea. The Secretary of War, Lord Barrington, had already told Parliament in 1751 that he was all for having 'as many Scottish soldiers as possible in the army' and 'of all the Scottish soldiers I should choose to have and keep in our army as many Highlanders as possible'.[3] A sea-change had taken place in government thinking, in part because the destruction of the Jacobite threat was now recognized to be so complete that the menace of Stuart counter-revolution had been removed once and for all. The Highlands, unlike Ireland, no longer posed an internal security threat and mass recruitment into the forces of the crown could therefore proceed with all speed. At the same time, however, the old ingrained fear of disaffection took time to wholly dissipate, and so Highland troops were not to be allowed to linger long in Scotland after training but were rapidly despatched overseas. Thus it was that the Highlanders soon came to be publicly acknowledged as the crack troops of imperial warfare, with experience of battle in North America, the West Indies and India, enduring long and arduous tours of duty in foreign climes lasting over several years from which many never returned, either dying in service or settling the expanding Empire in order to avoid the threat of rent racking and clearance in the homeland.

English perception of the '45 was crucial to an understanding of the high levels of recruitment eventually achieved. Highlanders had first impressed themselves on the British state as warriors, and formidable ones at that. The terrifying charge and slashing broadswords which routed Sir John Cope's regulars at Prestonpans in less than thirty minutes were not easily forgotten. Even in the carnage of Culloden the following year it was acknowledged by officers of the crown that the rebel army had performed with remarkable fortitude and almost suicidal tenacity. Over time, therefore, a myth developed and hardened. Jacobite clansmen had indeed followed the wrong cause but they had done so only at the behest of their chiefs. Throughout they had displayed not only heroism in battle but undying loyalty. In bestselling publications like *Young Juba: or the History of the Young Chevalier* and *Ascanius, or the Young Adventurer*, the story of the 'Prince in the Heather' enchanted a growing readership throughout the British Isles. They told how, after Culloden, Bonnie Prince Charlie was never betrayed by his followers despite the high price on his head. Government came to believe that these virtues of loyalty and courage were founded on the ethic of clanship, of a martial society which had long ago vanished from the rest of Britain. For this reason the government tried to keep Gaels together in 'Highland regiments' under their 'natural' leaders, the chiefs and *fir-tacsa*. Fraser's Highlanders (71st of Foot) had no fewer than six chiefs of clans among its officers, as well as several clan gentry. Paradoxically, therefore, while the British government was wholly bent on destroying clanship on the ground as a menace to the state, it was also at the same time trying to reinforce clan allegiances through recruitment to clan-based Highland regiments. The intriguing feature was that clanship was almost dead by the 1750s, through a cycle of decline which was soon to accelerate in the later eighteenth century because of enhanced commercialization of estates and clearance of their people. But the government continued to hold fast to the belief that the Highlander was a natural warrior, an assumption also constantly reinforced by Highland landowners who milked the glamorous and famed image of clanship in order to win profitable contracts from government for recruitment into their family regiments.

One of the reasons why Lowland and Border magnates were so much less successful in the business of eighteenth-century military entrepreneurship was that they lacked this key marketing advantage of clan reputation in the competitive bidding process. Another was that in the 1750s at least they did not benefit from the government's policy of using military patronage to draw the teeth of residual Jacobite dis-affection. During the Seven Years War some of this was targeted on recalcitrant Highland families. Thus Fraser's Regiment was not only headed by the son of an executed Jacobite but also included several kinfolk of notorious rebels among the officers. One of them was the brother of Ewen Macpherson of Cluny, who had famously hidden in a specially designed cage on Ben Alder in Badenoch for seven years after Culloden. He had set up the first private casino in Gaeldom, before finally escaping into permanent exile in France. Indeed, some support-ers of the 'old cause' were able to successfully rehabilitate themselves in the eyes of the crown by their loyal service in imperial war. While it would be wrong to exaggerate the number of former Jacobites in the new kilted battalions, the presence even of a few of them did give an ironic twist to the colonial campaigns in America. Several of the line regiments which had fought against Highlanders during the '45 now found themselves as comrades of the former rebels in the war against the French. Lascelle's 47th Foot had been shattered by the charge of the clans at Prestonpans. But on the Plains of Abraham, outside Quebec, they joined with Fraser's Highlanders to pursue the fleeing French in the decisive battle which won Canada for the British. General James Wolfe, the commander of the army that day, had himself faced the Jacobite clans on Culloden Moor as a junior officer in April 1746. He served in Barrell's Regiment, which was later known as Duroure's 4th Foot, and it had suffered the most intense and violent Highland charge on the left flank of the Hanoverian line at Culloden. During the Seven Years War, however, it combined with Highland levies to great effect in the Caribbean campaigns.

The foundation therefore had been laid for greater expansion of Highland recruitment between 1775 and 1783 and again, and in even greater numbers, in the French wars between 1793 and 1815. The higher echelons of the British military now became influenced by German military dogma which suggested that people of mountainous regions were especially suited to the martial life. David Stewart of Garth's *Sketches of the Character, Manners, and Present State of the Highlanders of Scotland, with Details of the Military Service of the Highland Regiments*, first published in 1822, was the most influential text on the Highland soldier in Victorian times. Stewart of Garth contended that the perfect warrior had been formed by 'nature' in Highland Scotland:

> Nursed in poverty he acquired a hardihood which enabled him to sustain severe privations. As the simplicity of his life gave vigour to his body, so it fortified his mind. Possessing a frame and constitution thus hardened he was taught to consider courage as the most honourable virtue, cowardice the most disgraceful failing.[4]

Enlightenment ideas further fortified beliefs. The 'stage' theory of the development of human civilization, propounded by such Scottish intellectuals as Adam Ferguson and John Miller, fitted perfectly with the stereotype of the Highlander as an outstanding soldier. It was contended that the Highlands remained fixed in a period long ago when militarism was a way of life. Ferguson, for instance, argued that the Gaels were not interested in the 'commercial arts' but by their very nature were more disposed to making war. A parallel notion also soon became popular. Highlanders could be easily spared from ordinary manual labour for the duties of soldiering because their economy was so impoverished compared with the rest of the British Isles that the loss in terms of resources to the state was minimal.

There was more than enough actual evidence during 'the Great War for Empire' to justify beliefs like these. Statesmen who were accustomed to the slow, hard slog of army and navy recruitment were astonished at the speed with which the first Highland regiments were formed. Simon Fraser obtained his commission to raise a new battalion in January 1757. By March of that year he had already recruited over 1,100 men under arms and during the war itself the new formation performed with great distinction. In another alliance Major Hector Munro won the Battle of Buxar in India in October 1764 with the help

of detachments of the 89th Regiment. This was the victory which effectively completed the British conquest of Bengal. Munro was no stranger
to the Highlands, having once hunted Cluny Macpherson as a fugitive
after Culloden. The Black Watch played a major role against the Indian
nations in the brutal campaign known as Pontiac's War in America in
1763. Among other Highland battle honours were the capture of the
great French fortress at Louisburg on Cape Breton, the key to the St
Lawrence river, and Wolfe's even more decisive victory over the French.

By 1757 the number of Highlanders had reached 4,200 out of a
total of 24,000 British regulars in North America. Despite only being
a sixth of the whole, they were able to maintain a high profile. Colonial warfare was different from the formalized rituals of the European
theatre. Guerrilla actions were much more common and raids, retreats
and ambushes were the stock-in-trade of the Cherokees, Micmacs and
other tribal allies of the French in the wilderness. The Highlanders
were not only among the most adept British troops at responding to
these tactics but were also some of the most ruthless in crushing the
Indian enemy. By its nature wilderness warfare was ferocious, with
prisoners and wounded liable to be tomahawked, scalped and disem-
bowelled. Gaels used the same techniques of total war employed by
'Butcher' Cumberland's men after Culloden in genocidal campaigns
against the Indian nations between 1760 and 1764.

But it was not all a series of uninterrupted triumphs. Those battalions posted to Guadeloupe and Havana lost countless men to
yellow fever and malaria. The habit of using Highlanders as shock
troops in battles of attrition could also sometimes have devastating
consequences. At Ticonderoga on 7 July 1758, the Black Watch,
which formed part of the British force, lost 8 officers, 9 sergeants and
299 other ranks killed, and 17 other officers, 10 sergeants and 306
other ranks wounded. Yet, by these bloody sacrifices the Gaels not
only finally sealed their loyalty to the House of Hanover but ensured
that the Highlands became the government's favourite recruiting
ground in the imperial wars of the future. The Highland levies had
come to be regarded as the expendable cannon fodder of the Empire
with feared reputations among the enemies of Britain. Stewart of
Garth recalled that to the French they were the 'Sauvages d'Écosse':

they believed that they would neither take nor give quarter, . . . and that no man had a chance against their broadswords; and that with a ferocity natural to savages, they made no prisoners, and spared neither man, woman nor child . . . they were always in the front of every action in which they were engaged.[5]

2

A long tradition based largely on innumerable regimental histories has it that the Highland battalions of the later eighteenth century were the direct heirs of the clans. Their values were also said to be those of clanship: courage, loyalty, endurance and, above all, an innate capacity for making violent war. Yet any resemblance between the old clans and the regiments was at best superficial, which was hardly surprising since recruitment boomed at the very time when Highland society was in the process of fundamental change from tribalism to capitalism. Indeed, the mania for raising family regiments does not fit into a model of neo-clanship but rather one of rampant commercialism. Landowners were now military entrepreneurs rather than patriarchal chieftains. They harvested the population of their estates for the army in order to make money, in the same way as they established sheep walks, cattle ranches and kelp shores. But such profiteering had to be managed behind the façade of clan loyalties and martial enthusiasms because it was these very attributes which gave the Highlands a competitive edge in the military labour market in the eyes of government during the later eighteenth century. Even sophisticated and cynical politicians like Henry Dundas were taken in. During the Napoleonic Wars he exuded praise for the clansmen and their 'chiefs', enthusiastically approved of the great scheme to embody even more of them in 1797, and applauded the Highland warriors for their hostility to the pernicious 'levelling and dangerous principles' of the urban radicals of the time.[6]

In fact, recruitment to the army provided many benefits for the Highland élites. Raising a regiment promised lucrative commissions not only for a landlord but also for his kinsmen and associates. It also conferred influence and patronage in the neighbourhood among other impoverished minor gentry who desperately sought regimental officerships and the secure incomes and pensions which came with them. Local power and standing were increased while military service also consolidated close connections with government. The rewards could be substantial. Sir James Grant, whose estates were heavily encumbered with debt, won a sinecure worth £3,000 a year and the lord lieutenancy of Inverness in 1794. Mackenzie of Seaforth, who like most Highland landowners suffered from acute and perennial financial difficulties, did even better. In quick succession he became Lord Lieutenant of Ross in 1794, Lord Seaforth in the English peerage in the same year, and, in 1800, Governor of Barbados. But there were also more direct and equally desirable advantages. Dividing up lands for soldiers could provide an estate with more regular rentals than were likely to accrue from the small tenantry whose payments were notoriously volatile because of partial harvest failure and market fluctuation. The military had a secure income not only when on active service but also as half-pay officers in peacetime and from pensions when they retired. There is evidence, therefore, that several proprietors showed a clear preference for securing these 'martial' tenants for their estates.

The Warrants or Beating Orders issued by the Secretary of War, allowing the raising of a new corps, authorized the recruitment of officers and men, the numbers involved and the bounties to be paid to recruits when they joined. The cost of bounties rose dramatically in the later eighteenth century as the army's needs for more and more rank and file seemed unending. Average bounty levels for Highland recruits were £3 per man in 1757 but had climbed to £21–£30 by 1794. Landlords in the north of Scotland pocketed bounties, but rather than paying them in full to recruits used land on their estates as a substitute reward to those who were prepared to join up. Tenants were also expected to supply a family member or, if not, a 'purchased man', whose bounty was paid by the tenant himself. Through this mechanism, landlords made huge profits which during wartime equalled and sometimes even surpassed the income from their agricultural earnings. Recruitment was indeed 'More Fruitful than the Soil'.[7] There was also an expectation by landowners that those who lived on their estates would accept recruitment. When this did not happen willingly, systematic coercion was employed. Estate records teem with examples. Alexander Macdonnel of Glengarry ordered his agent to 'warn out' a list of small tenants from his Knoydart property, they 'having refused to serve me'. Similarly, MacLean of Lochbuie, on the island of Mull, threatened to remove seventy-one tenants, cottars and their families in 1795 because they had not been prepared to provide sons for service. On several estates, the tradition of 'land for sons' became commonplace. In the papers of Lord Macdonald covering his extensive lands on Skye, a document is headed 'List of Tenants who have been promised Lands and an exchange of lands for their sons'. These contracts were often very specific, outlining the length of leases and the tenurial arrangements related to sons being traded for land. In the long run, however, they generated angry controversy. Many recruits never returned and were buried in foreign graves after falling in battle or, more commonly, dying from disease. To the families, therefore, their holdings had often been acquired or secured, quite literally, by the blood of their kinfolk. When these obligations were cast aside, for whatever reason, the people were likely to feel that a gross breach of trust had been committed. Lands for sons added an emotional edge to Highland history which was entirely missing from that of the rural Lowlands during improvement. This was another factor helping to explain the different emotional responses in each region to dispossession.

Donald MacLeod's *Gloomy Memories in the Highlands of Scotland* was just one of several polemics to draw attention in angry and emotive prose to this aspect of recruitment and which must have made a powerful impression on his Victorian readership. He declared: 'The children and nearest relations of those who sustained the honour of the British name in many a bloody field – the heroes of Egypt, Toulouse, Salamanca and Waterloo – were ruined, trampled upon, dispersed and compelled to seek an asylum across the Atlantic.'[8] Alexander Mackenzie, in his bestselling *The History of the Highland Clearances* (1883), also launched a bitter attack on those proprietors who had perpetuated crimes of betrayal against the nation's finest soldiers:

> in their names, the fathers, mothers, brothers, wives, of the invincible '78th' [a regiment raised on the estate of the Duke of Sutherland] had been remorselessly driven from their native soil . . . were Britain some

twenty years hence to have the misfortune to be plunged into such a crisis as the present, there will be few such men as the Highlanders of the 78th to fight her battles if another policy towards the Highlands is not adopted, that sheep and deer, ptarmigan and grouse, can do but little to save it in such a calamity.[9]

It should be remembered also that when Mackenzie published his powerful condemnation of landlordism in the 1880s, the Highland regiments were at the very pinnacle of their fame. One historian has noted that 'Highlanders were the most fêted of all Victorian soldiers', while another described how there was a 'Victorian cult of the High-landers'.[10] So potent was their appeal at the time that the Scottish military in general became Highlandized when Lowland regiments were ordered to be dressed in doublets and tartan trews.

Military entrepreneurship brought considerable short-term profit to proprietors but could also lead to long-term loss of public reputation for some of their descendants. Moreover, the earnings from the military economy only lasted for a relatively short time from the 1750s to the later 1790s. By that decade the numbers being recruited in the Highlands were in dramatic decline. Yet, over the period of good earnings, this ephemeral stream of estate income had boosted the consumerist culture of many landlords and so aggravated their long-term crisis of indebtedness.

Promises of land to recruits were also fraught with long-term danger. Without them recruitment could not have taken place on such an immense scale as the only alternative was to pay money bounties to each soldier. But that would have been intolerably costly, sometimes averaging expenditure up to a third or more of the rental income of a large estate, to recruit a single formation of regimental size. Also, in order not to remove the rent-paying tenants from work on the land, proprietors mainly tended to recruit semi-landless cottars who paid nothing in rent into the coffers of the estate. But cottar families then expected to be rewarded with some land in return for the service of their menfolk. The only way to satisfy these obligations was to break up larger holdings into crofts, or divide crofts into even smaller lots. On the Duke of Argyll's estate on the Ross of Mull in 1806, a number of those pressing for land were soldiers and their families. As a result, approval was given to divide up some of the medium-sized farms. Again, in Sleat on Skye and in Lewis, several townships were also crofted to accommodate veterans and their dependants. By anchoring an increasing part of the population in such semi-economic small-holdings, landlords reduced the possibility of building up more substantial and resilient farms. It was the very antithesis of the policy of land consolidation pursued throughout most of the Lowlands.

The subdivision of scarce land was soon made even worse by population growth which left large numbers of almost destitute smallholders relying on the potato crop when bi-employments, including military recruitment, went into decline or vanished altogether after 1815. These poor communities, however, did not, unlike those surveyed in the next chapter, have the resources to emigrate and so they clung on to their patches of land despite growing difficulties. Eventually, many land-lords came to the conclusion that they had no alternative but to force them out, if they were to avoid having to assume responsibility for their welfare, which might in turn bring financial ruin to themselves and their own families.

12

Rejecting the Highlands

Any violent opposition to authorities pursuing removal of tenants under due legal process would sooner or later lead to intervention by the forces of law and order and arrest of the offenders. Resistance must have been thought by many not only pointless but counter-productive. More effective by far, at least for the period of this chapter down to 1815, would be to reject absolutely the new ways in the Highlands by leaving the region. However, both government and the landed class of the north-west and the islands were implacably opposed to emigration in the later eighteenth century and early nineteenth. For the former, it meant the loss of a militarily valuable population when Britain was involved in two major wars. For the latter, emigration removed precious manpower from their estates which were needed for kelp burning, fishing and army recruitment. An implicit alliance formed of government strategic concern and landlord vested interest caused emigration to be banned altogether in 1775. Another attempt at prohibition was made in 1786 by Henry Dundas, Scotland's leading political manager of the day. Later, lobbying by Highland landowners at the height of the kelp boom in the early nineteenth century led to the passing of the Passengers Vessels Act in 1803. The legislation was ostensibly humanitarian in intent as it was purportedly placed on the statute book in order to improve conditions on board ship for passengers in vessels sailing to North America. The real objective, however, was to substantially raise the cost of passage and so deter future emigrants. In some cases fares more than doubled as a result of the legislation. The Act remained on the statute book until it was finally repealed in 1826. Parliament also voted to provide more than half a million pounds for transport projects in the Highlands, including the construction of the

Caledonian Canal, connecting northern Scotland from east to west, in order to stem the tide of outflow from the region through the provision of more employment. Despite these measures, however, and in the teeth of landlord opposition, emigration from the western Highlands and Islands reached hitherto unprecedented levels.

Rising emigration was a Britain-wide phenomenon. Numbers were so great in the 1760s that by 1775 as many as 10 per cent of the population of the American colonies over the long period of settlement had arrived there in the previous fifteen years. The humiliating loss of the thirteen colonies in 1783 confirmed in the official mind that an empire of colonization was not a good idea and the effort was redoubled to prevent further movement to the remaining colonies of British North America, later Canada. The provincial governors of Prince Edward Island, Cape Breton, Nova Scotia and Upper Canada were warned by London not to encourage migration from the British homeland.

These instructions may have partially helped to stem the tide. But they did not achieve complete success because, as will be shown later, Highland emigration previously channelled to what was now the United States began to slowly move north and built up new connections after 1783 with Britain's remaining North American provinces. Indeed, tensions emerged between the interests of London and those of the governors of the under-populated Canadian colonies. Immigrants arriving at their ports were not necessarily turned away or subjected to any significant opposition. For instance, in 1791 the governor of Nova Scotia provided both food and support to 650 West Highland emigrants who had landed at Pictou, in a vain attempt to encourage them to stay on the island and not continue on the journey to their planned destination in North Carolina. Eventually the British government did concede that the emigration policy was failing and tried to compromise by steering settlement towards the Canadian colonies of the Empire rather than to the now independent United States.

Between 1760 and 1815, Highland transatlantic emigration took two forms which were interconnected. The first consisted of the movement of civilian families and the second the settlement of demobilized Highland officers and rank and file who had been allocated American land grants at the end of service after the Seven Years War

(1756–63) and the American War of Independence (1776–83). Both emigrant streams were influenced by the attractions of cheap or free land across the Atlantic and given impetus by the economic tensions surfacing in the late-eighteenth-century Highlands. These threatened the grip of the peasantry on the land and their status as full tenants on the estates.

I

Tracing the migration of Highlanders to North America is not an easy task for the eighteenth century. Apart from the government-inspired *Register of Emigrants* in the years before the American War of Independence, the numbers involved have to be constructed from stray newspaper reports and some contemporary comments. We do know, however, that before the 1760s small numbers of Gaels, mainly from Argyll, were already moving in family and local parties to North Carolina, Georgia and New York. But it is reckoned that migration was limited to fewer than 3,000 leaving over the half-century from *c.*1700 to *c.*1760. Only after the end of the Seven Years War in 1763 did numbers rise to unprecedented levels, with nearly 10,000 emigrants between the early 1760s and 1775. It was the scale of this exodus and its local focus on the western Highlands and Islands which alarmed both landlords and government as to that total needed to be added the significant number of veterans from the Highland regiments who decided to remain and take land in America after demobilization in 1763. The Highland departures accounted for around 60 per cent of all Scottish emigration, though only 40 per cent of the Scottish population lived in the Highland region at the time. Between 1773 and 1776 only London had more emigrants than the Highlands, with the region having at least 18 per cent of all emigrants from Britain, and this from one of the most sparsely populated areas of the United Kingdom. Some contemporaries claimed that a frenzied emigration 'mania' had gripped the north of Scotland in these decades.

The migrations fell away during the American War and when it came to an end their orientation changed from the USA to British North America. Loyalists left the infant republic in large numbers for the remaining imperial territories to the north. One estimate has it that Scots, who had provoked considerable enmity for a number of reasons from American patriots, may have comprised one in five of the 30,000 loyalists who fled north. Nova Scotia was a favoured area of resettlement for Highlanders from North Carolina, while Scottish refugees from New York, many of them recent emigrants from Glengarry in western Inverness-shire, tended to make for what would become eastern Upper Canada. Even during the war, Scots families from the Mohawk Valley in New York had gone in order to avoid the vengeance of the Americans. The conflict in that area had descended into a bloody and very violent guerrilla war with savage reprisals and counter-reprisals on both sides. Highlanders had won a fearsome reputation both for their ferocity and as first-rate frontier guerrillas. It would have been suicidal for them to remain among their former enemies when peace was declared. Instead, they and the disbanded soldiers of the King's Royal Regiment of New York and the Royal Highland Emigrant Regiment sought refuge across the border in Canada. The Roman Catholic Macdonnels and their kinfolk formed a new community on the north bank of the St Lawrence River west of Montreal. One migrant wrote to her family back in Scotland that the 'McDonalds hope to found in the new land a new Glengarry'.[1] The name stuck and, over the following decades, the district attracted numerous emigrants from the western mainland of the Highlands and the neighbouring islands.

Canada and the maritime colonies now virtually completely supplanted the USA as places of settlement for the Gaels. Scottish transatlantic emigration after 1783 was very much Highland in origin, though the individualized and almost invisible movement to the USA left little record and its scale has almost certainly been underestimated. Around 14,000 emigrants may have left Scotland for British North America between 1776 and 1815 and probably as many as nine out of ten of them could have come from the Highlands. But the annual level of emigration was significantly lower than the early 1770s, almost certainly due to the immense disruption caused to the traditional migrant routes by war and the subsequent Loyalist diaspora. Remarkably, however, the connections with the Canadian areas of settlement were soon renewed, which was powerful evidence of the dense network of communications which now spanned the Atlantic and linked communities in the wilderness areas of the New World with those of their kindred and friends in remote parts of the Highlands.

Each of the new Canadian settlements became a strong magnet for people from the coastlands and glens of Gaeldom. Small colonies from the Uists and Glenfinnan were to be found on Prince Edward Island, while Pictou, Nova Scotia, was settled mainly from Rossshire. In five large emigrations between 1785 and 1793, people from Glengarry, Knoydart, Morar and Glenelg in western Inverness sailed to join their families and friends in the new Highland settlement of Glengarry County in western Quebec. Over 1,200 made the transatlantic crossing in these years, around 40 per cent of the entire migrant stream from the Highlands over the period. It was inevitable, therefore, that these concentrated settlements, often located in isolated districts, would become enduring outposts of Gaelic culture for several generations to come.

This was not a flight of the very poor or the dispossessed because migration by sea followed by resettlement across the Atlantic had costs. Emigration assisted by landowners, which became more common from the 1820s, was out of the question in this earlier period for the reasons already discussed. Indeed, landlords were so implacably opposed to the departures that in mainland west Inverness during the 1790s they were even prepared to place evictions on hold for a time because the recruitment of soldiers from their estates was providing such attractive returns. McDonnell of Glengarry offered his old followers a reduction in rental of 10 per cent if they promised to stay. The offer was rejected. The irony, of course, was that it was the policies of the landowners which prompted large-scale emigration in the first place. There were only two 'assisted' emigrations before 1815. One was the support that the tiny Catholic Church in Scotland gave to its adherents in South Uist because it feared Presbyterian proselytism in the southern Hebrides. A second was the formation of a fencible regiment for defence of Canada which was established in order to steer the exodus away from the United States by promising free land to soldiers and their families. The total recruited with dependants eventually reached 2,100 people. The poor could, of course, seek to cross the Atlantic by obtaining passage as indentured servants. In this system, the costs of the voyage were paid in advance by masters in the colonies in return for a period of bonded service. Data on how far that means of emigration was popular only exist in the customs returns for the peak movement years of 1774–5. They reveal that only 150 of the nearly 3,000 Scots documented in the records then travelled on an indentured passage and the majority of them were from the Lowlands.

The evidence from other sources is conclusive that it was mainly those tenants with some resources from the middling ranks of Highland society who made up the majority of the emigrant parties. These people had enough livestock to sell off to release cash to support the costs of the voyage and resettlement. One reason why the renewal of emigration reached a new peak in 1801–2 was that cattle fetched good prices in those years enabling them to be converted into good returns. The social composition of emigrant parties from western Inverness-shire to Glengarry County in Canada seems to have been fairly typical of the generality:

> three out of five emigrants were farmers, one out of eight was a craftsman and one out of four was a labourer or servant . . . the emigrants are described as 'the principal tenants', the better-off tenants, or (later) 'the best part of the dregs . . . of the commoners'. Clansmen of middling status and resources – tenants and craftsmen – therefore dominate the emigrant parties but some poorer members of the community also left.[2]

2

The main outlines of the sequence of emigration from the Highlands in this period are not in dispute. But the reasons why so many people from this region of Scotland should seek to leave in such large numbers are far from clear and are disputed by scholars. Certainly a new transport infrastructure for mass emigration from northern Scotland was in place by the second half of the eighteenth century. Also, the growth of Highland communities in North Carolina, Georgia and New York from the 1730s had laid the foundation for 'chain migration' or the development of a long-term connection between places in the Highlands and North America. The commercial relationship between Scotland and North

America was also revolutionized by the remarkable success of Glasgow in the transatlantic tobacco trade from the 1730s. The American trades helped to provide the transport for large-scale emigration from Scotland as most Highland communities were within relatively easy travelling distance of the Clyde ports and vessels were also often chartered from there to sail to the northern sea lochs to pick up emigration parties from there. It was, for instance, the growing trade in Canadian timber to Scotland in the early nineteenth century which partially helped to offset the impact of the Passenger Vessels Act of 1803 on emigration. The British timber market's demand for Canadian lumber radically increased as a result of wartime needs. The trade needed large vessels but they had low freights on the outward journey and the emigrant traffic to Upper Canada and the maritime provinces was therefore an effective means of utilizing surplus capacity and cutting costs.

The Highlands at all social levels had also become less insular by the later eighteenth century. Extensive recruitment of Gaels to the army in the three wars between 1757 and 1815 must have accustomed Highland society to greater mobility. This was even more likely when the government started to pay off officers and men from the army in colonial land rather than cash; in turn, these military settlements soon acted as magnets to kinsfolk at home. A key element in this Highland emigration was also the leadership provided to many emigrant parties by *fir-tacsa*, tacksmen or lesser gentry, who had either acquired land in, or had become familiar with, the transatlantic colonies, as a result of their service as officers in the British army.

All these influences facilitated mass emigration, but they could not in themselves cause it to happen. In the age before the steamship, transatlantic migration by sail was usually tantamount to permanent exile. Most of North America still remained a wilderness to Europeans, an alien land thought to be peopled by wild savages living in impenetrable forests. Few therefore embarked willingly on the long transatlantic voyage because of the well-publicized risks and dangers unless they had reasons for doing so because of pressing circumstances at home. In the search for direct causation, contemporary commentators and later scholars have addressed both the impact of conditions in the Highlands and the pull from opportunities in North America. Some argue that the increasing volume of emigration reflected the pressure of rising population, which led, in turn, to an outflow of 'surplus' peasants and their families. This is a hypothesis which at first glance has much to commend it. As noted in earlier chapters, numbers did increase substantially in northern Scotland in the later eighteenth century, the Highland economy was indeed poor and underdeveloped, and, when the emigration of Highland people is examined down to the middle decades of the nineteenth century, the Malthusian explanation does have real force. Population loss in the long run was inevitable because the economy proved incapable over time of generating an adequate level of employment for those who lived in the region.

However, the picture in the earlier period between 1760 and 1815 is considerably more complex and it is by no means certain that the demographic explanation is entirely satisfactory. There are several problems. First, though numbers were increasing, economic activity was also expanding. There were indeed difficult years, such as 1772–3, 1782–3 and 1801–2, which were brought about by partial harvest failure and so triggered emigration. In addition, the vast majority of the population continued to eke out an existence at, or only marginally above, subsistence level. Nevertheless, in these decades, there was also an increase in employment, especially in the western Highlands and Islands, where most emigrants came from, in kelp manufacture, fishing, illicit whisky making, the seasonal migrant economy in the Lowlands and, above all, military service. Landlord correspondence in these years actually reveals a fear of labour shortage on some estates, a concern which explains why most lairds were resolutely opposed to emigration. Second, as discussed earlier, the majority of those in the emigrant parties were not the very poorest or those closest to the margins but tenant families who had enough resources to meet the costs of emigration and resettlement.

A more convincing explanation can be found in a study of nine emigrant parties bound for Upper Canada between 1773 and 1802 from Glengarry and Glen Morriston, Knoydart, Eigg and the west coast, Loch Arkaigside, Glenelg and Lochiel which argues that 'economic transformation was the key underlying cause ... in this period'.[3] Where evidence is available, it shows that nine out of ten of those who left did so in family groups. Women formed between 44 and 51 per cent of the adults while children under the age of thirteen were at least 27 per cent on average and up to almost 50 per cent of passengers in half of these sailings to Canada. The average family size ranged from 4.6 to 5.7 people. Overwhelmingly, the emigrants came from contiguous districts and drew on extended networks of family and association. A community exodus of this kind confirmed 'the emigrants' total rejection of the place offered them in the trans-formed Highlands'.[4] In other words, their decision to leave was a forced choice. The people would doubtless have preferred to stay but escalating rentals and the fact or threat of eviction made that impos-sible in their eyes. They specifically complained not of over-population but of losing their land to incomers who would break up the trad-itional *bailes* and merge the lands into single, large pastoral farms.

It is important to recognize, however, that the people do not seem to have been opposed to all the new ways *per se*. An increase in trading activity had been a fact of life in the Highlands since the seventeenth century and, later, when settled in Canada, the emigrants became fully involved in commerce in their new homes. Rather, they appear to have strongly resented the increased share of their meagre incomes which they now had to devote to paying increased rent, the threat of eviction from their holdings, and the fear of being consigned to the function and status of quasi-labourers in small crofts. There were other options available to them in addition to that of emigration, including fishing, crofting or even movement for wage labour to the cities of the Lowlands. They chose Canada because it satisfied the peasant aspiration for land and since emigration allowed the whole community to remain together as a functioning social entity. In essence, therefore, mass emigration represented a radical opposition to how Highland society was changing in the last quarter of the eighteenth century. Yet, as an exercise in collective self-help it was a time-limited strategy. Most of those who remained after 1815 suf-fered the full impact of the postwar collapse in incomes and increasing encroachment of sheep on land occupied by their cattle stocks. Few had the resources by that time to follow the example of those who had been fortunate enough to go before in earlier decades.

The history of the emigrant Gael before 1815 is often in dramatic contrast to the much gloomier narrative of later times. For a start, the emigration parties left in the teeth of opposition from both the state and the overwhelming majority of landowners. They also for the most part achieved success. Virgin forest was cleared and by the end of the 1780s the settlements in Glengarry were already dotted with small log cabins built in tiny clearings. The emigrants had obtained what they sought: land, freedom from landlord oppression, the reconstitution of networks of family and friends, and the perpetuation of their traditional culture. The potential catastrophic loss of land and social disruption in Scotland had been avoided through the decision to emigrate. Several of these new Gaelic settlements flourished. By 1832, for instance, the population of Glengarry in Upper Canada had climbed to 8,500 and doubled again to 17,596 twenty years later. The vast majority of them were Scottish Gaels or their descendants.

More highly publicized was the Earl of Selkirk's settlement at Baldoon (named after his family estate in Wigtownshire) on Prince Edward Island. Nearly 1,000 Highlanders left for the area in 1803–4 under his tutelage. But the territory for colonization had been selected unwisely. The marshlands bred malarial mosquitoes, which soon spread disease of epidemic proportions. Baldoon languished until the war of 1812, when it was finally overrun by invading American forces. Selkirk's Red River settlement in Upper Canada did much better. But these colonizations did not bring easy or sudden riches. The Highland districts were often isolated and located on marginal arable land. But they did provide a new security at a modest standard of living, which for the most part was accepted by communities habituated in the old country to even lower levels of comfort.

Only through exploring the scattered evidence of correspondence, oral tradition, song and poetry can we obtain a more realistic picture of the actual mindset of these emigrant parties. The very fact of the continuous stream of people who left for the new settlements over many years suggests an optimism and a strong faith in the benefits of emigration. Surviving poetry is equally positive. A strong theme running through the verse is that of liberation from servility, akin to the exodus from Egypt of the Israelites under Moses. Some songs do reveal sorrow at leaving home and the fracturing of ancient connections with beloved landscapes, family and friends. But linked with this is often a sense of excitement as the bards contemplate a new life across the ocean. The mood is captured well in 'Fair is the Place' by Micheil Mór MacDhómhnaill's (Michael McDonald, *c.*1745–1815) after his arrival in Prince Edward Island in 1772:

O, 'S àlainn an T-àite	Fair is the Place
A, 's àlainn an t-àite	Fair is the place
Th' agam 'n cois na tràghad	I have here by the sea,
'N uair thig e gu bhith 'g	when it comes time to till it
àiteach ann	with the plough.
Leis a' chrann, leis a' chrann, O.	I shall make bread-land with
Ni mi 'n t-aran leis na gearrain	horses
'S an crodh-bainne chuir mu'n	and put the cows to graze;
bhaile;	we shall not be in want in
'S cha bhi annas oirnn 's an	spring,
earrach,	I wager.
Chuirinn geall, chuirinn geall.	
	Sparkling, diamond-like,
O, 's fraoidhneasach,	clear as candle-light,
daoimeanach,	is the salmon with his
Glan mar sholus choinnlean,	brilliance,
Am gradan le chuid	in every stream,
shoillseanach	Merrily sporting, leaping from
Annas gach allt, anns gach allt, O.	the pool
Mear ri mire, leum na linne	

Rory Roy Mackenzie (1755–?) was one of the Earl of Selkirk's colonists who first owned land in Prince Edward Island before migrating subsequently to Pictou. 'An Imrich' ('The Emigration'), was composed as he prepared to leave Scotland. He laments the new economic order in the Highlands but looks forward to better times across the Atlantic:

An Imrich

The Emigration

Ma 's e Selkirk na bàighe	If it be the benign Selkirk
Tha ri àite thoirt dhuinn,	who will grant us a place,
Tha mi deònach, le m' phàisdean,	with my children I am eager
Dhol gun dàil air na tuinn.	to sail without delay.
Siud an imrich tha feumail	It is necessary to emigrate,
Dhol 'nar leum as an tìr s'	to leave this land immediately,
Do dh'America chraobhach,	and go to wooded America
'S am bi saors' agus sìth.	where there will be freedom and peace.
Faigh an nall dhuinn am botul,	Bring us the bottle,
Thoir dhuinn deoch as mu'n cuairt;	pass a drink around to us;
'S mise a' fear a tha deònach	I am most eager
A'dhol a sheòladh a' chuain;	to set sail across the sea,
A'dhol a dh'ionnsaidh an àite	and to go to the place
Gus 'n do bhard am mòr-shluagh;	from which many have embarked;
A'dhol gu Eilein Naomh Màiri,	to go to St Mary's Isle,
'S cha bhi màl 'ga thoirt bhuainn.	and no rents will be exacted from us.
A dheagh Aonghais Mhic-Amhlaidh,	Now, worthy Angus Macaulay,
Tha mi 'n geall ort ro mhòr,	I will wager
Bho'n a sgrìobh thu na briathran	that since you wrote the instructions
'Us an gnìomh le do mheòir,	and their terms with your own hands,
Gu'n grad chuir thu gu'r n-ionnsaidh	
Long Ghallda nan seòl,	you will soon send us
'Us ruith-chuip air a clàraibh	a foreign vessel,
Thar nam bàrc-thonn le treòir.	foam on her deck,
	rushing powerfully over the waves.
Seo a' bhliadhna tha sàraicht'	This is a taxing year
Do dh'fhear gun àiteach, gun sunnd,	for one without a dwelling, without cheer,
'N uair théid càch 's a' mhìos Mhàrta	when in March others go
Ris an àiteach le sùrd.	to their ploughing eagerly.
Tha luchd-riaghlaidh an àite	The overlords here
Nis 'gar n-àicheadh gu dlùth,	reject us completely.
'S gur h-e an stiùuir a thoirt an iar dhi	To turn the rudder westward
Nì as ciataiche dhuinn.	is the most sensible course for us.

Ma 's e réiteachan chaorach
'N àite dhaoine bhios ann,
Gu'm bi Albainn an tràth sin
'S i 'na fàsaich do 'n Fhraing.
'N uair thig Bonipart' stràiceil
Le làimh làidir an nall,
Bidh na cìobairean truagh
   dheth
'Us cha chruaidh leinn an call.

If it be sheep-walks
which will replace men,
Scotland will then
become a wasteland for France.
When the arrogant Bonaparte
   comes
with his heavy hand,
the shepherds will be badly off,
and we will not grieve for them.

'S mo ghuidhe ma sheòlas sinn
Gu'n deònaichear dhuinn
Gu'm bi 'n Tì uile ghràs-mhor
Dh' oidhch' 's a' là air ar stiùir,
Gu ar gleidheadh 's ar teàrnadh
Bho gach gàbhadh 'us cùis,
'S gu ar tabhairt làn sàbhailt
Do thìr àghmhor na mùirn.

It is my wish, if we sail,
that it may be granted us
that the all merciful one
guide us night and day,
to save us and protect us
from every peril and need,
and to bring us safely
to the land of good cheer.

Gheibh sinn fearann 'us àiteach
Anns no fàsaichean thall;
Bidh na coillteau 'gan rùsgadh
Ged bhiodh cùinneadh orinn
   gann.
'N dràsd s' ann tha sinn 'nar
   crùban
'M bothain ùdlaidh gun taing,
'Us na bailtean fo chaoraich
Aig luchd-maoine gun dàimh.

We shall get land and a home
in the wilderness yonder;
the forests will be cleared
though money will be scarce.
Now we are cramped
in gloomy huts without
   recompense,
and the fields are occupied by
   sheep
owned by the unfriendly rich.

The final song comes from Anna Gillis of Morar, who sailed from Greenock to Quebec in 1786 with 500 others to settle eventually in Glengarry County. 'Canada Ard' or 'Upper Canada' reflects her views of the new colony and contains a tribute to Father Alexander (Scotus) MacDonnell, who accompanied the Knoydart emigrants of 1786 and continued to act as their pastor, leader and counsellor in Glengarry:

Canada Ard

Ann an Canada Ard
Tha gach sonas 'us àgh;
Bidh gach maoin ann a' fàs ri
    chéile.

Gu bheil cruithneachd a' fàs,
Luchdmhor, lìonte gu' bhàrr,
Ach trì mìosan thoirt dha de
    thearmunn.

Gheibhear siùcar à craobh
Ach an goc chur 'na taobh,
'Us cha dochair sin a h-aon de
    geugan.

Gheibh sinn mil agus fion,
'S gach ni eile gu'r miann;
Cha bhi uireasbhuidh sìon
    fo'n ghréin oirnn.

Maighstir Alasdair òg,
Mac Fear Scotais na sròil,
Sagart beannaicht' bha mór le
    éibhneas.

Dh'fhalbh e leinne mar naomh
Gus ar beatha bhi saor,
Mar dh'fhalbh iad le Maois Eipheit.

Fhuair sinn bailtean dhuinn fhìn,
Le còir dhainginn o'n rìgh,
'S cha bhi uachdrain a chaoidh
    'gar léireadh.

Upper Canada

In Upper Canada
there is every joy and delight;
all requirements will prosper
    together.

Wheat grows
abundantly, ready to harvest,
with only three months to bring it to
    full season.

Sugar may be gotten from a
    tree
if a tap be inserted in its side,
and not one of its branches
    damaged.

We shall have berries and wine
and all else that we desire;
we shall lack nothing under
    the sun.

Young Father Alexander,
son of Scotus of the banners,
the holy priest, was full of
    kindness.

Like a saint he brought us out
so that we would be free
as were those who followed Moses
    out of Egypt.

We got farms of our own
with proprietory rights from
    the king,
and landlords will no more oppress us.

The labour of carving out new communities from wilderness must have been hard, demanding, exhausting and often discouraging. But the Highland pioneers of this era had a number of advantages which at least helped successful settlement in British North America to progress. The imperial state may have been hostile for a time to the idea of populating Canada but it did recognize the responsibility to those families who had sacrificed a great deal in their loyalty to the crown before 1783. Thus, in June 1784, government bateaux carried Loyalists from their refugee camps in Quebec to the new townships, where they not only received land in the better areas but also provisions for two years, clothing, tools, some livestock and household plenishings which enabled a good start to be made in building homes and clearing land. All this then lowered the threshold of risk for later migrants, who could also hope for food and help in the crucial early years of resettlement. Moreover, the provincial governments had a different agenda from London. They saw colonization as a means of expansion and development and some governors took the view that the martial traditions of the Highlanders would also fashion a robust defensive barrier against attempted armed incursions from the USA. The result was that the local governments were often more than willing to assist with provisions and transport within Canada from the port of disembarkation to areas of resettlement. This was done in Quebec for emigrants from the Island of Eigg in 1790, in Nova Scotia in 1791 and again in Quebec in 1794.

In cases where support was not forthcoming, Scottish merchant houses in Montreal, Halifax and Quebec commonly subscribed substantial sums to assist indigent passengers on arrival. Eventually, even the British government conceded that emigration could not be prevented and so should be directed if possible towards the British colonies. The outbreak of war with the USA in 1812 and the attempted American invasion of Canada concentrated the minds of London politicians and encouraged them to support the settlement of loyal Highlanders to bolster the colony's defences. Thus in 1815 a scheme was established to offer 2,000 free passages to Canada with bedding and rations. In a sense, however, the state had been at the heart of the emigration process long before this because only government could provide land, the vital basis of settlement. For most of the period of this chapter, crown land in Canada was available in theory at least as a free grant. Concessions were usually 200 acres per recipient and, in the early years to 1797, even survey fees were covered by the state. Thereafter, however, full fees were levied on new settlers who often had to rent land initially or even share for a time with relatives who already possessed holdings.

The social composition of the emigrant parties was also a critical factor in adaptation to the colonial environment. This was usually a movement of entire communities, often several hundred strong. The people left as the families of those who had lived together for generations in the same Highland townships. There were large numbers of women and children who were fundamental if the new communities overseas were to grow and thrive. For instance, the emigration led by Archibald McMillan of Murlaggan from the Cameron country along Loch Arkaig in 1802 included some 448 people. Young children made up 32 per cent of the group and women over twelve years of age more than a half. Similarly, three vessels sailed from the small Scottish port of Duchainas in 1790 carrying 405 passengers from adjacent areas of Roman Catholic loyalty on the coastal mainland of Inverness-shire and the neighbouring islands. Among them were 111 heads of families and only twenty-five passengers travelled independently. Most crucially of all, family heads in virtually all the groups analysed were rent-paying tenants, the middle rank of Highland society. As long as they could keep their holdings intact until departure, they would hope to gain by selling cattle stocks as prices rose, cover the costs of the voyage and still have enough left over to help with resettlement in Canada.

Leadership was also vital to plan the ventures effectively, hire ships and then manage the complexities of land allocation in the colonies. For all this, the emigrants relied on their traditional leaders. In the Catholic districts, some were priests, such as the aforementioned Father Alexander MacDonnell, *Maighstir Alasdair*. Leaders were also drawn from the gentlemen of the clans, the *Daoine-Uaisle*, or clan gentry, *fir-tacsa*, and prominent tenants. These men had the necessary contacts, financial resources and often knowledge of colonial conditions. Several were half-pay army officers who had seen active service in the colonies. Above all, the leadership was held in respect by the people, an important advantage when difficult decisions had to be made. Their responsibilities did not end when the emigrants landed. In some districts, such as Glengarry County, leaders of the emigrant parties managed to secure positions as land surveyors and members of the land boards, where they were able to act as mediators between local crown officers and the people. Like the mass of emigrants they too had a basic stake in the success of colonization. The gentry of the clans were being squeezed out by the loss of favourable leases, the splitting of their holdings to accommodate crofting townships and the loss of traditional status in the community. Emigration not only offered them economic independence through landownership but perpetuated the social leadership they had possessed in clanship. Canada also held out the prospect of financial gain through populating their colonial properties with subtenants in the familiar manner practised in the Highlands for generations. Against this background, it is scarcely surprising that the survival and growth of these new settlements depended to a significant extent on the retention of conservative values and traditional social hierarchies.

3

The two great obstacles to Highland emigration between 1760 and 1815 were government prohibition and the impact of war. In both the American War of Independence and the French Revolutionary and Napoleonic Wars, civilian migration across the Atlantic fell away to very low levels. In the years of temporary cessation of conflict, however, such as after the Peace of Amiens in 1802, emigration returned quickly to prewar levels. Paradoxically, however, it was the colonial wars which gave some Gaels an effective way around government controls. The state had introduced during the Seven Years War a system of paying off demobilized soldiers with grants of colonial land. The policy was refined and expanded during the two subsequent conflicts of the later eighteenth century. It seemed a very sensible strategy. Dividing lots from the abundant empty lands of North America was an economical way of laying off troops, and thereafter they could also be used as a reserve army garrisoning at no cost those frontier areas threatened by the French or the newly independent Americans. As Chapter 11 showed, the scale of military recruitment in the Highlands was massive. Many of those who joined the colours never returned home when peace came in 1763 and 1783 but took advantage of the land settlement policies in America. In effect, they had exploited the opportunities for cheap state-subsidized emigration and the offer of free grants of land. Key aspects of government policy, preventing emigration, raising recruits in Scotland and paying them off in colonial land, were now in direct conflict with one another. As the leading authority on the subject has put it, through army recruitment, the Gaels were essentially being offered 'a free ticket across the Atlantic'.[5]

The militarization of the Highlands and the system of soldier demobilization had a number of effects on emigration. The most obvious is that a headcount solely of civilian migrants considerably underestimates the scale of the departures. A proclamation of 1763 awarded captains 3,000 acres of land, subaltern officers 2,000 and rank and file fifty acres each. As a result, 27,000 acres in New York colony were divided among the officers and non-commissioned officers of the 42nd and 77th Highland regiments. The grievous losses they had sustained in battle cannot alone account for the fact that only one in five men returned to the Highlands in the years of peace. Perhaps emigration through the medium of army service became even greater after the American War came to an end in 1783, because the terms of land grants provided by then were even more generous and included veterans' dependants. To take but one example, the demobilization of four battalions in what was later to become Upper Canada resulted in awards totalling 256,000 acres to 3,642 former soldiers and their families, numbering 1,056 women and children. It was scarcely surprising that these concentrations of Highlanders in North America soon became demographic and cultural points of connection, in turn drawing more kinfolk, friends and associates from the old country.

Emigration through military service was depicted in correspondence from soldiers as a route to advancement. A piper from Fraser of Lovat's 71st Highland Regiment wrote home in euphoric terms in 1778: 'I am as well as ever I was in my life, my pay is as good as one shilling and six pence per day and I hope my fortune within two years will be as good that I will have 200 acres of free land of my own in this country . . . if it had not been for this war this is the best country in the world.'[6] The contemporary commentator on Highland affairs John Knox noted how the military settlements acted as potent inducements for further emigration. Ex-soldiers who had acquired land settlements 'were desirous that their kindred and friends should come and partake of their good fortune'.[7] The movement from Eigg and Arisaig to Canada in 1790, for instance, was specifically linked to opportunities to join relatives and friends and secure crown lands close to the original military settlements. This type of chain migration was facilitated by the emergence of a corps of entrepreneurs, enterprising half-pay army officers, often former Highland tacksmen, who came back home to recruit and organize emigrant parties. They understood that the land they had acquired across the Atlantic would be of little value if they could not settle it with people to work their properties and pay them rents. Contrary to some of the racial prejudice emanating later from some circles in the Lowlands, the Highlands was plainly not a society devoid of commercial acumen and enterprise.

13
Passive Victims?

To many contemporary observers one of the most perplexing questions about clearances in the Highlands was the apparent failure of the people to show more resolute and widespread resistance to landlord policies of eviction. Even sympathetic supporters of the Gaels were frustrated about what they judged to be the weakness of protest. Hugh Miller, the famous self-taught geologist, wrote angrily in 1840: 'They [the Irish] are buying guns and will be bye-and-bye shooting magistrates and clergymen by the score; and Parliament will in consequence do a great deal for them. But the poor Highlanders will shoot no-one . . . and so they will be left to perish unregarded in their hovels.' One modern scholar raised the question directly: 'Why didn't the Scots peasant shoot his landlord?'[1] After all, the local sources of law and order in the Highlands seemed weak in the extreme, military force could only be summoned from a distance, and the geography of the Highlands and its scattered population made effective intervention difficult. What added to the puzzle was that the Gaels of the nineteenth century were descendants of the famed warrior race of the clans and in more recent times large numbers saw active and distinguished military service in the many Highland regiments of the period between 1756 and 1815. Tough veteran soldiers skilled in arms and used to violent conflict were common in most crofting communities.

It was significant that during the potato famine in the Highlands of the 1840s, organizers of relief for the stricken region employed the stereotype of a peaceful, submissive and stoical people who, though suffering great adversity, were not willing to break the laws of the land. The argument therefore ran that they were much more deserving of philanthropic support than the murderous peasantry of Ireland. Others asserted from a quite different perspective that the tranquillity of the Highlands was a great boon for investors as the real rental of a large Highland estate in 1830 was worth at least 20 per cent more than the nominal price because it had 'no *Tithes*, poor rates or *Incendiaries* to contend with'.[2]

It was undeniable that peasant disturbance was more threatening, organized and enduring in parts of Ireland than in Highland Scotland. Every decade between 1760 and 1840 was punctuated by at least one major agrarian rebellion across the Irish Sea. The secret societies of Rightboys, Whiteboys, Oakboys, Peep O' Day Boys and others were formidable associations. In some chronically disturbed districts, such as Tipperary, Antrim, Kilkenny and Limerick, they survived all efforts over many years by the forces of the crown, police and the judiciary to subdue them. They prided themselves as semi-military formations, bound together by oaths of loyalty and wearing special clothing to mark them out as outlawed subversives in open conflict against lawful authority. One government official, George Cornwall Lewis, described them as 'protective unions, steadily, determinedly and unscrupulously working at their objects but sleeping in apparent apathy so long as their *regulations* are not violated'.[3] These societies practised systematic intimidation, terrorism and murder on those, including soldiers, police and landowners, whom they believed transgressed the peasant codes of custom.

By contrast with much of rural Ireland, the Scottish Highlands seem a different world. Long after the major evictions there had come to an end, one observer found that crofters on the Gordon estate of South Uist in 1870 were living in such 'a state of slavish fear' that, though they had many grievances, they dared not admit them to the factor for fear he might drive them off the land. The same witness also noted how the people of South Harris were so 'paralysed by terror' that they were incapable of challenging the will of the landowner and his estate managers. Even during the land agitations of the 1880s, one speaker at a public meeting in Dunvegan, in Skye, openly admitted to his listeners: 'I am ashamed to confess it that I trembled more before the factor than I did before the Lord of Lords.'[4]

Much Gaelic poetry, especially that from the 1820s and thereafter, seemed to reflect in its melancholia and nostalgia the weakness of physical resistance to clearance. Sorley MacLean, the greatest Gaelic poet of the twentieth century, was withering in his criticism when he wrote in the 1930s: 'The Highlanders' resistance, physical and moral, was bound to be very weak and the poetry of the period reflects this impotence.'[5] For MacLean the verses were often 'the wail of a harassed and dejected people', such was the sense of hopelessness and despair that ran through so many of them.[6]

There has been no shortage of historical theories presented to explain the apparent fatalism of the crofting population. In England, too, it was reported that anti-enclosure riots of an earlier era were rare. Yet, as E. P. Thompson argued, this was not because enclosure was acceptable but because 'people learned early that to riot was hopeless'.[7] The same might be said about responses to clearance in the Highlands. Evictions took place under legal warrant and were protected by laws and regulations governing the rights of private property.

It is also sometimes suggested that the collective psyche of the Gael had been destroyed at Culloden and by the reign of state terror and the full-blooded attack on clan culture which followed that final and devastating defeat of Jacobitism. Others contend that the people were 'thoroughly perplexed, demoralized and disorientated' by the metamorphosis of the clan gentry into commercial landlords.[8] It was not an alien class of landowners who were in the main responsible for the evictions but the descendants of clan chiefs to whom the ancestors of the people had given allegiance for centuries. This, so it is argued, left the people not only leaderless but broken in spirit. So, as the old warrior spirit was crushed, the people sank into fatalism, a process then hastened by the enormous appeal of evangelical Protestantism which completed the transformation of a martial society into a timorous and God-fearing crofting community. Remarkably, as late as 1884, the Royal Commission on the Condition of Crofters and Cottars in the Highlands and Islands could report that despite all that had gone before in the region 'there is still on the side of the poor much reverence for the owner of the soil'.[9] That statement implied that many Gaels were still unable to sever their links with past loyalties and recognize themselves instead as a coherent class with rights and interests

independent of their landlords. Sorley MacLean made a broadly similar point when discussing aspects of the poetry of the clearance era.
He asserted that only rarely did landlords attract direct censure on
account of their policies of eviction. MacLean described instead 'the
absurd tendency to blame the factor more than the landowner and
the continued belief that if proprietors knew of the behaviour of their
managers injustices would be rectified'.[10]

I

There is now much more scholarly understanding of the constraints
on rural protest, not simply in the Scottish Highlands, but in societies
of a similar kind elsewhere. Studies of peasant revolts in Asia, Latin
America and Eastern Europe have detected common patterns. Small
farmers in general were usually slow to engage in collective protest
and when they did so found it difficult to maintain their campaigns
until their objectives had been achieved. As one scholar has it: 'the
powerless are easy victims'.[11] Protest undertaken by those in a position of weakness was usually doomed to failure as only those who
possessed some degree of tactical control over their own resources
had the capacity for effective resistance:

> The poor peasant or the landless labourer who depends on a landlord
> for the larger part of their livelihood, or the totality of it, has no tactical
> power: he is completely within the power domain of his lord or employer.
> Poor peasants and landless labourers, therefore, are unlikely to pursue
> the course of rebellion, unless they are able to rely on some external
> power to challenge the power which constrains them.[12]

Consider then the condition of the Highland people during the Age
of Clearances. They were certainly mainly devoid of power as land
which provided their source of subsistence was held only at the will
of proprietors. Landlords could also rely on the support of the legal
authorities and, if necessary, the police or military, at the behest of
local sheriffs, to maintain order. Especially after 1815, any residual
power the people might have possessed as a labour force needed for
kelp burning and herring fishing vanished as those by-employments

collapsed or stagnated in the 1810s and 1820s. Crofters and cottars were by then judged to be a 'redundant' population whose small possessions obstructed the ongoing expansion of profitable sheep farming. Any possibility of effective collective resistance across the Highlands was also made difficult because the small communities were widely dispersed, land transport was poor, and towns which might have acted as centres of organization and dissemination of opinion were few and far between.

External support for the plight of the people before the 1870s did come from a few writers and pamphleteers but none of them had any real political clout. The spiritual leaders of Gaeldom usually counselled restraint and moderation, and while some did speak out in defence of the dispossessed, any breaking of the law or violent resistance to civil authority was usually frowned upon. This response was not necessarily the result of some collaborative conspiracy with landlordism. Ministers were very aware that those who engaged in civil unrest were certain to be dealt with very severely by the courts. Imprisonment of the breadwinning menfolk could only compound the misery of their abandoned families while they served long sentences in gaol. Naturally, too, the clergy were wont to see injustice from a spiritual perspective. For instance, in its submission to the Napier Commission, the Free Church of Scotland, to which the vast majority of the West Highland and Hebridean crofters had rallied after the Disruption of 1843, asserted that it was wrong to try to prevent suffering by sinning. This life was 'a glen of tears' which had to be endured with courage and patience, though, in the end, justice and salvation would be meted out in eternity to both the bad and the good on earth.

The clergy of all denominations tended therefore to be generally a force for peace and social stability rather than potential leaders of communal insurrection. But active collaboration by ministers with estate managers in order to facilitate evictions was not as common as sometimes supposed, even if they had been appointed to their parishes through landlord patronage. In the case of the Sutherland estate, for example, Patrick Sellar wrote: 'I do not exaggerate the matter when I say that during the Riots no minister settled by the proprietors stirred one inch to support the law.'[13] He added that in only one instance did a member of the clergy 'exhort his flock to peace and to commune with us'.[14] Some of the Lowland press, like the *North British Daily Mail* and *The Witness*, the journal of the Free Church, could be counted on to show sympathy and were often deeply critical of landlordism. But no convincing intellectual challenge was mounted to the economic principles which underpinned the removals. Most mainstream opinion in Scotland before the second half of the nineteenth century held to the view that clearances were a necessary evil, an unfortunate but inevitable cost of agrarian progress.[15]

However, some interpretations of so-called Highland passivity are problematic. For instance, to use the history of Irish rural unrest as a comparator with the Highlands is to follow a false analytical trail. The scale and intensity of agrarian terrorism in Ireland was exceptional, not only within the British Isles but also across most of Western Europe, because of the very unusual nature of the political and religious circumstances in that country. The Irish state apparatus was monopolized by Protestants but the vast majority of the rural population in the central and southern regions of the country were Catholic and the penal laws assumed all of them were potentially disaffected to the state. For some peasant communities these religious fissures helped to establish a collective bond of union among the Catholic poor, an ideological cohesion, which helped to mobilize peasant movements. The Irish landed class was also alien in terms of both religion and ethnicity. Therefore the élites did not possess the hegemonic authority or the networks of social influence in the localities of the kind enjoyed by their counterparts across the Irish Sea. In mainland Britain rural stability mainly rested not on draconian law enforcement or military force but on many generations of family lordship, influence and assured hierarchy among the population. The Highlands should therefore be best compared not with Ireland but with the more representative experiences of the rural Lowlands and the English countryside.

Between 1760 and 1830 the dispossession of small tenants and cottars in the Lowlands, as argued previously, was a silent process which did not trigger overt opposition. However, modern scholarship has now shown that contemporaries may have significantly underestimated the extent and range of disturbance in the Highlands. Especially in the early stages of the expansion of sheep farming in the later eighteenth century, farmers from the Lowlands and Border country coming on to estates to consider their potential for sheep rearing were often set upon violently and given a bloody send-off. The clandestine stealing, maiming, mutilation and slaughter of sheep by night were, for obvious reasons, relatively risk-free and were the most popular forms of intimidation and retribution visited on the flockmasters. Anonymous letters sent to the families of sheep farmers threatening violent revenge were also common. In the 1810s sheep thefts on the Sutherland estate rose to around 1,500 animals a year and led to the formation of a protective organization, the Sutherland Association against Felony. But the poverty of the people ensured that these defensive measures were usually ineffective. As the Rev. Norman MacLeod recorded of Skye in 1841: 'The flocks of the large sheep farmers are annually thinned by those who feel the pinching of famine; and to such an extent is this system carried on that it has led to the proposal of establishing a rural police throughout the island.[16] Again, on the MacLeod estate on the same island, inflammatory notices were posted on the doors of churches which caused numerous sheep to be mutilated or killed. From other districts came reports of petty violence and simmering hatred of sheep farmers.

Yet, even if the vast majority of evictions passed off peacefully with little dissent or opposition, resistance did take place in some cases with sporadic but repeated incidents of protest. Thus far modern research has documented at least fifty such episodes, but that figure is almost certainly an underestimate because most of those which have been recorded to date only came to public notice because they attracted the attention of the contemporary press. However, from the known examples of opposition, the leading historian of the Highland disturbances has constructed the following useful typology:

> From the many examples of obstruction and resistance emerges an almost stylised mode of action. Typically the anti-eviction episode followed a pattern in these four stages:
>
> – The local law officer or the landlord's agent would attempt to serve the summons of removal on a village. The first time he might simply be turned away. The second time he would be subjected to petty

humiliation, usually at the hands of the womenfolk of the village. They might seize his papers and burn them under his nose. Sometimes the officer was stripped naked and chased off the land – or even pushed out to sea in an open boat without oars.

– A posse of constables led by a Sheriff and his assistants would arrive, often very early in the morning. Real resistance would follow: they would be assaulted with volleys of stones and sticks from a massed group of the common people. In the front line of the latter were, invariably, the women and boys, making most noise and taking the worst injuries. Sometimes men were reported at the front – often dressed as women. But most of the menfolk were to the rear, apparently as a second line of defence. The resistance was usually sufficiently vociferous and violent to push back the posse. Meanwhile, the common people might have made an appeal to some distant authority: the Prince Regent, the press, local worthies or even the landlord.

– Higher legal authorities would be alerted: the Solicitor General, or the Lord Advocate, or perhaps the Home Office. Repeatedly the local landowners, in an advanced state of panic, would attribute the disturbances to agitators with suspected connections with 'Radicalism'. Sometimes there was inflated talk of a 'Northern Rebellion' which helped persuade the authorities that military intervention was required – from Inverness, Fort William, Aberdeen or Glasgow.

– The news of impending military intervention was usually enough of itself to lead to a collapse of the resistance. Troops intervened on at least ten occasions but were never actually engaged in physical hostilities. The termination of resistance was frequently facilitated by the mediation of the local minister who produced a face-saving formula for the people. It generally took the form of a delay of removal, but rarely did anything to prevent the eventual clearance. Most of these incidents show the marks of desperation among the people – unpreparedness, absence of arms, lack of coordination, no clear leadership and the final collapse in the face of military intervention.[17]

One of the best documented of these episodes took place on the Argyllshire estate of Neil Malcolm of Poltalloch. He and his family were natives of the county and had made an immense fortune in the sugar and slave trades of the Caribbean. At the height of the potato famine in June 1848, Malcolm attempted to remove the small tenants of the township of Arichonan in North Knapdale, Argyll. At the first attempt to enforce the notices of eviction, the sheriff officer, factor and other employees of the estate were resisted with considerable violence and the attempt at removal collapsed in ignominy.

A month later another effort was made. This time the party numbered thirty-eight men, including a police escort. Even then the people seem not to have been intimidated: 'a mob of great number of evil disposed persons did then and there riotously and tumultuously assemble with the "common purpose" of opposing the eviction', as the report preserved in Justiciary Court Records described the incident.[18] The authorities were routed once again and forced to release the prisoners they had already taken during the action. Significantly, too, the inhabitants of Arichonan were helped by crofters and cottars from elsewhere in the neighbourhood in their struggle to resist dispossession.

Subsequently, charges were brought against fifteen individuals 'for mobbing and rioting, obstructing and deforcing [preventing with force an officer of the law doing his duty] and assaulting officers'. Most were tenants and a few others were cottars. Five of the fifteen were women. All the accused, except for one man who was exonerated, each received sentences of eight months' imprisonment.

The high profile of women in the Arichonan incident is intriguing; indeed, some have suggested that Highland riots were in effect women's riots. In a representative sample of thirty clearance and patronage disputes across the Highland region, women were involved in nineteen and in many of them they often took the lead while the menfolk at first held back. This was true of a series of disturbances at Culrain in 1820; Gruids in 1821; Durness in 1841; Sollas in 1849; Greenyards in 1854; Knockam and Elphim in 1852; and Coigach in 1852. Sometimes men appeared as transvestites, dressed in female clothing. The proactive role of women in peasant resistance was not unique to the Highlands. It was also an integral part of popular insurrectionism in Ireland, England, Holland, France and elsewhere. Wives and mothers were at the heart of the home and their determination to defend it and their families to the bitter end is hardly surprising. The loss of earnings of the menfolk by reason of arrest and imprisonment could condemn wives and children to a life of penury. Court records suggest there was a belief among the people that women would not experience prosecution and even if they did were likely to be treated more leniently by the judiciary. Men generally did tend to receive longer sentences, but there is no evidence that the authorities were unwilling to prosecute women with the full force of the law. If the military was summoned to help crush riotous behaviour they may initially have been surprised to be confronted by serried ranks of females pitching stones and screaming curses at them. But that did not prevent soldiers using rifle butts and even bayonets against women if those tactics were thought necessary in order to arrest them.

The example of Arichonan was fairly typical of the Highland riots. Violence was employed in the resistance, the forces of law and order were rebuffed for a time, but eventually the perpetrators were arrested and imprisoned. One exception to the rule was the attempted clearance of Coigach in Wester Ross in 1852–3. The officer who attempted to serve the eviction papers was stripped by the womenfolk and despatched almost naked in a boat across the loch. Six constables were then ordered to the district but were again given short shrift by angry women. The dispute lasted for over two years. Eventually the people were allowed to remain as the proprietor began to fear the bad publicity that might ensue if he called in the military to carry out a forced eviction. Coigach may have been one sign of changing times and of growing sympathy for the plight of the crofting communities outside the Highlands.

Another important advance in the assessment of protest has been exploration of the oral tradition, by studying the fragments of Gaelic poetry which have survived. Verse and song were the main vehicles of public expression and can provide a fascinating insight into the emotional world of the people. As noted earlier, some poetry of the time tended to convey depression and hopelessness. But other parts of the genre are much more robust and express feelings of rage, anger and eagerness for revenge on the perpetrators of clearance. Also, contrary to the opinion expressed by some writers, the verse does occasionally condemn landlords as well as their factors by name. Satirical poetry, in particular, that which belongs to the poetic tradition of *aoir*, or vituperation and condemnation, can be especially venomous.[19] Two examples are given below:

Aoir air Pàdraig Sellar	*Satire on Patrick Sellar*
Dòmhnall Bàillidh	Donald Baillie

Refrain:	Refrain:
Hò 'n ceàrd dubh, hè 'n ceàrd dubh;	Hò the black rogue, hè the black rogue;
Hò 'n ceàrd dubh dhaor am fearann.	Hò the black rogue, who raised the land-rent.

Chunnaic mise bruadar,	I saw a dream,
'S cha b' fluathach leam fhaicinn fhathast,	and I would not mind seeing it again;
'S nam faicinn e 'nam dhùsgadh,	if I were to see it while awake,
Bu shùgradh dhomh e rim latha.	it would make me merry all day.

Teine mòr an òrdagh	A big fire was ready
Is Roy 'na theis-mheadhoin,	and Roy was right in its middle,
Young bhith ann am prìosan,	Young was incarcerated,
'S an t-iarann mu chnàmhan Shellair.	and there was iron about Sellar's bones.

Tha Sellar an Cùl-Mhàillidh	Sellar is in Culmailly,
Air fhàgail mar mhadh-allaidh,	left there like a wolf,
A' glacadh is a' sàradh	catching and oppressing
Gach aon nì thig 'na charaibh.	everything that comes within his range.

Tha shròn mar choltar iarainn	His nose is like an iron plough-share
No fiacail na muice bioraich;	or the tooth of the long-beaked porpoise;
Tha ceann liath mar ròn air	he has a grey head like a seal
Is bòdhan mar asal fhireann.	and his lower abdomen resembles that of a male ass.

Tha rugaid mar chòrr-riabhaich	His long neck is like that of the crane,
Is iomhaigh air nach eil taairis,	and his face has no appearance of gentleness;
Is casan fada liadhach	his long, sharp-shinned legs
Mar shiaman de shlataibh mara.	

'S truagh nach robh thu 'm priosan
Rè bhliadhnan air uisg' is aran,
Is cearcall cruaidh de dh' iarann
Mud shliasaid gu làdir daingeann.

Nam faighinn-s' air raon thu
Is daoine bhith gad cheangal,
Bheirinn le mo dhòrnaibh
Trì òirlich a-mach dhed sgamhan.

Chaidh thu fhèin 's do phàirtidh
An àirde gu bràghe Rosail,
Is chuir thu taigh do bhràthar
'Na smàlaibh a suas 'na lasair.

Nuair a thig am bàs ort,
Cha chàirear thu anns an talamh,
Ach bidh do charcais thodharail
Mar òtrach air aodann achaidh.

Bha Sellar and Roy
Air an treòrachadh leis an
   Deamhan
Nuair dh'òrdaucg uad ab cinoaust
'S an t-slabhraidh chur air an
   fhearann.

Bha 'n Simpsonach 'na chù
Mar bu dùthchasach don
   mharaich',
Seacaid ghorm à bùth air,
'S triùbhsair de dh' aodach tana.

'S I pacaid dhubh an ùillidh
A ghiùlain iad chum an
   fhearainn-s',

resemble ropes of large sea-tangle.

What a pity that you were not in
   prison
for years, existing on bread and water,
with a hard shackle of iron,
strong and immovable, about your
   thigh.

If I could get at you on an open field,
with people tying you down,
I would pull with my fists
three inches [of flesh] out of your lungs.

You yourself and your party
went up the braes of Rosal,
and you set fire to your brother's
   house,
so that it burned to ashes.

When death comes upon you,
you will not be placed in the ground,
but your dung-like carcase will be
   spread
like manure on a field's surface.

Sellar and Roy
were guided by the very Devil,
when they commanded that the
   compass
and the chain be set to [measure]
   the land.

The Simpson man behaved like a dog
as befitted the nature of a seaman,
wearing a blue jacket from a shop
and trousers of thin cloth.

Ach chìthear fhathast bàitht' iad
Air tràilleach an cladach
　　Bhanaibh.

It was the black packet of the oil
that brought them to this land,
but they will yet be seen
　　drowned
[and thrown up] on seaweed on the
　　Banff shore.

Oran air Fear a bha a'
Fuadachadh nan. Gàidheal

Song on One Who was Evicting
Highlanders

An uair a thig an t-eug ort,
Leam fèin gur math, O raithill ò.

When death comes upon you,
I will think it fine.

Cuiridh sinn air dèlidh thur
Led lèine bhric, O raithill ò.

We will put you on a deal plank
in your speckled shirt.

Togaidh sinn gu h-uallach thu
Air guaillibh hear, O raithill ò.

We will lift you happily
on men's shoulders.

Cha tèid nì air d' uachdar
Ach buachar mairt, O raithill ò.

Nothing will go on top of you
except cow dung.

'S a-chaoidh cha chinn an
　　t-eòinean ort
No am feòirlinn glan, O raithill ò.

And never will a daisy grow
　　on you
or the clean blade of grass.

Ach cinnidh foghanain is feanntag
Aig ceann do chas, O raithill ò.

But thistles and nettles will grow at
　　your feet.
When a spadeful of earth is put on top
　　of you,

Nuair thèid spaid den ùir ort,
Bidh an dùthaich ceart, O raithill ò.

the country will be put to rights.

Bidh gach bochd is truaghan
A' bualadh bhas, O raithill ò.

Every poor person and weakling
will be clapping their hands.

Nam faighte air an tràigh thu	If you were found on the shore
An àite stamh, O raithill ò;	instead of kelp,
Gum biodh fear no dhà ann	there would be one or two people
A ghàireadh mach, O raithill ò.	who would laugh out loud.
Cha chuirte cist' no anart ort	No coffin or shroud would be put
Ach lèine bhreac, O raithill ò.	on you
	but a speckled shirt.
Gu bheil cridhe spìocach	There is a miserly heart
Ad chliabh a-steach, O raithill ò.	inside your chest.
Tha d' aodann mar am miaran,	Your face resembles a thimble,
A bhlianaich bhric, O raithill ò.	made of pock-marked lean meat.
'S e an t-òr a bha san laoighcionn	The gold that is in the calf-skin
Chuir daoine as, O raithill ò;	is what dispossessed the people;
Or na seiche ruaidhe,	the gold of the red hide,
'S cha bhuaidh cho math, O raithill ò.	and its influence is not so good.
Nan cailleadh to chlach bhuadhach,	If you lost the efficacious stone,
Bhiodh d' uain glè thearc, O raithill ò.	your lambs would be very scarce.
	My own curse be on you beyond others for ever more.
Mo mhallachd fhèin thar chàcha	
Gu bràtha leat, O raithill ò.	

[Roy: John Roy was land surveyor on the Sutherland estate.
Patrick Sellar: was factor (or manager) of the Sutherland estate from
1811 until 1817 and responsible for several controversial evictions.
Young: William Young was factor of the Sutherland estate, together
with Patrick Sellar, from 1811 until his dismissal in 1816 and also
responsible for several evictions.]

2

The well-known aphorism of the French historian Pierre Goubert that 'No peasant willingly surrenders land, be it only half a furrow' is a reminder that violent response to eviction was not unique to the Highlands.[20] But hostility to dispossession there seems to have been motivated not simply by fear of the loss of subsistence but by strongly held beliefs in *rights* to land. This was the repeated claim throughout the poetry of the clearances and was also a salient feature of the evidence given by crofter witnesses to the Napier Commission in 1882–3. Of principal importance in this respect was, as discussed earlier in the book, the concept of *duthchas*. The term has several meanings but they included the belief in the hereditary right of possession to land. It was not a legal concept but one based on custom and derived from the old clan tradition of land given in return for service. Occupation of a holding therefore was seen as being justifiable in moral terms and was in explicit conflict with the legal rights of private property in land. The Napier Commission recognized the inevitable conflict between the two concepts:

> The opinion was often expressed before us that the small tenantry of the Highlands have an inherited inalienable title to security of tenure in their possessions while rent and service are duly rendered which is an impression indigenous to the country though it has never been sanctioned by legal recognition, and has long been repudiated by the actions of the proprietors.[21]

The Earl of Selkirk, who organized several emigration schemes to Canada from the Highlands, had made a similar point seventy years before:

> According to the ideas handed down to them from their ancestors, and long prevalent among high and low throughout the Highlands, they were only defending their rights and resisting a ruinous unjust and tyrannical encroachment on *their* property.[22] [my italics]

Patrick Sellar, one of the managers of the Sutherland estate in the early nineteenth century and notorious for being charged with culpable homicide during an eviction, came up against these beliefs in the clearance of the Strath of Kildonan in 1812. The delivery of notices to quit their holdings triggered open opposition from the people. A petition from the tenants denied that they were in any way motivated by radical politics, as some might have suspected at the time. Instead, they contended that 'Mr Young [Sellar's fellow manager] would give us the first offer of our present possessions or provide us with such larach [holdings] that we may have some Hill Grass as the Highlanders mostly depends on the Hill Grass.' Sellar, who was a native of Lowland Morayshire, was astonished to learn that the tenants claimed 'they were entitled to keep possession of their Grounds and would allow no shepherd to come to the country'. Another observer at the time described how the Kildonan people had 'so much of the old Highland Spirit as to think the land their own'.[23]

The durability of these beliefs in the right to land was remarkable. As late as 1954 the Royal Commission on Crofting Conditions of that year noted:

> they have the feeling that the croft, its land, its houses are their own. They have gathered its stones and reared its buildings and occupied it as their own all their days.
>
> They have received it from their ancestors who won it from the wilderness and they cherish the hope they will transmit it to the generations to come.
>
> Whatever the legal theory they feel it to be their own.[24]

3

The most successful example of defiance against landlord authority in the Victorian Highlands before the 1880s was not in the secular sphere or in resistance to clearance but in the religious sphere and was occasioned by the Disruption of the Church of Scotland in 1843. The long-running controversy over landed rights of patronage had been a source of tension and protest in the parishes of Scotland since the early decades of the eighteenth century. The evangelical wing of the established church had always been in strident opposition to lay patronage as in their view it conferred arrogant and unacceptable secular authority over Christ's kingdom on earth. By the 1830s the tide of opinion in the General Assembly was running very favourably for the evangelicals and they determined to rid the church once and for all of this historic grievance. The growing crisis came to a head in 1842 when the Assembly passed the Claim of Right which proclaimed that only Jesus Christ had headship of the Church of Scotland and to recognize any other authority in its governance was tantamount to heretical rejection of His Divine supremacy. The Prime Minister, Robert Peel, in early 1843 summarily rejected the Claim as totally unacceptable because it could only lead to clerical tyranny over the state.

The evangelicals considered that they now had little choice but to break from the established church. Therefore on 18 May 1843, the first day of the annual General Assembly in Edinburgh, the retiring Moderator read out a long statement denouncing the British state for infringing the spiritual independence of the national Church of Scotland. He laid the paper on the table and then left the Assembly, followed *en masse* into the street by all his fellow evangelical ministers and elders. Later, they formally constituted themselves as the 'Free Protesting Church of Scotland' and signed the Deed of Demission by which over 450 clergy resigned from the establishment and surrendered their churches, manses and incomes in a remarkable demonstration of the power of religious principle and commitment.

This historic decision had major implications for the people of the western Highlands and Islands. By the time of the Disruption the region had become a stronghold of popular and enthusiastic evangelicalism with a history of intense and deeply emotional religious revivals. There was also a recent history of public and violent opposition by congregations to ministers settled on them by landlord patrons who were not only considered more restrained and moderate in their beliefs but were also sometimes viewed as clerical creatures of landlordism. Indeed, it is possible to detect a people's church already emerging out of the established order in parts of the Highlands before the Church of Scotland finally fractured in 1843. A key factor in this development was the influence of *Na Daoine*, translated as 'The Men'. They were lay preachers, so called to distinguish them from the ordained clergy, a spiritual élite, drawn mainly from better-off crofting and tradesman families, with powerful personal charisma, deep religious piety, detailed knowledge of the scriptures and, above all, an ability to blend the appeal of Christian spirituality with Gaelic tradition and imagery.

Their message gave hope of salvation in the next world and some consolation in the present to those suffering from the economic convulsions which gripped the western Highlands. Christian conversion was only possible through complete submission to the Will of God and a refusal to accept suffering was to question that divine authority. Evangelical teaching therefore provided a certainty amid the trauma of tumultuous social change and at the same time the promise of eternal reward in heaven for those who lived good and holy lives despite the travails they experienced on earth.

It came as little surprise then that when the new Free Church was founded it generated widespread and enthusiastic support among crofters and cottars. Even before it was established in 1843 the evangelical leadership in the Lowlands had been preparing the ground. Pamphlets and broadsheets in Gaelic were widely circulated. Delegations toured the region to seek popular support and ministers of an evangelical persuasion were urged to prepare their congregations for the coming crisis. When the schism finally came, entire districts quickly separated from the established church, and 'The Men', together with the large numbers of people whom they had influenced, collectively joined the Free Church. The religious division soon hardened into class division. The new church was no friend of landlords whose rights of patronage the evangelicals had challenged for generations. For their part, landowners, big farmers, factors and merchants mainly continued to adhere to the Auld Kirk, the established Church of Scotland. Many of them felt that the people had carried out an unprecedented act of collective defiance against their social superiors. For some time afterwards landlords organized a campaign of harassment and obstruction against the Free Church which normally took the form of refusing sites on their estates for church buildings. One magnate, Sir James Riddell, proprietor of Ardnamurchan, publicly and bitterly denounced those who had broken off from the establishment and asserted that if the crofters had shown such defiance in the religious sphere there was every chance that before too long they would also be likely to challenge the powers that be in the secular sphere.

It was to be another forty years before any such challenge did emerge in the crofting districts so one has to be cautious about drawing a simple cause-and-effect relationship between the Disruption of 1843 and the successful agitations over land reform which surfaced in the 1880s. Nevertheless, the popularity of the Free Church was yet another great breach in the relationship between élites and people in the western Highlands. Some have also suggested that 1843 and the aftermath was a collective victory for the interests of crofters over landlords which generated a stronger sense of community among the people. Members of the Free Church throughout Scotland were also committed supporters of the Liberal Party and they soon began to develop an interest in the plight of their co-religionaries in the Highlands which was to prove a key source of influential political support during the Crofters' War of the 1880s.

There is, however, another side to the issue of the relationship between the people of Gaeldom and evangelical religion which makes the discussion more complex. During the period of trauma and famine as the policy of clearance changed from resettlement to expulsion between the 1820s and 1850s it can also be plausibly argued that the religious transformation of that time helped to contain violent protest and peasant unrest. The people were probably already disorientated since for the most part the promoters of the revolution in land holding were their own hereditary leaders. In Highland Scotland, much of the population must have been in a condition of psychological confusion as the families of the old clan élites began to enforce widespread dispossession of peasant communities. In such a time of social convulsion, religious certainties could provide some comfort.

This had a number of facets. Patient acceptance of suffering was nothing less than pious submission to God's plan. During the potato famine, the Edinburgh Gaelic Schools Society stated: 'for He hath said I will never leave thee nor forsake thee. It is this word that your teachers are, day and night, occupied in dispensing to the starving families of the Highland and Islands.'[25] The proper response to suffering was the examination of conscience as a precondition to repentance. The experience of tragedy in this world could be explained as the result of personal wickedness and so those who were the victims of disaster might themselves be the causes of their own misfortune. This was the reaction, for example, of the people of Glencalvie in Strathconan who were obliged to seek refuge in the church at Croick in 1845 after being evicted from their lands. They scrawled a message on the windowsill of the kirk where they sought shelter that their plight was a dreadful punishment for sin. Also, the mighty who had inflicted pain would not go unpunished. But retribution belonged to God, not man; in one sermon the Rev. John Sinclair, minister of Bruan in Caithness, made the point explicitly: 'It is true that we often see the wicked enjoy much comfort and worldly ease, and the Godly chastened every morning; but this is a dreadful rest to the former and a blessed chastisement to the latter.'[26] The doctrines of Calvinism therefore gave spiritual certainty during the transition from clanship to clearance as the evangelicals concentrated the minds and emotions of the people on a highly personal struggle for grace and election. The miseries of this life were not therefore simply to be endured but were in themselves a necessary agony for those who wished to attain eternal salvation in the next.

This compelling set of beliefs had important implications for the response of the Highland population to the impact of dispossession. Resistance to clearance did take place but was still limited in relation to the overall scale of dislocation. But the beliefs disseminated with such emotional fervour by the missionaries and 'The Men' must have buttressed other forces making for stability and further diluted influences making for resistance. The evangelical gospel was not a theology of social justice but a faith designed to promote personal spiritual growth and commitment. It offered solace and the certainty of punishment for the oppressor, not by man but by God, and so deflected opposition in this life to the other side of the grave. The vision that suffering had to be endured as a necessary preparation for salvation was an obvious constraint on insurrection, and it was hardly surprising that the poet Mary MacPherson of Skye eloquently condemned evangelical preachers for their indifference to the poor conditions in which the people lived. Their concern with spiritual challenges and the eternal verities took precedence over mere secular problems.

14

Clearance and Expulsion

I

Until the 1860s emigration from the Scottish Highlands was an important numerical feature of the Scottish exodus as a whole. In the last four decades of the nineteenth century, however, and thereafter, the contribution of the region as a proportion of the general outflow of Scots fell dramatically as the towns, cities and Lowland country-side became by far the dominant sources of large-scale Scottish movement across the globe. Yet, for a number of years in the later 1840s and early 1850s, the Highland diaspora reached truly un-precedented levels. It is arguable that much of the international mobility of the Scottish people throughout the nineteenth century was led by the search for opportunity overseas. But in that period the great wave of Highland emigrants was primarily driven by subsist-ence crisis, clearance and peasant expropriation.

The essential background to the exodus was the lethal impact of the potato blight which had earlier devastated Ireland and some other parts of Europe in the years after 1845. The Highland crops suc-cumbed to the disease from the autumn of 1846, one year after the beginning of the Irish tragedy. Press reports from the north and west started to describe the stench of rotting potatoes, the key subsistence crop of the region, throughout the crofting townships, particularly those located in the Hebrides and the coastlands of the western main-land. In that area, with its moderate winters and rainy summers, the climatic conditions were exactly right for the rapid and destructive spread of the fungal disease *Phytophthora infestans*, to which there was no known antidote at the time. Early estimates for 1846 suggested

306

the potato crop had failed entirely in over 75 per cent of crofting parishes. The newspaper of the Free Church, *The Witness*, proclaimed in apocalyptic terms: 'The hand of the Lord has indeed touched us' and described the calamity 'unprecedented in the memory of this generation and of many generations gone by, even in any modern periods of our country's history'.[1] Unambiguous signs of famine soon emerged. While burial registers for most Highland areas in the 1840s are few and far between, in those that have survived deaths among the old and the very young rose significantly in late 1846 and the first few months of 1847. The *Scotsman* in December 1846 described how the numbers dying from dysentery were 'increasing with fearful rapidity among the cottar class'.[2] In the Ross of Mull, government relief officers reported that the mortality rate during the winter months was three times above the average for that time of year. Elsewhere in Harris, South Uist, Barra, Skye, Moidart and Kintail, influenza, typhus and dysentery were also spreading unchecked among the poor. The awful possibility that the Highlands might be engulfed in a human catastrophe of Irish proportions seemed to some observers to be only a matter of time.

But the potential disaster was averted, despite the fact that the potato blight continued to ravage the Highlands to a greater or lesser extent for almost a decade after 1846. By the summer of 1847 death rates had returned to normal levels and the threat of starvation receded. It seemed as if a terrible mortality crisis had been contained. The different experiences of Ireland (where over one million died) and the Highlands in this respect can be explained by a number of influences. An important factor was scale. In Ireland, the blight brought over three million people to the edge of starvation. In the Highlands, on the other hand, around 200,000 were seriously as risk, and this number diminished over time as the crisis increasingly centred on parts of the north-western coastlands, the northern isles of Orkney and Shetland, and the Hebrides. By 1848 only around a quarter (or fewer than 70,000) of the total population of the Highland region remained in need of famine relief.

The map of distress was complex. The southern, central and eastern Highlands did not escape entirely unscathed, but after 1847 relief operations were already being wound down in most of the parishes there, reflecting their more resilient economies. Here were less potato dependency and more reliance on grain and fish; a better ratio of land to population; and developed alternative occupations, such as commercial fishing and linen manufacture, in southern Argyll, Perthshire and eastern Inverness-shire. The concentrated and relatively small-scale nature of the Scottish famine meant that the emergency could be managed more effectively by the relief agencies of the day in contrast to the epochal crisis across the Irish Sea. The Scottish authorities were dealing with many thousands of potential victims, their counterparts in Ireland with millions. The vastly different magnitude of the two famines is best illustrated by the role of government. In Ireland the state, both local and national, was the principal source of relief during the crisis, whereas in the Highlands direct government intervention began in late 1846 and had come to an end by the summer of 1847. Two vessels were stationed as meal depots at Tobermory in Mull and Portree in Skye to sell grain at controlled prices while landowners in the stricken region were able to make application for loans under the Drainage and Public Works Act to provide relief work for the distressed people of their estates.

These initiatives apart, the main burden of the relief effort was borne by three great charities, the Free Church of Scotland, the Edinburgh Relief Committee and its Glasgow equivalent, which came together in early 1847 to form the Central Board of Management for Highland Relief. The Central Board had the responsibility for relieving destitution until its operations came to an end in 1850. The programme of support went through several phases. First in the field was the Free Church, eager to come to the aid of its numerous loyal congregations in the north-west and the islands. The schooner *Breadalbane*, built to carry ministers around the Hebrides, was pressed into service to take emergency supplies to the most needy communities. The Free Church was the only active agency during the most critical months of late 1846 and early 1847. Through its superb intelligence network of local ministers it was able to direct aid to those districts where the risk of starvation was greatest. The Free Church's relief operation was also free of any sectarian bias. Grateful thanks for supplies of grain were received from the Catholic areas of Arisaig and Moidart. Not the least of the Free Church's contribution was the imaginative plan to transport over 3,000 able-bodied men from the Highlands for temporary work on the Lowland railways.

The Central Board assumed control of relief operations in February 1847 and by the end of that year had established a huge fund for the aid of distress of nearly £210,000 (over £16,000,000 at 2017 values). This was probably the greatest sum ever raised in support of a single charitable cause in nineteenth-century Scotland. With this substantial resource behind it, the Board divided its relief responsibilities into two Sections. Edinburgh was entrusted with Skye, Wester Ross, Orkney, Shetland and the eastern Highlands, while Glasgow took charge of Argyll, western Inverness, the Outer Hebrides and the Inner Hebrides, apart from Skye. The distribution of meal was managed initially under the Sections' Local Committees, appointed from each parish or district from lists supplied by local clergymen. The objective was only to do enough to prevent absolute starvation and so allowances were limited to only one pound of meal per adult male per day and half of one pound for each woman. In order to ensure that the people were not to be corrupted into the feared state of indolent dependency, anathema to the Victorian mind, these meagre portions would only be provided in return for hard labour. So, in the spring and summer of 1847, gangs of men, women and children could be seen at work all over the western Highlands, the northern isles and the Hebrides at 'public' works, laying roads, building walls, digging ditches and constructing piers. Several of these so-called 'destitution roads' survive to this day as physical memorials to the greatest human crisis in the modern history of Gaeldom.

The relief effort contained the threat of starvation and the spread of famine-related diseases. In spring 1847, for instance, the Glasgow Section despatched 15,680 bolls of wheatmeal, oatmeal, peasemeal and Indian corn to the distressed districts. But critics in the hierarchy of the Central Board were soon complaining that the Highlanders were being encouraged to rely on 'pauperizing' assistance, the so-called 'labour test' was often ignored, and the distribution of meal was becoming too lavish. A campaign to establish a more rigorous system of relief started to gain momentum, partly inspired by the belief that destitution was likely to last longer than one season, and so major efforts had to be made to ensure that the Gaels could support themselves in the future.

Latent racism now came more to the surface. Vitriolic attacks against the 'indolent' Highlander who was being supported by the 'industrious' Lowlander began to be published in the pages of the *Scotsman*, the *Glasgow Herald* and other newspapers. Sir Charles Trevelyan, Assistant Secretary to the Treasury, the key figure in the famine relief strategies in Ireland, was now a powerful influence on the men who ran the Central Board. Trevelyan's position was unequivocal. He regarded both Irish and Highland Celts as profoundly racially inferior to Anglo-Saxons. It was his confirmed view that the potato famine was the judgement of God on a feckless people. They now had to be taught a crucial moral lesson in order to transform their values that they might be able to support themselves in the future rather than rely on the charity of others. Gratuitous relief was a veritable curse on society; in the words of Trevelyan: 'Next to allowing the people to die of hunger, the greatest evil that could happen would be their being habituated to depend upon public charity.'[3]

The outcome was the imposition of the hated 'destitution test' throughout the distressed region. By this system of extreme stringency a whole day's work was required in return for a pound of meal, the theory being that only those facing starvation would accept support on such terms. Trevelyan stressed that 'pauperism', or dependency on relief, could be avoided but by insisting that 'the pound of meal and the task of at least eight hours hard work is the best regime for this moral disease'.[4] An elaborate bureaucracy was set up to enforce this more demanding regime, consisting of an inspector-general, resident inspectors, relief officers and work overseers spread throughout all the districts which had been affected by failure of the potatoes. Most of the functionaries were retired or semi-retired naval officers ('heroes of the quarter-deck', as one observer put it) who were very experienced in enforcing strict discipline. Meal allowances were now to be issued only once a fortnight in order to impose habits of prudence by teaching the poor to spread their paltry issues of meal over an extended period rather than relying on being fed on a daily basis. Labour books were kept by the overseers in which the hours of work of each recipient were faithfully recorded, the fortnight's allowance for each family calculated with care and tickets issued for presentation to the meal dealers. The destitution test was resolutely imposed by relief officers who saw it as their duty to teach the people a moral lesson. Not surprisingly, however, it provoked deep hostility. One critic commented acidly that the scheme was 'starving the poor Highlanders according to the most approved doctrines of political economy . . . the Highlanders upon grounds of Catholic affinity, were to be starved after the Irish fashion'.[5] Free Church ministers protested loudly at the programme of 'systematized starvation' which unleashed angry hostility, particularly among the people of Skye and Wester Ross. Nevertheless, the test was enforced through 1848 and into 1849. In essence a great philanthropic endeavour had been transformed into an ideological crusade to reform a population judged to be inadequate and in need of character improvement. It was an extraordinary outcome.

However, the reasons why the Highlands did not starve were wider and deeper than the relief effort itself. Many landowners were active, at least for a period, in supporting the inhabitants of their estates in the early years of the crisis. For instance, only 14 per cent of all west Highland proprietors were censured by government officials for negligence, though in some other cases pressure had to be brought to bear to ensure that landowners met their obligations. In later years, as described below, estate policy in general became much less benevolent and more coercive. Civil servants even contrasted the positive role of Scottish proprietors with the indifference of many of their counterparts across the Irish Sea. A prime factor in the Scottish case was that many landlords had the financial resources to provide support to their small tenants. As described in Chapter 10, in the early nineteenth century there had been a great transfer of estates from the indebted hereditary landlord class of the region to new owners who were often rich tycoons from outside the Highlands. Over three quarters of all estates in the famine zone had been acquired by merchants, bankers, lawyers, financiers and industrialists by the 1840s. The affluent were attracted to the Highlands for sport, recreation, the romantic allure of the region and, not least, a basic desire for territorial acquisition. Typical of the breed was the new owner of Barra and South Uist, Colonel John Gordon, dubbed 'the richest commoner in Scotland', and Sir James Matheson, proprietor of Lewis and partner in the China opium house of Jardine, Matheson and Co. The economic muscle of this élite was able to complement and support the relief programmes of government and the charities, at least in the first years of the disaster.

The different stages of economic development of Ireland and Scotland were also of crucial importance. The Scottish famine took place in a rich industrialized society with much higher per capita wealth than Ireland. The proof was the army of Irish immigrants which had been drawn by this, settling in the western Lowlands from the late eighteenth century. Scotland had a dynamic industrial economy which offered a range of jobs in general and casual labouring to temporary and permanent migrants from the Highlands. Agricultural work, especially at the harvest, the fisheries, domestic service, building, dock labouring and railway navvying were just some of the outlets available in the booming southern economy. By the 1840s, temporary migration had become a very well-developed feature of Highland life. Not only did it provide a stream of income from the Lowlands but the peak months for seasonal movement, May to September, were also the times of maximum pressure on food resources when the old grain and potato harvests were running out and the new had still to be gathered.

These migration networks were of key importance during the potato famine. The years 1846 and 1847 were by happy coincidence a phase of vigorous development in the Lowland economy, stimulated in large part by the greatest railway construction boom of the nineteenth century. As a result there was an unprecedented demand for labourers, but employment in fishing and agriculture, both traditional outlets for Highland seasonal migrants, was also very buoyant. The combination of a very active labour market in the south and the unremitting pressure of destitution in the north prompted a great stream of people from the stricken region. In a sense, however, and despite the acute distress suffered by the poor, these first two years of the Great Highland Famine can be considered the relative quiet before the real social storm. A wave of widespread clearances and compulsory programmes of emigration were soon to be unleashed on the impoverished communities of Gaeldom.

2

The benevolence of urban philanthropists and several Highland magnates in providing support for the stricken population in 1846–7 cannot be denied. However, voices of disquiet and criticism started to reach a peak from 1848 onwards. In part this was because the Scottish economy was plunged into a deep industrial recession in that year. The depression was accompanied by serious cholera epidemics in some of the larger Lowland towns. Donor fatigue started to set in, not least because the question was now raised of why the Gaels should be offered such 'generous' support while many industrial communities suffered extreme privation with only limited help. The Scottish Poor Law reform of 1845 had set its face against relief for the able-bodied unemployed and, as a result, countless families were now sinking into miserable destitution in the manufacturing areas.

The Central Board's attempts to use its resources to invest in economic improvement in the western Highlands and Islands had also proven fruitless. The *Scotsman* editorials thundered that the charity of industrious, hard-working Lowlanders had been wasted to support 'Celtic laziness'.[6] On some of the great estates of the Highlands, where large sums had been spent on both famine relief and public works, the impact on long-term improvement was indeed slight. Sir James Matheson had provided over £107,000 in the island of Lewis between 1845 and 1850, or some £68,000 more than the revenue derived from his estate over that period. Similarly, between 1846 and 1850 £7,900 was spent on the Tiree and Ross of Mull properties by the Duke of Argyll on famine support together with other road and agricultural improvements. Expenditure on this scale helped to maintain the people, but, to the critics, the continuance of the crisis into its third and fourth years, despite such levels of funding, seemed to confirm that deployment of resources alone, however great they were, could not solve a problem now deemed to be chronic and deeply entrenched in the very fabric and values of Highland society.

The decision of the Central Board to give notice of the termination of its activities in 1850 finally concentrated minds. For the old and infirm, the only alternative was the Poor Law, which, of course, meant a considerable hike in the costs to local ratepayers. Ominously, numbers on the local poor rolls did rise dramatically from the early months of 1850. Then, an even more worrying scenario began to emerge. It was rumoured that, with the winding up of the operations of the Central Board, the government was contemplating the introduction of 'an able-bodied poor law' to combat the threat of starvation and the continued serious destitution in the Highlands. Such a decision would have given all those suffering from destitution the legal right to claim relief. One observer alleged that such measures 'were being talked of in high quarters as a remedy for the grievances' of the Highlands.[7] If implemented, a drastic increase in poor rates would have had a serious impact on the financial position of some proprietors. Strategies on several estates now started to move away from containment of the crisis to systematic dispersal of the people through mass eviction and forced emigration. Contemporaries argued that 'the terror of the poor rates' and 'the retribution of the poor' were the fundamental reasons for the harsh measures which would now have to be implemented.[8] From his vantage point in Whitehall, Sir Charles Trevelyan, who still continued to maintain a keen interest in Highland affairs, agreed that the possibility of a sharp rise in the poor rates 'would give a motive for eviction stronger than any which has yet operated'.[9]

It did not help that in these shifting political circumstances the price of black cattle, the main source of income for crofters, fell on average by more than 50 per cent between 1846 and 1852. The spiralling increases in tenant arrears could not be halted or reversed in such market conditions. Ironically, during the same period prices for both Cheviot and Blackface sheep, which had fluctuated earlier, now recovered and rose on an upward curve from the later 1840s until the early 1860s. Market forces were therefore strongly dictating investment in sheep walks and, with it, policies of clearance of small tenants and cottars, as the most secure route back to financial stability.

Another factor was likely to have a key influence on the unfolding trauma afflicting the people. Some large Highland estates which were insolvent but not yet sold off were managed by trustees for creditors of the owner. They included the lands of Walter Frederick Campbell, proprietor of most of Islay; Norman MacLeod of MacLeod and Lord

Macdonald in Skye and North Uist; Sir James Riddell (Ardnamurchan); Macdonnel of Glengarry (Knoydart); and Maclaine of Lochbuie (Mull), among others. Administration of lands under trust was much more rigorous in law than where a solvent proprietor had personal freedom of action. When a voluntary trust was established, the trustee, normally an Edinburgh accountant or lawyer, possessed all powers of decision making and the owners had to relinquish control over the entire estate. In law, the single responsibility of the trustee was to make funds available to begin repayment of creditors, organize the property to make possible its sale in whole or in part to pay debts, and maintain the revenue stream at a sufficient level to cover public burdens, interest payments and the costs of management. In addition, when an estate was managed under a judicial trust, the trustee was exempted from any law requiring the use of estate revenues for the relief of the poor.

Not surprisingly, therefore, most trustees found it difficult to avoid the removal of crofters and cottars as the conversion of lands to profitable sheep farming was the surest and quickest method of maximizing income. As one contemporary newspaper put it: 'When the lands are heavily mortgaged, the obvious though harsh resource is dispossessing the small tenants, to make room for a better class able to pay rent. This task generally devolves on south country managers or trustees, who look only to money returns, and who cannot sympathize with the peculiar situations and feelings of the Highland population.'[10] A similar comment came from Professor John Stuart Blackie, an influential advocate of the rights of the Gael, some years later: 'A trustee on a bankrupt's estate . . . cannot afford to be generous: women may weep and widows may starve; the trustee must alone attend to the interest of the creditors.'[11] Significantly, historians have noted that some of the most heartless evictions of these years, like those in North Uist and Knoydart, took place on lands managed by trustees.

In the gathering storm, a deep conflict of values and ideologies surfaced and became as relevant as economics and law to the final outcome for the people. Lowland attitudes to the Highlands in the Victorian era were profoundly ambivalent and varied in tone and emphasis over time. On the one hand, by the 1840s, the development of romantic Highlandism had made the region a fashionable tourist destination for the élites of British society. Also, the Highlands had become famed as the kindergarten of the kilted regiments which had brought glory to Scotland and helped increase the standing of the nation within the Union and Empire. But there was also a darker side to Lowland perceptions which became increasingly influential. One of the first works arguing for the intrinsic inferiority of the Celtic race was John Pinkerton's *Dissertation on the Origin and Progress of the Scythians or Goths*, published many years before in 1787. He scorned the Celtic peoples as the aborigines of Europe who were being inevitably displaced by superior Anglo-Saxon Teutonic peoples. The Celts were therefore in mass retreat to the very fringes of European civilization in Ireland and northern Scotland. Pinkerton considered that the expected final disappearance of the Celtic races was evidenced by the nature of their poetry and song, which was 'wholly melancholic' as might be expected of 'a weak and dispirited people'. The culture of Lowland Scotland by contrast was 'replete with that warm alacrity of mind, cheerful courage and quick wisdom which attend superior talents'.[12] The correspondence of Patrick Sellar, the notorious land manager of the Duke of Sutherland and afterwards a sheep farmer, suggests that his attitude may have been influenced by the writings of the Pinkerton genre. He too was wont to describe the Gaels as 'aborigines'.

Pinkerton's analysis was founded on the eighteenth-century Enlightenment belief that different races developed over time at different stages. The new science of anthropology was also interested in the classification of race and the ways in which the Enlightenment idea of man as the product of his environment could best be understood. Even if the views of Pinkerton and his ilk were shared by only a small intellectual minority in the eighteenth century, they still helped to lay one of the key foundations for the later flourishing of racist thought, particularly the assumption that the Celt was unambiguously inferior to the Anglo-Saxon. By the middle decades of the nineteenth century in Scotland, this distinction came to be seen by some as the mark of a profound racial division between the Highlands and the Lowlands.

In the first half of the nineteenth century, race became an even more popular part of medical and scientific research. George Combe's *The Constitution of Man* (1828) was one of the bestsellers of the age and was followed by Robert Knox's 'mono-maniacally racialist and virulently anti-Celticist volume', *The Races of Men* (1850). Knox, one of Edinburgh's leading medical teachers and anatomists, had moved south to London in the wake of his notorious connection to the Burke and Hare murders in the capital in 1828. The Teutonic–Celtic distinction was becoming further refined, the former associated with industriousness, a strong work ethic, ambition and enterprise, the latter with indolence, sloth and dependency. The remarkable advances which had been made in commerce, industry and agriculture were surely proof positive of the strong and energetic racial attributes of the Lowland population. On the other hand, the economic failures of the Highlands should be primarily explained in terms of Celtic inadequacy.

The famine crisis made these views even more influential. The two most important Scottish newspapers of the time, the *Scotsman* and the *Glasgow Herald*, began to give their support, as did the main Highland journal, the *Inverness Courier*, an organ which was traditionally sympathetic to landlordism. In their columns the new orthodoxy of the famine experience from 1847–8 onwards was reiterated time and again, and often in the most vitriolic terms. The Gael was by nature indolent, and his innate laziness had been fortified by the liberal distribution of charity from the pockets of hardworking Lowlanders. The failure of the Highland economy to recover despite such massive dispensation of aid was therefore absolute confirmation of the racial inferiority of the population of the region.

Coincidentally, too, the 1840s were, in the view of one historian, 'a watershed in the surging growth of Anglo-Saxonism', as ideas of Teutonic greatness developed by comparative philologists were combined with notions of Caucasian superiority in the work of those interested in the science of man.[13] In Scotland these perspectives were often analysed in territorial and ethnic terms. The London *Times* despatched a special commissioner to the north to investigate why Britain, a country so pre-eminent and advanced, could possibly contain within its borders an area of such profound poverty and threatened starvation. His explanation was also couched in terms of racial differentiation. The journalist was very keen to stress that not all of the north of Scotland was afflicted by the disease of moral inadequacy. In parts of the region, 'the Danish or Norwegian race' of Aberdeen, Caithness, Shetland and Orkney was thriving because they were accustomed to hard work in a challenging climate and terrain. In a physical sense, they could also be clearly identified by their fair hair and blue eyes. Despite the bleak and inhospitable environment in which they lived, there was no famine in these areas. By contrast, in the neighbouring county of Sutherland, the land of the Celt, poverty was endemic, the turf huts were filthy and filled with smoke, and the failure of the potatoes was catastrophic. The inference was clear. The famine was not the result of biology or economics. Fundamentally, it came about because of racial differences of character, values and attitudes.

What had emerged therefore by 1848/9 were irreconcilable differences between the traditional values of the people and the prevailing ideologies of much contemporary capitalism, improvement and Victorian social morality. Those who subscribed to them seemed to have little comprehension of the Highland labour cycle which meant great effort in spring, summer and autumn but much less work during the winter months. These seasonal rhythms were intrinsic to a pastoral economy, subsistence agriculture and the climatic challenges of daily life in the western Highlands and Islands. But to many outside they conflicted with the Victorian belief in the moral and material value of regular and disciplined toil. Also offensive to this mentality was the traditionalist expectation of the Celt that his social superiors had the responsibility to offer support in times of need. It was a conflict of two world views but in which only those who were committed to the virtues of self-help, independence and initiative had the monopoly of power and authority. For, unlike the pattern in Lowland rural society, where rulers and ruled shared broadly similar sets of social and cultural expectations, the Highland experience seems more akin to one of colonial dominion imposed on the region by outside influences:

> Colonialism is a relationship of domination between an indigenous (or forcibly imported majority) and a minority of foreign invaders. The fundamental decisions affecting the lives of the colonised people are made and implemented by the colonial rulers in pursuit of interests that are defined in a distant metropolis. Rejecting cultural compromises with the colonised population, the colonisers are convinced of their own superiority and their ordained mandate to rule.[14]

Of course, there is no exact fit between this definition and the course of nineteenth-century Highland history. The Gaels were not being dominated by a foreign power. But there are several aspects of their experience which suggest the impact of internal colonialism on Gaeldom. By the early Victorian era most estates were being sold off to affluent southerners, the élite of big farmers was mainly recruited from outside the Highlands and the ideology of those in authority over the people, whether they were natives from Gaeldom or elsewhere, was shaped by an ethos of market capitalism ultimately derived from the Lowland and wider British experience. Some thinkers in the Lowland citadels of learning during the Scottish Enlightenment had also posited a stage theory of development by arguing that humans evolved from barbarity to eventual civility over different phases of time. This concept did not automatically lead to the racialized differentiation of Celts and Anglo-Saxons but did provide a foundation for Victorian intellectuals to do so in later years.

Apart from landowners, their factors, and the Lowland accountants and lawyers who became trustees of insolvent estates, the key players in the unfolding scenario were two public officials, Sir Charles Trevelyan and Sir John McNeil. Both had had a major influence on the policies of the Central Board and even when its operations ceased in 1850 maintained a strong interest in Highland affairs. It was McNeil's Report to the Board of Supervision in Scotland, published in 1851, which finally and authoritatively discredited charitable relief as a solution to the Highland problem and presented a powerful case for large-scale emigration of the 'surplus' population as the only possible way forward. The Report led to the passage of the Emigration Advances Act of 1851, which provided loans at low interest to those proprietors willing to 'encourage' emigration from their estates. This legislation can be seen as a catalytic factor triggering a major increase in clearance and 'compulsory' emigration. Both McNeil and Trevelyan became deeply involved in the foundation and then the management of the Highland and Island Emigration Society, which supported an exodus of nearly 5,000 people to Australia between 1851 and 1856. Trevelyan was the chairman and the principal influence on the Society, while McNeil was his trusted lieutenant.

By 1850, Trevelyan himself had become convinced that mass emigration, including, if warranted, the use of coercion, was the only corrective for the deep-seated social ills of the Highlands. The failures of charity and relief had already inflicted moral damage on the population: 'The only immediate remedy for the present state of things is Emigration, and the people will never emigrate while they are supported at home at other people's expense. This mistaken humanity has converted the people . . . from the clergy downwards into a Mendicant Community.'[15] He proposed instead a grandiose programme to 'emigrate' 30,000–40,000 of the people of the western Highlands and Islands. 'A national effort' would be necessary in order to rid the land of 'the surviving Irish and Scotch Celts'. The exodus might then allow for the settlement of racially superior peoples of Teutonic stock in the districts from which the Gaels had been removed. Trevelyan welcomed 'the prospects of flights of Germans settling here in increasing number – an orderly, moral, industrious and frugal people, less foreign to us than the Irish or Scotch Celt, a congenial element which will readily assimilate with our body politic'.[16] The *Scotsman* was in full agreement with the diagnosis that expulsion was now the only recourse: 'Collective emigration is, therefore, the removal of a diseased and damaged part of our population. It is a relief to the rest of the population to be rid of this part.'[17]

3

Over the two decades from 1841 to 1861 many west Highland parishes experienced an unprecedented fall in population, primarily caused by large-scale emigration. Uig in Lewis lost almost a half of its total population, the island of Jura nearly a third, several parishes in Skye a quarter or more, and Barra a third. In the whole of the region covering the west coast north of Ardnamurchan and the Inner and Outer Hebrides, the total population decline averaged around 30 per cent. It was by far the greatest volume of emigration in such a short period, not only in the nineteenth-century Highlands, but in the modern history of Scottish Gaeldom. Over 10,000 emigrants were 'assisted' to move to Canada, mainly from four great landed estates, those of the Dukes of Argyll and Sutherland, John Gordon of Cluny and Sir James Matheson. A further 5,000 left for Australia under the auspices of the Highland and Island Emigration Society. But these are the emigrants who can be accounted for because they were supported by landlords or charities and so feature in contemporary documentation. The trails of the many who moved overseas by other means have left little trace in the historical record and remain anonymous within the overall statistical evidence. We do know, however, that the exodus of this period was principally from the Hebrides, and especially from the islands which had suffered most during the potato famine, particularly Lewis, North Uist, South Uist, Barra, Tiree, Mull and Skye.

But the famine clearances were not exclusive to those locations. Research has confirmed they took place in twenty-two Highland parishes with a population in all of nearly 77,000. Some of them were on the western mainland and the Inner Hebrides. For example, between 1847 and 1851 the Lowland lawyer F. W. Clark, the new proprietor of the island of Ulva, off Mull, cut the population back from 500 to 150 souls through a systematic process of eviction. At Knoydart, in western mainland Inverness-shire, a series of particularly brutal removals reduced the numbers on the estate from 600 to little more than seventy over a five-year period.

Coercion was employed widely and systematically. The officials of the estates reckoned that it was the poorest who were most reluctant to move, even though they were in the most desperate circumstances of all. The mechanism employed to ensure that they went came to be described as 'compulsory emigration'. Families were offered the bleak choice between outright eviction or removal together with assistance to take ship across the Atlantic with costs of passage covered by proprietors. As the Chamberlain for the Matheson estate, in Lewis, put it in April 1851: 'none could be called to emigrate and they need not go unless they please but all who were two years and upwards in arrears would be deprived of their land at Whitsunday . . . the proprietor can do with his land as he pleases'.[18] Thirty years later a Church of Scotland minister from Lewis recalled:

> Some people say it was voluntary. But there was a great deal of forcing and these people were sent very much against their will. That is very

well known and people present know that perfectly well. Of course, they were not taken in hand by the police and all that, but they were in arrears and had to go, and remonstrated against going.[19]

The Chamberlain, John Munro Mackenzie, and his sub-factors had carried out a thorough examination of the condition and prospects for each tenant in all the Lewis crofting townships. The exercise identified around 2,500 men, women and children designated for emigration. However, of the first 1,512 selected, only forty-five were willing to take up the estate's offer of support for the voyage to Canada. But by 1855 Mackenzie had virtually reached his target of 2,500 men women and children through a combination of threats of eviction, confiscation of cattle stocks from those in rent arrears and the suspension of famine relief.

So it was that a huge increase in clearance throughout the region became linked with a dramatic expansion of emigration. In early 1848, William Skene, Secretary of the Edinburgh Section of the Central Board, had predicted that the termination of relief operation proposed for 1850 would immediately cause 'a very great and very extensive "Highland Clearing"'.[20] He was soon to be proven correct. Of the Summonses or Writs of Removal granted at Tobermory Sheriff Court on Mull, a mere handful were awarded to proprietors in 1846 and 1847. But over 81 per cent of those issued between 1846 and 1852 were granted between 1848 and 1852. This was the typical pattern elsewhere. The processes of coercion reached unprecedented levels as the intensity and scale of clearance became evident. Between 1848 and 1851, Sir James Matheson in Lewis obtained no fewer than 1,367 summonses of removal against his tenants. In some districts in Skye it was said that eviction had become so widespread that men feared to leave their families to go south to work for the season. The highly experienced government official, lugubriously named Sir Edward Pine Coffin, who had experience of famine relief in Mexico and Ireland as well as Highland Scotland, was so alarmed that he expressed himself in unusually colourful prose. Coffin condemned the landed classes for seeking to bring about 'the extermination of the population' and asserted that eviction was now so rampant it would lead to 'the unsettling of the foundations of the social system' and so 'the enforced depopulation of the Highlands'.[21]

According to contemporary reports and evidence later given to the Napier Commission in the 1880s, some of the most brutal 'compulsory emigrations' took place on the island estates of John Gordon of Cluny in Barra, Benbecula and South Uist. Gordon, of Cluny Castle in Aberdeenshire, reputed to be the wealthiest commoner in Scotland at the time, had bought the properties from the insolvent hereditary owners, the MacNeills of Barra. He was a former military officer, but his wealth came from the rich farming lands of the north-east and six slave plantations in the Caribbean which he had inherited from his father and an uncle. Between 1848 and 1851 the Gordon estates shipped off almost 3,000 destitute tenant and cottar families across the Atlantic to the port of Quebec. It was alleged that those who resisted were forced on to the emigrant vessels. Their very poor and weak condition on arrival was condemned and reported back to London in angry prose by immigration officials.

Three key sources provide insights into how the managers of Highland estates went about the business of removal and compulsory emigration. The first is the report by Thomas Goldie Dickson, a trustee of the Ardnamurchan Estate of Sir James Riddell, written in 1852; secondly, the diary of John Munro Mackenzie, for 1851; and, thirdly, the correspondence of John Campbell of Ardmore, Chamberlain of the Duke of Argyll's lands in Tiree and the Ross of Mull.[22]

A striking feature in all three cases was the careful investigations carried out of the lives and personal circumstances of the people before any action was taken. The economic conditions of each tenant and his capacity to pay rent were of paramount concern but they were by no means the only evidence to be scrutinized before decisions on which families to evict were made. Character, age and health were among the other key matters which were given considerable weight. Each household was visited and detailed enumerations were collected. On the basis of these facts, the futures of whole families and communities were decided. The poorest were always the main targets. The Duke of Argyll put the issue in plain terms in a note to his Chamberlain in spring, 1851: 'I wish to send out those whom we would be obliged to feed if they stayed at home – to get rid of that class is the object'[23] (underlined in source). He had earlier issued John Campbell with instructions to eradicate and 'emigrate' crofters paying below

£10 rental as well as all cottar families on the Mull lands. On Lewis a special feature of the clearance programme was the emptying of those townships formerly involved in the now-redundant kelp manufacture and, at the same time, the building up of other communities on the island which were committed to the more profitable fishing economy.

But decisions were not simply based on disinterested economic calculation. Ideologies, values and attitudes were also part of the equation. Some Lowland trustees, lawyers and accountants, in particular, came north with a set of social and moral prejudices about the racial inferiority of the Gael which undoubtedly influenced their thinking on who should go and who might be allowed to stay. One of the leading accountants of the day, George Auldjo Jamieson, in an address to the Royal Society of Edinburgh, had noted the contrast between the Saxon race of the Lowlands, which he lauded as the land of independence and progress, as opposed to the Gaelic Highlands, inhabited by a Celtic race corrupted by dependence on charity and backwardness. It was also significant that in 1851 Sir James Matheson advised the Canadian immigration authorities in Quebec in advance of the arrival of the first shiploads of people from his estate that they should be dispersed rather than kept together in the same communities. He contended that would be 'the best means of eradicating those habits of indolence and inertness to which their impoverished condition must in some measure be attributed'.[24]

These views coloured the decision-making processes to a considerable extent. Indeed, some estate managers come across in the sources as rigorous guardians of Victorian morality rather than as impartial administrators. While the 'respectable poor' might be protected and saved from removal, others were less fortunate. In April 1848, for instance, John Campbell issued 'a goodly number' of 'removing summonses'. Some were for rent arrears but others were for such offences as 'selling whisky', 'unruly conduct', 'extreme laziness and bad conduct'. 'Bad characters' were also likely to suffer eviction.[25] Thomas Goldie Dickson also made life-changing decisions for the people of the Ardnamurchan estate on grounds which were far removed from economic criteria alone.[26] Dugald McDonald, the blacksmith at Sunart, had few rent arrears but 'was of intemperate habits' and so 'must be removed and another smith procured'. Another unfortunate was James

McMaster, who not only had substantial rent arrears but 'was living with a Woman not his wife'. Even more extraordinarily, Duncan Henderson of Kilmory was described as 'a clever man, a little too much so'. The decision was therefore that he 'must be sequestrated for safety'. Hugh McPherson 'does nothing all winter . . . An ill-dressed and evidently lazy fellow.' In this and other estates, managers had total power over the lives of crofters, who held land on annual tenure, and cottars, who had no legal rights to land at all. Several used this authority to impose the virtues of self-help, the work ethic and 'respectability' on a population deemed to be inferior in all these respects. Also striking was the callousness of the decisions; the very old, the sick and even the dying were not exempt from the programme of removals.

For a people already brought low by years of failing crops this must have seemed like a reign of terror and, not surprisingly, long after these events their infamy lived on among the emigrant communities overseas. The following satirical poem, suffused with anger, was penned by Eugene Ross (or Rose), a native of Ardtun in the Ross of Mull, to mark the death of the aforesaid John Campbell of Ardmore, known widely as the 'Factor Mhòir', the Big Factor, because of his height. The 'Big Angus' referred to in the text was Angus McVicar, Campbell's sub-factor. Both were natives of the island of Islay.

'Cumha a' Bhailldh Mhoir'
Uisdean Ros

Tha sgeul an duthaic, s' tha sin sunndach ga
Gu bheil am Baillidh 'na shineadh, 's gun trid air ach leine
'S e gun chomas na bruidhneadh, gun sgriobhadh, gun leughadh
'S gu bheil cul-taice nan Ileach 'na shineadh 's chan eirich

'S nuair theid iaddon bhata ni sinn gair a bhios eibhinn
'S nuair chruinnicheas sinn comhla bidh sin nag ol air a cheile
Uisge-beatha math Gaidhealach, fion laidir is seudar;
'Scha bhi sinn tuileadh fo churam on a sgiursadh 'a bheist ud

Gum bi a' Factor air thoiseach san t-sloc sa bheil Satan,
'S Aonghas Mor as a dhearahaidh, 's lasair theine ri mhasan,

Leis na rinn thu de ainneart air mnathan 's paisdean,
'S an sluagh bha san duthaic rinn sgiursadh far saile

S' nuair a chulaig iad an Canada gun do chaidl a' bheist ud,
Chaidh an tein-eibhinn fhadadh is chaidh bratach ri gugan:
'S ann an sin a bha lan aighear, s' iad a' tachairt ri cheile,
S' chaidh iad a bha lan aighear, s' thug iad cliu gun do
      dh'eug thu.

'Lament for Factor Mòr'
Eugene Ross

There is news in the land that we rejoice to hear –
that the Factor is laid out without a stitch on him but a shroud,
without the ability to speak and unable to read or write;
the champion of the Islay folk is laid low, and will never rise
      again.

When they go to the boat we will laugh with glee,
and when we gather together, we will drink toasts to one another
with a good Highland whisky, with strong wine and cider,
and we will not be worried any longer, since that beast has been
      vanquished.

The Factor will have the pre-eminence in Satan's pit,
and Big Angus will be right behind him, with a flame of fire up his
      buttocks,
because of all the oppression that you inflicted on women and
      children,
and the people of the country that you drove mercilessly overseas.

When they heard in Canada that that beast had expired,
bonfires were lit and banners were attached to branches;
people were cock-a-hoop with joy, as they met one another,
and they all got down on their knees and praised God that you
      had died.[27]

3

The micro-history of John Campbell's evictions on the Ross of Mull and the island of Tiree provide some revealing insights on how they were conducted and the response of the people to them. Even before the potatoes failed in 1846, the 8th Duke of Argyll and his managers had determined by 1840 to carry out large-scale removals on the Ross and Tiree of crofters and cottars and replace them with medium-sized mixed farms and extensive sheep runs which would be mainly rented by Islay kinsmen and associates of his factor, John Campbell. It was argued that this strategy would finally provide some economic stability to districts over-populated by impoverished and destitute families. In the Ross the better land lay to the south and this was where over 60 per cent of the people lived at the census of 1841. By that year the population of the Ross had risen to 2,500, more than half of whom were cottars paying no rental or only minimal amounts. The removals were to be targeted at them in particular and the settlements of the richer land of the southern Ross in general. There were ten townships in that area with 167 households and a total population of 928 in 1841. By 1861 three had been left virtually untouched and the remaining seven cleared in whole or in part. The number of households fell to ninety-seven and the population of South Ross to 391, less than half that of 1841.

The first to be cleared was Shiaba, '*nan sia ba*' ('of the six cows'), in the far south-east corner of the Ross. There had been a township there since early medieval times. Shiaba had some of the best land in the district and so paid an above-average rental. As well as houses, byres and stackyards, this substantial settlement boasted kailyards, stone enclosures, a schoolhouse, shop, fishermen's huts and two water mills. The remains of a small medieval chapel were within walking distance. None of the twelve main tenants were in arrears and for many years had paid their rents on time. Notices of eviction were served on them in 1845, before the onset of the potato disease, and again a second time in 1847 from the Factor Mor demanding their immediate removal. The news sent tremors of alarm throughout the Ross as Shiaba was the most prosperous township in the district, with much arable land for the cultivation of oats as well as potatoes.

It even paid some of the in-kind rental in coal. More impoverished settlements now looked to their own fate in the future with dread.

On 1 June 1847 an appeal signed by seven of the tenants was sent to the Duke of Argyll together with a letter from Shiaba's oldest inhabitant, aged nearly 100, Neil MacDonald, who signed himself 'ex-soldier':

> ... having paid rent to your grace's ancestors for upwards of sixty years I beg leave to send prefixed a petition by myself and the other tenants in Shiaba. Trusting that your Grace will give us a favourable reply to it's [sic] prayers as it would be a great hardship and quite unprecedented to remove a man of my age, who, as natural to suppose, is drawing close to the house appointed for all living. Trusting that your Grace will order an answer soon.[28]

The petition itself read:

> Unto His Grace The Duke of Argyll
>> The Petition of the undersigned tenants in Shiaba, Ross of Mull
>> Humbly showeth
>
> That the petitioners and their forefathers had been tenants in Shiaba about sixty years and in other estates in the Ross since time immemorial.
>
> That the petitioners were lately warned to flit [leave] and remove from their respective possessions, although they were not in arrears of rent, but, on the contrary, have paid the same regularly, though they had large families to support – numbering, including, cottars, upwards of one hundred persons neither of whom received any aid or were a burden on the parish.
>
> That the whole farm has lately been let in one lot to one individual who is not native of the Ross and neither he, nor any of his ancestors, ever possessed any lands under your Grace's noble ancestors.
>
> That a few days ago the incoming tenant came with shepherds and men to value the sheep belonging to the petitioners without giving them previous intimation, but as he had not the money and could not find a cautioner for the payment of the price, and is under good character – all the surrounding tenants and others being afraid of him – they would not deliver the stock.

May it, therefore, please your Grace to take our petitioners' case into consideration and give instructions whether they are to be removed under the circumstances above stated – and if so they trust that they will be accommodated with land on other parts of the estate. And your Grace's petitioners beg to pray accordingly.

Writer – Neil MacDonald ex-soldier

Signatories: Alexander MacGillvary, Archie MacGillvary, Donald McKinnon, John Campbell, John McKinnon, Allan McDougall, Duncan McCormick[29]

A tone of deference and even submissiveness runs through the petition but also articulated is the age-old claim of the people to the land because of past service to the ducal family and long residence on the township and the estate. There is no evidence that the Duke ever replied. The evictions went ahead. Some families who had decided to go to Canada were taken off by ship from the *Traig Bhan*, the beach below Shiaba. Others were moved into townships on the poorer north of the Ross and an unknown number left for Glasgow. A cattle dealer from Factor Mor's home island of Islay became sole tenant of the virtually deserted lands of Shiaba.

On the neighbouring island of Tiree, the social crisis triggered by the failure of the potatoes was if anything more acute than in the Ross of Mull. Population had been rising at an accelerating rate there: *c.*1750, 1,509; 1801, 2,776; 1841, 4,900. These were increases of 84 per cent from 1750 to 1801 and a further 79 per cent between 1801 and 1841. They were unsustainable even if the famine had not taken place, especially with the collapse or stagnation of the by-employments of kelp burning and fishing. The root cause of the teeming numbers had been the reckless subdivision of land into crofts which were then fragmented again by the expansion of the cottar class, who by 1841 comprised over a third of all the inhabitants on the island. The packing in of small tenants to provide labour for kelping was a principal factor. Another had been the long-term effect of soldier recruitment during the Napoleonic Wars: 'the minute subdivision of the land was much increased by the family of Argyll having raised three or four regiments for government during the last war and residences were afforded to those soldiers on their return'.[30] By the 1840s it was said that the people of Tiree had become 'a vast semi-pauper population'.[31] The 8th Duke of Argyll was candid enough to blame the policies or lack of them by his predecessors since the late eighteenth century for the social evils which threatened a human calamity after 1846:

> I thought it my duty to remember that the improvidence of their fathers [of the inhabitants] had been at least seconded, left unchecked by any active measures, or by the enforcement of any rules of my own predecessors who had been in possession of the estate.
>
> I regarded my self, therefore, as representing those who had some share in the responsibility, although that responsibility was one of omission and not of commission.[32]

When John Campbell, the Duke's chamberlain, arrived in Tiree in January 1847 the impact of the potato blight on the people was instantly apparent. The inhabitants were in 'a state of absolute starvation', a judgement later confirmed by relief officials who considered the island to be one of the most distressed in the Hebrides.[33] In that year alone the estate had to spend £5,403 on famine relief and employment projects to keep the people alive. Perhaps predictably, as circumstances improved, the Duke of Argyll embarked on a large-scale scheme of emigration, especially of the poorest class. At the considerable additional cost of £3.80 per person, the estate supported the emigration of 1,354 men, women and children, principally to Canada, between 1847 and 1851. Many years later, the Duke considered the investment worthwhile. The 'old pauperized class' had been eradicated: 'the detritus of the old subdivided cottars and subtenants . . . also in great measure the remains of the old kelp burning population'.[34] Strict controls over any future subdivision were imposed and, as in the Ross of Mull, crofts were consolidated into larger farms. Controversy remains on the extent of coercion employed to manage the exodus. Certainly many wanted to leave and petitioned the estate for help to do so. But not everyone did. There is abundant evidence in John Campbell's correspondence of numerous eviction notices being delivered, confiscation of cattle stocks from those in arrears and the cutting back on famine relief to force people out.

Landlords, government officials and managers of estates had, of course, a quite different perspective from that of the small tenants and cottars who were 'emigrated' to Canada and Australia. For the élites emigration by coercion was an unfortunate but necessary evil. From their perspective, by removing the most distressed and vulnerable people from the Western Isles, a human catastrophe had been avoided. The potato crisis was not over by the early 1850s, but relief from the Lowlands had come to an end and opposition to further charitable support had hardened. Most proprietors were also hostile to the expenditure of large sums on relief as the famine entered its fourth year and the future continued to look bleak. For them, the enforcement of mass emigration was much more acceptable than risking a major crisis of mortality on their estates and exposing themselves to bankruptcy and forced sale of their lands.

In large part it was the clearances of the later famine period that marked out the experience of the western Highlands and Islands as different from the history of dispossession in the rest of Scotland. These removals were unleashed against communities still suffering from the ravages of a major destitution crisis. They affected many on the Hebridean islands, were concentrated in both time and space and for the most part designed to drive out the poorest families and the 'redundant population'. Several were enforced by draconian means with little concern for humanity or the welfare of the people. Racialist assumptions undeniably helped to fashion those responsible for the strategy of dispossession.

These evictions by their extreme and often callous nature were therefore unique in the history of the many clearances that had taken place over generations in the Scottish countryside since the seventeenth century. They left a deep mark and their memory endured, while most of those that had gone before were lost to history.

15
Turning of the Tide

I

Mass clearance in the Highlands had ended by the later 1850s, though some individual evictions continued. Also, in early 1856, after a full decade of misery, conditions began to improve for the majority of the population. The potato crop once again regained its former abundance, though it never regained its former dominance in the Highland diet. Instead, there was a very marked increase in the consumption of imported meal. So significant was this that it became common practice to feed the indigenous grain crop and part of the potato crop to the cattle to sustain them during the winter months while reserving imported meal for human consumption. An equally important expansion occurred in the purchase of tea, sugar, jam and tobacco. Until the 1850s these articles had mainly been rare and expensive luxuries, but by the 1890s tea drinking had become universal in the crofting districts and a familiar part of the domestic way of life.

These alterations in diet were the most obvious manifestations of more fundamental changes in the nature of crofting society in the aftermath of the famine. To some extent, the declining significance of the potato may have reflected the relaxation of population pressure in some districts as emigration persisted and the ranks of the cottar class were thinned in most localities outside the Long Island. But the new dietary patterns were also to be found in the Outer Hebrides, where the old problems of population congestion and land hunger remained. A greater variety in foodstuffs, in fact, was simply one part of a wider and deeper social transition which affected *all* areas of life. In the 1870s and 1880s the majority of the population of the western

Highlands became less dependent on the produce of the land for survival and even more reliant on the two sources of income and employment, fishing and temporary migration, which had proved most resilient during the famine itself. They entered more fully into the cash economy, selling their labour for cash wages and buying more of the necessities of life with their earnings rather than producing them themselves.

Manufactured clothes and shoes, 'shop produce' as they were known in the region, steadily replaced the home-made varieties in the two generations after the famine. A new mechanism of credit facilitated these developments. Shopkeepers, merchants and fish curers supplied credit on which meal and clothes were bought until seasonal earnings from fishing and temporary migration became available. The running accounts were then partly paid off on the basis of these returns, but more often than not debts persisted from year to year. In Strath in Skye, 'Every man is in a hurry to get the spring work past and be off to his work on sea and land all through the kingdom and when they return, if their earnings have succeeded well, they pay the shop, and the shopman supplies them on credit, as they require it.'[1] In Lewis, the fishing crews purchased on credit in the curers' shops the meal, clothing and other necessities required for their families. Settlement took place at the end of the season; fishermen were credited with the price of fish delivered by them to the curers and were debited with the price of their purchases.

The new structure depended ultimately on five factors: the recovery of the prices for Highland black cattle; a steep fall in world grain prices in the 1870s and 1880s; a revolutionary expansion in steam navigation in the western Highlands; the growth of the indigenous fishing industry; and a further increase in the scale of temporary migration and casual employment outside the Highlands. These specific influences need also to be viewed against the longer perspective of the decisive change in the economic circumstances of the west Highland population which took place from the later 1850s and continued into the 1860s and 1870s. The period from the end of the Napoleonic Wars to the potato famine had been one of contracting income and falling employment. Then the three decades after the crisis saw a significant recovery in both earnings and jobs which was not wholly offset by either rising costs or new demographic pressures. Even given the important qualifications which will be discussed below when living standards are considered in more detail, there had been a relative improvement in circumstances.

Price trends, between the 1850s and the 1870s, were to the advantage of the people in the crofting region. This was a dramatic reversal of the pattern before 1846. Cattle prices continued the recovery which had begun in 1852. Crofters' two-year-old heifers in Lewis, selling at 30s.–£2 in 1854 fetched £4–£5 by 1883. Those tenants who possessed small stocks of sheep gained from the upward swing in prices which lasted until the late 1860s. The fact that they were much better fed on grain and potatoes during the winter months added to the marketability of cattle. The principal aim was now one of maximizing the potential of stock not simply in the traditional manner to pay rent but as a source of the funds employed to purchase meal and other commodities.

A further expansion in sea transport facilitated both cattle and sheep exports and grain imports. In the early 1850s a single small steamer had plied the route between the Clyde and Portree in Skye once every fortnight. Three decades later two larger vessels sailed to Skye and Lewis every week and a further three ships visited Barra and North and South Uist. These developments in communications were both cause and effect of the changing way of life in the region and the basis of the closer involvement of the people in the money economy. Above all, they allowed the population of more areas to take full advantage of the sustained fall in world grain prices which took place after the opening up of the interior areas of North America by railroad and the new steamship connections established with the purchasing countries in Europe. In the early 1840s meal imported from the Clyde sold at an average of £2.2s. per boll in the Outer Hebrides; by the 1880s average prices were close to 16s. per boll. It was the enormous decline in costs which encouraged the practice of feeding cattle on grain produced at home and allowed earnings from cattle sales and other activities to be devoted to the purchase of cheap meal from outside.

Pivotal to the whole system of increased trade, credit and money transactions was a vast expansion in seasonal employment opportunities. The indigenous white and herring fisheries of the Outer Hebrides achieved a new level of activity and prosperity. Fishing stations were set up at Castlebay, Lochboisdale and Lochmaddy. The number of fish-curing companies increased from seven in 1853 to fifty in 1880. In the early 1850s about 300 small boats were active; three decades later around 600. The organization and capitalization of the industry were dominated by men from the east coast, but Hebrideans gained from the new opportunities for seasonal employment. The developing steamer services and the injection of capital from the east had given the winter white fishery in particular a fresh and vigorous stimulus. Casual jobs were also available on the sporting estates as stalkers and ghillies and in the labour squads needed to build the infrastructure of roads and lodges of the new recreation economy. There were seasonal opportunities, too, in sheep smearing, which involved working a mixture of butter, tar and grease into the fleeces to afford protection against vermin: 'Since one man could only smear about twenty sheep a day and since a quarter of a million were annually smeared in Inverness-shire alone, labour was obviously much in demand ... During the 1860s and 1870s the wages paid for casual labour of this type rose steadily and more or less doubled between 1850 and 1880.'[2]

Finally, the expansion in temporary migration which had begun during the famine was sustained after it. Virtually all sectors – agricultural work in the Lowlands, domestic service in the cities, the merchant marine, general labouring (such as in the gasworks of the larger towns) – produced more opportunities for Highland temporary migrants than before. Because of this, 'seasonal' migration more often became 'temporary' movement with absences extending not simply for a few weeks or months but for the greater part of a year or even longer. The seasonality of different work peaks made it possible to dovetail different tasks outside the Highlands and at the same time alternate labour in the crofting region with work opportunities elsewhere.

The classical example of the latter cycle was the interrelationship between the winter white fishery in the Minch, the spring herring fishery in the same waters and the east-coast herring fishery during the summer months. This last was the most dynamic sector and the source of a great stream of income which percolated through the entire Inner and Outer Hebrides in the 1860s and 1870s. From 1835 to 1854 the annual average cure in Aberdeenshire and Banffshire increased moderately from 428,343 to 495,879 barrels. In the 1860s and 1870s, however, the industry boomed. The average cure rose from 602,375 barrels between 1865 and 1874 to 902,665 in the period 1875–84. During the same phase the number of herring boats on the east coast grew by 51 per cent while the total of fishermen and boys rose by 60 per cent from 1854 to 1884. An increased field of employment opened up in consequence for the population of the western Highlands and Islands. It was estimated that 30,000 men and women came in a great annual migration to the fishing ports up and down the east coast from the Gaelic-speaking areas of the far west. On the surface, therefore, the evidence for improvement in living standards seemed compelling.

The emigration of some of the poorest classes of Highland society did allow a more rapid recovery from the trauma of the crisis of the 1840s than would otherwise have been the case. Cottars and squatters often placed a burden on the over-stretched resources of crofters and these pressures doubtless diminished when the numbers of these semi-landless people went into decline during the famine and its immediate aftermath. The period from 1856 to the later 1870s did appear to be one of considerable material progress in the western Highlands. Crofting rents on several estates were paid more regularly than before and the problem of accumulating arrears was not as serious. Consumer goods were imported on a much larger scale. The gathering of shellfish for consumption during the summer months, a practice which had long been one of the principal manifestations of the chronic poverty of the region, seems to have declined, though it retained its importance as a source of cash income into the second half of the twentieth century. Numerous contemporary commentators who could recall the deprivation of earlier times were also sure that a considerable amelioration had taken place in the decades which followed the famine.

Nevertheless, the majority of the people continued to endure an existence of poverty and insecurity after 1860. Life was still precarious and could easily degenerate into destitution if any of the fragile supports of the population temporarily crumbled. Between 1856 and 1890 there was a series of bad seasons which recalled some of the worst years of the potato blight. In 1864 'the cry of destitution in Skye has been as loud as ever and yet from no part of the Highlands has there been a more extensive emigration'.[3] Conditions on Mull were at that time also briefly reminiscent of the tragic days of the 1840s. On the Duke of Argyll's estate rent arrears escalated, especially among the small tenants. Food, seed and labour had to be provided for the people who had suffered great hardship since 1862. Four years later distress was again experienced by the population of an island which had sustained a decline in the numbers of its inhabitants from 10,054 to 7,240 between 1841 and 1861. In the Bunessan area 'many of the poor are actually starving'.[4] Once again meal was made available and public works started. It was successive bad seasons in 1881–2, affecting the whole of the western Highlands, which not only caused much suffering but also provided the initial economic impetus for the great crofters' revolt of that decade. Over 24,000 people received relief in these years. Conditions deteriorated once more in 1888. In the Outer Hebrides 'actual starvation' was predicted and the inhabitants once more were supported by charitable organizations from the Lowland cities. The chamberlain of the Lewis estate himself estimated that there had been at least nine seasons between 1853 and 1883 when the proprietor had had to advance varying amounts of seed and meal to the crofters.

At best, then, 'recovery' was modest and continued to be punctuated by years of distress. Typhus remained common in some localities because of poor living conditions and poor sanitation. Cattle continued to share living accommodation with human beings. Domestic squalor persisted and disconcerted observers from outside the Highlands accustomed to higher standards. Mass clearances were a thing of the past, but insecurity of tenure remained a fact of life: 'Others, not a few, continue quietly evicting by legal process and clearing by so-called voluntary emigration. The lawyer's pen supersedes the soldier's steel.'[5] Moreover, the heavy impact of landlord authority was felt in other ways.

It is known that successful action to control subdivision was already taking place on some properties, especially along the western mainland, before the famine. This probably helps to explain why several parishes in that region had already reached their peak populations by the census of 1841. However, in most areas of the Outer Hebrides after the famine, regulations against subdivision of crofts were still lax. Nevertheless, for the remainder of the crofting region, there is abundant evidence not only that opposition to subdivision was more widespread after the 1850s but that the mechanisms of control had become more efficient. The result was that by the 1880s, along the west coast north of Ardnamurchan, in Mull and in other islands of the Inner Hebrides, the cottar class was disappearing rapidly or had vanished entirely from the social structure. The fear of the burdens they might inflict on the poor rates, bitter memories of the famine, and the assumption that the proliferation of poor cottar families had been a principal and powerful cause of earlier grievous destitution combined to harden opposition to them. These influences ensured subletting was often crushed whatever the human costs. It was yet another sign of the radical change in landlord policy which had taken place since the early nineteenth century. The boom in labour-intensive activities encouraged fragmentation of holdings to c.1820; their collapse or stagnation thereafter caused a trend back towards consolidation of holdings into sheep farms which grew stronger during and after the great subsistence crisis.

Control of subdivision meant that no additional or separate households could any longer be created within a single tenancy. Only one member of a tenant or cottar family was permitted to set up home after marriage on the lot. Even that could only be done by sharing the father's house until he died. In practice, however, regulation was even tighter than this and often designed to reduce rather than simply regulate the numbers of households. As one observer put it: 'landlords . . . *weed out* families by twos or threes . . . an absolute veto was placed upon marriage . . . when a young man is guilty of that he may look for a summons of removal'.[6]

These were not the exaggerated claims of an over-enthusiastic pamphleteer. Duncan Darroch, proprietor of the Torridon estate in Wester Ross, later admitted to the Napier Commission that the regulations which prevailed on his property meant that the young emigrated 'and the elderly members generally go on the poor's roll and, as they die out, the cottages are taken down'.[7] In Arisaig it was alleged that the offspring of families who reached the age of twenty-one had to go and live elsewhere unless allowed to remain 'with the written sanction of the proprietor'.[8] There had in the past been a good deal of subdivision of crofts on some parts of the Lochaber estate of Cameron of Lochiel. By the later 1840s, however, these practices were outlawed:

> The present proprietor is enlarging rather than subdividing and his regulations against the increase of population are of the most stringent and Malthusian character. Two families are strictly prohibited from living upon one croft. If one of a family marries, he must leave the croft; and a case has even been brought under my notice, in which the only son of a widow, who is in joint possession of a croft with his mother, has been told that if he marries he will be compelled to leave the estate. Severe penalties are also threatened against the keeping of lodgers. The unlucky crofter who takes a friend under his roof, without first obtaining the consent of Lochiel, must pay for the first offence a fine of £1; and, for the second, shall be removed from the estate.

There is ample evidence in the Cameron of Lochiel papers that summonses of removal were issued to any crofters who infringed these regulations.[9]

Control of subdivision in Lochcarron meant that 'families as they grow up are sent out to shift for themselves'. In Ardnamurchan and Mull landlords not only restricted subletting but also pulled down houses on the death of the occupants in order to cause 'a thinning of numbers'.[10] On the Duke of Argyll's estate in Mull the regulations against subdivision were also rigorously enforced, and the older tradition of subletting to kinfolk had disappeared entirely.[11] Instead, the children of tenants had no alternative but to go. At Glenshiel regulations against subletting were given as the main reason for a sharp decline in marriages. Attempts to limit subdivision on the Macdonald estates in Skye had begun before the famine but were only partially effective. From the 1850s, however, it became the 'inevitable rule ... that subdivision of lands by crofters is rigorously prohibited'.[12] Eldest sons were informed that they alone had the right to succeed to the croft held by the father on the basis of primogeniture. It therefore was in their interest to prevent the holding from being divided among other members of the family. Elsewhere on the island controls were enforced with equal resolution. One tacksman on the Macleod estates ensured that at marriage the couple would have to move. It was alleged that 'If a son married in a man's family, the father dared not give him shelter even for a night.'[13]

This degree of intervention in family life and the attack on the old traditions of inheritance ensured that crofting society remained far from settled in tranquillity in these decades. The simmering tensions finally came to the surface on the Isle of Skye in 1882. The disturbances there in that year came to be known as 'the Battle of the Braes'. It had several features associated with the sporadic and familiar outbreaks of lawlessness in the past. The protest began in the townships of Gedintailor, Balmeanach and Peinchorran, which constituted the district known as Braes on Lord MacDonald's estate on the east coast of Skye, some eight miles south of the island's capital of Portree. The crofters petitioned the landlord to have traditional grazing rights on Ben Lee returned to them. The factor rejected the request, but the people replied by stating they would no longer pay rent to Lord MacDonald until their rights were restored. The landlord then attempted to serve summonses of removal on a number of tenants on the grounds that they were in rent arrears. On 7 April 1882, however, the sheriff officer serving the summonses was accosted by a crowd of around 500 people, and the notices were taken from him and burned. Ten days later, the law returned in force, strongly supported this time by a force of fifty Glasgow policemen. They managed to arrest those who had assaulted the sheriff officer but not before about a dozen constables received injuries at the hands of a large crowd of men and women throwing stones and wielding large sticks. The Battle of the Braes was followed by similar actions of protest at Glendale in Skye at the end of 1882.

These disturbances had several features which recalled the ineffectual protests against clearance in the decades before the 1860s: the use of rudimentary weapons; the central role of women; deforcement of the officers of the law; intervention by the police; and the localized nature of resistance. However, the Battle of the Braes has come to be regarded as a historic event because it signalled a decisive change of direction from past episodes of protest. For one thing, it had been the people who first took the initiative to try to regain grazing rights which they had lost over seventeen years before. This disturbance was therefore proactive rather than reactive. For another, the rent strike, which had been employed with deadly effect on numerous Irish estates in earlier years, was a new tactic which proprietors found difficult to combat without contemplating mass eviction, a policy that was becoming politically unacceptable by the 1880s. The Battle of the Braes and other disturbances suggested that landlordism was now encountering a different type of opposition, but it remained small in scale, confined to only a few estates in Skye, and at this stage the authorities were only dealing with a minor land dispute. This soon changed. Previous episodes of resistance had petered out in failure and imprisonment for the participants, but the Braes skirmish was the prelude to more widespread acts of subordination which were sustained on a number of Highland estates for several years afterwards and involved the consolidation of rent strikes, occupation of sheep farms, destruction of farm fences, collective assaults on sheriff officers, and the mutilation and killing of livestock. The *Scotsman* reported in some alarm in October 1884 that:

> men are taking what does not belong to them, are setting all law at defiance, and are instituting a terrorism which the poor people are unable to resist . . . Rents are unpaid, not because the tenants cannot pay them, but because in some cases they will not, and in some cases they dare not.

The paper claimed that if the law was not enforced quickly 'the condition of the islands will soon be as bad as that of Ireland three years ago'.[14]

The *Scotsman* was prone to exaggeration on the issue as a stout supporter of the landlord interest. There was little 'Irish'-style agrarian terrorism in the Highlands at this time, and most disturbances were confined to a few districts. The western mainland was peaceful for the most part and even in the Hebrides, where there was most overt discontent, disturbance was mainly concentrated in Skye and, to a lesser extent, Lewis. Direct action did occur in South Uist, Tiree and Harris but tended to be much more intermittent than elsewhere. In part the notion that the entire region was aflame and lawlessness everywhere rampant was the result of the extraordinary success of the publicity given to the disturbances in the Scottish and English press.

However, the incidents in Skye were deemed so serious that the government sent an expeditionary force to the island, the first since the time of the last Jacobite rising in the eighteenth century. The decision unleashed an almost hysterical reaction from some of the press. A violent armed confrontation between troops and people was eagerly anticipated as the *North British Daily Mail* carried such sensational headlines as, 'Threatened General Rising of Crofters' and 'Dunvegan Men on the March to Uig'. The sixteen newspaper correspondents who were sent from the south and two artists from the *Graphic* and the *Illustrated London News* were disappointed, however, when the expected violent conflict did not materialize. Marine detachments did stay on in Skye until 1885 and on their departure from Uig in June of that year they received a friendly farewell reception from the local people. The troops stationed at Staffin seem to have developed a particularly close association with some of the inhabitants. According to one observer they had shown a considerable interest in the young women of the district: 'They gave more of their time to the god of love than to the god of war'![15]

In fact, the distinguishing feature of the events of the 1880s, or the 'Crofters' War' as it came to be described, was not so much the spread of violence, intimidation and lawlessness throughout the Highlands as the fusion of an effective political campaign for crofters' rights with a high-profile series of acts of resistance, of which the refusal to pay rents and the 'raiding' of old lands were the most significant. By the early 1880s a crofting lobby had grown up in the southern cities consisting of land reformers, Gaelic revivalists, second- and third-generation Highland migrants, and radical liberals. From these groups and existing committees there was formed the Highland Land Law Reform Association (HLLRA), *Comunn Gaidhealach Ath-Leasachadh an Fhearainn*, with a strategy loosely based on that of the Irish Land League. It sought fair rents, security of tenure, compensation for improvements and, significantly, redistribution of land. The Association took the motto '*Is Treasa na Tighearna*', 'The People are Stronger Than the Lord'. The development was crucial. Not only did the HLLRA link the crofters' cause with external political interests, it also, through proliferating branches and district committees, helped to end the localism which had impeded collective action in the past.

The most remarkable example of this new attitude came with the appointment of a Royal Commission into the condition of the crofters and cottars in the Highlands and Islands under the chairmanship of Lord Napier and Ettrick. The government had responded to the threat of even more extensive civil unrest and growing public sympathy for the Gaels. The Commission took evidence throughout the crofting region from spring to the winter of 1883 and its report was finally published in 1884. When it appeared it was much criticized, not surprisingly by landlords, who saw 'communism looming in the future' as controls on their powers of private ownership had been recommended.[16] It was also criticized by a majority of the people because they thought it fell far short of their aspirations. The recommendations ignored the problem of the cottars and were confined to those who possessed holdings rented at more than £6 and less than £30 per annum. Nevertheless, the Napier Commission's Report was a symbolic victory for the crofting agitation as, for the first time, a public body had admitted the validity of the land rights of the people, even though they were not recognized in law. The Royal Commission also proposed that the state should provide a degree of protection for the interests of the crofters. The report was reluctant to offer perpetual security of tenure but advocated that government should instead assist crofters to purchase their holdings. It was a radical change from the kind of assumptions which had governed external intervention in the Highlands during the famine years of the 1840s and 1850s.

The subsequent legislation, enshrined in the Crofters Holdings (Scotland) Act, 1886, differed in some key respects from the Commission's recommendations, but it too represented a decisive break with the past and began a new era of landlord–crofter relations in the Highlands. Security of tenure for crofters was guaranteed as long as rent was paid; fair rents would be fixed by a land court; compensation for improvements was allowed to a crofter who gave up his croft or was removed from it; crofts could not be sold but might be bequeathed to a relative and, with certain restrictions, the compulsory enlargement of holdings could be considered by the land court.

This legislation did not immediately find favour with the land reformers, especially since it gave only very minor concessions to crofters' demands for more land. But its historic significance should not be underestimated. The Crofters Act made clearances of the old style impossible, breached the sacred rights of private property, controlled landlord–crofter relations through a government body and afforded the crofting population secure possession of their holdings. The balance of power between landlords and small tenants had been irrevocably altered after 1886, but in fact that was already becoming apparent earlier. In December 1884, Cameron of Lochiel noted that the current of political and public opinion was flowing fast against the landed interest. The following month about fifty Highland proprietors and their representatives met at Inverness to discuss the crofting agitation and agreed to provide crofters with leases, consider revision of rents and guarantee compensation for improvements in an attempt to draw the teeth of discontent. It was a remarkable and tardy attempt at developing a more benevolent form of landlordism introduced only because of the weakening position of the landed élites. The proposals were rejected as the HLLRA decided that they confirmed that the landowners were finally on the run. As the *Oban Times* gleefully reported: 'the Highland lairds are on their knees'.[17] Final victory seemed only a matter of time.

In historical perspective the events of the 1880s are indeed remarkable. Crofters had not managed to secure the return of lands from which they had been removed during the clearances; that would have amounted to expropriation of property and remained politically unthinkable. Yet by imposing legislation which made the tenancy of a croft heritable, the state had in effect deprived the landlord of most of his former rights of ownership. No other class or group in late-nineteenth-century mainland Britain were given such protection as were the crofters of the Highlands in this way. How and why they managed to achieve such privileges is the question which will be discussed in the final section of this chapter.

The agitation in Skye was triggered in part by economic problems. The winter of 1882–3 was reckoned to have been one of the worst since the disasters of the 1840s. The potato crop was partially destroyed and earnings of migrant labourers from the east-coast fisheries, a key source of income in Skye and the Long Island, had fallen dramatically. Problems became more acute after a great storm in October 1882 which damaged or destroyed many boats, nets and much fishing gear. The resulting stress may help to explain why no-rent campaigns became so popular within the crofting community. Even when there was some

TURNING OF THE TIDE

recovery from the difficulties of 1882–3, cattle prices fell throughout most of the remainder of the decade. By the late 1880s two-year-old heifers which might have fetched £7 or £8 in 1883 were worth less than £2. The period was also one of difficulty in sheep farming as the British market for wool and mutton was swamped by imports from the Antipodes. The big flockmasters suffered most, with many surrendering their leases and wholesale conversion of sheep farms to deer forests took place. Small-tenant income was also affected as, by this time, it was also usual for crofters to keep a few sheep.

It is very possible these continuing economic difficulties in the western Highlands fuelled social tensions. Yet there had been bad times before and little unrest. The people had accepted suffering as God's judgement or as part of the natural law, not as a consequence of the injustice of man. But the difference in the 1880s may have been partly because the generation of that decade had become accustomed to the better times of the 1860s and 1870s and might have felt a sense of frustrated expectations as their living standards collapsed. Nevertheless, the movement of the 1880s was not one of the hungry and distressed. If it had been it would probably not have endured for long. Economic factors, therefore, do not really explain how a few minor land disputes became the catalyst for a widespread land agitation which eventually resulted in a political and social revolution in the Highland region.

One factor was a changing attitude among the people; some contemporary observers commented that they now had more iron in their souls. Certainly the Gaelic poetry of the land war period, as analysed by Sorley MacLean, in the 1930s transmits a more powerful mood of confidence and optimism, and even before the Battle of the Braes there was evidence on some Highland estates of a new level of tenant truculence. By 1880, for example, on the Sutherland estate, agents were apparently willing to allow rent arrears and breach of regulations, rather than provoke the people into further acts of defiance. It is also interesting to note that virtually all the famous incidents of the Crofters' War were triggered by the local populations rather than responses to landlord action as had been the pattern in the past.

This new-found confidence may reflect the growth of a new generation in the western Highlands. All commentators stressed that it was young men and women who were the backbone of protest. They had been brought up in the better times of the 1860s and 1870s and had not known at first hand the anguish of the famine decades which had demoralized so many of the generation of their parents and grandparents. The press often drew attention to the fact that many of the older people in the crofting townships were sometimes timorous and meek while the young were bold, defiant and truculent. A decisive factor prompting them to action was the example of the Irish. Rural agitation in Ireland had led in 1881 to a famous victory when Gladstone's government passed the Irish Land Act. This granted to tenants the rights known as the '3 Fs': fair rents determined by a land court, fixed tenure as long as the rent was paid, and free sale of the tenant's interest in the farm which allowed for compensation for improvements. The Irish victory had obvious implications for Highland crofters. In part, information on the Irish agitation was conveyed through the regional Highland press, especially in the columns of the *Highlander*, edited by John Murdoch, who had lived in Ireland. Indeed, it was suggested by some that he devoted most issues of his journal more to Irish than to Highland matters. Even more important, however, was the personal connection between Skye and Ireland. From about 1875 many Skye men became labourers in Campbeltown and Carradale fishing boats for the summer season in Irish waters, and there can be little doubt that these annual sojourns gave them experience of such Irish tactics as rent strikes. Indeed, the Irish connection goes a long way to explaining why, in its early years, the agitation concentrated mainly on Skye. In a letter to Lord MacDonald's Edinburgh agent, his factor on the island noted:

> Shortly before the term of Martinmas a body of young men, the sons of tenants, most of whom had been fishing at Kinsale in Ireland and had imbibed Irish notions, came to my office and presented a petition which they had almost the whole tenants to sign, to the effect that they demanded the grazing of Ben Lee in addition to their present holdings without paying any additional rent.[18]

But despite the new boldness of the men of Skye the dispute would probably not have lasted for long if it had not been for significant changes in external attitudes to the land issue. As late as the 1850s protests against clearances had been effectively crushed, the law enforced and the rights of landed property upheld, but such robust assertions of proprietorial privilege had become politically unacceptable thirty years later. At first the due process of law in Skye was followed against assaults on sheriff officers and land raiding. Both police and military were brought in, but the government recognized that it could not contemplate the full use of force because public and political opinion would be hostile to such tactics. The only alternative therefore, was eventually to concede some of the crofters' demands in order to restore law and order.

The climate of opinion was already changing in the 1870s. In 1879, for example, the estate of Leckmelm on Lochbroom was purchased by A. C. Pirie, an Aberdeen paper manufacturer. He tried to organize 'improvements' on his property, which resulted in some evictions, but even these small-scale removals brought forth a huge outcry in the Highlands and resounding condemnation from all sections of the national press, with the predictable exception of the *Scotsman*. Four years later the Liberal politician J. B. Balfour referred to 'a considerable body of vague and floating sentiment in favour of ameliorating the crofters' condition' which had influenced several members of the Liberal Party'.[19] These feelings were apparent at the very highest levels of government. They were shared by the Prime Minister, William Ewart Gladstone, himself and the Home Secretary in 1882, Sir William Harcourt. Harcourt had a key role to play in the unfolding events in the Hebrides as he had spent many years on yachting holidays there and developed a sympathy for the condition of the people of the area. His decisions confirmed that. In November 1882 he refused permission for a military expedition to be sent to Skye and in the same month suggested to Gladstone that a Royal Commission be established instead. Significantly he observed that among 'decent people' there was now a view that the crofters had real grievances, and, in the age of an extending franchise, such opinions could not easily be ignored. In 1884 the suffrage was extended to men owning at least £10 or paying the same amount annually in rental. This included many crofters. A year later five Members of Parliament were elected from the Crofters' Party.

These latent sympathies for the crofters were exploited to the full by pro-crofter propagandists, of whom one of the most effective was Alexander McKenzie, editor of the *Celtic Magazine*. McKenzie had been using this publication to draw attention to the social problems of the western Highlands since 1877. In 1883, however, he published his bestseller, *A History of the Highland Clearances*, which conveyed in emotive prose the harrowing details of some of the most notorious removals. It was not a work of historical detachment but a compendium of landlord misdeeds. Works like McKenzie's portrayed Highland proprietors as heartless tyrants who had ruthlessly betrayed their responsibilities and their people.

The contemporary press also played a key role in publicizing the crofters' cause and influencing public opinion in their favour. Here was a publicity machine with which even the wealthiest landowner could not hope to compete. As one reporter who covered the events of the 1880s noted later: 'Printed paper in the shape of newspapers proved the most deadly tool against the Highland landowners.'[20] The fact that coverage was so extensive, not only on the part of the Scottish papers but also in the English press, reflected the deep interest which existed throughout the country in the Highland problem. This new awareness was facilitated by the revolution of communications in the Western Isles. By the 1880s a network of steamer connections had spread throughout the Inner and Outer Hebrides. In addition, the telegraph now allowed eyewitness reports of disturbances to be published soon after they took place, and this made the Crofters' War one of the first popular agitations in Britain in which the media of the day played a significant part not only by reporting but also by actually helping to influence the course of events.

External political and cultural forces were also important. Crofter political awareness was raised by the methods and campaigns of Charles Stewart Parnell's Irish Nationalist Party and the Irish Land League. Though the disturbances in the north were not as some suggested a 'Fenian conspiracy', there can be little doubt about the general Irish impact, especially through the writings and speeches of the charismatic John Murdoch, editor of the *Highlander*, who had been politically active in Ireland for several years before and was acquainted with some of the leading personalities of the Irish agitation. There was also powerful support from the Highland societies which were now active in the Lowland towns. Until the 1870s they had been almost exclusively devoted to convivial and cultural pursuits, but by the end of that decade the Federation of Celtic Societies was being criticized in some quarters as being far too political. Activists, such as the eloquent and energetic Professor John Stuart Blackie of the University of Edinburgh, projected a potent message of combined literary romanticism and political radicalism. The regional Highland press was increasingly sympathetic, notably the *Oban Times* from 1882, when Duncan Cameron became editor, and provided a faithful and detailed record of speeches and meetings of the HLLRA at local level which lent both cohesion and momentum to the agitation. Land reformers in mainland Britain and Ireland took up the crofters' cause and it received particularly important support from reformist sections of the Liberal Party in Scotland. Second-generation Highlanders in the southern cities were also deeply influential in certain areas.

This motley alliance came together to become an effective crofters' lobby. The people of the disturbed districts had helped themselves, but they gained a great deal from the unparalleled levels of external support which provided experienced leadership, political muscle and organizing expertise. The most remarkable demonstration of this contribution came in the months after the setting up of the Napier Commission. Government may have seen this as a way of defusing tension and deflecting opposition, but instead it became a catalyst for further agitation and the creation of a more effective organization, especially when it became apparent that the witnesses to the Royal Commission would be guaranteed immunity from intimidation. This was a crucial development since bitter memories of the reign of terror of the clearance period endured among the older men whose evidence of past events was vital to the crofters' case. Until the Napier Commission sat for the first time in May 1883 at the Braes in Skye, every effort was made to prepare evidence. Alexander McKenzie and John Murdoch toured the region and provided advice, and at the end of 1883 the HLLRA of London published three pamphlets in Gaelic and English addressed to the crofting community, highlighting past wrongs and encouraging agitation in favour of security of tenure, fair rents and reallocation of land, as well as other aims. Local people were urged to form district branches and use peaceful and constitutional methods in pursuit of their demands. When branches were established, rules were drawn up by central headquarters in London.

But the crofters' movement did not simply become the creature of external sympathizers in these years, although they did contribute a great deal. One of the most significant events in the organizational process had been the decision taken by west-coast fishermen at a mass meeting in the port of Fraserburgh in the north-east in August 1883 to form land reform associations on their return home. Furthermore, subversive and illegal activity on some estates persisted despite the official opposition of the HLLRA. The successes achieved represented a joint victory for the crofters and their new allies, who were able effectively to exploit the new and more sympathetic climate of opinion which had emerged in the last quarter of the nineteenth century. It was this which generated the power and tactical leverage that previous generations had lacked.

Conclusion

Before the middle of the eighteenth century the vast majority of Scottish families, whether living in the Highlands or rural Lowlands, had a place on the land, however small, as tenants, subtenants and cottars. A century later, and in many parts much earlier, that old world had passed away into history across the Lowlands and had also changed radically north of the Highland line.

In the Lowlands by the 1830s only a few had legal rights to land for specified periods of time as possessors of farm leases. There was but one regional exception to the pattern – the settlement of crofter families in the moorlands of the north-east counties as an economical way of bringing waste land into regular cultivation. But there, as everywhere else in the Lowlands, the old landholding population of cottars had vanished. An entire social class which had numbered between a quarter to a third of the population in many rural parishes in old Scotland was no more. Those who now worked the improved landscape were landless wage-earning servants and labourers. Rural tradesmen with smallholdings within the *fermetouns* of the past had abandoned them when they were broken up and often moved off to neighbouring villages, where they paid rent for their homes and sold their skills and wares in the competitive market place for monetary return. In areas of pastoral husbandry like the Borders, the hill country of southern Lanarkshire and the western parishes of Angus and Aberdeenshire, the development of large-scale stock farming for sheep and cattle squeezed out the people and left whole districts stripped of the indigenous population. In some parts only the scattered cottages of shepherds and a few hamlets survived to mark where human habitation had once existed. The loss of landholding must have caused stress, pain and anxiety as a centuries-old way of life came to an end within a few decades in the later eighteenth century. But the majority of the dispossessed in the Lowlands were spared large-scale destitution or long-term unemployment because critically the first phase of the agricultural and industrial revolutions down to the end of the Napoleonic Wars in 1815 significantly increased demand for rural labour. Former tenants and cottars might have to move and find work in villages, towns and cities. Many who had once had the status of rent-paying farmers faced downward mobility into the massed ranks of the landless wage earners. But there is little evidence that many of them were thrown on the mercies of the local Poor Law authorities as a consequence of their displacement. The cushion of rising employment levels during the period of major structural agrarian change partly helps to account for the intriguing level of silence and stability in the Lowland countryside at the time. Nor should the fundamental point be forgotten that many people in the countryside, and perhaps the majority, left for the towns and overseas not because they were forced to do so but because they saw there greater opportunities for advancement and a better standard of living.

In the Highlands, the patterns of change were more convulsive but varied across the region. On the fringes, in southern Argyll, Highland Perthshire, eastern Inverness-shire and Easter Ross, much of the Lowland style of farming was replicated but to a more limited and nuanced extent. The great river valleys which breached the Highland massif from end to end were now by the 1840s for the most part colonized by sheep walks of immense breadth and extent. The people whose ancestors had worked the land in these straths from time immemorial had gone, sometimes across the Atlantic or to the cities and towns of the south or been removed to live in minuscule crofts on the coastlands or barren moors in the interior judged by landowners to have some potential for reclamation by hard labour. Many of the settlements optimistically planned to support a thriving fishery for the crofters in the eighteenth century, like Tobermory, Bunessan, Lochcarron, Plockton, Lochaline, Tobermory, Dornie, Shieldaig and others, now became slum villages, packed with the dispossessed and destitute poor in the wake of the extensive clearances which became common after c.1820.

But it was indeed ironic, in light of the notoriety of the 'Highland clearances', that many crofters still clung on to some land, despite much trouble, strife and misery, along the coasts of the western and northern Highlands and on many of the Hebridean islands, at the same time as total landlessness became the lived experience of the vast majority of people in the rural Lowlands. At the census of 1861 the four Highland counties, even after famine and clearance, had a population of nearly 300,000, 36,000 more than in 1801. The Highland total was also some 20,000 greater than the Border counties at the same census. Of course, there had been a substantial haemorrhage of people through migration and emigration in the intervening years without which the population totals would have been much higher. But that was the pattern in all rural counties in Scotland in Victorian times. By the later nineteenth century, demographic historians have conclusively shown that only a single region, the west-central counties of concentrated industrialism, was actually gaining people from elsewhere. All other country parishes from the far north to the English border by that time were losing their inhabitants by net out-migration, sometimes on a large scale. Several of the smaller Hebridean islands like Eigg, Muck, Ulva, Lismore and Rum had been swept clear of their inhabitants by clearance. But elsewhere, particularly in the Outer Hebrides of Barra, Harris, Lewis and South Uist, population recovered after the destitution, widespread removals and compulsory emigrations of the famine years. Having a stake in the land, however small, was actually more common in the Western Highlands and Islands per head of regional population than in the Lowland counties at the end of the era of dispossession. And after the passage of the Crofters Holdings Act of 1886 those who dwelled on these small lots of land were protected from summary eviction and rack renting.

Clearance is an omnibus term with a whole range of implications. The forcing out of people by factors, sheriff officers and police in the Highlands is the most notorious and best documented in press sources of the time and has by far the highest profile in popular understanding of clearance. However, a myriad set of influences and pressures made for loss of land in addition to these familiar and dramatic events. These included: the impact of increases in rental; division of larger holdings to impose living space for soldier veterans among existing tenantry; landlord unwillingness to accept accumulation of rent arrears; refusal to provide relief when crops failed; prohibition of working on kelp shores; confiscation of cattle to meet accumulated arrears; refusal to assign leases to sitting tenants; relocation of cottars and small tenants to crofting townships and new villages; punitive prohibition of illicit whisky making so undermining local peasant economies; rigorous prevention of subdivision of land among kinfolk; long-run attrition of multi-tenancies until single occupiers became the sole tenants on compact enlarged farms; and the combined interaction of internal pressures to leave coupled with the lure of land overseas or higher wages and better opportunities in towns. Nature as well as man could also have a critical effect on migration from those parts where people lived close to the edge of subsistence. In the Highlands, for instance, serious harvest failure in 1836–7, followed by the even more devastating impact of the potato blight between 1846 and 1855, must have forced many to flee their holdings without notices of eviction needing to be enforced. In later times too it was more common for townships to be abandoned rather than cleared.

With the exception of the famine, all of these factors to a greater or lesser extent were common across the length and breadth of Scotland and not confined to any one region. This, therefore, was indeed the Scottish clearances. If so, a fundamental question then comes into focus. If dispossession was Scotland-wide, why has loss of land come to be exclusively associated in the popular mind with the Highlands?

Dispossession was undeniably more disruptive in most of Gaeldom and collective acts of clearance more common and dramatic. Landowners broke up traditional townships by adding them to sheep walks and introducing crofting settlements which were often populated by peasant families displaced to make way for large pastoral farms. These crofts were not designed to provide a full living subsistence from land alone. On the contrary, they were shaved down to a planned minimum size in order to force the occupying families to labour in fishing and kelp gathering and burning. Many proprietors also encouraged the unregulated splitting of land among cottars and squatters by packing more people into their estates to expand the labour force for these bi-employments.

However, the whole system proved to be not only unstable but ephemeral, as most growth sectors collapsed or stagnated after the end of the Napoleonic Wars, leaving a hugely increased population anchored in pitifully small patches of land, where they scraped a living from potatoes and meagre earnings from temporary migration for work in the Lowlands. Eventually, as far as the proprietors were concerned, only sheep farming offered a viable and long-term economic alternative. But, tragically, pastoralism offered little in the way of employment and was more of a mortal threat to the possession of land by the peasantry. Because of factors outside their own direct control, west Highland and Hebridean landlords certainly had fewer long-term options than their Lowland counterparts as no sustained industrial or urban development became established in the region which could have drawn people willingly from the land. Nonetheless, geographical impediment and market influence were not the only reasons why the region eventually degenerated into an overpopulated rural slum. Many landowners also bore some responsibility for this disastrous outcome.

A few years after the potatoes failed in 1846 some proprietors, especially in the Hebrides, unleashed an unprecedented wave of larger-scale clearances. Some of them were enforced with casual brutality by estate factors and sheriff officers on very poor communities which had not entirely recovered from the hunger and immiseration of famine. The objective was explicit and overt: it was once and for all to cut out from the population those families deemed incapable of paying secure rental, together with many of the cottar and squatter class which paid nothing at all. To ensure that they were fully and finally expelled from the Highlands, schemes of 'compulsory emigration' were introduced to transport the 'redundant population' across the seas to Canada and Australia, from there never to return. There can be little doubt that racist dogma also scarred the history of this period. The correspondence of relief officials, government servants, trustees of estates and opinion columns in some Scottish newspapers abound with references to the lazy, feckless and inadequate Celts, who had to be forced from their habitual indolence to earn their bread abroad so that the Highlands might be spared the 'Leprosy of Ireland'. Nothing close to this kind of trauma ever took place in the Lowlands during the entire cycle of dispossession.

There is also the issue of the traditional values of the Gael to be considered. They included the belief, inherited from the old martial society, in the right to land and, even after the death of clanship, that the élites had an obligation to protect the people on the lands in return for rental and service. It hardly needs saying that forced eviction was likely to be the grossest violation of that expectation. Also important was the vexed issue of 'land given in return for sons', a key feature of the recruiting mania during the three great wars between 1756 and 1815. Sometimes the agreements between proprietors, tenants and cottars to secure holdings in return for military service were entered into for fixed periods, but others were for life. These solemn contracts did lead to the deaths of fathers and brothers in battle and from disease overseas. When they were broken and families cleared as landowners went bankrupt in the bad times after 1820, bitterness, resentment and a sense of betrayal were likely to be aroused and passed down through the generations in the oral culture and traditions of the people.

Expectations of this kind had long gone from the Lowlands by the time dispossession began there in earnest. This is not to suggest that having a stake in the land was not important to tenants and cottars elsewhere in Scotland. Before the age of improvement the connection between land and people was fundamental: to be without a patch of land in a subsistence-based society threatened not only penury but survival itself. Yet the values did differ. Traces of benevolent paternalism existed in the Lowlands after the 1750s, but essentially the relationship between landlord and tenant had by then become economic in nature. The land was seen as an asset from which proper value should be extracted. The tack or lease specified the length of tenure to a holding for a given period and there was broad social acceptance that the proprietor had a right to take back the tenancy at the end of the agreed term of occupancy, or indeed even earlier if any of the clauses in it were neglected or broken.

By comparison with the north-west and the islands, therefore, dispossession seems to have caused much less dislocation in most parts away from the upland districts of the Borders and other zones of hill country where pastoralism offered the most profitable option by the later eighteenth century. Indeed, even before the rural revolution itself there had long been a widespread culture of mobility among Lowland cottars, servants and small tenants. They seem to have moved regularly between farms, estates, communities and parishes within the bounds of traditional localities and regions. Historians of migration have used this level of short-distance mobility to help explain the basis of the extensive long-distance movement to northern and central Europe and Ulster in the early modern period.

In addition, the consolidation of farms under single husbandmen in arable districts was a gradual and protracted process, mainly carried out by the normal method of letting and reletting of holdings at end of term. Cottars were forced to surrender their plots of land, but there was the possibility of finding work in rural villages and small towns, which, unlike those of the same type in the Highlands, often had a sustainable economic future because of the successful expansion of country textile industries. But the vexatious nature of that process should not be underestimated. Cottar families left the traditional townships for an uncertain future in which new opportunities existed but could not necessarily be guaranteed. The experience was one of dispersal and not always of carefully planned transfer from an old to a new environment. The silence of the people should not be interpreted as the happy acceptance of a life-changing process.

It was, however, their good fortune that during the first stages of improvement demand for labour on arable and mixed farms increased and for a time wages of servants and day labourers rose also in order to secure enough workers. A massive advantage, of course, was the industrialization and urbanization of the Lowlands, which took place close to most rural districts. This conjuncture helped draw people off the land and so made Highland-type congestion less likely in the southern countryside. The methods of hiring and housing agricultural labour also ensured that over time a rough equilibrium of supply and demand for male and female farm servants was normally achieved in most years. Those unable to gain a hire at the fairs had to move on. Accommodation went with the job so to be without a fee was also to be without a place to live. As a result it was often the slum districts of the cities which became over-populated with migrants from the countryside, rather than the rural parishes of Lowlands Scotland.

The issue of comparative chronologies should also be taken into account. Dispossession in the Lowlands took place in the period from the later seventeenth century but outside the Borders was concentrated in the decades between the 1760s and the 1820s. This was a time when landlord authority and the rights of property were rarely effectively challenged. When they were, as in the early 1790s by the forces of French and Paineite-inspired radicalism, the regime showed tough resilience, and opposition to the rule of the propertied élite soon disintegrated. This remained a rigidly hierarchical society and the widespread impact of the writings of the classical economists like Smith, Ricardo and Mill gave continued intellectual legitimacy to the rights of private property and freedom of enterprise within the market.

The earlier time frame of Lowland dispossession also meant that most of the physical remains of the old townships and cottar huts had long disappeared by the middle decades of the nineteenth century. Lowland improvement was nothing if not thorough. The stoneworks from traditional townships were recycled to create new buildings and construct the many miles of drystone dykes and walls which soon stretched unendingly across the countryside. Rural areas took on an antique mantle as if the farm steadings, roads and fields created in the age of improvement had existed since time immemorial. Only in some upland districts in the Borders and a few other places can some traces still be found of the marks of runrig cultivation.

In contrast, the story of clearance and emigration retains a visible physicality in the Highlands and Islands, with the many ruins of abandoned settlements surrounded by old cultivation beds covered in bracken. What happened in the past is much more obvious. In part this is because clearances in the Highlands had a quite different chronology from elsewhere in Scotland. They began later than in the south and still had only limited impact by the last quarter of the eighteenth century. They also lasted for nearly a hundred years, a much longer time frame than dispossession in the Lowlands. Not until the later 1850s did mass removals come to an end in the north-west Highlands and Islands. Indeed, some of the most controversial and highly publicized evictions took place earlier in that decade.

Moreover, by the 1840s the climate of opinion in Britain about unregulated free enterprise was slowly beginning to change. While laissez-faire ideology remained dominant, a new strain of humanitarianism started to question some of the established certainties of economic liberalism. The Victorians were not simply rigid ideologues obsessed with private interest and material gain as the stereotype has it. The 'Condition of England' question was coming to the fore and with it a host of social issues such as child labour, factory legislation, female labour and the plight of the poor. Larger questions about property and equality and the obligations of society were also beginning to emerge. It was this mood change which helped to make the novels of Charles Dickens and his depiction of contemporary social problems and abuses so popular.

This broader context helps to explain the developing sympathy for the plight of the Highland people and the vitriolic condemnation of landlordism published in pamphlets and articles by the likes of Donald McLeod, Hugh Miller, Donald Ross and others in the 1840s and 1850s. Crucially, these authors came to describe clearances not simply as a consequence of economic crisis but as a social and cultural disaster which threatened the destruction of an ancient civilization. No charge of this kind was ever levelled at the removals in the Lowlands during the eighteenth century. The national press both in Scotland and in England now started to send reporters to the Highlands who published stories to describe some of the more lurid clearance events, especially those which took place during the potato famine. An influential readership existed for these reports among the upper classes both north and south of the Border since the Highlands by this time had become a mecca for élite tourism and deer stalking. Press commentaries, together with political concerns about the paucity of recruits for the famed Highland regiments during the Crimean War (1853–6) as a result of rising emigration, attracted concern for the people suffering from the evictions and their consequences.

Then, during the last quarter of the nineteenth century, 'the land question' came into focus as a paramount issue in British politics. Landlordism was now under sustained political attack, fuelled in part by the publication of John Bateman's comprehensive survey, *The Great Landowners of Great Britain and Ireland* (1883), which showed in detail the quite remarkable concentration of landed power in the United Kingdom. The disputes in Ireland and Highland Scotland came to be publicized as confirmation of the abuses of landlord authority, especially during and after the Irish Land War and the crofting agitation of the 1880s. The Crofters' War and the subsequent investigation by the Royal Commission chaired by Lord Napier put the clearances in the Highlands well and truly on the British political map. Oral evidence collected by the Commission from aged eye witnesses to the events of the past proved to be particularly telling. At no time did dispossession in the Lowlands ever attract even a fraction of this public attention. The Lowland removals had ended many decades before the 1880s. In the public and literary domain they were already lost to history. Clearances to the late-Victorian mind became exclusively associated with Highland Scotland.

The tide was certainly flowing strongly against Highland landlords by the later nineteenth century and given powerful additional impetus by the publication of Alexander Mackenzie's *The History of the Highland Clearances* (1883). Mackenzie, a Highlander from Gairloch in Wester Ross, was editor of the *Celtic Magazine* and one of the most accomplished Scottish journalists of the age. His achievement was to bring together all the scattered critical reports on clearances into a single large volume which became the definitive guide to landlord iniquity and the most widely read handbook about the evictions. It strongly influenced the modern writings of John Prebble, Ian Grimble and others who successfully embedded dispossession of the clansmen at the heart of a Greek tragedy set in the Scottish Highlands. A famed warrior race which suffered brutal repression in the eighteenth century by the British state, was first abandoned and then betrayed by its tribal leaders, to whom they and their ancestors had given blood loyalty for centuries. The motive of the former clan chiefs, now landlords, was base: nothing other than the temptation of greed and the lust for riches. In a final act of treachery, the betrayed were forced off the land and shipped across the oceans to far-off countries. They left behind them empty glens and crumbling settlements as silent testimony of man's inhumanity to man.

The narrative is compelling and poignant but one in which some uncomfortable truths rarely intrude: the limitations of natural endowment in the Highlands; a marked increase of population on poor land with no long-term alternative for subsistence or employment for a people who had always lived close to the edge of subsistence in the old clan-based society; the destruction of infant Highland manufacturing by Lowland competition; bankruptcy of the traditional landed class; the overwhelming power of market capitalism; and the absence of any viable long-term alternative to pastoral husbandry. These were all factors of fundamental importance and cannot be ignored in any serious examination of the history of the Highlands. There is no question, however, that those who seek to defend the people affected by these forces have in the main avoided or downplayed them. Instead, they have opted for the single explanation of human wickedness, a resolution of the problem which does not fit with the historical evidence which is now to hand.

An impartial verdict on Highland landlordism during the age of clearances is unlikely to reach clear-cut conclusions. Some of the wealthier magnates, such as the Dukes of Argyll and Sutherland, and a few of the new breed of tycoon-landowners, like Sir James Matheson in Lewis, spent small fortunes for a time in attempts to bring viable economies and employment opportunities to their estates, but to little or no avail. Their doctrinaire plans failed to bring the people with them. Distance from markets and unrelenting competition from steam- and coal-based Lowland industrialism were also just too powerful. Some proprietors agonized over decisions which would lead to evictions. Others avoided clearance for many years against the advice of their managers, although it was in their economic interest to have acted sooner. Only when properties became insolvent and hereditary families had to abandon their patrimonies did the trustees for their creditors act to enforce the most draconian removals of all. It is also the case that many Highland landowners won praise from both government and the Free Church during the first crisis years of the potato famine for the provision of relief at their own expense to the starving poor of their estates. Civil servants publicly congratulated them on their support which in their view was in stark and positive contrast with the inadequacy of their counterparts across the Irish Sea. Yet benevolence soon changed to systematic policies of expulsion as the Highland crisis persisted and deepened.

Indeed, there is another side to Highland landlordism which warrants consideration. Human will and subjective decision, underplayed by some historians in their focus on the power of demographic and economic forces, must also be considered in any satisfactory analysis. In the case of most landed families, the temptations of consumerism seem to have had an easy victory over financial rectitude. Material display in houses, internal furnishings and clothing was deemed essential by the Victorian élite to confirm and perpetuate gentlemanly status and social rank. But many Highland lairds seem to have been congenitally incapable of trying to live within their means on a sustained basis and of tailoring their lifestyles in the southern capitals to the modest incomes of their properties in the north. There was, for example, the extraordinary case of Sir Duncan Campbell of Barcaldine, the owner of extensive lands near Oban in Argyll. His finances had been in serious difficulty for some time and in 1842 the 30,000-acre estate, in the ownership of his family for centuries, was sold to pay off debts. Yet, on the eve of this disaster, Campbell had a huge extension built in the 1830s to Barcaldine House, which was designed by a fashionable London architect and intended to provide space for a new library. This in effect was nothing other than an act of financial suicide.

Moreover, the radical restructuring of their estates by several landlords in the western Highlands and Islands in the late eighteenth century led to the widespread introduction of tiny smallholdings which were not viable in the long run as sources of subsistence and led to a further splintering of crofts and even more dependency on the potato crop while population continued to rise. The maintenance of some connection with the land, however slight, served to impede permanent migration and instead encouraged reliance on temporary movement to the seasonal labour markets of the Lowlands.

The objective of this crofting policy was to exploit what some at least among the landed class knew to be ephemeral wartime profits from kelp and other enterprises. This can only be described as an outrageous gamble. The windfall gains were mainly squandered on servicing debt and consumer expenditure and little on long-term investment which may or may not have significant long-term benefit. The croft system which proprietors embedded in the north-west and the islands also made it impossible for a middling tenant class to emerge which might have given the region some resilience in the difficult years after 1815. But, in addition, landlords aided and abetted the reckless subdivision of holdings among kinfolk and most took little action to impose effective controls even when the rationale for packing estates with labour power vanished after *c.*1820. This negligence then led eventually and inevitably to further large-scale clearances as wartime employment and profits dried up in the years of peace and destitution spread across the crofting townships like a malignant virus.

Annex A
The Highland Clearances as Holocaust: Excerpts from Popular Histories, 1974–2000

1. The victims of the Clearances [were] subjects of intense hatred such as the gypsies and the Jews were to experience under the Nazis and other groups in the Western World.

    F. G. Thomson, *The Highlands and Islands* (London, 1974), p. 61.

2. Like the shipping-off of the Polish and other Jews in cattle trucks.

    David Craig, *On the Crofter's Trail* (London, 1990), p. 72.

3. Sellar's crimes against the people of Strathnaver, Grimble said, were to be ranked with those of Heydrich, the man who perpetrated unspeakable acts against the Jews in Prague in the Second World War.

    Professor Eric Richards, discussing the views of
    Ian Grimble in Eric Richards, *The Highland Clearances*:
    People, Landlords and Rural Turmoil (Edinburgh, 2000), p. 10.

4. Sutherland's managers kept records of their shipments of people with the obsessional thoroughness of an Eichmann.

    David Craig, *On the Crofter's Trail* (London, 1990), p. 129.

5. The policy of genocide could scarcely have been carried out further.

    D. C. Thomson and Ian Grimble, eds., 'Introduction',
    The Future of the Highlands (London, 1968).

    Paul Basu, *Highland Homecomings* (London, 2007), p. 197.

Annex B
Tenant Structure on Four Lowland Estates, 1675–1824

Table A Tenant structure: estate of
Lord Melville (Fife), 1675–1780

Year	Total no. of tenants	No. of tenants in multiple tenancies	Percentage of tenants in multiple tenancies
Barony of Balgonie			
1675	18	2	11.0
1720	39	6	15.0
1730	72	?	?
1740	85	3	3.5
1750	74	4	5.0
1760	81	4	5.0
1770	77	3	4.0
1780	76	4	5.0
Lordship of Melville			
1715	45	5/6	11/13
1730	50	6	12.0
1740	43	3	7.0
1750	40	1	5.0
1760	66	0	0
1770	63	2	3.0*
1780	55	3	4.5*

*These were all examples of smallholders, most of them tradesmen, who were sharing possessions.

The post-1780 rentals were not specific enough on smallholder numbers to allow multiple tenancy percentages to be calculated.

Source: Extracted from SRO, GD26/5/251–95 Leven and Melville Muniments, *passim*.

Table B Tenant structure: Panmure estate (Angus), 1728–1824

Year	Total no. of tenants	No. of tenants in multiple tenancies	Percentage of tenants in multiple tenancies
Lethnot and Navar			
1728	37	11	29.7
1736	38	10	26.3
1758	33	6	18.2
1775	31	2	6.5
1785	31	2	6.5
1824	25	2	8.0
Edzel			
1728	79	14	17.7
1736	75	16	21.3
1758	68	7	10.3
1764	65	6	9.2
1775	65	6	9.2
1785	65	6	9.2
1824	63	6	9.5

Source: SRO, Dalhousie Muniments, GD45/18/506–2091, *passim*.

Table C Tenant structure: Strathmore estate (Angus), 1690–1721

A. *Narrow and wider circles of Glamis, 1690*

No. of tenants	154
No. of tenants in multiple tenant possessions	126
No. of possessions	42
No. of multiple tenant possessions	26

B. *Lordship of Glamis, 1721*

No. of tenants	132.0
No. of tenants in multiple tenant possessions	112.0
No. of possessions	33.0
No. of multiple tenant possessions	14.0
Percentage of multiple tenant possessions	42.4

Source: NRA(S) 885, Earl of Strathmore Papers, Boxes 53, 65, 148.

Table D Tenant structure: estate of Earl of Morton (Fife), 1694–1795

Year	Total no. of tenants	No. of tenants in multiple tenancies	Percentage of tenants in multiple tenancies
1694	31	11	36
1705	35	14	40
1715	32	10	31
1717	34	10	30
1726	39	9	23
1735	50	10	20
1742	65	2	3
1795	75	0	0

Source: SRO, GD150, 2061, Morton Papers, Rentals, 1694, 1705, 1715, 1717, 1726, 1735, 1742, 1795.

Annex C
Summonses and Decreets of Removal: Selected Lowland Sheriff Courts, 1662–1800

Cupar sheriff court: Summonses and Decrets of Removal

Year	End of tack	Arrears		Breach of tack	No written tack		Bankrupt	Other	Unknown		Totals
	Tnt.	Tnt.	Subtnt.	Tnt.	Tnt.	Subtnt.	Tnt.	Tnt.	Tnt.	Subtnt.	
1751	0	1	0	0	0	0	0	0	0	0	1
1760	2	2	0	0	0	0	0	0	5	0	9
1770	4	4	1	0	1	1	1	0	8	2	22
1780	0	2	0	0	0	0	0	0	1	0	3
1785	2	0	0	0	1	0	0	0	25	3	31
1790	11	2	0	0	7	0	0	0	7	2	29
1800	33	13	2	1	15	0	1	1	5	0	71
Totals	52	24	3	1	24	1	2	1	51	7	166
Percentages	31.3	14.5	1.8	0.6	14.5	0.6	1.2	0.6	30.7	4.2	100

Source: SRO, Sheriff Court Processes (Cupar), SC 20/5/1–62.

Dunblane sheriff court: Summonses and Decreets of Removal

Year	End of tack Tnt.	Subtnt.	Arrears Tnt.	Subtnt.	Breach of tack Tnt.	No written tack Tnt.	Subtnt.	Other Tnt.	Unknown Tnt.	Subtnt.	Totals
1729–65	0	0	0	0	0	0	0	0	0	0	0
1766	0	0	1	0	0	2	0	0	3	1	7
1770	0	0	2	0	0	0	0	1	3	2	8
1780	3	1	2	0	1	5	0	0	2	1	15
1790	10	0	3	0	0	2	1	0	4	1	21
1800	13	0	2	1	0	3	0	0	3	0	22
Totals	26	1	10	1	1	12	1	1	15	5	73
Percentages	35.6	1.4	13.7	1.4	1.4	16.4	1.4	1.4	10.5	6.8	100

Source: SRO, Sheriff Court Processes (Dunblane), SC 44/22/1–62.

Peebles sheriff court: Summonses and Decreets of Removal

Year	End of tack		Arrears		No written tack		Other	Unknown	Totals
	Tnt.	Subtnt.	Tnt.	Subtnt.	Tnt.	Subtnt.	Tnt.	Tnt.	
1662–1704	0	0	0	0	0	0	0	1	1
1750	0	0	0	0	0	0	0	2	2
1760	0	0	0	0	0	0	0	2	2
1770	0	0	1	1	1	0	1	2	6
1780	0	0	0	0	0	0	0	0	0
1790	2	1	2	0	1	1	0	0	6
1800	0	0	0	0	0	0	0	0	0
Totals	2	1	3	1	2	1	1	7	17
Percentages	11.8	5.9	11.8	5.9	11.8	5.9	5.9	41.2	100

Source: SRO, Sheriff Court Processes (Peebles), SC SF42/5/1–53.

Linlithgow sheriff court: Summonses and Decrees of Removal

Year	End of tack Tnt.	Arrears Tnt.	No written tack Tnt.	Unknown Tnt.	Subtnt.	Totals
1737	0	0	0	0	1	1
1749	0	0	0	2	0	2
1770	1	0	2	2	0	5
1800	3	1	7	2	0	13
Totals	4	1	9	6	1	21
Percentages	19.0	4.8	42.9	28.6	4.8	100

Source: SRO, Sheriff Court Processes (Linlithgow), SC 41/6/1–22.

Annex D
Estimated Net Out-Migration from Ayr, Angus, Fife, Lanarkshire, 1755–1790s

The level of migration into or out of any given area over a specific time period can only be accurately calculated if four vital statistics are known: the population levels at the start and end of the period, and the numbers of both births and deaths. The difference between the latter two reveals the natural rate of increase, while the difference between the two successive censuses give the actual change in population level. By subtracting the natural increase from the actual population change a crude measure of the level of net in- or out-migration becomes apparent. However, variations in both nuptiality and fertility ratios can mean that gains and losses may imply other consequences than simply rates of human mobility.

Demographic data for the eighteenth century are sparse by comparison with later periods. On a national scale and prior to the first national census of 1801, only the Webster enumeration of 1755 and that of the OSA in the 1790s are of any use to the historian in this context. Unfortunately, however, there are no data on fertility and mortality rates for later-eighteenth-century Scotland comparable to those of enumeration. Thus, to even approximately measure the scale of migration, it becomes necessary to estimate the rate of natural increase. This has been done here by using the crude national average rate of population increase of 6 per cent per decade or 0.6 per cent per annum.

Table 1 below together with Tables A–D provide population counts for the four counties at the two periods followed by the actual change in numbers. The estimated percentage multipliers on the county sheets are arrived at for each parish by multiplying the assumed national percentage yearly rise of population (i.e. 0.6 per cent) of the appropriate number of years between the two population counts. For example, a parish which gave 1790 as the date of its *OSA* report would have an estimated multiplier of 35 x 0.6 per cent or 21.0 per cent. Thus, with this estimated natural increase, the estimated level of net in- or out-migration is deduced as described above and the figure can then be expressed as a percentage of the original population level of 1755. The estimated mean percentage multiplier for each county, as indicated in Table 1, is simply the average figure calculated from the total of those multipliers of each parish as shown on the tables for each county in Tables A–D. It should be borne in mind, however, that local variation in both nuptiality and fertility could affect these figures.

Table 1 Estimated net out-migration from the four counties, 1755–1790s

County	Population 1755	Population 1790s	Actual change	Estimated mean percentage multiplier
Angus	68,593	91,601	+23,008	21.2
Fife	80,970	87,224	+6,254	21.3
Ayrshire	59,009	73,511	+14,502	21.8
Lanarkshire	80,300	151,234	+70,934	21.8

County	Estimated natural increase	Estimated Net out-migration	Net out-migration as percentage of 1755 population
Angus	14,542	+8,466	+12.3
Fife	17,247	−10,993	−13.6
Ayrshire	12,864	+1,638	+2.8
Lanarkshire	17,505	+53,429	−66.5

Source: OSA.

To move beyond the generalized picture, a migration factor analysis was conducted. From the *OSA* reports, four independent factors were examined which might have influenced migration at the parish level. These were: reduction of cottar numbers, industrial presence, farm consolidation and the presence of villages or towns. This exercise deals in the numbers and percentages of parishes in the four counties examined, *not* those of population as such. In other words, the importance of a specific factor, and its impact on population movements, is not gauged here by the actual size of the estimated migration flows but by the number of cases of parishes demonstrating this coincidence of presumed cause and effect. For example, the absence of some kind of industrial presence was associated with out-migration in 33.3 per cent of the forty-five Ayrshire parishes analysed, but this does not imply that the lack of some kind of industry accounted for one third of out-migration from Ayrshire parishes.

Tables 2 and 3 lay out the numerical and percentage results of the single (and in some cases) combined factor analysis for the three counties. As can be seen, it is divided into two main sections: those parishes demonstrating net out-migration and those demonstrating net in-migration. These two groups were isolated in turn from the database and then checked against the individual factors laid out in the left-hand column. For each of the two groups in each county the actual number of parishes with the particular factor present is given in the first column and this figure is then expressed as a percentage of the total number of parishes.

It should be noted that in all four counties the denominator used to calculate percentages is slightly less than the actual total number of parishes because, in a few cases, there were no usable data given in the *OSA*. Note also that only where a particular factor, such as industrial presence, was indicated in the parish account can the result be relied upon, since it is possible that in some cases other factors – assumed here to be absent – were simply not mentioned in the *OSA* reports.

These results shown in Tables 2 and 3 give some indication of the explanatory power of the various factors *vis-à-vis* the in- or out-flows of population since they outline the percentage of parishes in which the specific and presumed causes and effects were associated with each other.

Table 2 Estimated migration in the shires of Ayr, Angus and Fife, 1755–1790s: factor analysis

Factor(s)	Ayr (45 parishes) no./percentage	Angus (52 parishes) no./percentage	Fife (59 parishes) no./percentage
Parishes demonstrating net out-migration, 1755–90s			
No industrial presence	15/33.3	26/50.0	25/42.2
Farm consolidation	11/24.4	12/23.1	14/23.7
No villages, towns, etc.	3/6.7	24/46.2	26/44.1
Cottar nos. reduced	3/6.7	8/15.4	8/13.6
Parishes demonstrating net in-migration, 1744–90s			
Industrial presence	15/33.3	11/21.2	10/16.9
No farm consolidation	19/42.2	16/30.8	13/22.0
Villages, towns, etc.	19/42.2	12/23.1	10/16.9
Cottars exist	2/4.4	6/11.5	5/8.5

Source: OSA.

Tables 4 and 5 attempt to extend this analysis further by combining the results of both sides of a particular hypothesis. If it is assumed that in this period the absence of an 'industrial presence' from a parish would have acted as a 'push' factor and that, conversely, the existence of some kind of industry would have functioned as a 'pull', then in Ayrshire, for instance, this total hypothesis is supported by the results from 66.6 per cent of parishes, and so on. However, given the caveat

Table 3 Estimated migration in the shire of Lanark, 1755–1790s: factor analysis

Factor(s)	No. of cases	Percentage of total
Parishes demonstrating net out-migration, 1755–90s		
No industrial presence	8	21.1
Farm consolidation	10	26.3
No villages, towns, etc.	9	23.7
Cottar numbers reduced	8	21.1
Parishes demonstrating net in-migration, 1755–90s		
Industrial presence	8	21.1
No farm consolidation	11	28.9
Villages, towns, etc.	6	15.8
Cottars exist	3	7.9

Source: OSA.

entered above on the reliability of presumed 'negative' evidence, the hypotheses built into the 'migration' figures, the results of this exercise must be treated with caution. Nevertheless, both the factor and combined-factor analysis indicate a broadly similar result. The existence or reduction of the cottar class was not associated in more than about one fifth of Ayr, Angus and Fife parishes with a static or increasing population on the one hand or a decreasing population on the other. Only the Lanarkshire figures marginally rise above this average. On the other hand, the industrial village/town and consolidation variables ranked very much higher as factors associated with mobility. This short statistical exercise suggests that the results of cottar displacement were far from simple.

Table 4 Estimated migration in the shires of Ayr,
Angus and Fife, 1755–1790s: combined factor analysis

Combined factors	Combined percentage figures for the three counties			
	Ayr	Angus	Fife	Mean
(O) No industrial presence + (I) Ind. Pres.	66.6	71.2	59.1	65.6
(O) Farm consolidation + (I) No farm consolidation	66.4	53.9	45.7	55.3
(O) No villages etc. + (I) Villages etc.	48.9	69.3	61.0	59.7
(O) Cottars reduced + (I) Cottars exist	11.1	26.9	22.1	20.0

Notes: (O) = data set representing parishes that recorded net out-migration,
1755–1790s.

(I) = data set representing parishes that recorded net in-migration, 1755–1790s.

Source: OSA.

Table 5 Estimated migration in the shire of Lanark,
1755–1790s: combined factor analysis

Combined factors	Combined percentage figures for Lanarkshire
(O) No industrial presence + (I) Industrial presence	42.4
(O) Farm consolidation + (I) No farm consolidation	55.2
(O) No villages etc. + (I) Villages, etc.	39.5
(O) Cottars reduced + (I) Cottars exist	29.0

Notes: (O) = data set representing parishes that recorded net out-migration,
1755–1790s.
   (I) = data set representing parishes that recorded net in-migration, 1755–1790s.

Source: OSA.

Table A Estimated net out-migration from Lanarkshire parishes, 1755–1790s

Parish	Pop. 1755	Pop. 1790s	Actual change	Estimated % of age multiplier	Estimated natural increase	Estimated net out-migration	Net out-m. as % of 1755 pop.
Avendale/Strathaven	3,551	3,343	−208	21.6	767	−975	27.5
Biggar	1,098	937	−161	21.6	237	−398	36.3
Blantyre	496	1,040	+542	21.6	107	+435	+87.7
Bothwell	1,561	2,707	+1,146	23.4	365	+781	+50.0
Cadder	2,396	1,769	−627	22.2	532	−1,159	48.4
Cambuslang	934	1,288	+354	21.6	202	+152	+16.3
Cambusnethan	1,419	1,684	+265	21.6	307	−42	3.0
Carluke	1,459	1,730	+271	22.2	324	−53	3.6
Carmichael	899	781	−118	22.8	205	−323	35.9
Carmunnock	471	570	+99	22.8	107	−8	1.7
Carnwath	2,390	3,000	+610	22.8	545	+65	+2.7
Carstairs	845	924	+79	22.8	193	−114	13.5
Covington	521	484	−37	14.4	75	−112	21.5
Crawford	2,009	1,490	−519	21.6	434	−953	47.4
Crawford-John	765	590	−175	21.0	161	−336	43.9
Culter	422	326	−96	21.6	91	−187	44.3
Dalserf	765	1,100	+335	21.6	165	+170	22.2
Dalziel	351	478	+127	22.2	78	+49	14.0

Dolphington	302	200	−102	21.6	65	−167	55.3
Douglas	2,009	1,715	−294	21.6	434	−728	36.2
Dunsyre	359	360	+1	21.6	78	−77	21.5
Glasford	559	788	+229	22.2	124	+105	+18.8
Glasgow	23,546	61,945	+38,399	21.6	5,086	+33,313	+141.5
Gorbals of Glasgow	3,000	5,000	+2,000	21.6	648	+1,352	+45.1
Barony of Glasgow	3,905	18,451	+14,546	21.6	844	+13,702	+350.9
Gowan	4,389	8,318	+3,929	22.2	974	+2,955	+67.3
Hamilton	3,815	5,017	+1,202	21.6	824	+378	+9.9
East Kilbride	2,029	2,359	+330	22.2	450	−120	5.9
Lamington	599	417	−182	22.2	133	−315	52.6
Lanark	2,294	4,751	+2,457	22.2	509	+1,948	+84.9
Lesmahagow	2,996	2,810	−186	22.2	665	−851	28.4
Liberton	708	750	+42	21.6	153	−111	15.7
New/East Monkland	2,713	3,560	+847	22.2	602	+245	+9.0
Old/West Monkland	1,823	4,000	+2,187	22.8	413	+1,774	+97.8
Pettimain	330	386	+56	22.2	73	−17	5.2
Rutherglen	988	1,860	+872	22.2	219	+653	+66.1
Shotts	2,322	2,041	−281	22.8	529	−810	34.9
Stonehouse	823	1,060	+237	21.6	178	+59	7.2
Symington	264	307	+43	22.8	60	−17	6.4
Walston	479	427	−52	22.2	106	−158	33.0
Wistoun & Roberton	1,102	740	−362	21.6	238	−600	54.5

Source: OSA.

Table B Estimated net out-migration from Angus parishes, 1755–1790s

Parish	Pop. 1755	Pop. 1790s	Actual change	Estimated % of age multiplier	Estimated natural increase	Estimated net out-migration	Net out-m. as % of 1755 pop.
Aberlemno	943	1,033	+90	21.0	198	108	11.5
Airly	1,012	865	−147	22.2	225	372	36.8
Arbirlot	865	1,055	+190	21.0	182	+8	+0.9
Arbroath	2,098	4,676	+2,578	22.2	466	+2,112	+100.7
Auchterhouse	600	600	0	22.2	137	137	22.8
Barrie	689	796	+107	21.6	149	42	6.1
Brechin	3,181	e5,000	+1,819	21.0	668	+1,151	+36.2
Careston	269	260	−9	21.0	56	65	24.2
Carmylie	730	700	−30	21.0	153	−183	25.1
Cortachy & Clova	1,233	1,020	−213	22.2	274	−487	39.5
Craig	935	1,314	+379	21.0	196	+183	+19.6
Dun	657	500	−157	21.0	138	−295	44.9
Dundee	12,477	e24,000	+11,523	22.2	2,770	+8,753	+70.2
Dunnichen	612	872	+260	21.6	132	+128	+20.9
Edzell	862	963	+101	21.0	181	−80	9.3
Essie & Nevay	500	630	+130	22.8	114	+16	+3.2

Fern	500	490	−10	21.0	105	−115	23.0
Fernell	509	620	+111	21.6	110	+1	+0.2
Forfar	2,450	4,625	+2,175	21.0	515	+1,660	+67.8
Glamis	1,780	2,040	+260	16.8	299	−39	2.2
Glenisla	1,852	1,018	−834	21.6	400	−1,234	66.6
Guthrie	584	571	−13	22.2	130	−143	24.5
Inverarity	996	929	−67	21.0	209	−276	27.7
Inverkeilor	1,286	1,747	+461	21.0	270	+191	+14.9
Kettins	1,476	1,100	−376	22.8	337	−713	48.3
Kingoldrum	780	600	−180	22.8	178	−358	45.9
Kinnell	761	830	+69	21.0	160	−91	12.0
Kinnettles	616	621	+5	22.2	137	−132	21.4
Kirkden	563	727	+164	21.0	118	+46	+8.2
Kirriemuir	3,409	e4,500	+1091	22.2	757	+334	+9.8
Lethnot	635	505	−130	21.0	133	−263	41.4
Liff & Bervie	1,311	1,790	+479	22.8	299	+180	+13.7
Lintrathen	1,165	e900	−265	22.8	266	−531	45.6
Lochlee	686	608	−78	22.2	152	−230	33.5
Logie & Pert	696	999	+303	21.6	150	+153	+22.0
Lunan	208	291	+83	21.0	44	+39	+18.8

(continued)

Parish	Pop. 1755	Pop. 1790s	Actual change	Estimated % of age multiplier	Estimated natural increase	Estimated net out-migration	Net out-m. as % of 1755 pop.
Lundie & Foulis	586	648	+62	21.0	123	-61	10.4
Mains of Fintry	709	878	+169	22.2	157	+12	+1.7
Maryton	633	529	-104	22.7	144	-248	39.2
Menmuir	743	900	+157	21.0	156	+1	+0.1
Monifieth	1,421	1,218	-203	22.8	324	-527	37.1
Monikie	1,345	1,278	-67	21.0	283	-350	26.0
Montrose	4,150	6,194	+2,044	21.0	872	+1,172	+28.2
Muirhouse	623	462	-161	22.8	142	-303	48.6
Newtyle	913	594	-319	21.6	197	-516	56.5
Oathlaw	435	430	-5	21.0	91	-96	22.1
Panbride	1,259	1,460	+201	21.0	264	-63	5.0
Rescobie	798	934	+136	22.8	182	-46	5.8
Ruthven	280	220	-60	22.2	62	-122	43.6
St Vigeans	1,592	3,336	+1,774	22.8	363	+1,411	+88.6
Strathmartin	368	340	-28	22.8	84	-112	30.4
Strickathrow	529	672	+143	21.0	111	+32	+6.1
Tannadice	1,470	1,421	-49	21.0	309	-358	24.4
Tealing	735	802	+67	21.6	159	-92	12.5

Note: e = estimated population figure as shown in relevant parish account.

Source: OSA.

Table C Estimated net out-migration from Fife parishes, 1755–1790s

Parish	Pop. 1755	Pop. 1790s	Actual change	Estimated % of age multiplier	Estimated natural increase	Estimated net out-migration	Net out-m. as % of 1755 pop.
Abbot's Hall	1,348	2,136	+788	21.6	291	+497	+36.9
Abdie	882	e600	-222	20.4	168	-390	47.5
Aberdour	1,198	1,280	+82	21.0	252	-170	14.2
Anstruther Easter	1,100	1,000	-100	21.0	231	-331	30.1
Anstruther Wester	385	370	-15	21.0	81	-96	24.9
Auchterderran	1,194	1,200	+6	21.0	251	-245	20.5
Auchtermuchty	1,308	1,439	+131	22.2	290	-159	12.2
Auchtertool	389	334	-55	22.2	86	-141	36.3
Ballingry	464	220	-244	21.6	100	-344	74.1
Balmerino	563	703	+140	21.6	122	+18	+32.0
Beath	1,099	e450	-649	21.0	231	-880	80.1
Burntisland	1,390	1,210	-180	21.0	292	-472	34.0
Cameron	1,295	1,165	-130	22.8	295	-425	32.8
Carnbee	1,293	1,041	-252	22.8	295	-547	42.3
Carnock	583	970	+387	21.6	126	+261	+44.8
Ceres	2,540	2,320	-220	21.6	549	-769	30.3

(*continued*)

Parish	Pop. 1755	Pop. 1790s	Actual change	Estimated % of age multiplier	Estimated natural increase	Estimated net out-migration	Net out-m. as % of 1755 pop.
Collessie	989	949	−40	21.6	214	−254	25.7
Crail	2,173	1,710	−463	21.0	456	−919	42.3
Creich	375	306	−69	21.6	81	−150	40.0
Cults	449	534	+85	21.6	97	−12	2.7
Cupar of Fife	2,192	3,702	+1,510	22.8	500	+1,010	+46.1
Dairsie	469	540	+71	21.0	99	−28	6.0
Dalgety	761	869	+108	22.8	174	−66	8.7
Denino	598	383	−215	22.8	136	−351	58.7
Dunbog	255	235	−20	21.0	54	−74	29.0
Dunfermline	8,552	9,550	+998	21.6	1,847	−849	9.3
Dysart	2,367	4,862	+2,495	22.2	526	+1,969	+83.2
Elie	642	620	−22	24.0	154	−176	27.4
Falkland	1,792	2,195	+1,403	21.0	376	+1,027	+57.3
Ferry-Port-on-Craig	621	875	+254	21.0	130	+124	+20.0
Flisk	318	331	+13	21.0	67	−54	17.0
Forgan	751	875	+124	22.8	171	−47	6.3
Inverkeithing	1,694	2,210	+516	22.8	386	+130	+7.7

Kemback	420	588	+168	22.2	93	+75	+17.9
Kennoway	1,240	1,350	+110	21.0	260	−150	12.1
Kettle	1,621	1,759	+138	21.0	340	−202	12.5
Kilconquhar	2,131	2,013	−118	21.0	448	−566	26.6
Kilmany	785	869	+84	22.8	179	−95	12.1
Kilrenny	1,348	1,086	−262	21.0	283	−545	40.4
Kinghorn	2,389	1,768	−621	22.8	545	−1,166	48.8
Kinglassie	998	1,200	+202	21.0	210	−8	0.8
Kingsbarns	871	807	−64	21.6	188	−252	28.9
Kirkcaldy	2,296	2,673	+377	21.0	482	−105	4.6
Largo	1,396	1,913	+517	21.6	302	+215	+15.4
Leslie	1,130	1,212	+82	18.0	203	−121	10.7
Leuchars	1,691	1,620	−71	22.8	386	−457	27.0
Logie	413	425	+12	22.2	92	−80	19.4
Markinch	2,188	2,800	+612	22.2	486	+126	+5.8
Monimail	884	1,101	+217	21.6	191	+26	+2.9
Moonzie	249	171	−78	22.8	57	−135	54.2
Newburgh	1,347	1,664	+317	22.2	299	+18	+1.3
Newburn	438	456	+18	23.4	103	−85	19.4
Pittenweem	939	1,157	+218	21.0	197	+21	+2.2

(continued)

Parish	Pop. 1755	Pop. 1790s	Actual change	Estimated % of age multiplier	Estimated natural increase	Estimated net out- migration	Net out-m. as % of 1755 pop.
St Andrews & St Leonards	4,590	5,008	+418	21.0	964	-546	11.9
St Monance	780	832	+52	21.0	164	-112	14.4
Saline	1,285	950	-335	22.8	293	-628	48.9
Scoonie	1,528	1,675	+147	21.6	330	-183	12.0
Strathmiglo	*1,095	980	-115	21.0	230	-345	31.5
Torryburn	1,635	1,600	-35	21.6	353	-388	23.7
Wemyss	3,041	3,025	-16	21.6	657	-673	22.1

Notes: e = estimated population figure as shown in relevant parish account.

*Given total (1775) = 1,695. This is thought to be too high since the 1754 total was c.1,100.

Source: OSA.

Table D Estimated net out-migration from Ayrshire parishes, 1755–1790s

Parish	Pop. 1755	Pop. 1790s	Actual change	Estimated % of age multiplier	Estimated natural increase	Estimated net out-migration	Net out-m. as % of 1755 pop.
Ardrossan	1,297	1,518	+221	21.6	280	−59	4.6
Auchinleck	887	775	−112	21.6	192	−304	34.3
Ayr	2,964	4,647	+1,683	21.6	640	+1,043	+35.2
Ballantrae	1,049	770	−279	21.0	220	−499	47.6
Barr	858	750	−108	21.6	185	−293	34.2
Beith	2,064	2,872	+808	21.6	446	+362	+17.5
Colmonell	1,814	1,100	−714	21.0	381	−1,095	60.4
Coylton	527	667	+140	21.0	111	+29	+5.5
Craigie	551	700	+149	21.0	116	+33	+6.0
New Cumnock	1,497	1,200	−297	21.6	323	−620	41.4
Old Cumnock	1,336	1,632	+296	21.6	289	+7	+0.5
Dailly	839	1,607	+768	21.6	181	+587	+70.0
Dalmellington	739	681	−58	22.2	164	−222	30.0
Dalry	1,498	2,000	+502	22.2	333	+169	+11.3
Dalrymple	439	380	−59	21.0	92	−151	34.4
Dreghorn	887	830	−57	21.0	186	−243	27.4

(*continued*)

Parish	Pop. 1755	Pop. 1790s	Actual change	Estimated % of age multiplier	Estimated natural increase	Estimated net out-migration	Net out-m. as % of 1755 pop.
Dundonald	983	1,317	+334	22.2	218	+116	+11.8
Dunlop	796	779	−17	21.6	172	−189	23.7
Fenwick	1,113	1,281	+168	22.8	254	−86	7.7
Galston	1,013	1,577	+564	21.0	213	+351	+34.7
Girvan	1,103	1,725	+622	21.6	238	+384	+34.8
Irvine	4,025	4,500	+475	21.0	845	−370	9.2
Kilbirny	651	700	+49	21.6	141	−92	21.7
West Kilbride	885	698	−187	21.6	191	−378	42.7
Kilmarnock	4,405	6,776	+2,371	21.0	925	+1,446	+32.8
Kilnaurs	1,094	1,147	+53	22.2	243	−190	17.4
Kilwinning	2,541	2,360	−181	22.2	564	−745	29.3
Kirkmichael	710	956	+246	21.6	153	+93	+13.1
Kirkoswald	1,168	1,335	+167	21.6	252	−85	7.3
Largs	1,164	1,025	−139	21.0	244	−383	32.9
Loudoun	1,494	2,308	+814	21.6	323	+491	+32.9
Mauchline	1,169	1,800	+631	21.6	253	+378	+32.3
Maybole	2,058	3,000	+942	21.0	432	+510	+24.8

Monkton & Prestwick	e582	717	+135	22.2	129	+6	+1.0
Muirkirk	745	e1,100	+355	21.6	161	+194	+26.0
Newton-upon-Ayr	e581	1,750	+1,169	21.0	122	+1,047	+180.0
Ochiltree	1,210	1,150	−60	22.2	269	−329	27.2
Riccarton	745	e1,000	+255	22.2	165	+90	+12.1
St Quivox	499	1,450	+951	22.2	111	+840	+168.3
Sorn	1,494	2,779	+1,285	25.2	377	+908	+60.8
Stair	369	518	+149	21.6	80	+69	+18.7
Stevenson	1,412	2,425	+1,013	21.6	305	+708	+50.1
Stewarton	2,819	e2,400	−419	22.2	626	−1,045	37.1
Straiton	1,123	934	−189	21.6	243	−432	38.5
Symington	359	610	+251	22.2	80	+171	+47.6
Tarbolton	1,356	e1,200	−165	24.6	336	−501	36.7

Note: e = estimated population figure as shown in relevant parish account.

Source: OSA.

Annex E
Summons of Removing,
Sutherland, 1810

Summons of Removing:
Alex Ross agt.
Johyn Gordon and others
1810
Mandate filed 4 April 1810
Thos. Gunn
Dornoch 23 May 1810
Precept Extracted
By Thomas Gunn

George Cranston Esquire advocate Sheriff Depute of the shire of
Sutherland to . . . .
. . . . my officers in that part Generally and Sever-
ally specially Constituted

Greeting

Forasmuch as it is humbly meant and shown to me by Alexander
Ross, Tacksman or Principall Tenant of Navidale, Cain and others
aftermentioned lying in the Parishes of Loth & Kildonan and County
of Sutherland that by the act of Sederunt of the Lords of Council and
Session dated the fourteenth day of December seventeen hundred and
fifty six Entituled Act anent Removings, it is provided that it shall be
lawfull /

lawfull to the Heritor or other Setter of the Tack in his option either
to use the order prescribed by the Act of Parliament made in the year

fifteen hundred and fifty five intituled Act anent the Warning of Tenants and thereupon to pursue a Removing and Ejection or to bring his
action of Removing against the tenants before the Judge Ordinary
and such action being called before the Judge Ordinary at least forty
days before the Term of Whitsunday shall be held equal to a Warning
exacted in terms of the forsaid Act and the Judge shall thereupon proceed to determine the Removing in terms of that Act in /

in the same manner as if a Warning had been executed in terms of the
foresaid Act of Parliament And True it is that John Gordon in Cain,
Elizabeth Sutherland mother to the said John Gordon there, George
Mackay, in Cainmore, Robert Gunn, Gilbert Mitchell, James Mac-
kenzie, George Mackenzie, Ann Polson, Charlotte MacLeod, John
Murray, Joseph Mitchell, John Sutherland and Bessy Macleod all in
Navidale or in parts or pendicies thereto belong and all movable ten-
ants at the Will of the Pursuer from their respective possessions and
Occupation and although the Pursuer intends to have them removed
therefrom at the term of Whitsunday next Yet they mean as /

mean as the Pursuer is informed to keep violent possession and will not
remove unless compelled. Therefore the said John Gordon in Cain, Elizabeth Sutherland, George Mackay, in Cainmore, Robert Gunn, Gilbert
Mitchell, James Mackenzie, George Mackenzie, Ann Polson, Charlotte
MacLeod, John Murray, Joseph Mitchell, John Sutherland and Bessy
Macleod, Defenders Ought to and Should be Decerned and Ordained
by Decreet and Sentence of me or my Substitute to flit and Remove
themselves, Wives Bairns family, servants Subtenants and Cottars
Defenders and whole good and effects furth and from

the possession of the said Lands and others at the terms of Removall
after mentioned viz from the Houses Gardens and Grass at the time
of Whitsunday Eighteen hundred /

/ hundred and ten and from the arable land under crop at the Separa-
tion of crop Eighteen hundred and ten from the Ground and to leave
the same Void and ridd to the end the Pursuer or others in his name
may at the forsaid respective terms enter thereto and peaceasbly Bruil

and enjoy the same in all coming hereaftr Conform to the Laws and daily practice of Scotland used and observed in the like cases Herefor my Will is and I command and Charge You that you in his Majestys name and authority & mine lawfully summon Warn and Charge the said John Gordon, Elisabeth Sutherland, George McKay, Robrt Gunn, Gilbert Mitchell, James Mackenzie, George Mackenzie, Ann /

Ann Polson, Charlotte MacLeod, John Murray, Jospeh Mitchell, John Sutherland, and Bessy MacLeod, Defenders personally or at their respective dwelling places to compear before me or by Substitute at Dornoch at Ordinary Court place thereof the thirtieth day of March current in the hous of Cain with continuation of days to answer at the Instance of this and pursuand in the matter lybeiled with Certification as I give According to Justice. The which to do etc. Given under the hand of the Clerke of Court at Dornoch the Seventh day of March 1810.

Dornoch 30th March 1810	[signed] Wm Taylor
Sh Clk	
Lodged with execution with	[signed] Wm Taylor
Dornoch 4 April 1810 Sh Sub Judge	

The Pursuer compearing by Hugh Leslie writer as his procr as per lawful mandate who produced summons and execution against the Defenders and craved decreet and the Defenders being called and all failing to compear.

The Sheriff holds the Defenders as confessed and decerns against them in the Removing in terms of the Lybell.

Rob Mackid

Source: NRS, Sheriff Court Records, SC9/7/60/Bundle 1810E, Item A.

Bibliography

MANUSCRIPT SOURCES

National Archives, Kew, London

H045/OS.1794	Papers relating to British Association for the Relief of Distress in Ireland and Scotland
T1/4201	Papers relating to Distress in the Highlands, 1837, including correspondence and report of Robert Grahame
HD45/1080	Potato Famine in Ireland and Scotland, 1846–8
CO 384; CO 42	Petitions and other materials relating to Highland emigration

National Register of Archives (Scotland)

874	Dr John Berry Papers
859	Sir Alexander F. Douglas-Home Papers
0094	Earl of Glasgow Papers
2177	Hamilton Papers
792	Earl of Southesk Papers
885	Earl of Strathmore Papers

Hamilton Public Library

631/1	Burrell Journals, 1763–1808, 46 volumes

National Library of Scotland

Acc. 4322	Lockhart of Lee Papers
Acc. 5474	Lockhart of Lee Papers
Acc. 5976	Lockhart Papers
Acc. 8217	Stuart of Castlemilk Papers
Acc. 8220	Stuart of Castlemilk Papers
Session Papers:	Campbell (1717–1816), Douglas (1752–71), Elphinstone (1780–81), Hermand (1756–1820), Kames (1752–68), Kilkerran (1736–57), Meadowbank (1750–1814), and Pitfour (1740–74) Collections
Dep. 313	Sutherland Estate Papers

National Records of Scotland

SC20/5	Sheriff Court Processes, Cupar
SC44/22	Sheriff Court Processes, Dunblane
SC37/8	Sheriff Court Processes, Hamilton
SC38/22	Sheriff Court Processes, Lanark
SC41/6	Sheriff Court Processes, Linlithgow
SC42/5	Sheriff Court Processes, Peebles
GD16	Airlie Muniments
GD288	Balfour of Balbirnie Muniments
GD5/497	Bertram of Nisbet Papers
GD1/732	Blantyre Papers
RH2/8/75	Cunninghame of Auchinharvie Papers
GD45	Dalhousie Muniments
GD3	Eglinton Muniments
GD179/3697	Handaxwood Papers
GD26	Leven and Melville Muniments
GD150	Morton Papers
GD213/54	Oswald of Auchincruive Papers
GD86/770	Berwick Poll Tax Lists, 1693
E79/8/A	Midlothian Poll Tax Lists, 1693
GD178/2	Selkirk Poll Tax Lists, 1893
E70/13	West Lothian Poll Tax Lists, 1693
CH2/35/9	Biggar Presbytery Records
CH2/56/4	Carluke Kirk Session Records
CH2/57/2	Carmichael Kirk Session Records

CH2/60/3	Carnwath Kirk Session Records
CH2/63/2	Carstairs Kirk Session Records
CH2/72/1	Covington Kirk Session Records
CH2/522/1	Crawford Kirk Session Records
CH2/451/1	Culter Kirk Session Records
CH2/953/2	Douglas Kirk Session Records
CH2/115/1	Dunsyre Kirk Session Records
CH2/522/4	Kirkpatrick Kirk Session Records
CH2/404/1	Lamington Kirk Session Records
CH2/301/2	Pettinain Kirk Session Records
CH2/376/4	Roberton Kirk Session Records
CH2/363/2	Walston Kirk Session Records
CH2/376/3	Wiston Kirk Session Records
CH1/2/86	General Assembly Papers
CH1/187	General Assembly Papers
AD58/81	(Lord Advocate's Papers). Reports on conditions of various estates in the Highlands and Islands, 1846–7
AD58/82	Free Church Relief Fund, 1846
AD58/83	Threatened Evictions at Strathaird, Skye, 1850
AD58/84	Conditions in the Isle of Harris
AD58/85	Conditions in Barra and South Uist, 1846–9
AD58/89	Miscellaneous letters re. Highland Destitution to Lord Advocate
AD14/47/628	Precognition as to the alleged death of Widow Anne Gillies from starvation, 18 March 1847
HD	Highland Destitution. Collection of government correspondence and all material relating to the activities of the Edinburgh Section of the Central Board, its officers and local committees, 1846–50
HD4/1–6	Papers of the Highland and Island Emigration Society, 1851–9
AF7/85	Reports by the General Inspector (Fisheries) for the West Coast, 1845–52
CS 279	Court of Session. Petitions in Sequestrations, 1839–56
CS 277	Sederunt Books in Sequestration
SC59/2/4–14	Sheriff Court Processes, Tobermory
SC9/7/128–30	Sheriff Court Processes, Dornoch
SC32/5/1–2	Sheriff Court Processes, Portree
SC33/17/27–34	Sheriff Court Processes, Stornoway
RH 2/4	Home Office (Scotland). Domestic Entry Books

CH2/190/7	Presbytery of Inveraray Records
CH2/230/4	Presbytery of Skye Records
CH2/557/10	Synod of Argyll Records
GD 112	Breadalbane Muniments
GD 170	Campbell of Barcaldine MSS
GD 64	Campbell of Jura Papers
GD 201	Clanranald Papers
GD 305	Cromartie Estate Papers
GD 208	Loch Muniments
GD 221	Lord Macdonald Papers
GD 174	Maclaine of Lochbuie Papers
GD 1	Riddell Papers
AF 49	Riddell Papers
GD 248	Seafield Muniments
GD 46	Seaforth Muniments
CS 96/1686	Accounts of Donald Maclean and Co., Merchants and Fishcurers, Kyleakin
RH 21/44/1	Roman Catholic Register of Baptisms, Deaths, Marriages, Arisaig, 1839–60
RH 21/48/2	Roman Catholic Register of Baptisms, Deaths, Marriages, Moidart, 1830–55

OLD PARISH REGISTERS

Ardchattan (504/2); Ardnamurchan (505/3); Barvas (86/2); Bracadale, Campbeltown (507/6); Clyne; Creich (46/2); Dornoch (47/2); Edderachillis (49/2); Farr (50/2); Glenorchy (512/3); Harris (111/1); Iona (538/1); Kilfinichen (542/2); Lochs (87/1); North Uist (113/1); Portree (114/2); Stornoway (88/2); Strathy (50/2/1); Strontian (505/2); Tiree (551/2).

CENSUS ENUMERATORS' SCHEDULES, 1841, 1851 AND 1861 CENSUS

Ardchattan; Ardnarnurchan; Arisaig and Moidart; Gigha; Glenorchy; Inverchaolin; Jura; Kilchoman; Killarow; Kildalton; Kilchrennan; Kilfinan; Kilfinichen; Kilninian; Lismore; Morvern; Tiree; Coll; Torosay; Barra; Bracadale; Dores; Duirnish; Glenelg; Harris; Kilmallie; Kilmonivaig; Kilmorack; Kilnuir; Kiltarlity; N. Uist; S. Uist; Portree; Sleat; Small Isles; Snizort; Strath; Urquhart; Applecross; Barvas; Gairloch; Kintail; Lochalsh; Lochbroom; Lochcarron; Lochs; Stornoway; Uig; Glensheil; Assynt; Clyne; Creich; Dornoch;

Durness; Edderachillis; Farr; Kildonan; Lairg; Loth; Rogart; Tongue; Campbeltown; Craignish; Dunoon; Glassary; Inveraray; Kilbrandon; Kilcalmonell; Killean; Kilmodan; Kilmartin; Kilmore; Kilninver; N. Knapdale; S. Knapdale; Lochgoilhead; Sadell; Southend; Strachur; Ardersier; Boleskine; Cromdale; Croy; Inverness; Kingussie; Kirkhill; Laggan; Moy and Dalarossie; Petty; Alness; Avoch; Contin; Cromarty; Dingwall; Edderton; Fearn; Fodderty; Killearnan; Kilmuir Easter; Kiltearn; Kincardine; Knockbain; Logie Easter; Nigg; Resolis; Rosemarkie; Rosskean; Tain; Tarbat; Urquhart and Logie Wester; Urray; Golspie; Abbey Parish, Paisley, 1851.

ARGYLL AND BUTE DISTRICT ARCHIVES, LOCHGILPHEAD

CO 6–13   Parochial Board Minutes, Argyllshire Parishes

SCOTTISH CATHOLIC ARCHIVES, COLUMBA HOUSE, EDINBURGH

Oban Letters

MITCHELL LIBRARY, GLASGOW

MS 21506   Letterbook on Highland Emigration of Sir John McNeill, 1852

IN PRIVATE HANDS

Argyll Estate Papers (Inveraray Castle)
Cameron of Locheil Papers (Achnacarry Castle)
Hamilton Muniments (Lennoxlove)
Mackenzie of Gairloch MSS (Conon House)
Macleod of Macleod Muniments (Dunvegan Castle)
Diary of John Munro Mackenzie, 1851 (Courtesy of Ms M. Buchanan)

NEWSPAPERS AND PERIODICALS

Edinburgh Evening Courant, 1750–75
Edinburgh Review
Glasgow Herald

Inverness Advertiser
Inverness Courier
Illustrated London News
John O'Groats Journal
The Scotsman
The Times
Witness

PARLIAMENTARY PAPERS (PP)

Reports from the Select Committee appointed to inquire into the expediency of encouraging emigration from the United Kingdom, 1826, IV; 1826–7, V

Letters Addressed to Mr F. Maule by R. Grahame relative to the Distress of the Highlands of Scotland, 1837, LI

Report from the Select Committee appointed to inquire into the condition of the Population of the Highlands and Islands of Scotland, and into the practicablity of affording the People relief by means of Emigration, 1841, VI

Report of the Agent General for Emigration on the Applicability of Emigration to relieve Distress in the Highlands (1837), 1841, XXVI

Report from the Commissioners appointed for inquiring into the Administration and Practical Operation of the Poor Laws in Scotland, 1844, XXVII–XXXVI

Documents relative to the Distress in Scotland in 1783, 1846, XXXVII

Report from the Select Committee on Railway Labourers, 1846, XIII

Colonial Land and Emigration Commissioners, Annual Reports, 1845–58

Board of Supervision for Relief of the Poor in Scotland, Annual Reports, 1846–56

Reports of Commissioners, Inspectors of Factories, 1846, XV

Papers relative to Emigration to the British Provinces in North America, 1847–60

Return of Applications for Advances under the Drainage Act, 1847, XXXIV

Correspondence relating to the measures adopted for the Relief of Distress in Ireland and Scotland, 1847, LIII

Report to the Board of Supervision by Sir John McNeill on the Western Highlands and Islands, 1851, XXVI

Copies or Extracts of Despatches relative to Emigration to the North American Colonies, 1851, XL

First Report of Select Committee on Emigrant Ships, 1854, XIII

Communications with regard to the Administration of the Poor Law in the Highlands of Scotland, 1854–5, XLVI

Return of Population and Poor Rates, Scotland (1853), 1854–5, XLVII

Royal Commission on the Employment of Children, Young Persons and Women in Agriculture (1867), 1870, III

Reports as to the Alleged Destitution in the Western Highlands and Islands, 1883, LIX

Report and Evidence of the Commissioners of Inquiry into the Condition of the Crofters and Cottars in the Highlands and Islands of Scotland, 1884, XXXII–XXXVI

Report on the Condition of the Cottar Population of the Lews, 1888, LXXX

Royal Commission on Labour. The Agricultural Labourer (Scotland), 1893, XXXVI

Royal Commission (Highlands and Islands, 1892). Reports and Minutes of Evidence, 1895, XXXVIII–XXXIX

Report to the Secretary for Scotland by the Crofters Commission on the Social Condition of the People in Lewis as compared with Twenty Years Ago, 1902, LXXXIII

Report on the Sanitary Conditions of the Lews, 1905, XXXIV

UNPUBLISHED THESES

Adams, I. H., 'Division of Commonty in Scotland', Ph.D. thesis, University of Edinburgh, 1967

Anderson, Christine B., 'Uncovering and Recovering Cleared Galloway', unpublished Ph.D. thesis, University of Massachusetts at Amherst, 2015

Balfour, Roderick A. C. S., 'Emigration from the Highlands and Western Isles of Scotland to Australia during the Nineteenth Century', unpublished M.Litt. thesis, University of Edinburgh, 1973

Bourke, P. M.A., 'The Potato Blight, Weather and Irish Famine', unpublished Ph.D. thesis, National University of Ireland, 1965

Cameron, James M., 'A Study of the Factors That Assisted and Directed Scottish Emigration to Upper Canada, 1815–1855', unpublished Ph.D. thesis, University of Glasgow, 1970

Carpenter, S. D. M., 'Patterns of Recruitment of the Highland Regiments of the British Army, 1756 to 1815', unpublished M.Litt. thesis, University of St Andrews, 1977

Clapham, P., 'Agrarian Reform on the Airlie Estate', M.Phil. thesis, University of Strathclyde, 1990

Docherty, Denis, 'The Migration of Highlanders to Lowland Scotland in the Nineteenth Century with Special Reference to Paisley', BA dissertation, Department of History, University of Strathclyde, 1979

Hildebrandt, R. N., 'Migration and Economic Change in the Northern Highlands during the Nineteenth Century', unpublished Ph.D. thesis, University of Glasgow, 1980

Livingstone, Alastair, 'The Galloway Levellers', unpublished M.Phil. thesis by research (University of Glasgow, 2009)

Lobban, R. D., 'The Migration of Highlanders into Lowland Scotland, c. 1750–1890 with Special Reference to Greenock', unpublished Ph.D. thesis, University of Edinburgh, 1969

Lodge, Christine, 'The Clearers and the Cleared: Women, Economy and Land in the Scottish Highlands, 1800–1900', unpublished Ph.D. thesis, University of Glasgow, 1996

Morrison, J., 'Rural Society in the Lothians, 1790–1850', M.Litt. thesis, University of Strathclyde, 1985

Shaw, Catherine Douglas, 'Enclosure and Agricultural Development in Scotland', unpublished D.Phil. thesis, University of Oxford (2009)

Walker, D. B., 'The Agricultural Buildings of Greater Strathmore, 1770–1920', Ph.D. thesis, University of Dundee, 1983

BOOKS

Adam, R. J., ed., *John Home's Survey of Assynt* (Edinburgh, 1960)

——, ed., *Papers on Sutherland Estate Management* (Edinburgh, 1972)

Adams, I. H., *Directory of Commonties* (Edinburgh, 1971)

——, ed., *Descriptive List of Plans in the Scottish Record Office*, vols. 1–3 (Edinburgh, 1966, 1970, 1974)

Adams, Ian, and Meredyth Somerville, *Cargoes of Despair and Hope: Scottish Emigration to North America, 1603–1803* (Edinburgh, 1993)

Aitchison, Peter, and Andrew Cassell, *The Lowland Clearances* (East Linton, 2003)

Allan, J. R., *The North-East Lowlands of Scotland* (London, 1934)

Anderson, Michael, 'The Demographic Factor', in T. M. Devine and Jenny Wormald, eds., *The Oxford Handbook of Modern Scottish History* (Oxford, 2012)

——, *Scotland's Populations from the 1850s to Today* (Oxford, 2018), pp. 25–6

Anon., *The Depopulation System in the Highlands* (Edinburgh, 1849)

Ansdell, Douglas, *The People of the Great Faith: The Highland Church, 1690–1900* (Stornoway, 1998)

Anthony, R., *Herds and Hinds* (East Linton, 1997)

Argyll, The Duke of, *Crofts and Farms in the Hebrides* (Edinburgh, 1883)

Armstrong, W. A., 'Labour I: Rural Population Growth, Systems of Employment and Incomes', in G. E. Mingay, ed., *The Agrarian History of England and Wales*, vol. VI: *1750–1850* (Cambridge, 1989)

Auld, Alexander, *Ministers and Men in the Far North* (Wick, 1868)

Bailyn, Bernard, *Voyagers to the West* (New York, 1988)

Bangor-Jones, Malcolm, 'From Clanship to Crofting: Landownership, Economy and the Church in the Province of Strathnaver', in John R. Baldwin, ed., *Firthlands of Ross and Sutherland* (Edinburgh, 1986)

——, 'Land Assessments and Settlement History in Sutherland and Easter Ross', in John R. Baldwin, ed., *Firthlands of Ross and Sutherland* (Edinburgh, 1986)

——, 'The Long Trek: Agricultural Change and the Great Northern Drove', in John R. Baldwin, ed., *Firthlands of Ross and Sutherland* (Edinburgh, 1986)

——, 'The Strathnaver Clearances', in Scottish Vernacular Buildings Working Group, *North Sutherland Studies* (Glasgow, 1987)

——, *Historic Assynt* (Assynt, 1996)

——, *The Assynt Clearances* (Assynt, 2001)

Basu, Paul, 'Sites of Memory, Sources of Identity: Landscape Narratives of the Sutherland Clearances', in J. A. Atkinson, I. Banks and G. MacGregor, eds., *Townships to Farmsteads: Rural Settlement Studies in Scotland, England and Wales* (Oxford, 2000)

——, *Highland Homecomings: Genealogy and Heritage Tourism in the Scottish Diaspora* (Oxford, 2007)

Beatson, R., *General View of the Agriculture of the County of Fife* (Edinburgh, 1797)

Beckett, J. V., 'Landownership and Estate Management', in G. E. Mingay, ed., *The Agrarian History of England and Wales*, vol. VI: *1750–1850* (Cambridge, 1989)

Bennett, Margaret, ed., *Recollections of an Argyll-shire Drover and Other West Highland Chronicles* (Ochtertyre, 2013)

Berg, M., *The Age of Manufactures* (London, 1985)

Bil, Albert, *The Shieling, 1600–1840* (Edinburgh, 1990)

Bonnyman, Brian, *The Third Duke of Buccleuch and Adam Smith* (Edinburgh, 2014)

Botfield, Beriah, *Journal of a Tour Through the Highlands* (Norton Hall, 1830)

Brannagan, Kenneth, *From Clan to Clearance: History and Archaeology of the Isle of Barra, c.850–1850* (Oxford, 2005)

Brown, C. G. *The Social History of Religion in Scotland since 1700* (London, 1987)

——, 'Religion and Social Change', in T. M. Devine and R. Mitchison, eds., *People and Society in Scotland*, vol. I, *1760–1830* (Edinburgh, 1988)

——, 'Protest in the Pews. Interpreting Presbyterianism and Society in Fracture during the Scottish Economic Revolution', in T. M. Devine, ed., *Conflict and Stability in Scottish Society, 1700–1850* (Edinburgh, 1990)

Brown, P. H. *Scotland before 1700 from Contemporary Documents* (Edinburgh, 1893)

Brown, Robert, *Remarks on the Earl of Selkirk's Observations on the Present State of the Highlands of Scotland* (Edinburgh, 1806)

Browne, James, *A Critical Examination of Dr MacCulloch's Work on the Highlands of Scotland* (Edinburgh, 1825)

Bumstead, J. M., *Lord Selkirk: A Life* (East Lancing, 2009)

Cage, R. A., *The Scottish Poor Law, 1745–1845* (Edinburgh, 1981)

Calder, T. T., *Sketch of the Civil and Traditional History of Caithness* (Glasgow, 1861)

Callander, R., *A Pattern of Landownership in Scotland* (Haughend, 1987)

Cameron, A. D., *Go Listen to the Crofters: The Napier Commission and Crofting a Century Ago* (Stornoway, 1986)

Cameron, David Kerr, *The Ballad and the Plough* (London, 1978)

——, *Willie Gavin, Crofter Man* (London, 1980)

——, *Cornkister Days* (London, 1984)

Cameron, J. Stewart, *A History of the Ross of Mull* (Bunessan, 2013)

Campbell, R. H., 'The Scottish Improvers and the Course of Agrarian Change in the Eighteenth Century', in L. M. Cullen and T. C. Smout, eds., *Comparative Aspects of Scottish and Irish Economic and Social History, 1600–1900* (Edinburgh, 1977)

——, 'The Landed Classes', in T. M. Devine and R. Mitchison, eds., *People and Society in Scotland*, vol. I, *1760–1830* (Edinburgh, 1988)

—— and A. S. Skinner, eds., *The Origin and Nature of the Scottish Enlightenment* (Edinburgh, 1982)

Campey, Lucille H., *After the Hector: The Scottish Pioneers of Nova Scotia and Cape Breton* (Toronto, 2004)

——, *An Unstoppable Force: The Scottish Exodus to Canada* (Toronto, 2008)

Cannadine, David, *The Decline and Fall of the British Aristocracy* (New Haven, Conn., 1990)

Carruthers, Gerard, and Colin Kidd, eds., *The International Companion to John Galt* (Glasgow, 2017)

Cathcart, A., *Kinship and Clientage: Highland Clanship 1451–1609 (Northern World)* (London, 2006)

Cavendish, A. E. J., *An Rèisimeid Chataich: The 93rd Sutherland Highlanders* (London, 1928)

Clapham, Peter, 'Agricultural Change and Its Impact on Tenancy: The Evidence of Angus Rentals and Tacks, *c*.1700–1850', in T. M. Devine and A. J. G. Cummings, eds., *Industry, Business and Society in Scotland since 1700* (Edinburgh, 1994)

Clyde, Robert, *From Rebel to Hero: The Image of the Highlander, 1745–1830* (East Linton, 1995)

Cobbett, W., *The Parliamentary History of England from the Earliest Period to 1803*, vol. XIV (1816)

——, *Tour in Scotland* (London, 1833)

Cockburn, Henry, *Circuit Journeys* (Edinburgh, 1888)

——, *Journal of Henry Cockburn*, 2 vols. (Edinburgh, 1874)

Cowley, D. C., *Strath of Kildonan: An Archaeological Survey* (Edinburgh, 1993)

Craig, David, *On the Crofter's Trail* (London, 1990)

Cregeen, E. R., ed., *Argyll Estate Instructions: Mull, Morvern and Tiree, 1771–1805* (Edinburgh, 1964)

——, 'The Changing Role of the House of Argyll in the Scottish Highlands', in N. T. Phillipson and Rosalind Mitchison, eds., *Scotland in the Age of Improvement* (Edinburgh, 1970)

Cullen, L. M., and T. C. Smout, eds., *Comparative Aspects of Scottish and Irish Economic and Social History, 1600–1900* (Edinburgh, 1977)

——and——, 'Introduction', in L. M. Cullen and T. C. Smout, eds., *Comparative Aspects of Scottish and Irish Economic and Social History, 1600–1900* (Edinburgh, 1977)

Dalgleish, Chris, *Rural Society in the Age of Reason* (New York, 2003)

Dawson, Alastair G., *So Foul and Fair a Day: A History of Scotland's Weather and Climate* (Edinburgh, 2009)

Defoe, D., *A Tour of the Whole Island of Great Britain* (London, 1971 edn)

Devine, T. M., 'Glasgow Colonial Merchants and Land, 1770–1815', in J. T. Ward and R. G. Wilson, eds., *Land and Industry: The Landed Estate in the Industrial Revolution* (Newton Abbot, 1971)

——, ed., *Lairds and Improvement in the Scotland of the Enlightenment* (Glasgow, 1979)

——, 'Social Stability and Agrarian Change in the Rural Lowlands of Scotland, 1780–1840', in T. M. Devine, ed., *Lairds and Improvement in the Scotland of the Enlightenment: The Proceedings of the Ninth Scottish Historical Conference, University of Edinburgh, 1978* (Glasgow, 1979)

——, 'The English Connection and Irish–Scottish Development in the Eighteenth Century', in T. M. Devine and D. Dickson, eds., *Ireland and Scotland, 1600–1850: Parallels and Contrasts in Economic and Social Development* (Edinburgh, 1983)

——, ed., *Farm Servants and Labour in Lowland Scotland, 1770–1914* (Edinburgh, 1984)

——, 'Pastoralism and Highland Migration', in A. Poitrineau, ed., *Élevage et Vie Pastorale dans les Montagnes d'Europe au Moyen Age et à l'Époque Moderne* (Clermont Ferrand, (1984)

——, 'Scottish Farm Labour during the Agricultural Depression, 1870–1914', in T. M. Devine, ed., *Farm Servants and Labour in Lowland Scotland, 1770–1914* (Edinburgh, 1984)

——, 'Scottish Farm Service in the Agricultural Revolution, 1780–1840', in T. M. Devine, ed., *Farm Servants and Labour in Lowland Scotland, 1770–1840* (Edinburgh, 1984)

——. 'Women Workers, 1850–1915', in T. M. Devine, ed., *Farm Servants and Labour in Lowland Scotland, 1770–1840* (Edinburgh, 1984)

——, *The Great Highland Famine: Hunger, Emigration and the Scottish Highlands in the Nineteenth Century* (Edinburgh, 1988)

——, 'Highland Landowners and the Highland Potato Famine', in L. Leneman, ed., *Perspectives of Scottish Social History* (Edinburgh, 1988)

——, 'Introduction', in T. M. Devine and R. Mitchison, eds., *People and Society in Scotland*, vol. 1, *1760–1830* (Edinburgh, 1988)

——, 'Scottish Society, 1760–1830', in T. M. Devine and R. Mitchison, eds., *People and Society in Scotland*, vol. 1, *1760–1830* (Edinburgh, 1988)

——, 'Stability and Unrest in Rural Scotland and Ireland, 1760–1840', in R. Mitchison and P. Roebuck, eds., *Economy and Society in Scotland and Ireland, 1500–1939* (Edinburgh, 1988)

——, 'Unrest and Stability in Rural Ireland and Scotland, 1760–1840', in R. Mitchison and P. Roebuck, eds., *Economy and Society in Scotland and Ireland, 1500–1939* (Edinburgh, 1988)

——, 'Urbanisation', in T. M. Devine and R. Mitchison, eds., *People and Society in Scotland*, vol. 1, *1760–1830* (Edinburgh, 1988)

——, 'Social Responses to Agrarian Improvement: The Highland and Lowland Clearances in Scotland, 1500–1850', in R. A. Houston and I. D. White, *Scottish Society, 1500–1800* (Cambridge, 1989)

——, ed., *Conflict and Stability in Scottish Society, 1700–1850* (Edinburgh, 1990)

——, 'The Failure of Radical Reform in Scotland in the Late Eighteenth Century: The Social and Economic Context', in T. M. Devine, ed., *Conflict and Stability in Scottish Society, 1700–1850* (Edinburgh, 1990)

——, *The Tobacco Lords* (Edinburgh, 1990 edn)

——, 'The Paradox of Scottish Emigration', in T. M. Devine, ed., *Scottish Emigration and Scottish Society* (Edinburgh, 1992)

——, *Clanship to Crofters' War: The Social Transformation of the Scottish Highlands* (Manchester, 1994)

——, *The Transformation of Rural Scotland* (Edinburgh, 1994)

——, 'Why the Highlands Did Not Starve: Ireland and Highland Scotland during the Potato Famines', in S. J. Connolly, R. A. Houston and R. J. Morris, eds., *Conflict, Identity and Economic Development: Ireland and Scotland 1600–1939* (Lancaster, 1995)

——, 'The Great Landlords of Lowland Scotland and Agrarian Change in the Eighteenth Century', in S. Foster, A. I. Macinnes and R. MacInnes, eds., *Scottish Power Centres from the Early Middle Ages to the Twentieth Century* (Glasgow, 1998)

——, 'Irish and Scottish Development Revisited', in David Dickson and Cormac O'Grada, eds., *Refiguring Ireland: Essays in Honour of L. M. Cullen* (Dublin, 2003)

——, *Scotland's Empire, 1600–1815* (London, 2003)

——, *Clearance and* Improvement: *Land, Power and People in Scotland 1700–1900* (Edinburgh, 2006).

——, 'Soldiers of Empire', in John M. Mackenzie and T. M. Devine, eds., *Scotland and the British Empire* (Oxford, 2011)

——, *To the Ends of the Earth: Scotland's Global Diaspora 1750–2010* (London, 2011)

——, 'A Global Diaspora', in T. M. Devine and Jenny Wormald, eds., *The Oxford Handbook of Modern Scottish History* (Oxford, 2012)

——, *The Scottish Nation, 1700–2007* (London, 2006); updated as *The Scottish Nation: A Modern History* (London, 2012)

—— and A. J. G. Cummings, eds., *Industry, Business and Society in Scotland since 1700* (Edinburgh, 1994)

—— and D. Dickson, eds., *Ireland and Scotland, 1600–1850: Parallels and Contrasts in Economic and Social Development* (Edinburgh, 1983)

——, C. H. Lee and G. C. Peden, eds., *The Transformation of Scotland* (Edinburgh, 2005)

—— and R. Mitchison, eds., *People and Society in Scotland*, vol. I: *1760–1830* (Edinburgh, 1988)

—— and Jenny Wormald, eds., *The Oxford Handbook of Modern Scottish History* (Oxford, 2012)

—— and J. R. Young, eds., *Eighteenth Century Scotland: New Perspectives* (East Linton, 1999)

de Vries, J., *European Urbanisation, 1500–1800* (London, 1987)

Dickson, T., ed., *Scottish Capitalism: Class, State and Nation from before the Union to the Present* (London, 1980)

Dodgshon, R. A., *Land and Society in Early Scotland* (Oxford, 1981)

——, 'Agricultural Change and Its Social Consequences in the Southern Uplands of Scotland, 1660–1780', in T. M. Devine and D. Dickson, eds., *Ireland and Scotland, 1600–1850* (Edinburgh, 1983)

——, 'West Highland Chiefdoms, 1500–1745', in R. Mitchison and P. Roebuck, eds., *Economy and Society in Scotland and Ireland 1500–1919* (Edinburgh, 1988)

——, '"Pretense of blude" and "place of thair duelling": The Nature of Scottish Clans, 1500–1745', in R. A. Houston and I. D. Whyte, eds., *Scottish Society, 1500–1800* (Cambridge, 1989)

——, *From Chiefs to Landlords: Social and Economic Change in the Western Highlands, 1493–1820* (Edinburgh, 1998)

——, *The Age of the Clans* (Edinburgh, 2002)

——, 'The Clearances and the Transformation of the Scottish Countryside', in T. M. Devine and Jenny Wormald, eds., *The Oxford Handbook of Modern Scottish History* (Oxford, 2012)

——, *No Stone Unturned: A History of Farming, Landscape and Environment in the Scottish Highlands and Islands* (Edinburgh, 2015)

Donnachie, Ian L., and Innes MacLeod, *Old Galloway* (Newton Abbot, 1974)

Dovring, F., 'The Transformation of European Agriculture', in *The Cambridge Economic History of Europe* (Cambridge, 1965)

Dunn, Charles W., *Highland Settler: A Portrait of the Scottish Gael in Cape Breton and Eastern Nova Scotia* (Toronto, 1953)

Durkacz, V. E., *The Decline of the Celtic Languages* (Edinburgh, 1983)

Dwyer, J., R. A. Mason and A. Murdoch, eds., *New Perspectives on the Politics and Culture of Early Modern Scotland* (Edinburgh, n.d.)

Dziennick, Matthew P., *The Fatal Land: War, Empire and the Highland Soldier* (London, 2015)

Fenton, Alexander, and Kenneth Veitch, *Scottish Life and Society: Farming and the Land* (Edinburgh, 2011)

Fenyö, Krisztina, *Contempt, Sympathy and Romance: Lowland Perceptions of the Highlands and the Clearances during the Famine Years 1845–1855* (East Linton, 2000)

Ferguson, W., 'The Electoral System in the Scottish Counties before 1832', in Stair Society, *Miscellany II* (Edinburgh, 1984)

Findlater, Rev. Eric J., *Highland Clearances: The Real Cause of Highland Famines* (Edinburgh, 1855)

Flinn, M. W., 'Malthus, Emigration and Potatoes in the Scottish North West, 1770–1870', in L. M. Cullen and T. C. Smout, eds., *Comparative Aspects of Irish and Scottish Economic and Social Development, 1690–1900* (Edinburgh, 1977)

Forsyth, David, ed., *A Global Force: War, Identities and Scotland's Diaspora* (Edinburgh, 2016)

——, ed., *Bonnie Prince Charlie and the Jacobites* (Edinburgh, 2017)

Foyster, Elizabeth, and Christopher A. Whatley, eds., *A History of Everyday Life in Scotland 1600 to 1800* (Edinburgh, 2010)

Fraser, W. H., 'Patterns of Protest', in T. M. Devine and R. Mitchison, eds., *People and Society in Scotland*, vol. 1: *1760–1830* (Edinburgh, 1988)

Fry, Michael, *Wild Scots* (London, 2005)

Fullarton, W., *General View of the Agriculture of the County of Ayr* (Edinburgh, 1793)

Galt, John, and James Kinsley, eds., *Annals of the Parish* (Oxford, 1980)

Gibson, A. J. S., and T. C. Smout, *Prices, Food and Wages in Scotland 1550–1760* (Cambridge, 1995)

Gibson, Rob, *The Highland Clearances Trail* (Edinburgh, 1983)

——, *Toppling the Duke: Outrage on Ben Bhraggie* (Evanton, 1996)

——, *The Highland Clearances Trail* (Edinburgh, 2006)

Goodare, Julian, *The Government of Scotland 1560–1625* (Oxford, 2004)

Gordon, Alastair G., *A Sutherland Trail: A History of the Gordons of Dallagan, Griarnachary and Drumearn* (London, 2005)

Gore, John, ed., *Creevey's Life and Times* (London, 1934)

Gouriévidis, Laurence, *The Dynamics of Heritage: History, Memory and the Highland Clearances* (Farnham, 2010)

Gray, Malcolm, *The Highland Economy 1750–1850* (Edinburgh, 1957)

——, 'North East Agriculture and the Labour Force, 1790–1875', in A. A. MacLaren, ed., *Social Class in Scotland: Past and Present* (Edinburgh, 1976)

——, 'Migration in the Rural Lowlands of Scotland, 1750–1850', in T. M. Devine and D. Dickson, eds., *Ireland and Scotland, 1600–1850* (Edinburgh, 1983)

——, 'The Social Impact of Agrarian Change in the Rural Lowlands', in T. M. Devine and R. Mitchison, eds., *People and Society in Scotland*, vol. 1: *1760–1830* (Edinburgh, 1988)

——, *Scots on the Move: Scots Migrants 1750–1914* (Dundee, 1990)

Green, Daniel, ed., *Cobbett's Tour in Scotland* (Aberdeen, 1984 edn)

Greenshields, J. B., *Annals of the Parish of Lesmahagow* (Edinburgh, 1864)

Grimble, Ian, *The Trial of Patrick Sellar* (London, 1963)

Groves, Percy, *History of the 93rd Sutherland Highlanders* (Edinburgh, 1895)

Hamilton, H., *Life and Labour on an Aberdeenshire Estate, 1735–50* (Aberdeen, 1946)

——, *An Economic History of Scotland in the Eighteenth Century* (Oxford, 1963)

Handley, J., *Scottish Farming in the Eighteenth Century* (Edinburgh, 1953)

——, *The Agricultural Revolution in Scotland* (Glasgow, 1963)

Harper, M., *Emigration from North-East Scotland* (Aberdeen, 1988)

Headrick, J., *Agriculture of Angus* (Edinburgh, 1813)

Heron, Robert, *Observations made in a Journey through the Western Counties of Scotland*, vol. II (Perth, 1793)

Hesse, David, *Warrior Dreams: Playing Scotsmen in Mainland Europe* (Manchester, 2014)

Hobsbawm, E. J., et al., eds., *Peasants in History* (Oxford, 1980)

——, 'Scottish Reformers of the Eighteenth Century and Capitalist Agriculture', in E. J. Hobsbawm et al., eds., *Peasants in History* (Oxford, 1980)

Holderness, B. A., *Pre-Industrial Britain: Economy and Society, 1500–1700* (London 1976)

——, 'Prices, Productivity and Output', in G. E. Mingay, ed., *The Agrarian History of England and Wales, vol. VI, 1750–1850* (Cambridge, 1989)

Hopkins, P., *Glencoe and the End of the Highland War* (Edinburgh, 1990)

Houston, R. A., and I. D. Whyte, eds., *Scottish Society, 1500–1800* (Cambridge, 1989)

Hume, John R., and Michael S. Moss, *Scotch Whisky: A History of the Scotch Whisky Distilling Industry* (Edinburgh, 2000)

Hunter, James, *The Making of the Crofting Community* (Edinburgh, 1976 and new edn 2000)

——, *A Dance Called America: The Scottish Highlands, the United States and Canada* (Edinburgh, 1994)

——, *Last of the Free: A History of the Highlands and Islands of Scotland* (Edinburgh, 1999)

——, *Scottish Exodus: Travels Among a Worldwide Clan* (Edinburgh, 2005)

——, *Set Adrift upon the World: The Sutherland Clearances* (Edinburgh, 2015)

Johnson, Samuel, *A Journey to the Western Islands of Scotland in 1773* (Oxford, 1924 edn)

Johnston, Thomas, *History of the Working Classes in Scotland* (Glasgow, c.1920)

——, *Our Scots Noble Families* (Glasgow, new edn 1999)

Jonsson, Fredrik Albritton, *Enlightenment's Frontier: The Scottish Highlands and the Origins of Environmentalism* (New Haven, Conn., 2013)

Keith, T. S., *General View of the Agriculture of the County of Aberdeenshire* (Edinburgh, 1814)

Kennedy, Allan, *Governing Gaeldom: The Scottish Highlands and the Restoration State, 1660–1688* (Leiden, 2014)

Knox, John, *A View of the British Empire more Especially Scotland* (London, 1785)

Knox, Robert, *The Races of Men* (Philadelphia, 1850)

A. Kussmaul, *A General View of the Rural Economy of England, 1538–1840* (Cambridge, 1990)

Leneman, L., *Living in Atholl* (Edinburgh, 1986)

——, ed., *Perspectives of Scottish Social History* (Aberdeen, 1988)

Lenman, B., *The Jacobite Risings in Britain 1689–1746* (London, 1980)

Lewis, G. C., *On Local Disturbances in Ireland and on the Irish Church Question* (London, 1836)

Lindsay, Nick, *Dalreavoch-Sciberscross, Strathbrora, Sutherland: A Report of an Archaeological Survey* (Brora, 2009)

Lockhart, D. G., 'The Planned Villages', in M. L. Parry and T. R. Slater, eds., *The Making of the Scottish Countryside* (London, 1980)

Logue, K. J., *Popular Disturbances in Scotland, 1780–1815* (Edinburgh, 1980)

Lythe, S. G. E., *The Economy of Scotland in Its European Setting, 1550–1625* (Edinburgh, 1960)

McCarthy, Angela, ed., *A Global Clan* (London, 2006)

——, 'The Scottish Diaspora since 1815', in T. M. Devine and Jenny Wormald, eds., *The Oxford Handbook of Modern Scottish History* (Oxford, 2012)

MacCoinnich, Aonghas, 'Siol Torcail and Their Lordship in the Sixteenth Century', in Islands Book Trust, *Crossing the Minch: Exploring the Links between Skye and the Outer Hebrides* (Port of Ness, 2008)

——, *Native and Stranger: Plantation and Civility in the North Atlantic World: The Case of the Northern Hebrides, 1570–1637* (Leiden, 2015)

MacColl, Allan W., *Land, Faith and the Crofting Community: Christianity and Social Criticism in the Highlands of Scotland, 1843–1893* (Edinburgh, 2006)

McCrone, David, *The New Sociology of Scotland* (London, 2017)

Macdonald, James, *General View of the Agriculture of the Hebrides* (Edinburgh, 1811)

McDonald, R. A., *The Kingdom of the Isles. Scotland's Western Seaboard c.1000–c.1336* (East Linton, 1997)

MacAskill, John, ed., *The Highland Destitution of 1837* (Woodbridge, 2013)

MacDonnell, Margaret, ed., *The Emigrant Experience: Songs of Highland Emigrants in North America* (Toronto, 1982)

McGeachy, Robert A. A., *Argyll 1730–1850* (Edinburgh, 2005)

McGowan, Douglas, ed., *The Stonemason: Donald MacLeod's Chronicle of Scotland's Highland Clearances* (Westport, Conn., 2001)

MacGregor, Martin, 'Gaelic Barbarity and Scottish Identity in the Later Middle Ages', in Dauvit Broun and Martin MacGregor, eds., *Mìorun Mòr nan Gall, 'The Great Ill-Will of the Lowlandes?' Lowland Perceptions of the Highlands, Medieval and Modern* (Glasgow, 2007)

——, 'Civilising Gaelic Scotland: The Scottish Isles and the Stewart Empire', in Éamonn Ó Ciardha and Micheál Ó Siochrú, eds., *The Plantation of Ulster: Ideology and Practice* (Manchester, 2012)

Macinnes, Allan I., 'Scottish Gaeldom: The First Phase of Clearance', in T. M. Devine and Rosalind Mitchison, eds., *People and Society in Scotland*, vol. 1, *1760–1830* (Edinburgh, reprinted 1991)

——, *Clanship, Commerce and the House of Stuart* (East Linton, 1996)

——, 'Commercial Landlordism and Clearance in the Scottish Highlands: The Case of Arichonan', in J. Pan-Montojo and F. Pedersen, eds., *Communities in European History: Representations, Jurisdictions, Conflicts* (Pisa, 2007)

——, 'A' Ghaidhealtachd and the Jacobites', in D. Forsyth, ed., *Bonnie Prince Charlie and the Jacobites* (Edinburgh, 2017)

MacInnes, John, *The Evangelical Movement in the Highlands of Scotland* (Aberdeen, 1951)

——, *Duathchas nan Gàidheal: Selected Essays of John MacInnes*, ed. Michael Newton (Edinburgh, 2006)

MacKay, Alexander, *Sketches of Sutherland Characters* (Edinburgh, 1889)

MacKay, Angus, ed., *Autobiographical Journal of John MacDonald, Schoolmaster and Soldier, 1770–1830* (Edinburgh, 1906)

——, *The Book of MacKay* (Edinburgh, 1906)

MacKay, Robert, *History of the House and Clan of MacKay* (Edinburgh, 1829)

Mackenzie, Alexander, *The History of the Highland Clearances* (Inverness, 1883)

——, ed., *The Trial of Patrick Sellar* (Inverness, 1883)

MacKenzie, George, *General View of the Agriculture of the Counties of Ross and Cromarty* (London, 1834)

MacKenzie, John, ed., *Popular Imperialism and the Military 1850–1950* (Manchester, 1992)

MacKenzie John M., and T. M. Devine, eds., *Scotland and the British Empire* (Oxford, 2011)

Mackillop, Andrew, '*More Fruitful Than the Soil': Army, Empire and the Scottish Highlands, 1715–1815* (East Linton, 2000)

MacLaren, A. A., ed., *Social Class in Scotland, Past and Present* (Edinburgh, 1976)

McLean, Marianne, *The People of Glengarry: Highlanders in Transition, 1745–1820* (Montreal, 1991)

MacLeod, Donald, *Gloomy Memories in the Highlands of Scotland* (Glasgow, 1892)

MacLeod, Norman, *Reminiscences of a Highland Parish* (London, 1863)

Macphail, I. M. M., *The Crofters' War* (Stornoway, 1989)

Martin, M., *A Description of the Western Isles of Scotland* (2nd edn, Edinburgh, 1970)

Meek, Donald, *Tuath is Tighearna: Tenants and Landlords* (Edinburgh, 1995)

Miller, Hugh, *Sutherland as It was and Is* (Edinburgh, 1843)

——, *My Schools and Schoolmasters* (Edinburgh, 1854)

Miller, James, *The Gathering Stream: The Story of the Moray Firth* (Edinburgh, 2012)

Mingay, G. E., ed., *The Agrarian History of England and Wales*, vol. VI: *1750–1850* (Cambridge, 1989)

——, 'Introduction', in G. E. Mingay, ed., *The Agrarian History of England and Wales*, vol. VI: *1750–1850* (Cambridge, 1989)

Mitchell, Joseph, *Reminiscences of My Life in the Highlands*, 2 vols. (London, 1883)

Mitchison, Rosalind, *Agricultural Sir John: The Life of Sir John Sinclair of Ulbster* (London, 1962)

——, 'The Government and the Highlands, 1707–1745', in N. T. Phillipson and R. Mitchison, eds., *Scotland in the Age of Improvement* (Edinburgh, 1970)

——, *A History of Scotland* (London, 1970)

——, 'The Highland Clearances', *Scottish Economic and Social History*, vol. 1 (1981)

——, 'The Poor Law', in T. M. Devine and R. Mitchison, eds., *People and Society in Scotland*, vol. I: *1760–1830* (Edinburgh, 1988)

——, *The Old Poor Law in Scotland* (Edinburgh, 2000)

—— and P. Roebuck, eds., *Economy and Society in Scotland and Ireland 1500–1939* (Edinburgh, 1988)

Mokyr, Joel, *The Enlightened Economy: Britain and the Industrial Revolution, 1700–1850* (London, 2009)

Morton, Graeme, and Trevor Griffiths, eds., *A History of Everyday Life in Scotland 1800 to 1900* (Edinburgh, 2010)

Moss, Michael, *The Magnificent Castle of Culzean and the Kennedy Family* (Edinburgh, 2002)

Mulock, Thomas, *The Western Highlands and Islands of Scotland Socially Considered* (Edinburgh, 1850)

Munro, R. W., and Jean Munro, *Tain through the Centuries* (Edinburgh, 2005)

Naismith, J., *General View of the Agriculture of the County of Clydesdale* (Edinburgh, 1794)

Neat, Timothy, *The Horseman's Word* (Edinburgh, 2002)

Nenadic, Stana, 'The Rise of the Urban Middle Classes', in T. M. Devine and R. Mitchison, eds., *People and Society in Scotland*, vol. I: *1760–1830* (Edinburgh, 1988)

——, *Lairds and Luxury: The Highland Gentry in Eighteenth-Century Scotland* (Edinburgh, 2007)

——, ed., *Scots in London in the Eighteenth Century* (Lewisburg, Pa, 2010)

Newby, Andrew, *Ireland, Radicalism and the Scottish Highlands, c.1870–1912* (Edinburgh, 2006)

Osterhammel, Jürgen, *Colonialism: A Theoretical Overview* (Princeton, 2005)

Overton, M., 'Agricultural Revolution? Development of the Agrarian Economy in Early Modern England', in A. R. H. Baker and D. J. Gregory, eds., *Explorations in Historical Geography* (Cambridge, 1984)

Parker, A. W., *Scottish Highlanders in Colonial Georgia* (Athens, Ga, 1997)

Parrish, Woodbine, *Two Reports on the Subject of Illicit Distillation in Scotland* (London, 1816)

Parry, M. L., and T. R. Slater, eds., *The Making of the Scottish Countryside* (London, 1980)

Paterson, Audrey, 'The New Poor Law in Nineteenth Century Scotland', in Derek Fraser, ed., *The New Poor Law in the Nineteenth Century* (London, 1976)

Paton, David, *The Clergy and the Clearances: The Church and the Highland Crisis, 1790–1850* (Edinburgh, 2006)

Phillipson, N. T., and R. Mitchison, eds., *Scotland in the Age of Improvement* (Edinburgh, 1970)

Pinkerton, John, *An Enquiry into the History of Scotland Preceding the Reign of Malcolm III or the Year 1056 Including the Authentic History of that Period*, 2 vols. (London, 1794)

Pittock, Murray, *Culloden* (Oxford, 2016)

Pollard, Tony, ed., *Culloden: The History and Archaeology of the Last Clan Battle* (Barnsley, 2009)

Porter, J. H., 'The Development of Rural Society', in G. E. Mingay, ed., *The Agrarian History of England and Wales*, vol. VI: *1750–1850* (Cambridge, 1989)

Prebble, John, *The Highland Clearances* (Harmondsworth, 1969)

Pritchett, John P., *The Red River Valley: A Regional Study* (New Haven, Conn., 1942)

Ray, Celeste, *Highland Heritage* (Chapel Hill, NC, 2001)

Richards, Eric, *The Leviathan of Wealth: The Sutherland Fortune in the Industrial Revolution* (London, 1973)

——, 'Patterns of Highland Discontent, 1790–1860', in R. Quinault and R. Stevenson, eds., *Popular Protest and Public Order* (London, 1974)

——, *A History of the Highland Clearances* (Edinburgh, 1985)

——, *Patrick Sellar and the Highland Clearances: Homicide, Eviction and the Price of Progress* (Edinburgh, 1999)

——, *The Highland Clearances* (Edinburgh, 2000)

——, *Debating the Highland Clearances* (Edinburgh, 2007)

——, *The Highland Clearances: People, Landlords and Rural Turmoil* (Edinburgh, 2008)

——and Monica Clough, *Cromartie: Highland Life 1650–1914* (Aberdeen, 1989)

Roberts, J. L., *Clan, King and Covenant* (Edinburgh, 2000)

Robertson, James, *General View of the Agriculture in the Southern Districts of the County of Perth* (London, 1794)

Robertson, P., *Report of the Trial of Patrick Sellar* (Edinburgh, 1816)

Revd Mr Roger, *General View of the Agriculture of Angus* (Edinburgh, 1794)

Ross, Alasdair, 'Improvement on the Grant Estates in Strathspey in the Later Eighteenth Century', in Richard W. Hoyle, ed., *Custom, Improvement and the Landscape in Early Modern Britain* (Farnham, 2011)

Ross, Walter, *A Discourse upon the Removing of Tenants* (Edinburgh, 1782)

Roy, William, *The Great Map: The Military Survey of Scotland 1747–55* (reproduced Edinburgh, 2007)

Sage, Donald, *Memorabilia Domestica: Parish Life in the North of Scotland* (Wick, 1899)

Sellar, E. M., *Recollections and Impressions* (Edinburgh, 1908)

Sellar, Patrick, 'Farm Reports: County of Sutherland: Strathnaver, Morvich and Culmaily Farms', in John F. Burke, ed., *British Husbandry Exhibiting the Farm Practice in Various Parts of the United Kingdom* (London, 1834)

Sellar, Thomas, *The Sutherland Evictions of 1814: Former and Recent Statements Respecting Them Examined* (London, 1883)

Semple, D., ed., *Renfrewshire Poll Tax Returns* (Glasgow, 1864)

Shanin, T., ed., *Peasants and Peasant Societies* (London, 1971)

Shaw, J. S., *The Management of Scottish Society, 1707–1764* (Edinburgh, 1983)

Sibbald, Sir Robert, *Provision for the Poor in Time of Dearth and Scarcity* (Edinburgh, 1699)

Simmons, Andrew, ed., *Burt's Letters from the North of Scotland and as related by Edmund Burt* (Edinburgh, 1998 edn)

Sinclair, Sir John, ed., *The Statistical Account of Scotland, 1791–97* (Edinburgh, 1791–7), 21 vols. New edn by I. Grant and D. J. Withrington (Wakefield, 1975–9)

——, *General View of the Agriculture of the Northern Counties and Islands of Scotland* (Edinburgh, 1795)

——, *Analysis of the Statistical Account of Scotland* (Edinburgh, 1825)

Slater, T. R., 'The Mansion and Policy', in M. L. Parry and T. R. Slater, eds., *The Making of the Scottish Countryside* (London, 1980)

Smith, Donald C., *Passive Obedience and Prophetic Protest: Social Criticism in the Scottish Church, 1830–1945* (New York, 1987)

Smout, T. C., *A History of the Scottish People* (London, 1969)

——, 'The Landowner and the Planned Village in Scotland, 1730–1830', in N. T. Phillipson and R. Mitchison, eds., *Scotland in the Age of Improvement* (Edinburgh, 1970)

——, 'Famine and Famine-Relief in Scotland', in L. M. Cullen and T. C. Smout, eds., *Comparative Aspects of Irish and Scottish Economic and Social Development, 1690–1900* (Edinburgh, 1977)

——, 'The Strange Intervention of Edward Twistleton: Paisley in Depression, 1841–3', in T. C. Smout, ed., *The Search for Wealth and Stability* (London, 1979)

——, 'Land and Sea: The Environment', in T. M. Devine and Jenny Wormald, eds., *The Oxford Handbook of Modern Scottish History* (Oxford, 2012)

Somers, R., *Letters from the Highlands* (London, 1848)

Somerville, A., *The Autobiography of a Working Man* (London, 1848)

Speck, W. A., *The Butcher* (London, 1981)

Sprott, Gavin, *Robert Burns: Pride and Passion* (Edinburgh, 1996)

Spurlock, R. S., *Cromwell and Scotland* (Edinburgh, 2007)

Stevenson, D., *Alasdair MacColla and the Highland Problem in the Seventeenth Century* (Edinburgh, 1980)

Stewart, David, *Sketches of the Character, Manners and Present State of the Highlanders of Scotland*, 2 vols. (Edinburgh, 1822)

Stowe, Harriet B., *Sunny Memories of Foreign Lands*, 2 vols. (London, 1854)

Streets, Heather, *Martial Races* (Manchester, 2004)

Stuart, John, ed., *List of Pollable Persons within the Shire of Aberdeen, 1696* (Aberdeen, 1844), 2 vols.

Sutherland, Alexander, *A Summer Ramble in the North Highlands* (Edinburgh, 1825)

Symon, J. A., *Scottish Farming, Past and Present* (Edinburgh, 1959)

Thompson, F. G., *The Highlands and Islands* (London, 1974)

Thomson, James, *The Value and Importance of the Scottish Fisheries* (London, 1849)

Thomson, D. C., and Ian Grimble, eds., *The Future of the Highlands* (London, 1968)

Timperley, L., 'The Pattern of Landholding in Eighteenth-Century Scotland', in M. L. Parry and T. R. Slater, eds., *The Making of the Scottish Countryside* (London, 1980)

Tindley, Annie, *The Sutherland Estate, 1850–1920: Aristocratic Decline, Estate Management and Land Reform* (Edinburgh, 2010)

Treble, J. H., 'The Standard of Living of the Working Class', in T. M. Devine and R. Mitchison, eds., *People and Society in Scotland*, vol. I: *1760–1830* (Edinburgh, 1988)

Trevor-Roper, H. R., 'The Invention of Tradition: The Highland Tradition of Scotland', in E. J. Hobsbawm and T. Ranger, eds., *The Invention of Tradition* (Cambridge, 1983)

Whatley, C. A., 'The Experience of Work', in T. M. Devine and R. Mitchison, eds., *People and Society in Scotland*, vol. I: *1760–1830* (Edinburgh, 1988)

——, 'How Tame were the Scottish Lowlanders during the Eighteenth Century?', in T. M. Devine, ed., *Conflict and Stability in Scottish Society, 1760–1850* (Edinburgh, 1990)

Whetstone, A. E., *Scottish County Government in the Eighteenth and Nineteenth Centuries* (Edinburgh, 1981)

Whittington, G., 'Agriculture and Society in Lowland Scotland, 1750–1870', in G. Whittington and I. D. Whyte, eds., *An Historical Geography of Scotland* (London, 1983)

—— and I. D. Whyte, eds., *An Historical Geography of Scotland* (London, 1983)

Whyte, Ian, *Agriculture and Society in Seventeenth-Century Scotland* (Edinburgh, 1979)

—— and K. A. Whyte, 'Some Aspects of the Structure of Rural Society in Seventeenth Century Lowland Scotland', in T. M. Devine and D. Dickson, eds., *Ireland and Scotland, 1600–1850* (Edinburgh, 1983)

—— and ——, 'Poverty and Prosperity in a Seventeenth Century Scottish Farming Community', in R. Mitchison and P. Roebuck, eds., *Scotland and Ireland: A Comparative Study of Development* (Edinburgh, 1987)

Wight, A., *Present State of Husbandry in Scotland* (Edinburgh, 1778).

Wightman, Andy, *The Poor Had No Lawyers* (Edinburgh, 2010)

Withers, Charles W. J., 'Rural Protest in the Highlands of Scotland and in Ireland, 1850–1930', in R. A. Houston and R. J. Morris, eds., *Conflict, Identity and Economic Development: Ireland and Scotland, 1600–1939* (Preston, 1995)

——, *Urban Highlanders* (East Linton, 1998)

Withrington, D. J., 'Schooling, Literacy and Society', in T. M. Devine and R. Mitchison, eds., *People and Society in Scotland*, vol. I: *1760–1830* (Edinburgh, 1988)

Wolf, E. R., 'On Peasant Rebellions', in T. Shanin, ed., *Peasants and Peasant Societies* (London, 1971)

Womack, Peter, *Improvement and Romance – Constructing the Myth of the Scottish Highlands* (Basingstoke, 1989)

ARTICLES

Adam, R. J., 'Agricultural Statistics of Scotland, 1855–58', *Transactions of the Highland and Agricultural Society*, new series (1855–7; 1857–9)

Adams, I. H., 'The Land Surveyor and His Influence on the Scottish Rural Landscape', *SGM*, 84 (1968)

—— and I. D. Whyte, 'The Agricultural Revolution in Scotland: Contributions to the Debate', *Area*, 9 (1977)

——, —— and M. L. Parry, 'The Agricultural Revolution in Scotland: Contributions to the Debate', *Area*, 10 (1978)

Anon., 'The Highlands: Men, Sheep and Deer', *Edinburgh Review*, 106 (1957)

Anon., 'Report on the Disease of the Potato Crop in Scotland in the Year 1845', *Transactions of the Highland and Agricultural Society*, new series (1845–7)

Anon., 'Reports on the Disease of the Potato Crop in Scotland for the Year 1846', *Transactions of the Highland and Agricultural Society*, new series (1847–9)

Aymard, Maurice, 'The History of Nutrition and Economic History', *Journal of European Economic History*, 2 (1973)

Bangor-Jones, Malcolm, 'Sheep Farming in Sutherland in the 18th Century', *Agricultural History Review*, 50 (2002)

Black, J., 'On the Agriculture of Aberdeen and Banff Shires', *Transactions of the Highland and Agricultural Society, 1870–1*, 4th series, III, pp. 33–4

——, 'Report on Cottage Accommodation in the District of Buchan, Aberdeenshire', *Transactions of the Highland and Agricultural Society*, 5 (1851–3)

Brodie, P., 'On Green Crops', *Prize Essays and Transactions of the Highland Society of Scotland*, I (1799)

Cathcart, Alison, 'The Statutes of Iona: The Archipelagic Context', *Journal of British Studies*, 49:1 (2009)

Clark, D., 'On the Agriculture of the County of Argyll', *Transactions of the Highland and Agricultural Society*, 4th series, X (1878)

Clerk, Duncan, 'On the Agriculture of the County of Argyll', *Transactions of the Highland and Agricultural Society*, 4th series, X (1878)

Cregeen, Eric R., and Annie Tindley, 'The Creation of the Crofting Townships in Tiree', *Journal of Scottish Historical Studies*, 35:2 (2015)

Denton, J. B., 'Land Drainage etc., by Loans', *Journal of the Royal Agricultural Society of England*, 4:ii (1868)

Devine, T. M., 'The Rise and Fall of Illicit Whisky-Making in Northern Scotland, 1780–1840', *Scottish Historical Review* 54 (1975)

——, 'Temporary Migration and the Scottish Highlands in the Nineteenth Century', *Economic History Review*, 2nd series, XXXII (1979)

——, 'Highland Migration to Lowland Scotland, 1760–1860', *Scottish Historical Review*, 62 (1983)

——, 'The Union of 1707 and Scottish Development', *Scottish Economic and Social History*, 5 (1985)

——, 'The Highland Clearances', *Recent Findings in Economic and Social History*, 4 (1987)

Dodgshon, R. A., 'The Removal of Runrig in Roxburghshire, 1680–1766', *Scottish Studies*, 16 (1972)

——, 'The Nature and Development of Infield–Outfield in Scotland', *Transactions of the Institute of British Geographers*, 59 (1973)

——, 'Farming in Roxburghshire and Berwickshire on the Eve of Improvement', *Scottish History Review*, LIV, no. 158 (1975)

——, 'Runrig and the Communal Origins of Property in Land', *Juridical Review*, 20 (1975)

——, 'Towards an Understanding and Definition of Runrig: The Evidence for Roxburghshire and Berwickshire', *TIBG*, 64 (1975)

——, 'Coping with Risk: Subsistence Crises in the Scottish Highlands and Islands, 1600–1800', in *Rural History*, 15:1 (2004)

Fairhurst, Horace, 'The Surveys for the Sutherland Clearances', *Scottish Studies*, 8 (1964)

——, 'Rossal: A Deserted Township in Strathnaver', *Proceedings of the Society of Antiquaries in Scotland*, 100 (1967)

Fenton, A., 'The Rural Economy of East Lothian in the Seventeenth and Eighteenth Centuries', *Transactions of East Lothian Antiquarian and Field Naturalists Society*, 9 (1963)

Flinn, M. W., 'Trends in Real Wages, 1750–1850', *Economic History Review*, 2nd series, XXVII (1974)

Geddes, A., 'The Changing Landscape of the Lothians, 1600–1800, as Revealed in Old Estate Plans', *SGM*, 54 (1938)

Gibson, A., 'Proletarianisation? The Transition to Full-Time Labour on a Scottish Estate, 1723–1787', *Continuity and Change*, 53 (1990)

Gould, J. D., 'European Inter-Continental Emigration, 1815–1914: Patterns and Causes', *Journal of European History*, 8 (1979)

Gouriévidis, Laurence, 'Patrick Sellar', *Études Écossaises*, 10 (2005)

Gray, Malcolm, 'The Highland Potato Famine of the 1840s', *Economic History Review*, 2nd series, 7 (1954–5)

——, 'The Consolidation of the Crofting System', *Agricultural History Review*, 5 (1957)

——, 'Scottish Emigration: The Social Impact of Agrarian Change in the Rural Lowlands, 1775–1875', *Perspectives of American History*, VII (1974)

Harrison, B., 'Philanthropy and the Victorians', *Victorian Studies* (1966)

Hart, Jenifer, 'Sir Charles Trevelyan at the Treasury', *English Historical Review*, LXXV (1960)

Horsman, Reginald, 'Origins of Racial Anglo-Saxonism in Great Britain before 1850', *Journal of the History of Ideas*, XXXVII (1976)

Houston, R. A., 'Geographical Mobility in Scotland, 1652–1811', *Journal of Historical Geography*, 11 (1985)

Hunt, E. H., and F. W. Botham, 'Wages in Britain during the Industrial Revolution', *Economic History Review*, 2nd series, XL (1987)

Hunter, James, 'Sheep and Deer: Highland Sheep Farming, 1850–1900', *Northern Scotland*, 2 (1975)

James, Steve, 'The Flawed Legacy of Scottish Popular Historian John Prebble', https://www.wsws.org/en/articles/2001/03/preb-m21.html, accessed 17 March 2018

Jones, M. A., 'The Background to Emigration from Great Britain in the Nineteenth Century', *Perspectives in American History*, 7 (1973)

Kay, G., 'The Landscape of Improvement: A Case Study of Agricultural Change in North-East Scotland', *SGM*, 78 (1962)

Kidd, Colin, 'Race, Empire and the Limits of Nineteenth Century Scottish Nationhood', *The Historical Journal*, 46:4 (2003)

Ladurie, E. Le Roy, 'L'aménorrhée de famine (XVIIe–XXe siècles)', *Annales*, 24 (1969)

Lebon, J. H. G., 'The Face of the Countryside in Central Ayrshire during the Eighteenth and Nineteenth Centuries', *SGM*, 62 (1946)

——, 'The Process of Enclosure in the Western Lowlands', *SGM*, 62 (1946)

Little, J. L., 'Agricultural Improvement and Highland Clearance: The Isle of Arran 1766–1829', *Scottish Economic and Social History*, vol. 19 (1999)

Lockhart, D. G., 'Sources for Studies of Migration to Estate Villages in North East Scotland', *Local Historian*, 14 (1980)

Macdonald, James, 'On the Agriculture of the County of Sutherland', *Transactions of the Highland and Agricultural Society*, 4th series, XII (1880)

Macdonald, William, 'On the Agriculture of Inverness-shire', *Transactions of the Highland and Agricultural Society*, 4th series, IV (1872)

McGregor, A., 'On the Advantages of a Government Grant for Emigration from the Highlands and Islands of Scotland', *Quarterly Journal of Agriculture*, XI (1840–41)

MacGregor, Martin, 'The Statutes of Iona – Text and Context', *Innes Review*, 57:2 (2006)

Macinnes, A. I., 'Crown, Clan and *Fine*: The "Civilising" of Scottish Gaeldom', *Northern Scotland*, 13 (1993)

MacInnes, John, 'A Gaelic Song of the Sutherland Clearances', *Scottish Studies*, 8 (1964)

McIntosh, Alastair, 'Wild Scots and Buffoon History', *The Land*, 1 (2006)

McKay, Margaret, 'Nineteenth Century Tiree Emigrant Communities in Ontario', *Oral History Journal*, 9 (1981)

Mckichan, Finlay, 'Lord Seaforth and Highland Estate Management in the First Phase of Clearance', *Scottish Historical Review*, 86 (2007)

Mackillop, Andrew, 'The Political Culture of the Scottish Highlands from Culloden to Waterloo', *Historical Journal*, 46 (2003)

Mackinnon, Iain, 'Colonialism and the Highland Clearances', *Northern Scotland*, 8 (2017)

Maclauchlan, Thomas, 'The Influence of Emigration on the Social Condition of the Highlands', *Transactions of the National Association for the Promotion of Social Science* (1863)

Maclean, Samuel (Sorley), 'The Poetry of the Clearances', *Transactions of the Gaelic Society of Inverness*, vol. 38 (1937–41)

Macmillan, D. S., 'Sir Charles Trevelyan and the Highland and Island Emigration Society, 1849–1859', *Royal Australian Historical Society Journal*, XLIX (1963)

Mearns, Alexander B., 'The Minister and the Bailiff: A Study of Presbyterian Clergy in the Northern Highlands during the Clearances', *Scottish Church History Society Records*, 29 (1990)

Meuvret, J., 'French Demographic Crises', in D. V. Glass and D. E. C. Eversley, eds., *Population in History* (London, 1965)

Mitchison, R., 'The Movements of Scottish Corn Prices in the Seventeenth and Eighteenth Centuries', *Economic History Review*, 2nd series, XVIII (1965)

——, 'The Making of the Old Scottish Poor Law', *Past and Present*, 63 (1974)

Morgan, V., 'Agricultural Wage Rates in Late Eighteenth Century Scotland', *Economic History Review*, 2nd series, XXIV (1971)

Morton, A. S., 'The Levellers of Galloway', *Transactions of the Dumfriesshire and Galloway Natural History Society and Antiquarian Society*, 3rd series, vol. 19 (1936)

Murdoch, Alexander, ed., 'A Scottish Document Concerning Emigration to North Carolina in 1772', *North Carolina Historical Review*, 67 (1990)

Newsome, Albert R., 'Records of Emigrants from England and Scotland to North Carolina, 1774–75', *North Carolina Historical Review*, 11 (1954)

Parry, M. L., 'Secular Climatic Change and Marginal Agriculture', *TIBG*, 64 (1975)

——, 'The Abandonment of Upland Settlement in Southern Scotland', *Scottish Geographical Magazine*, 92 (1976)

—— and D. Mill, 'A Scottish Agricultural Revolution?', *Area*, 8 (1976)

David Paton, ' "Brought to a Wilderness": The Rev. David MacKenzie of Farr and the Sutherland Clearances', *Northern Scotland*, 13 (1993)

R. Perren, 'Markets and Marketing', in G. E. Mingay, ed., *The Agrarian History of England and Wales*, vol. VI: *1750–1850* (Cambridge, 1989)

Post, J. P. D., 'Famine, Mortality and Epidemic Disease in the Process of Modernisation', *Economic History Review*, 2nd series, XXIX (1976)

Prevost, W. A. J., 'Letters Reporting the Rising of the Levellers in 1724', in *Transactions of the Dumfriesshire and Galloway Natural History Society and Antiquarian Society*, 3rd series, vol. 44 (1967)

Richards, Eric, 'Highland Emigrants to South Australia in the 1850s', *Northern Scotland*, 5 (1982)

——, 'The *Military Register* and the Pursuit of Patrick Sellar', *Scottish Economic and Social History*, 16 (1996)

——, 'Patrick Sellar and His World', *Transactions of the Gaelic Society of Inverness*, 61 (1999)

Robinson, W. P., 'Richard Oswald the Peacemaker', *Ayrshire Archaeological and Natural History Society Collections*, 2nd series, III (1959)

'Sir John Clerk of Penicuik's Journie into Galloway in 1721', *Transactions of the Dumfriesshire and Galloway Natural History and Antiquarian Society*, 3rd series, vol. 41 (1962–3)

Skirving, R. S., 'On the Agriculture of East Lothian', *Transactions of the Highland and Agricultural Society*, 4th series, V (1873)

Smout, T. C., 'Scottish Landowners and Economic Growth, 1650–1850', *Scottish Journal of Political Economy*, 11 (1964)

——, 'Tours in the Scottish Highlands from the Eighteenth to the Twentieth Centuries', *Northern Scotland*, 5 (1983)

—— and A. Fenton, 'Scottish Agriculture before the Improvers – an Exploration', *Agricultural History Review*, 13 (1965)

Stewart, David, 'Observations on the Origins and Cause of Smuggling in the Highlands and Islands of Scotland', *Quarterly Review of Agriculture*, 1 (1828)

Third, B. M. W., 'Changing Landscape and Social Structure in the Scottish Lowlands as Revealed by Eighteenth Century Estate Plans', *SGM*, 71 (1955)

——, 'The Significance of Scottish Estate Plans and Associated Documents', *Scottish Studies*, I (1957)

Thompson, E. P., 'English Trade Unionism and Other Labour Movements before 1790', *Society for the Study of Labour History*, Bulletin 17 (1968)

Tindley, Annie, 'The Creation of the Crofting Townships in Tiree: Introductory Note', *Journal of Scottish Historical Studies*, vol. 35 (2015)

—— and Eric Richards, 'Turmoil among the Crofters: Evander McIver and the "Highland Question" 1873–1903', *Agricultural History Review* 60:2 (2012)

Walker, B., 'The "Great Rebuilding" on a Scottish Estate', *SGM*, 101:3 (1985)

Walker, Stephen P., 'Agents of Dispossession and Acculturation: Edinburgh Accountants and the Highland Clearances', *Critical Perspectives in Accounting*, 14 (2003)

Watson, J. A. S., 'The Rise and Development of the Sheep Industry in the Highlands and the North of Scotland', *Transactions of the Highland and Agricultural Society of Scotland*, 5th series, 44 (1932)

Wheeler, Philip T., 'The Sutherland Crofting System', *Scottish Studies*, 8 (1964)

Whittington, G., 'Was There a Scottish Agricultural Revolution?', *Area*, 7 (1975)

Whyte, I. D., and K. A. Whyte, 'Continuity and Change in a Seventeenth Century Scottish Farming Community', *Agricultural History Review*, 32 (1984)

Withers, Charles W. J., 'Highland Migration to Dundee, Perth and Stirling, 1753–1891', *Journal of Historical Geography*, 4 (1985)

——, ' "Give us land and plenty of it": The Ideological Basis to Land and Landscape in the Scottish Highlands', *Landscape History* (1990)

——, 'Place, Memory, Monument: Memorialising the Past in Contemporary Highland Scotland', *Ecumene*, 3 (1996)

——, 'Landscape, Memory, History: *Gloomy Memories* and the Nineteenth-Century Scottish Highlands', *Scottish Geographical Journal*, 121 (2005)

Wordie, J. R., 'The Chronology of English Enclosure, 1500–1914', *Economic History Review*, 2nd series, XXXVI (1983)

Acknowledgements

I have incurred several personal and academic debts in the course of researching and writing this book.

My darling wife, Catherine, and all our family, have as usual been unstinting in their loving and patient support, even when their husband, father and grandfather drifted off yet again to reflect on some puzzling questions about the past.

Ideas for this book have been fashioned, rejected and refined over many years of teaching undergraduates and supervising doctoral students at three Scottish universities: Strathclyde, 1969–97; Aberdeen, 1998–2004; and Edinburgh, 2005–14. There is nothing like daily interaction with bright and committed students to enable thinking and rethinking on the essential issues of a historical project.

I also wish to extend warm thanks to members of my family, friends and colleagues who have given me practical assistance throughout the writing of the book: Professor Michael Anderson (University of Edinburgh), Noreen Devine, Kathryna Glennon, Sean Glennon, Dorothy Kidd (National Museums Scotland), Elizabeth Lyons, Gerry Lyons and James Patrick.

The research on the chapters on Lowland rural transformation and the history of famine in the Highlands depended to a very great extent on the impeccable work of two skilled research assistants, Willie Orr and Peter Clapham, both of whom are my former students. I acknowledge their invaluable contributions as well as the generous financial help of the UK Economic and Social Research Council for both of those projects.

This volume could not have been completed without the superb technical support and patient work of Margaret Begbie, on whose support I have long relied over the years and who has never failed me at any time. Professor Angela McCarthy of Otago University provided valuable advice and also read the proofs of the book with consummate care.

Three scholars from the disciplines of anthropology, economics and history very kindly sent me copies of their research theses. I am most grateful to Christine B. Anderson, 'Uncovering and Recovering Cleared Galloway', unpublished Ph.D. thesis, University of Massachusetts at Amherst (2015); Catherine Douglas Shaw, 'Enclosure and Agricultural Development in Scotland', unpublished D.Phil. thesis, University of Oxford (2009); and Alastair Livingston, 'The Galloway Levellers', unpublished M.Phil. thesis by research, University of Glasgow (2009).

I wish to thank Stuart A. Paterson for sending me his evocative poem 'The fields that once were Home' and for giving permission to reprint it in Chapter 5 of the book.

Warm thanks also go to Peter Aitchison and Andrew Cassell, formerly of BBC Scotland. Their fascinating radio programme 'The Lowland Clearances', transmitted in May and June 2003, was the first to raise the media profile of a subject long forgotten. It was also great fun working with Peter and Andrew in the great outdoors during the project.

I am grateful to the management and staffs of two important sites, Auchindrain Historic Township near Inveraray and the Highland Folk Museum at Newtonmore, for information and guidance on their artefacts and buildings. For anyone interested in the issues covered in this book, both are 'must see' destinations.

The long list of sources in the Bibliography will confirm how much I have depended on the professional expertise of many archivists and librarians not only for making available material in their own care but also for facilitating access to manuscripts in private hands.

I have now worked with Simon Winder, my editor at Penguin, for nearly twenty years. Each of the five books on the history of Scotland, empire and diaspora which have been published during that time bears the imprint of his wise counsel, honest criticism and stimulating ideas. I could not have wished for a better editor. I also wish to thank him as a senior figure in a major international publishing house for his willingness to bring the history of the Scottish people to a global readership.

Simon's patient and efficient editorial assistant, Ellen Davies, was immensely supportive and also found time to take on the role of part-time picture researcher for the book.

I have also been most fortunate in having a copy-editor for this book as scrupulous and thorough as Mark Handsley.

The staff at Penguin Random House have once again excelled in their consummate professionalism. I am especially grateful to Richard Duguid, Daisy Taylor, Louise Willder, Pen Vogler and Rebecca Lee for their support. No author could have asked for more.

My agent, Andrew Lownie, has been with me for as long as Simon. His prudent advice has been a constant feature over the years as have his faultless negotiating skills in contract after contract with publishers to our mutual benefit! I will always be greatly in Andrew's debt.

Several scholars have built a new intellectual edifice over the past generation or so which allows a better understanding of Scottish rural history than hitherto. There are too many of them to mention by name here, but I do wish to thank all of these fellow labourers in the field for their many publications which are listed in the Bibliography. Without their work this book would not have been possible.

Some among them have also by their writings opened up routes to new insights and fresh perspectives. They include the late Eric Cregeen, Robert Dodgshon, the late Alexander Fenton, the late Malcolm Gray, James Hunter, Allan M. Macinnes, Andrew Mackillop, Marianne McLean, Donald Meek, the late Eric Richards, Christopher Smout, Ian Whyte and Charles Withers. I am very pleased to publicly acknowledge their stimulating and pathbreaking work.

This book is dedicated with warmth, respect and admiration to the memory of a great scholar and modest man, Malcolm Gray (1918–2008).

Tom Devine
Scoor House
Isle of Mull

July 2017

Notes

INTRODUCTION

1. Robert A. Dodgshon, 'The Clearances and the Transformation of the Scottish Countryside', in T. M. Devine and Jenny Wormald, eds., *The Oxford Handbook of Modern Scottish History* (Oxford, 2012), p. 131.

1. LAND AND CLANSHIP

1. Samuel Johnson, *A Journey to the Western Islands of Scotland in 1773* (London, 1870), p. 32.
2. Andrew Simmons, ed., *Burt's Letters from the North of Scotland* (Edinburgh, 1998 edn), p. 74.
3. Cited in T. C. Smout, 'Tours in the Scottish Highlands from the Eighteenth to the Twentieth Centuries', *Northern Scotland*, vol. 5, 1983, p. 120.
4. Robert A. Dodgshon, *From Chiefs to Landlords* (Edinburgh, 1998), p. 21.
5. Malcolm Gray, *The Highland Economy 1750–1850* (Edinburgh, 1957), pp. 23–4.
6. *OSA*, III, p. 90.
7. *Burt's Letters*, pp. 191–3.
8. Johnson, *Journey to the Western Islands*, p. 84.
9. M. Martin, *A Description of the Western Isles of Scotland* (2nd edn, Edinburgh, 1970), p. 101.
10. Cited in R. A. Dodgshon, 'West Highland Chiefdoms, 1500–1745', in R. Mitchison and P. Roebuck, eds., *Economy and Society in Scotland and Ireland 1500–1939* (Edinburgh, 1988), p. 13.
11. Cited in R. A. Dodgshon, ' "Pretense of blude" and "place of thair dwelling": The Nature of Scottish Clans, 1500–1745', in R. A. Houston and I. D. Whyte, eds., *Scottish Society, 1500–1800* (Cambridge, 1989), p. 181.

2. THE LONG DEATH OF CLANSHIP

1. A. I. Macinnes, 'Crown, Clan and *Fine*: The "Civilising" of Scottish Gaeldom', *Northern Scotland*, 13, 1993.

2. M. Martin, *A Description of the Western Isles of Scotland* (2nd edn, ?1716).

3. D. Defoe, *A Tour of the Whole Island of Great Britain* (London, 1971 edn), p. 663.

4. Quoted in R. Mitchison, 'The Government and the Highlands, 1707–1745', in N. T. Phillipson and R. Mitchison, eds., *Scotland in the Age of Improvement* (Edinburgh, 1970), p. 31.

5. Allan I. Macinnes, '*A' Ghaidhealtachd* and the Jacobites', in David Forsyth, ed., *Bonnie Prince Charlie and the Jacobites* (Edinburgh, 2017), p. 165.

6. D. Stevenson, *Alasdair MacColla and the Highland Problem in the Seventeenth Century* (Edinburgh, 1980), *passim*.

7. Quoted in A. I. Macinnes, 'Scottish Gaeldom, 1638–1651: The Vernacular Response to the Covenanting Dynamic', in J. Dwyer, R. A. Mason and A. Murdoch, eds., *New Perspectives on the Politics and Culture of Early Modern Scotland* (Edinburgh, n.d.), p. 84.

8. *Gentleman's Magazine*, IX, June 1739.

9. W. A. Speck, *The Butcher* (London, 1981), p. 183.

10. Cited in B. Lenman, *The Jacobite Risings in Britain 1689–1746* (London, 1980), p. 281.

11. Samuel Johnson, *A Journey to the Western Islands of Scotland in 1773* (Oxford, 1924 edn), p. 51.

3. BEFORE IMPROVEMENT

1. Citations in this paragraph are from S. G. E. Lythe, *The Economy of Scotland in Its European Setting, 1550–1625* (Edinburgh, 1960), pp. 24–5.

2. Ibid., pp. 3–4.

3. Cited in Peter Aitchison and Andrew Cassell, *The Lowland Clearances* (East Linton, 2003), p. 18.

4. Cited in A. J. S. Gibson and T. C. Smout, *Prices, Food and Wages in Scotland 1550–1760* (Cambridge, 1995), p. 231.

5. Sir Robert Sibbald, *Provision for the Poor in Time of Dearth and Scarcity* (Edinburgh, 1699), pp. 2–3.

6. Ian Whyte, *Agriculture and Society in Seventeenth-Century Scotland* (Edinburgh, 1979), p. 168.

7. NRA(S) 879, Douglas-Home Papers, 55/3, Sir Robert Pollock to the Duke of Douglas anent his Grace's estate in Dundee, 7 December 1759.
8. Malcolm Gray, 'The Social Impact of Agrarian Change in the Rural Lowlands', in T. M. Devine and R. Mitchison, eds., *People and Society in Scotland*, vol. I: *1760–1830* (Edinburgh, 1988), p. 54.

4. FORGOTTEN HISTORY: DISPOSSESSION IN THE BORDERS

1. P. H. Brown, *Scotland before 1700 from Contemporary Documents* (Edinburgh, 1893), p. 122.
2. Robert A. Dodgshon, 'Agricultural Change and Its Social Consequences in the Southern Uplands of Scotland, 1600–1780', in T. M. Devine and David Dickson, eds., *Ireland and Scotland 1600–1850* (Edinburgh, 1983), p. 51. This seminal essay has helped to shape this part of the chapter.
3. Ibid., pp. 52–3.
4. NRA(S), Douglas-Home Papers, 256/1, Report of Robert Ainslie, 7 September 1769.
5. Robert Heron, *Observations made in a Journey through the Western Counties of Scotland* (Perth, 1793), vol. II, p. 32.
6. *OSA*, Smalholm, County of Roxburgh, http://stat-acc-scot.edina. ac.uk/link 1791–99, vol. 3, p. 218. Accessed 18 February 2017.
7. *OSA*, Kelso, County of Roxburgh, http://stat-acc-scot.edina.ac.uk/ link, 1791–99, vol. 10, p. 87. Accessed 18 February 2017.
8. Cited in Robert Dodgshon, 'The Clearances and the Transformation of the Scottish Countryside', in T. M. Devine and Jenny Wormald, eds., *The Oxford Handbook of Modern Scottish History* (Oxford, 2012), p. 144.
9. 'Sir John Clerk of Penicuik's Journie into Galloway in 1721', *Transactions of the Dumfriesshire and Galloway Natural History and Antiquarian Society*, vol. 41, p. 186.
10. Cited in Peter Aitchison and Andrew Cassell, *The Lowland Clearances* (East Linton, 2003), pp. 35–6.
11. A. S. Morton, 'The Levellers of Galloway', *Transactions of the Dumfriesshire and Galloway Natural History and Antiquarian Society*, 3rd series, vol. 44 (1967).

5. RESISTANCE

1. *Caledonian Mercury*, 21 April 1724.
2. Robert Heron, *Observations made in a Journey through the Western Counties of Scotland* (Perth, 1793), vol. II, p. 27.
3. Cited in Alistair Livingston, 'The Galloway Levellers', unpublished M.Phil. thesis by research, University of Glasgow, 2009, p. 61. Mr Livingston's work is a mine of useful information on this subject.
4. Cited in Alistair Livingston, 'Galloway Levellers – 1724', p. 11, http://westlandwhig.blogspot.co.uk/2008/03/galloway-levellers-events-of-1724.html.
5. Ibid.
6. W. Prevost, 'Letters Reporting the Rising of the Levellers in 1724', *Transactions of the Dumfriesshire and Galloway Natural History and Antiquarian Society*, 3rd series, vol. 44 (1967), p. 200.
7. Cited in Peter Aitchison and Andrew Cassell, eds., *The Lowland Clearances* (East Linton, 2003), p. 44.
8. Prevost, 'Letters Reporting the Rising of the Levellers', p. 196.
9. *Caledonian Mercury*, 2 June 1724.
10. Ibid., 16 June 1724.
11. Cited in Ian L. Donnachie and Innes MacLeod, *Old Galloway* (Newton Abbott, 1974), pp. 59–60.
12. Ibid., p. 57.
13. Cited in Livingston, 'Galloway Levellers', p. 69.
14. Comment by Christopher A. Whatley, cited in Aitchison and Cassell, *Lowland Clearances*, p. 50.

6. TRANSFORMATION AND LANDLORDISM

1. Cited in Eric Richards, *The Highland Clearances* (Edinburgh, 2000), p. 73.
2. NRS, GD/46/17/36, Lord Seaforth to Colin Mackenzie, 1 July 1811.
3. Stana Nenadic, *Lairds and Luxury* (Edinburgh, 2007), p. 209.
4. David Stewart, *Sketches of the Character, Institutions and Customs of the Highlanders of Scotland* (Edinburgh, 1822), p. 153.
5. Nenadic, *Lairds and Luxury*, p. 209.
6. Sir John Sinclair, *General View of the Agriculture of the Northern Counties and Islands of Scotland* (Edinburgh, 1795), pp. 111–12.
7. Cited in R. A. Dodgshon, *From Chiefs to Landlords* (Edinburgh, 1998), p. 242, quoting from NAS, GD46/17/55.

8. 'A Supplement, Containing an Account of the Present State of Husbandry, and the Improvements recently introduced', in Lord Kames, *The Gentleman Farmer* (6th edn, Edinburgh, 1815), p. 537.

7. CLEARANCE BY STEALTH

1. Daniel Green, ed., *Cobbett's Tour in Scotland* (Aberdeen, 1984 edn), pp. 14–15, 17, 27.
2. NRA (S) 859, Sir Alexander F. Douglas-Home Papers; HPL, 631/1, John Burrell Journals, 1763–1808; NRS, GD 224/590/1, Buccleuch Muniments, Report concerning the improvements proposed to be made upon the Duke of Buccleuch's Estate in the County of Selkirk, William Keir, September 1802.
3. NRA (S) 859, Sir Alexander F. Douglas-Home Papers, Report of Robert Ainslie, 7 September, 1769. All subsequent references to Ainslie's plan come from this Report.
4. Malcolm Gray, 'Scottish Emigration: The Social Impact of Agrarian Change in the Rural Lowlands, 1775–1875', *Perspectives of American History*, VII (1974), p. 135.
5. *OSA* (Lanarkshire), p. 498.
6. HPL, 631/1, John Burrell's Journals, 8 July 1777 (1771?).
7. *OSA* (Lanarkshire), p. 422.
8. Ibid. (Ayrshire), p. 212.
9. HPL 631/1, Journals of John Burrell, Copy Letter, Burrell to Mr. Barron Mure, 8 January 1774.
10. Ibid., entries for 17 and 27 July 1774.
11. NRA(S) 855, Earl of Strathmore Papers, 160/3, W. Gammack to A. Burnett, 15 June 1754.
12. W. Fullarton, *General View of the Agriculture of the County of Ayr*, Edinburgh, 1793), pp. 69–70.
13. HPL 631/1, John Burrell's Journals, 18 and 28 April 1772.
14. Ibid., 20 May 1772.
15. There are numerous examples of this in court processes; see, for instance, NRS SC38/22/6, SC38/22/20, SC38/22/14.
16. NLS, Session Papers, Douglas Collection, vol. 9, Answers for his Grace Alexander, Duke of Gordon . . . (1770).
17. Ibid., Douglas Collection, vol. 1, Thos. Baillie of Polkemmet vs. Wm. Wardrope (1759); Douglas Collection, vol. 4, Petition of John and Donald Fraser (1762); Douglas Collection, vol. 1, Petition of Marquis of Tweedale and Tutors (1760); Hermand Collection, vol. 1, Petition of John Crediton

(1767); Hermand Collection, vol. 1, Petition of Janet Fulton (1770). These are but a sample of the much larger number of such cases.

18. The data which follow are derived from *OSA* parish reports.

19. James Black, 'Report on Cottage Accommodation in the District of Buchan, Aberdeenshire', *Transactions of the Highland and Agricultural Society*, 5 (1851–3), p. 93.

20. Malcolm Gray, *Scots on the Move: Scots Migrants 1750–1914* (Dundee, 1990), p. 15.

8. WHATEVER HAPPENED TO THE COTTARS?

This chapter incorporates material from Chapter 8 of T. M. Devine, *The Transformation of Rural Scotland* (Edinburgh, 1999 edn).

1. J. Naismith, *General View of the Agriculture of the County of Clydesdale* (Edinburgh, 1794), pp. 52–4.

2. *OSA* (Fife), p. 471.

3. Ibid. (Angus), p. 532.

4. Ibid. (Ayrshire), parish of Colmonell.

5. Ibid., parish of Kilwinning.

6. *OSA* (Aberdeenshire), *passim*.

7. NRS, Sheriff Court Processes (Hamilton), SC37/8/18, Lybell of Removing by J. Crawford (1779); SC37/8/20, Lybell of Removing by M. Baillie (1783).

8. NRS, Dalhousie Muniments, GD45/18/2268, Memorandum on Edzell Estate (1767).

9. *OSA* (Ayrshire), parish of Colmonell.

10. NRS, CH2/376/3, Kirk Session of Wiston, 7 June 1752.

11. NRS, HR581/4, Heritors' Meetings, Douglas parish, November 1764.

12. *OSA* (Lanarkshire), p. 143.

13. J. Naismith, *General View of Lanarkshire*, pp. 52–4. (*Clydesdale?*)

14. *OSA* (Fife), p. 372.

15. Ibid. (Ayrshire), parish of Sorn.

16. Ibid. (Lanarkshire), pp. 583–6.

17. C. A. Whatley, 'How Tame were the Scottish Lowlanders?', in T. M. Devine, ed., *Conflict and Stability in Scottish Society, 1700–1850* (Edinburgh, 1990), p. 21.

18. Ibid., pp. 21–2; C. G. Brown, 'Protest in the Pews', in Devine, *Conflict and Stability*, pp. 83–105, and C. G. Brown, *The Social History of Religion in Scotland since 1700* (London, 1987), p. 104.

19. Whatley, 'How Tame were the Scottish Lowlanders?', p. 21.
20. NRS, Sheriff Court Processes (Cupar), SC20/5/29.
21. Ibid. (Dunblane), SC44/22/33.
22. A recent major study of Scottish Criminality, Anne-Marie Kilday, *Crime in Scotland, 1660–1960* (London, 2018), comes to a similar conclusion.

9. THE LOWLANDS AFTER DISPOSSESSION

1. J. Black, 'On the Agriculture of Aberdeen and Banff Shires', *Transactions of the Highland and Agricultural Society, 1870–1*, 4th series, III, pp. 33–4.
2. Cited in David Kerr Cameron, *The Cornkister Days* (London, 1984), p. 219.
3. Ibid., p. 220.
4. David Kerr Cameron, *The Ballad and the Plough* (London, 1978), p. 36.
5. Ibid., p. 214.
6. The Horseman's Creed as recorded in an initiation ceremony in Angus. Timothy Neat, *The Horseman's Word* (Edinburgh, 2002), p. 59.
7. Ibid., p. 54.
8. *Farmer's Magazine*, XIII (1812), pp. 413–14.
9. Ibid., XXI (1820), p. iii. For other references to stability in the rural Lowlands in the period 1815–36, see PP, *Report from the Select Committee appointed to inquire into the Present State of Agriculture and Persons employed in Agriculture in the United Kingdom*, 1833, p. v, QQ.2745–6, 2755; BPP, *First Report from the Select Committee appointed to inquire into the State of Agriculture and into the causes and extent of Distress which still presses on some branches thereof*, 1836, VIII , QQ.19180, 10367, 12223, 14064.
10. Quoted in R. Anthony, *Herds and Hinds* (East Linton,1997), p. 37.
11. Ibid.
12. Cited in T. M. Devine, ed., *Farm Servants and Labour in Lowland Scotland, 1770–1914* (Edinburgh, 1996 edn), p. 108.
13. Ibid., p. 253.
14. M. Harper, *Emigration from North-East Scotland* (Aberdeen, 1988), p. 22.
15. Cited in Anthony, *Herds and Hinds*, p. 94.

10. MORE PEOPLE, LESS LAND

1. PP, VI (1841), *First and Second Reports from the Select Committee on Emigration (Scotland)*, Evidence of Rev. Norman McLeod, pp. 115–18.

2. Ibid., evidence of Charles Baird.
3. James Hunter, *Set Adrift upon the World* (Edinburgh, 2015), p. 235.
4. Cited in ibid., pp. 272–3.
5. Malcolm Gray, *The Highland Economy 1750–1850* (Edinburgh, 1957), p. 95.
6. Norman MacLeod, *Reminiscences of a Highland Parish* (London, 1863), pp. 393–6.
7. Gray, *Highland Economy*, p. 100.
8. NRS, Lord Advocate's Papers, AD58/83, Petition of the Tenants of Strathaird, Isle of Skye, 20 May 1850.
9. *Report for 1847 of Central Board of Management of the Fund raised for the Relief of the Destitute Inhabitants of the Highlands and Islands of Scotland* (Edinburgh, 1847), p. 10.
10. NA, Treasury Papers, T1/4201, R. Grahame to Fox Maule, 14 April 1837.
11. James Macdonald, *General View of the Agriculture of the Hebrides* (Edinburgh, 1811), p. 235.
12. Email message to T. M. Devine from Professor Michael Anderson, 17 July 2017.
13. E. R. Creegen, ed., *Argyll Estate Instructions, Mull, Morvern and Tiree, 1771–1805* (Edinburgh, 1964), pp. 30–31.
14. James Robertson, *General View of the Agriculture in the Southern Districts of the County of Perth* (London, 1794), p. 39.
15. NA, Treasury Papers, T1/4201, R. Grahame to Fox Maule, 6 May 1837.
16. *North British Daily Mail*, 13 September 1847.
17. NA, Treasury Papers, T1/4201, Grahame–Fox Maule Correspondence, March–May, 1837.

11. HARVESTING MEN

1. *Gentleman's Magazine*, IX (June 1739).
2. Cited in S. E. M. Carpenter, 'Patterns of Recruitment of the Highland Regiments of the British Army, 1756 to 1815', unpublished M.Litt. thesis, University of St Andrews (1977), p. 33.
3. W. Cobbett, *The Parliamentary History of England from the Earliest Period to 1803*, vol. XIV (1816), p. 278.
4. David Stewart of Garth, *Sketches of the Character, Manners, and Present State of the Highlanders of Scotland* (repr. Edinburgh, 1877), vol. I, p. 303.
5. Ibid.
6. Cited in Robert Clyde, *From Rebel to Hero: The Image of the Highlander, 1745–1830* (East Linton, 1995), p. 187.

NOTES

7. Andrew Mackillop, *'More Fruitful than the Soil'* (East Linton, 2000), *passim*. See also Matthew P. Dziennick, *The Fatal Land* (London, 2015).
8. Donald MacLeod, *Gloomy Memories in the Highlands of Scotland* (Glasgow, 1892), p. 1.
9. Alexander Mackenzie, *The History of the Highland Clearances* (Inverness, 1883), pp. 168–9.
10. Heather Streets, *Martial Races* (Manchester, 2004), p. 180; John Mackenzie, ed., *Popular Imperialism and the Military 1850–1950* (Manchester, 1992), p. 38.

12. REJECTING THE HIGHLANDS

1. Cited in Marianne McLean, *The People of Glengarry: Highlanders in Transition 1745–1820* (Montreal, 1991), p. 97.
2. Ibid., p. 209.
3. Ibid., p. 206.
4. Ibid., p. 209.
5. Andrew Mackillop, *'More Fruitful Than the Soil'* (East Linton, 2000), p. 184.
6. Cited in ibid., p. 185.
7. John Knox, *A View of the British Empire more Especially Scotland* (London, 1785), p. 127.

13. PASSIVE VICTIMS?

1. Cited in James Hunter, *The Making of the Crofting Community* (Edinburgh, 1976 and new edn 2000), p. 89; D. G. Macrae, Review of M. Gray, *The Highland Economy*, *Economica*, new series, vol. 25 (1958), p. 141.
2. Cited in Eric Richards, *A History of the Highland Clearances* (Edinburgh, 1985), vol. 2, p. 295.
3. G. C. Lewis, *On Local Disturbances in Ireland and on the Irish Church Question* (London, 1836), p. 124.
4. Cited in I. M. M. Macphail, *The Crofters' War* (Stornoway, 1989), p. 120.
5. Samuel (Sorley) MacLean, 'The Poetry of the Highland Clearances', *Transactions of the Gaelic Society of Inverness*, vol. 38 (1937–41), pp. 296–300.
6. Ibid.
7. E. P. Thompson, 'English Trade Unionism and Other Labour Movements before 1790', *Society for the Study of Labour History*, Bulletin 17 (1968), p. 20.

8. Allan I. Macinnes, 'Scottish Gaeldom: The First Phase of Clearance', in T. M. Devine and Rosalind Mitchison, eds., *People and Society in Scotland*, vol. I: *1760–1830* (Edinburgh, reprinted 1991), p. 72.

9. PP, 1884, vol. XXXII, *Report of the Commissioners of Inquiry into the Condition of the Crofters and Cottars in the Highlands and Islands of Scotland*, p. 36.

10. MacLean, 'Poetry of the Highland Clearances', pp. 296–7.

11. Donald E. Meek, *Tuath is Tighearna* (Edinburgh, 1995), p. 18.

12. E. R. Wolf, 'On Peasant Rebellions', in T. Shanin, ed., *Peasants and Peasant Societies* (London, 1971), p. 268.

13. R. J. Adam, ed., *Papers on Sutherland Estate Management* (Edinburgh, 1972), Patrick Sellar to James Loch, 7 May 1816.

14. Ibid.

15. Wolf, 'On Peasant Rebellions', p. 268.

16. PP, VI, 1841, *Select Committee on Emigration (Scotland)*, p. 80.

17. Eric Richards, *Debating the Highland Clearances* (Edinburgh, 2007), pp. 70–71.

18. NAS, Justiciary Court Records, JC26/808 Judicial declaration of Catherine McLachlan, 9 August 1868.

19. Richards, *Debating*, p. 71.

20. Cited in T. M. Devine, *The Scottish Nation* (London, 2012), p. 165.

21. Quoted in Charles Withers, ' "Give us land and plenty of it": The Ideological Basis to Land and Landscape in the Scottish Highlands', *Landscape History* (1990), 12, pp. 45–54.

22. Cited in Richards, *History of the Highland Clearances*, vol. 2, p. 181.

23. Cited in Withers, ' "Give us land" ', p. 52.

24. PP, VIII (1953–4), *Report of the Commission of Enquiry into Crofting Conditions*, pp. 35–6.

25. Quoted in V. E. Durkacz, *The Decline of the Celtic Languages* (Edinburgh, 1983), p. 99.

26. Quoted in A. Auld, *Ministers and Men in the Far North* (Wick, 1868), p. 54.

14. CLEARANCE AND EXPULSION

This chapter incorporates material drawn from T. M. Devine, *To the Ends of the Earth* (London, 2011), Chapter 5.

1. *Witness*, 21 November 1846.

2. *Scotsman*, 12 December 1846.

3. NRS, HD6/2, Treasury Correspondence, Trevelyan to Baird, 19 March 1847.

4. Ibid.

5. Thomas Mulock, *The Western Highlands and Islands of Scotland Socially Considered* (Edinburgh, 1850), pp. 81–2.

6. *Scotsman*, 30 July 1850.

7. Anon., *The Depopulation System in the Highlands* (Edinburgh, 1849), p. 23.

8. D. Clark, 'On the Agriculture of the County of Argyll', *Transactions of the Highland and Agricultural Society*, 4th series, X (1878), p. 95; Mulock, *Western Highlands*, p. 66.

9. NRS, HD7/76, Trevelyan to W. Skene, 26 June 1848.

10. *Scotsman*, 25 August 1849.

11. Cited in Stephen P. Walker, 'Agents of Dispossession and Acculturation. Edinburgh Accountants and the Highland Clearances', *Critical Perspectives in Accounting*, 14 (2003), p. 820.

12. John Pinkerton, *An Enquiry into the History of Scotland Preceding the Reign of Malcolm III* (Edinburgh, 1794), p. 339.

13. Reginald Horsman, 'Origins of Racial Anglo-Saxonism in Great Britain before 1850', *Journal of the History of Ideas*, XXXVII (1976), p. 387.

14. Jürgen Osterhammel, *Colonialism: A Theoretical Overview* (Princeton, 2005), pp. 16–17. Cited in Iain Mackinnon, 'Colonialism and the Highland Clearances', *Northern Scotland*, 8, 2017, p. 25.

15. NRS, HD4/1, Letterbook of Highland and Island Emigration Society (HIES) (1), Trevelyan to Miss Neave, 20 January 1852.

16. NRS, HD4/2, Letterbook of HIES (2), Trevelyan to Sir J. McNeil, 14 August 1852 and Commissary-General Miller, 30 June 1852.

17. *Scotsman*, 26 July 1851.

18. MS Diary of J. M. Mackenzie, 1851, Chamberlain of Lewis, 5 April 1851.

19. PP, *Report and Evidence of the Commissioners of Inquiry into the Condition of the Crofters and Cottars in the Highlands and Islands of Scotland*, 1884, XXXII–XXXVI, *Napier Commission*, QQ.1430, 16967–8.

20. NRS, HD7/47, William Skene to Sir Charles Trevelyan, 21 February 1848.

21. *Destitution Papers*, Second Report of the Edinburgh Section (1849). Sir E. P. Coffin to W. Skene, 29 June 1848.

22. NRS, AF49/6, Report of T. G. Dickson as acting for the trustee on Sir James M. Riddell's estate; Diary of J. M. Mackenzie, 1851; Inverary Castle (IC), Argyll Estate Papers, Bundles 1522–31.

23. IC, Argyll Estate Papers, Bundle 1558, Duke of Argyll to J. Campbell, 5 May 1851.

24. PP, *Papers Relative to Emigration to the the British Provinces in North America*, XXII (1852), Sir J. Matheson to A. C. Buchanan, 10 October 1851.

25. IC, Argyll Estate Papers, Bundle 1804, List of tenants and cottars warned of removal, 1850; Bundle 1623, Campbell to Duke of Argyll, 25 April 1854.

26. All examples come from T. G. Goldie's report in NS, AF49/6.

27. Donald E. Meek, ed., *Tuath is Tighearna: Tenants and Landlords* (Edinburgh, 1995), p. 204.

28. Cited in J. Stewart Cameron, *A History of the Ross of Mull* (Bunessan, 2013), p. 250.

29. *Scotsman*, 8 June 2005.

30. PP, VI (1841), *Select Committee on Emigration, 1841*, p. 87.

31. The Duke of Argyll, *Crofts and Farms in the Hebrides* (Edinburgh, 1883), p. 18.

32. Ibid., p. 64.

33. IC, Argyll Estate Papers, Bundle 1522, J. Campbell to Duke of Argyll, 21 August 1844.

34. *Napier Commission*, pp. 22–71.

15. TURNING OF THE TIDE

1. *Napier Commission*, p. 386, Q.5265.

2. James Hunter, *The Making of the Crofting Community* (Edinburgh, 1976 and new edn 2000), p. 109.

3. Thomas Maclauchlan, 'The Influences of Emigration on the Social Condition of the Highlands', *Transactions of the National Association for the Promotion of Social Science*, 1863.

4. IC, Argyll Estate Papers, Bundle 1764, Correspondence of 9 December 1862.

5. *Napier Commission*, p. 195.

6. Rev. Eric J. Findlater, *Highland Clearances: The Real Cause of Highland Famines* (Edinburgh, 1855), p. 9.

7. *Napier Commission*, pp. 12–13.

8. Ibid., p. 2083, Q.32793.

9. Achnacarry Castle, Cameron of Lochiel Papers, Attic Chest, R.H. Top Drawer, Bundle 15, E. Cameron to Lochiel, 7 November 1846, 26 March 1847; R. Somers *Letters from the Highlands* (London, 1848), pp. 124–5.

10. PP, *Report to the Board of Supervision by Sir John McNeill on the Western Highlands and Islands* (1851), xxvi, p. 38.

11. The Duke of Argyll, *Crofts and Farms in the Hebrides* (Edinburgh, 1883), p. 23.

12. *Napier Commission*, p. 2217, QQ.35050, 35057.

13. Ibid. p. 343, Q.6169.

14. *Scotsman*, 15 and 18 October 1884.

15. Cited in I. M. M. Macphail, *The Crofters' War* (Stornoway, 1989), p. 120.

16. Cited in Hunter, *Making of the Crofting Community*, p. 225.

17. *Oban Times*, 24 January 1885.

18. Cited in Macphail, *Crofters' War*, p. 38.

19. Cited in Hunter, *Making of the Crofting Community*, p. 143.

20. Cited in Macphail, *Crofters' War*, p. 11.

Index

ALLEN LANE
an imprint of
PENGUIN BOOKS

Also Published

David Wallace-Wells, *The Uninhabitable Earth: A Story of the Future*

Randolph M. Nesse, *Good Reasons for Bad Feelings: Insights from the Frontier of Evolutionary Psychiatry*

Anand Giridharadas, *Winners Take All: The Elite Charade of Changing the World*

Richard Bassett, *Last Days in Old Europe: Triste '79, Vienna '85, Prague '89*

Paul Davies, *The Demon in the Machine: How Hidden Webs of Information Are Finally Solving the Mystery of Life*

Toby Green, *A Fistful of Shells: West Africa from the Rise of the Slave Trade to the Age of Revolution*

Paul Dolan, *Happy Ever After: Escaping the Myth of The Perfect Life*

Sunil Amrith, *Unruly Waters: How Mountain Rivers and Monsoons Have Shaped South Asia's History*

Christopher Harding, *Japan Story: In Search of a Nation, 1850 to the Present*

Timothy Day, *I Saw Eternity the Other Night: King's College, Cambridge, and an English Singing Style*

Richard Abels, *Aethelred the Unready: The Failed King*

Eric Kaufmann, *Whiteshift: Populism, Immigration and the Future of White Majorities*

Alan Greenspan and Adrian Wooldridge, *Capitalism in America: A History*

Philip Hensher, *The Penguin Book of the Contemporary British Short Story*

Paul Collier, *The Future of Capitalism: Facing the New Anxieties*

Andrew Roberts, *Churchill: Walking With Destiny*

Tim Flannery, *Europe: A Natural History*

T. M. Devine, *The Scottish Clearances: A History of the Dispossessed, 1600-1900*

Robert Plomin, *Blueprint: How DNA Makes Us Who We Are*

Michael Lewis, *The Fifth Risk: Undoing Democracy*

Diarmaid MacCulloch, *Thomas Cromwell: A Life*

Ramachandra Guha, *Gandhi: 1914-1948*

Slavoj Žižek, *Like a Thief in Broad Daylight: Power in the Era of Post-Humanity*

Neil MacGregor, *Living with the Gods: On Beliefs and Peoples*

Peter Biskind, *The Sky is Falling: How Vampires, Zombies, Androids and Superheroes Made America Great for Extremism*

Robert Skidelsky, *Money and Government: A Challenge to Mainstream Economics*

Helen Parr, *Our Boys: The Story of a Paratrooper*

David Gilmour, *The British in India: Three Centuries of Ambition and Experience*

Jonathan Haidt and Greg Lukianoff, *The Coddling of the American Mind: How Good Intentions and Bad Ideas are Setting up a Generation for Failure*

Ian Kershaw, *Roller-Coaster: Europe, 1950-2017*

Adam Tooze, *Crashed: How a Decade of Financial Crises Changed the World*

Edmund King, *Henry I: The Father of His People*

Lilia M. Schwarcz and Heloisa M. Starling, *Brazil: A Biography*

Jesse Norman, *Adam Smith: What He Thought, and Why it Matters*

Philip Augur, *The Bank that Lived a Little: Barclays in the Age of the Very Free Market*

Christopher Andrew, *The Secret World: A History of Intelligence*

David Edgerton, *The Rise and Fall of the British Nation: A Twentieth-Century History*

Julian Jackson, *A Certain Idea of France: The Life of Charles de Gaulle*

Owen Hatherley, *Trans-Europe Express*

Richard Wilkinson and Kate Pickett, *The Inner Level: How More Equal Societies Reduce Stress, Restore Sanity and Improve Everyone's Wellbeing*

Paul Kildea, *Chopin's Piano: A Journey Through Romanticism*

Seymour M. Hersh, *Reporter: A Memoir*

Michael Pollan, *How to Change Your Mind: The New Science of Psychedelics*

David Christian, *Origin Story: A Big History of Everything*

Judea Pearl and Dana Mackenzie, *The Book of Why: The New Science of Cause and Effect*

David Graeber, *Bullshit Jobs: A Theory*

Serhii Plokhy, *Chernobyl: History of a Tragedy*

Michael McFaul, *From Cold War to Hot Peace: The Inside Story of Russia and America*

Paul Broks, *The Darker the Night, the Brighter the Stars: A Neuropsychologist's Odyssey*

Lawrence Wright, *God Save Texas: A Journey into the Future of America*

John Gray, *Seven Types of Atheism*

Carlo Rovelli, *The Order of Time*

Mariana Mazzucato, *The Value of Everything: Making and Taking in the Global Economy*

Richard Vinen, *The Long '68: Radical Protest and Its Enemies*

Kishore Mahbubani, *Has the West Lost It?: A Provocation*

John Lewis Gaddis, *On Grand Strategy*

Richard Overy, *The Birth of the RAF, 1918: The World's First Air Force*

Francis Pryor, *Paths to the Past: Encounters with Britain's Hidden Landscapes*

Helen Castor, *Elizabeth I: A Study in Insecurity*

Ken Robinson and Lou Aronica, *You, Your Child and School*

Leonard Mlodinow, *Elastic: Flexible Thinking in a Constantly Changing World*

Nick Chater, *The Mind is Flat: The Illusion of Mental Depth and The Improvised Mind*

Michio Kaku, *The Future of Humanity: Terraforming Mars, Interstellar Travel, Immortality, and Our Destiny Beyond*

Thomas Asbridge, *Richard I: The Crusader King*

Richard Sennett, *Building and Dwelling: Ethics for the City*

Nassim Nicholas Taleb, *Skin in the Game: Hidden Asymmetries in Daily Life*

Steven Pinker, *Enlightenment Now: The Case for Reason, Science, Humanism and Progress*

Steve Coll, *Directorate S: The C.I.A. and America's Secret Wars in Afghanistan, 2001 - 2006*

Jordan B. Peterson, *12 Rules for Life: An Antidote to Chaos*

Bruno Maçães, *The Dawn of Eurasia: On the Trail of the New World Order*

Brock Bastian, *The Other Side of Happiness: Embracing a More Fearless Approach to Living*

Ryan Lavelle, *Cnut: The North Sea King*

Tim Blanning, *George I: The Lucky King*

Thomas Cogswell, *James I: The Phoenix King*

Pete Souza, *Obama, An Intimate Portrait: The Historic Presidency in Photographs*

Robert Dallek, *Franklin D. Roosevelt: A Political Life*

Norman Davies, *Beneath Another Sky: A Global Journey into History*

Ian Black, *Enemies and Neighbours: Arabs and Jews in Palestine and Israel, 1917-2017*

Martin Goodman, *A History of Judaism*

Shami Chakrabarti, *Of Women: In the 21st Century*

Stephen Kotkin, *Stalin, Vol. II: Waiting for Hitler, 1928-1941*

Lindsey Fitzharris, *The Butchering Art: Joseph Lister's Quest to Transform the Grisly World of Victorian Medicine*

Serhii Plokhy, *Lost Kingdom: A History of Russian Nationalism from Ivan the Great to Vladimir Putin*

Mark Mazower, *What You Did Not Tell: A Russian Past and the Journey Home*

Lawrence Freedman, *The Future of War: A History*

Niall Ferguson, *The Square and the Tower: Networks, Hierarchies and the Struggle for Global Power*

Matthew Walker, *Why We Sleep: The New Science of Sleep and Dreams*

Edward O. Wilson, *The Origins of Creativity*

John Bradshaw, *The Animals Among Us: The New Science of Anthropology*

David Cannadine, *Victorious Century: The United Kingdom, 1800-1906*

Leonard Susskind and Art Friedman, *Special Relativity and Classical Field Theory*

Maria Alyokhina, *Riot Days*

Oona A. Hathaway and Scott J. Shapiro, *The Internationalists: And Their Plan to Outlaw War*

Chris Renwick, *Bread for All: The Origins of the Welfare State*

Anne Applebaum, *Red Famine: Stalin's War on Ukraine*

Richard McGregor, *Asia's Reckoning: The Struggle for Global Dominance*

Chris Kraus, *After Kathy Acker: A Biography*

Clair Wills, *Lovers and Strangers: An Immigrant History of Post-War Britain*

Odd Arne Westad, *The Cold War: A World History*

Max Tegmark, *Life 3.0: Being Human in the Age of Artificial Intelligence*

Jonathan Losos, *Improbable Destinies: How Predictable is Evolution?*

Chris D. Thomas, *Inheritors of the Earth: How Nature Is Thriving in an Age of Extinction*

Chris Patten, *First Confession: A Sort of Memoir*

James Delbourgo, *Collecting the World: The Life and Curiosity of Hans Sloane*

Naomi Klein, *No Is Not Enough: Defeating the New Shock Politics*

Ulrich Raulff, *Farewell to the Horse: The Final Century of Our Relationship*

Slavoj Žižek, *The Courage of Hopelessness: Chronicles of a Year of Acting Dangerously*

Patricia Lockwood, *Priestdaddy: A Memoir*

Ian Johnson, *The Souls of China: The Return of Religion After Mao*

Stephen Alford, *London's Triumph: Merchant Adventurers and the Tudor City*

Hugo Mercier and Dan Sperber, *The Enigma of Reason: A New Theory of Human Understanding*

Stuart Hall, *Familiar Stranger: A Life Between Two Islands*

Allen Ginsberg, *The Best Minds of My Generation: A Literary History of the Beats*

Sayeeda Warsi, *The Enemy Within: A Tale of Muslim Britain*

Alexander Betts and Paul Collier, *Refuge: Transforming a Broken Refugee System*

Robert Bickers, *Out of China: How the Chinese Ended the Era of Western Domination*

Erica Benner, *Be Like the Fox: Machiavelli's Lifelong Quest for Freedom*

William D. Cohan, *Why Wall Street Matters*

David Horspool, *Oliver Cromwell: The Protector*

Daniel C. Dennett, *From Bacteria to Bach and Back: The Evolution of Minds*

Derek Thompson, *Hit Makers: How Things Become Popular*

Harriet Harman, *A Woman's Work*

Wendell Berry, *The World-Ending Fire: The Essential Wendell Berry*

Daniel Levin, *Nothing but a Circus: Misadventures among the Powerful*

Stephen Church, *Henry III: A Simple and God-Fearing King*

Pankaj Mishra, *Age of Anger: A History of the Present*

Graeme Wood, *The Way of the Strangers: Encounters with the Islamic State*

Michael Lewis, *The Undoing Project: A Friendship that Changed the World*

John Romer, *A History of Ancient Egypt, Volume 2: From the Great Pyramid to the Fall of the Middle Kingdom*

Andy King, *Edward I: A New King Arthur?*

Thomas L. Friedman, *Thank You for Being Late: An Optimist's Guide to Thriving in the Age of Accelerations*

John Edwards, *Mary I: The Daughter of Time*

Grayson Perry, *The Descent of Man*

Deyan Sudjic, *The Language of Cities*

Norman Ohler, *Blitzed: Drugs in Nazi Germany*

Carlo Rovelli, *Reality Is Not What It Seems: The Journey to Quantum Gravity*

Catherine Merridale, *Lenin on the Train*

Susan Greenfield, *A Day in the Life of the Brain: The Neuroscience of Consciousness from Dawn Till Dusk*

Christopher Given-Wilson, *Edward II: The Terrors of Kingship*

Emma Jane Kirby, *The Optician of Lampedusa*

Minoo Dinshaw, *Outlandish Knight: The Byzantine Life of Steven Runciman*

Candice Millard, *Hero of the Empire: The Making of Winston Churchill*

Christopher de Hamel, *Meetings with Remarkable Manuscripts*

Brian Cox and Jeff Forshaw, *Universal: A Guide to the Cosmos*

Ryan Avent, *The Wealth of Humans: Work and Its Absence in the Twenty-first Century*

Jodie Archer and Matthew L. Jockers, *The Bestseller Code*

Cathy O'Neil, *Weapons of Math Destruction: How Big Data Increases Inequality and Threatens Democracy*

Peter Wadhams, *A Farewell to Ice: A Report from the Arctic*

Richard J. Evans, *The Pursuit of Power: Europe, 1815-1914*

Anthony Gottlieb, *The Dream of Enlightenment: The Rise of Modern Philosophy*

Marc Morris, *William I: England's Conqueror*

Gareth Stedman Jones, *Karl Marx: Greatness and Illusion*

J.C.H. King, *Blood and Land: The Story of Native North America*

Robert Gerwarth, *The Vanquished: Why the First World War Failed to End, 1917-1923*

Joseph Stiglitz, *The Euro: And Its Threat to Europe*

John Bradshaw and Sarah Ellis, *The Trainable Cat: How to Make Life Happier for You and Your Cat*

A J Pollard, *Edward IV: The Summer King*